ORIENS CHRISTIANUS

Hefte für die Kunde des christlichen Orients

Band 75

ORIENS CHRISTIANUS

Hefte für
die Kunde des christlichen Orients

Im Auftrag der Görres-Gesellschaft

herausgegeben von Julius Aßfalg und Hubert Kaufhold

Band 75 · 1991

OTTO HARRASSOWITZ · WIESBADEN 1991

Manuskripte, Besprechungsexemplare und Sonderdrucke werden erbeten an:
Prof. Dr. Julius Aßfalg, Kaulbachstr. 95, 8000 München 40

Gedruckt mit Unterstützung der Görres-Gesellschaft
und der Deutschen Forschungsgemeinschaft auf säurefreiem Papier.
Gesamtherstellung: Imprimerie Orientaliste, Leuven. Printed in Belgium

ISSN 0340-6407
ISBN 3-447-03180-8

INHALT

Anschriften der Mitarbeiter VII

Abkürzungen VIII

EDMUND BECK (†)
Der syrische Diatessaronkommentar zu der Perikope von der Sünderin, Luc. 7,36-50 1

ANDREW PALMER
The History of the Syrian Orthodox in Jerusalem 16

HUBERT KAUFHOLD
Der Ehrentitel »Jerusalempilger« (syrisch *maqdšāyā*, arabisch *maqdisī*, armenisch *mahtesi*) 44

OMERT J. SCHRIER
Chronological Problems Concerning the Lives of Severus bar Mašqā, Athanasius of Balad, Julianus Romāyā, Yoḥannān Sābā, George of the Arabs and Jacob of Edessa 62

JOSEPH HABBI
Synodalité de l'Église d'Orient de Séleucie-Ctésiphon 91

S. A. M. ADSHEAD and K. ADSHEAD
Topography and Sanctity in the North Syrian Corridor 113

FREDERIK WISSE
The Naples Fragments of Shenoute's 'De certamine contra diabolum' 123

LESLIE S. B. MACCOULL
The Coptic *Triadon* and the Ethiopic *Physiologus* 141

ERICA C. D. HUNTER
An Inscribed Reliquary from the Middle Euphrates 147

WAHEED HASSAB ALLA
Discours pour la fête de la croix attribué à Saint Cyrille d'Alexandrie 166

DORA PIGUET-PANAYOTOVA
L'église d'Iškhan: patrimoine culturel et création architecturale . . 198

BERICHTE
Georgischer Sommerkurs in Tbilisi (A. Schmidt) 254

Internationales Symposium: Die Bibel in der armenischen Kultur (Chr. Burchard) 255

Personalia (J. Aßfalg) 258
Totentafel (J. Aßfalg) 261

Besprechungen

S. Ronchey, Indagini sul martirio di san Policarpo, Roma 1990 (M. van Esbroeck) 263

Basile de Césarée: Sur le baptême, par U. Neri — J. Ducatillon, Paris 1989 — Aphraate le sage persan: Les exposés. Tome II. Exposés XI-XXIII, par M.-J. Pierre, Paris 1989 (W. Gessel) 263

H. R. Drobner und Ch. Klock, Studien zu Gregor von Nyssa und der christlichen Spätantike, Leiden-New York-København-Köln (W. Gessel) . 264

Jean Chrysostome: Trois catéchèses baptismales, par A. Piédagnel et L. Doutreleau, Paris 1990 (W. Gessel) 265

B. R. Suchla, Corpus Dionysiacum I. Pseudo-Dionysius Areopagita: De divinis nominibus, Berlin-New York 1990 (W. Gessel) 266

A. Kowalski, Perfezione e giustizia di Adamo nel Liber Graduum, Roma 1989 (M. van Esbroeck) 267

A. Böhlig, Gnosis und Synkretismus. Gesammelte Aufsätze zur spätantiken Religionsgeschichte. 1. Teil, Tübingen 1989 (W. Gessel) 267

W. Selb, Orientalisches Kirchenrecht. Band II: Die Geschichte des Kirchenrechts der Westsyrer (von den Anfängen bis zur Mongolenzeit), Wien 1989 (H. Kaufhold) 268

W. Selb, Sententiae Syriacae, Wien 1990 (H. Kaufhold) 269

Yūḥannōn Dōlabānī, Maḵtḇōnūṯō ḏ-pāṭrīyarkē ḏ-Antīōk d-suryōyē trīṣai šuḇḥō Glane/Losser 1990. — Ǧōrǧ Anṭūn Kirāz, ʿIqdu ʾl-ǧumān fī aḫbār as-suryān, Glane/Losser 1988. — Hanna Aydin, Die syrisch-orthodoxe Kirche von Antiochien, Glane/Losser 1990 (H. Kaufhold) 272

Suhail Qāšā, Taʾrīḫ abrašīyat al-Mauṣil li-s-suryān al-kāṯūlīq, Baghdad 1985 — Mīḫāʾīl al-Ǧamīl, Taʾrīḫ wa-siyar kahnat as-suryān al-kāṯūlīq min 1750-1985, ohne Ort, ohne Jahr (ca. 1986) (H. Kaufhold) 274

XXIV. Deutscher Orientalistentag vom 26. bis 30. September 1988 in Köln, Ausgewählte Vorträge. Hgb. v. W. Diem und A. Falaturi, Stuttgart 1990 (H. Kaufhold) 274

G. Riße, »Gott ist Christus, der Sohn der Maria«, Bonn 1989 (M. van Esbroeck) 276

K. Weitzmann - H. L. Kessler, The frescoes of the Dura Synagogue and christian art, Washington D.C. 1990 (W. Gessel) 277

E. G. Farrugia, R. F. Taft and G. K. Piovesana (ed.), Christianity among the Slavs. The Heritage of Saints Cyril and Methodius, Rome 1988 (M. van Esbroeck) 278

L. Padovese (ed.), Turchia: la Chiesa e la sua storia I. Roma 1990 (W. Gessel) . 279

H. Paprocki, La promesse du Père. L'expérience du Saint Esprit dans l'église orthodoxe, Paris 1990 (W. Gessel) 279

ANSCHRIFTEN DER MITARBEITER

Dr. S. A. M. ADSHEAD und Dr. K. ADSHEAD, University of Canterbury, Christchurch 1, Neuseeland.

Dr. WAHEED HASSAB ALLA, Impasse de la Forêt, 24, CH-1700 Fribourg.

Prof. Dr. JULIUS ASSFALG, Kaulbachstraße 95/III, D-8000 München 40.

Prof. Dr. Dr. P. EDMUND BECK OSB (†), Abtei, D-8354 Metten.

Prof. Dr. CHRISTOPH BURCHARD, Kisselgasse 1, D-6900 Heidelberg 1.

Prof. Dr. WILHELM GESSEL, Gerhart-Hauptmann-Straße 19, D-8905 Mering.

Dr. JOSEPH HABBI, Chaldean Patriarchate, Bagdad, Iraq.

Dr. ERICA C. D. HUNTER, Faculty of Oriental Studies, Sidgwick Avenue, Cambridge, CB3 9DA, England.

Prof. Dr. Dr. HUBERT KAUFHOLD, Brucknerstraße 15/I, D-8000 München 80.

Dr. LESLIE MAC COULL, Society for Coptic Archaeology (North America), 2800 Wisconsin Avenue N.W., Washington, D.C. 20007, U.S.A.

Univ.-Dozent Dr. ANDREW N. PALMER, Quintuslaan 13, NL-9722 RT Groningen, Niederlande.

Dr. DORA PIGUET-PANAYOTOVA, rue Miollis 27, F-75015 Paris.

Dr. ANDREA B. SCHMIDT, Goldsteinstraße 109, D-6000 Frankfurt am Main 71.

Dr. OMERT J. SCHRIER, Langemoor 10, NL-2151 VE Nieuw-Vennep, Niederlande.

Prof. Dr. P. MICHEL VAN ESBROECK, SJ, Seestraße 14, D-8000 München 40.

Dr. FREDERIK WISSE, Faculty of Religious Studies, McGill University, 3520 University Street, Montréal, Qué. H3A 2A7, Canada.

ABKÜRZUNGEN

AnBoll	= Analecta Bollandiana
Bardenhewer	= O. Bardenhewer, Geschichte der altkirchlichen Literatur, Freiburg i.B., I^{2} 1913, II^{2} 1914, III^{3} 1923, IV 1924, V 1932.
Baumstark	= A. Baumstark, Geschichte der syrischen Literatur mit Ausschluß der christlich-palästinensischen Texte (Bonn 1922)
BGL	= Bibliothek der griechischen Literatur
BHG	= Bibliotheca Hagiographica Graeca
BHO	= Bibliotheca Hagiographica Orientalis
BK	= Bedi Kartlisa. Revue de kartvélologie
BKV^{2}	= Bibliothek der Kirchenväter, 2. Auflage
BSOAS	= Bulletin of the School of Oriental and African Studies
BullSocArchCopt	= Bulletin de la Société d'Archéologie Copte
ByZ	= Byzantinische Zeitschrift
CChr. SL	= Corpus Christianorum, Series Latina, Turnhout 1953ff.
ChrOst	= Der christliche Osten
CSCO	= Corpus Scriptorum Christianorum Orientalium
CSEL	= Corpus Scriptorum Ecclesiasticorum Latinorum
DACL	= Dictionnaire d'archéologie chrétienne et de liturgie
DHGE	= Dictionnaire d'histoire et de géographie ecclésiastiques
DThC	= Dictionnaire de théologie catholique
EI	= The Encyclopaedia of Islam. New Edition
GAL	= C. Brockelmann, Geschichte der arabischen Literatur I-II (Leiden ^{2}1943-49)
GALS	= C. Brockelmann, Geschichte der arabischen Literatur — Supplementbände I-III (Leiden 1937-42)
GAS	= F. Sezgin, Geschichte des arabischen Schrifttums, Leiden 1970ff.
GCS	= Die griechischen christlichen Schriftsteller der ersten drei Jahrhunderte
Graf	= G. Graf, Geschichte der christlichen arabischen Literatur I-V = Studi e testi 118 (Città del Vaticano 1944), 132 (1947), 146 (1949), 147 (1951) und 172 (1953).

HO	= B. Spuler (Hrsg.), Handbuch der Orientalistik
JSSt	= Journal of Semitic Studies
JThS	= Journal of Theological Studies
LQF	= Liturgiegeschichtliche Quellen und Forschungen
LThK	= Lexikon für Theologie und Kirche (²1957 ff.)
MUSJ	= Mélanges de l'Université Saint-Joseph (Beyrouth)
OLZ	= Orientalistische Literaturzeitung
OrChr	= Oriens Christianus
OrChrA	= Orientalia Christiana Analecta
OrChrP	= Orientalia Christiana Periodica
OrSyr	= L'Orient Syrien
OstkSt	= Ostkirchliche Studien
PG	= P. Migne, Patrologia Graeca
PL	= P. Migne, Patrologia Latina
PO	= Patrologia Orientalis
POC	= Proche-Orient Chrétien
PTS	= Patristische Texte und Studien (Berlin)
RAC	= Reallexikon für Antike und Christentum
RE	= Realencyklopädie für protestantische Theologie und Kirche (Leipzig ³1896-1913)
REA	= Revue des Études Arméniennes
RGG	= Die Religion in Geschichte und Gegenwart (³1957 ff.)
ROC	= Revue de l'Orient Chrétien
RRAL	= Rendiconti della Reale Accademia dei Lincei
ThLZ	= Theologische Literaturzeitung
ThWNT	= G. Kittel † — G. Friedrich (Hrsg.), Theologisches Wörterbuch zum Neuen Testament
TU	= Texte und Untersuchungen zur Geschichte der altchristlichen Literatur
VigChr	= Vigiliae Christianae
ZA	= Zeitschrift für Assyriologie
ZAW	= Zeitschrift für die alttestamentliche Wissenschaft
ZDMG	= Zeitschrift der Deutschen Morgenländischen Gesellschaft
ZKG	= Zeitschrift für Kirchengeschichte
ZNW	= Zeitschrift für die neutestamentliche Wissenschaft und die Kunde der älteren Kirche
ZSem	= Zeitschrift für Semitistik und verwandte Gebiete

EDMUND BECK (†)

Der syrische Diatessaronkommentar zu der Perikope von der Sünderin, Luc. 7,36-50

Die folgende Übersetzung und Erklärung der Ausführungen des Ephräm zugeschriebenen Diatessaronkommentars zu Luc. 7,36-50 geht von dem syrischen Text aus, der sich in Leloirs Edition (Chester Beatty Monographs No. 8) als X 8-10 (S. 42,21-46,5) findet. Zur sachlichen und sprachlichen Erklärung ziehe ich die von mir edierten Werke Ephräms heran, hier vor allem den Sermo de Domino Nostro (CSCO 270, syr. 116), in dem öfters und ausführlich unsere Perikope zitiert und verwertet wird.

1) X 8a (S. 42,21-24)

Text: *»hânâ lam ellū nbīyā hwâ, yâdaʿ hwâ d-ḥaṭṭâytâ hī«. a(n)t dēn d-yâdaʿ a(n)t lâh, ō Šemʿōn, aykan šbaqtâh d-teʿol la-smâkâk? ellâ âf lâ men hâdē īdaʿt d-alâhâ hū, d-âf lâ l-ṣebyâneh kasyâ, d-aytyâh l-hâdē, eškaḥt d-teklē.*

Übersetzung: »Wäre dieser ein Prophet, dann wüßte er, daß es eine Sünderin ist«. Du, o Simon, der du sie kennst, wie hast du es geduldet, daß sie dein Gastmahl betrete? Doch du hast auch daraus nicht erkannt, daß er Gott ist, daß du seinen geheimen Willen, der diese (Frau) (herbei)führte, auch nicht hindern konntest.

Erklärung: Der Kommentar setzt ganz abrupt mit einem Zitat mitten aus der Erzählung ein, mit Luc. 7,41. Im Zitat fehlt, gegen VS und Peš, nach *yâdaʿ hwâ* das: *man hī w-mâ ṭebbâh*, worauf in Peš das *d-ḥaṭṭâytâ hī* des Kommentars folgt, wofür VS breiter: *d-a(n)ttâ hī ḥaṭṭâytâ* hat. Ephrâm zitiert die gleiche Stelle in Sermo de Dom. N. S. 38,6f. mit der ganz gleichen Auslassung. Er setzt das Zitat fort durch das auf *d-ḥaṭṭâytâ hī* folgende *hâdē d-qerbat leh* = »diese, die ihn berührt hat«, wie die Peš (nur *hây* statt *hâdē*) und die VS (nur ohne *hây*/*hâdē*). Davon weicht sehr stark der griech. Text ab, der einheitlich den Zusatz »die ihn berührt« folgendermaßen voranstellt: (*eginōsken an tis kai potapē*) *hē gynē hētis haptetai autū hoti hamartōlos estin.*

Was erklären nun der Kommentar und Ephräm zu dem in gleicher Kurzform zitierten Gedanken des Pharisäers, daß »dieser, wenn er ein Prophet wäre, wüßte, daß sie eine Sünderin ist«? Beide werfen dem Pharisäer vor, daß er den Herrn nicht erkenne, obwohl gewisse Umstände ihn hätten belehren können. In der Angabe dieser Umstände weichen nun Ephräm und der Kommentar völlig voneinander ab. Ephräm nimmt dabei das Verhalten der Sünderin zu den Füßen der Herrn hinzu und sagt in Sermo de Dom. N. S. 38,8ff. »Wir aber wollen den Pharisäer verlachen und sagen: wäre er einsichtig gewesen, dann hätte er von jener Sünderin, die unseren Herrn berührte, gelernt, nicht (nur) daß er ein Prophet war, sondern der Herr der Propheten ist. Denn die Tränen der Sünderin bezeugten, daß sie nicht einen Propheten versöhnten, sondern jenen, der als Gott über ihre Sünden erzürnt war.« Ganz anders der Kommentar. Er bleibt im Bereich des zitierten Satzes und gewinnt eigenartig und kühn schon daraus ein seelisches Motiv, das den Pharisäer hätte zur Einsicht der Größe des Herrn bringen können. Der Kommentar spricht hier direkt zum Pharisäer: »Wie hast du, der du die Sünderin kanntest, es über dich gebracht, sie in dein Gastmahl eintreten zu lassen? Das kann doch wohl nicht dein freier Wille gewesen sein. Du hättest daraus erkennen sollen, daß hier der göttliche Erlöserwille des Herrn wirksam war, den du nicht hindern konntest.« Eine kühne Deutung des Textes, die man bei Ephräm hätte erwarten können, die sich aber dort nicht fand.

2) X 8b (S. 42,24-44,8)

Text: *»trēn lam ḥayyâbīn īt hwaw l-gabrâ mawzfânâ, ḥad d-ḥamešm(ʾ)â wa-ḥrēnâ d-ḥamšīn«. wa-d-nawdaʿ galyâīt d-bâtreh akteb ḥawbâthōn emar lwât Šemʿōn Prīšâ: »l-baytâk lam ʿellet mayâ l-reglay lâ ya(h)bt«. šapīr lâ ya(h)b hwâ mayâ, d-lâ tebṭal lâh takšeftâ d-demʿē d-ḥaṭṭâytâ la-mzaddqânâh ṭayybat. lâ aḥmat nūrâ mayâ da-šyâgtâh, meṭul da-b-reḥmtâh dīlâh demʿēh d-ḥaṭṭâytâ râtḥân hway. qarrbat leh taḥnantâ ḥnīgtâ l-haw d-ya(h)b lâh mawhabtâ ḥsīmtâ.*

Übersetzung: »Zwei Schuldner hatte ein Ausleiher, der eine von fünfhundert, der andre von fünfzig«. (Luc. 7,41). Und um offen wissen zu lassen, daß er gegen ihn (den Pharisäer) ihre Schuld(briefe) schrieb, sagte er zu Simon dem Pharisäer: »In dein Haus trat ich ein, Wasser für meine Füße gabst du nicht«. (Luc. 7,44). Treffend hatte er kein Wasser gegeben, damit nicht das (Buß)flehen der Tränen, welches die Sünderin ihrem Rechtfertiger bereitet hatte, zwecklos würde. Kein Feuer hatte ihr Badewasser angewärmt; denn von ihrer eignen Liebe glühten die Tränen der Sünderin. Sie brachte schmerzvolle Bitten jenem dar, der ihr das beneidenswerte Geschenk (der Verzeihung) gab.

Erklärung: Das erste Zitat ist der Anfang der Parabel von den zwei Schuldnern, die der Herr dem Pharisäer vorbringt, mit dem *gabrâ mawzfânâ* der VS sin. statt des *mârē ḥawbâ* der Pš und der VS cur. Das *gabrâ mawzfânâ* hat auch Ephrâm, der in Serm. de Dom. N. S. 43,6 ausführlicher die Stelle zitiert und für das kürzende *ḥad d-ḥamešm(')â wa-ḥrēnâ d-ḥamšīn* des Kommentars den vollen Text bietet mit: *ḥad lam ḥayyâb hwâ dīnârē ḥamešm(')â wa-ḥrēnâ dēn dīnârē ḥamšīn*, wobei er das *wa-ḥrēnâ* des Kommentars und der Peš bietet und nicht das *w-ḥad* der VS.

Mit dem folgenden zweiten Zitat will der Kommentar zeigen, daß der Herr seine Parabel von den zwei Schuldnern nicht gegen die Sünderin angeführt hat, daß sie sich vielmehr gegen den Pharisäer richtet, obwohl zweifellos der große Schuldschein mit ihr zu verbinden ist. Der Kommentar übergeht die an die Parabel anschließende Zwischenfrage des Herrn mit der Antwort des Pharisäers und zitiert den Anfang der darauf folgenden Kritik des Herrn an seinen Gastgeber in Luc. 7,44: »Ich betrat dein Haus; Wasser gabst du meinen Füßen nicht«. Diese Deutung geht von meiner Übersetzung des: *bâtreh (akteb ḥawbâthōn)* mit »gegen ihn« aus, die noch zu rechtfertigen ist.

Für gewöhnlich hat *bâtar* die Bedeutungen von post (örtlich und zeitlich) und secundum, die Brockelmann in seinem Lexicon allein angibt. Leloir übersetzt in seiner dem syrischen Text beigegebenen lateinischen Version: secundum hoc (mit neutrischer Fassung des pronomen suffixum!), das ebenso in seiner Übersetzung zur Edition des armenischen Textes sich findet. Dieses secundum hoc gibt keinen Sinn. Nun zitiert schon der Thesaurus zu *bâtar* Stellen, in denen es die Bedeutung »gegen« gewinnt. Ich kann dafür aus Ephräm eine Stelle anführen, wo wie im Kommentar von einer Schuldverschreibung die Rede ist, nämlich Carm. Nis. 45,4. Hier sagt Ephräm gegen Häretiker, die die Auferweckung des Körpers leugneten, zunächst, daß dem Körper Hunger, Wachen und Dürsten angehören, ein Kapital, ohne das die Seele nicht reich werden kann. Sie wird reich durch die Zinsen der Talente des Körpers. »Und an Stelle seiner Zinsen *šṭârâ d-ḥawbâtâ ktab(ū) bâtreh(!) saklē* = stellten die Toren einen Schuldbrief gegen ihn (den Körper) aus, indem sie ihn ohne Auferstehung machten«.

Das zweite Zitat (Luc. 7,44) ist also in dem angegebnen Sinn mit dem ersten (Luc. 7,41) zu verbinden. Mit beißender Ironie lobt hier der Kommentar den Pharisäer dafür, daß er dem Gast die Füße nicht wusch; denn er habe damit die Ersatzhandlung der Sünderin möglich gemacht. Dabei wird der Umstand ergänzt, daß das Wasser zum Waschen der Füße gewärmtes Wasser zu sein pflegt. An seine Stelle treten die heißen Tränen der Sünderin, ein origineller Gedanke des Kommentars, den ich bei Ephräm nicht fand. Ephräm zitiert Luc. 7,44 in Sermo de Dom. N. S. 16,13ff. in der Form des Kommentars und nennt dazu das Unterlassen der Waschung der Füße der Herrn durch den Pharisäer »eine Verweigerung des Gebührenden« und das Netzen mit den Tränen der Sünderin »eine Erstattung des Gebührenden«. Daran fügt er ähnliche Erklärungen für ihre zwei weiteren Handlungen mit den Worten: »Mit Salbe hast du mich nicht gesalbt, ein Zeichen der Nachlässigkeit. Diese aber hat mit duftendem Öl meine Füße gesalbt, ein Zeichen ihres Eifers. Du hast mich nicht geküßt, ein Zeichen des Hasses. Diese aber hat nicht aufgehört, meine Füße zu küssen, ein Zeichen der Liebe.« Der Kommentar dagegen bleibt in seiner Erklärung bei den Tränen der Sünderin und führt dazu im Folgenden einen ganz eignen Gedanken durch.

3) X 8c (S. 44,9-13)

Text: *nâšūteh sḥât hwât b-dem'ēh w-ettnīḥat w-alâhūteh tamân 'al agrâ perqat. d-tesḥē gēr nâšūteh hū balḥōd maṣyâ hwât, d-tasḥē dēn ḥṭâhē d-lâ methzēn alâhūteh hū meškḥâ hwât. hī b-dem'ēh ašīgat ḥellâ d-'al reglaw w-hū b-mellaw ḥawwar kutmâtâ d-'al besrâh. asḥyateh hī b-dem'ēh ṭam(')âtâ w-asḥyâh hū b-mellaw qadīšâtâ. sḥâ hū men ḥellâ wa-hfak asḥyâh lâh dīlâh men 'awlâ. sḥay gēr reglaw b-dem'ē w-ya(h)b mellaw šubqân ḥṭâhē.*

Übersetzung: Seine Menschheit wurde gewaschen mit ihren Tränen und sie erquickte sich. Und seine Gottheit hat dort zum Lohn erlöst. Denn gewaschen werden konnte nur seine Menschheit. Die unsichtbaren Sünden aber abzuwaschen konnte (nur) seine Gottheit. Sie wusch weg mit ihren Tränen den Staub auf seinen Füßen und er wusch weiß mit seinen Worten die Makel auf ihrem Fleisch. Sie wusch ihn mit ihren unreinen Tränen und er wusch sie mit seienen heiligen Worten. Er wurde vom Staub abgewaschen und umgekehrt wusch er sie selber von der Lasterhaftigkeit. Gewaschen wurden seine Füße von Tränen und seine Worte gaben die Verzeihung der Sünden.

Erklärung: Ganz eigenartig ist der christologische Gedanke, den hier der Kommentar an das Waschen der Füße des Herrn durch die Tränen der Sünderin knüpft. Das Waschen der Füße konnte nur an der körperlichen Menschheit des Herrn geschehen. Die als Belohnung folgende Vergebung der unsichtbaren Sünden konnte nur das Werk seiner geistigen Gottheit sein. Das setzt der Kommentar fort in Sätzen, die mit dem Gegensatz von Körper und Geist spielen. Dabei sind im ersten Beispiel die Makel auf dem Fleisch der Sünderin nicht konkret, sondern bildhaft zu verstehen; es sind ihre »unsichtbaren« Sünden, wie es kurz zuvor hieß, und sie können so den Gegensatz bilden zu dem Staub auf den Füßen des Herrn. Es folgt der Gegensatz der »unreinen Tränen« der Sünderin zu den »heiligen Worten« des Herrn. Zuletzt in einer sachlichen Wiederholung eine Gegenüberstellung des Staubes auf Christi Füßen zu der Lasterhaftigkeit der Sünderin, des Waschens der Füße durch die Tränen zu der Vergebung der Sünden durch das Wort.

Zu dem Bild von den Makeln auf dem Fleisch der Sünderin kann aus Ephräm Hy. de fide 85,12 angeführt werden, wo er seine Sünden *kutmâtâ da-b-hadâmay* = »Makel auf meinen Gliedern« nennt. Und auch er gebraucht für die Tilgung der Makel das Verb *ḥawwar* = weißwaschen in der Schlußbitte der zitierten Strophe: *ḥawwar kutmât(ī)* = (o Herr) tilge meine Makel! Darüber hinaus erscheinen bei Ephräm drei bildhafte Ausdrücke für die unsichtbaren menschlichen Sünden, die er aus der trichotomischen Dreiteilung des Menschen in Körper, Seele und Geist gewinnt. In Hy. de fide 5,19 spricht er von der Sündhaftigkeit aller Christen seiner Zeit mit den Worten: *ḥbârâtâ b-gušman, šūmâtâ b-nafšan, kutmâtâ b-rūḥan* = »Wunden an unserem Körper, Geschwüre an unserer Seele, Makel an unserem Geist«. Das will sagen: wir Christen sind alle ganz und gar sündig. Dabei steht das Bild »Wunden auf unserem Körper« auf gleicher Stufe mit »Makel an unserem Geist«, wo die bildhafte Bedeutung von selbst gegeben ist. Es sei auch noch der Zusammenhang angeführt, in dem Ephräm dieses allgemeine Schuldbekenntnis ablegt. Er sagt dazu: »Statt also zu forschen, welche Arznei uns nütze, haben wir uns (im Arianismus) auf unsern Arzt gestürzt, um seine Natur und Geburt zu erforschen«.

Sprachlich sei zu unserem Abschnitt noch angemerkt, daß der Kommentar hier durchgehend für das Waschen der Füße das Verb *sḥâ/asḥī* hat; das *ṣabba'* (humectavit) der Peš und VS erscheint nicht. Für dieses *sḥâ* sei aus Ephräm Hy. de crucifixione 4,16 zitiert, wo es im Zusammenhang mit der Taufe in den Worten erscheint: »Die Völker wurden getauft *w-sḥaw weṣṭref(ū) wa-hwaw ḥadtē* = und sie wurden gewaschen und gereinigt und sie wurden neu«. Und zu dem *ettnīḥ*, das der Kommentar im ersten Satz mit *sḥâ* verbindet, sei Hy. de epiphania 7,15 angeführt, wo *nūḥ* zusammen mit *sḥâ* und wiederum in Verbindung mit der Taufe auftritt in dem Satz: »Der müde Körper badet sich (*sâḥē*) und wird erquickt (*nâ'aḥ*) von seiner Mühe«.

4) X 9a (S. 44,14-17)

Text: *»a(n)t lam lâ nšaqtân(ī) w-hī men d-'ellat lâ šelyat reglay la-mnaššâqū«. »w-meṭul hânâ šbīqīn lâh ḥṭâtēh sagī(')ē«. »l-haw gēr d-qalīl šbīq leh, z'ōr maḥeb«. 'am hâdē da-mqīm w-maššar 'al hadâmaw da-d-pagrâ hwaw wa-mgaššmē: ṣabb'at gēr w-šawwyat w-mešḥat.*

Übersetzung: »Du hast mich nicht geküßt und sie hat, seit sie eintrat, nicht aufgehört, meine Füße zu küssen«. (Luc. 7,45). »Und deshalb sind ihr ihre vielen Sünden vergeben«. (Luc. 7,47a). »Wem fürwahr wenig verziehen ist, der liebt wenig«. (Luc. 7,47b). Dabei gibt er kund und bekräftigt er von seinen Gliedern, daß sie die eines Körpers waren und (daher) körperlich. Denn (er sagt:) sie benetzte und wischte ab und salbte.

Erklärung: Der Kommentar begann mit dem Zitat von Luc. 7,39 und erklärte das »hic si propheta esset sciret quia peccatrix est« auf eigne Weise. Dann gab er den Anfang der Parabel von den zwei Schuldnern aus Luc. 7,41 und verband damit Luc. 7,44, den Vorwurf des Herrn gegen den Pharisäer, ihm bei seinem Eintritt die Füße nicht gewaschen zu haben, woraus dann der Kommentar das Thema von den Tränen der Sünderin gewann. Jetzt fährt er weiter mit einem neuen, dem letzten Zitat, das aus drei Bruchstücken besteht. Es beginnt mit Luc. 7,45, wo in Fortführung von Luc. 7,44 von der zweiten Handlung der Sünderin, von ihrem Küssen der Füße des Herrn, die Rede ist. Der Kommentar übergeht dann Luc. 7,46, den Vers, der von der Salbung der Füße spricht, und bringt den Anfang von Luc. 7,47 in der Form: »propter hoc remissae sunt ei sua peccata multa« mit Auslassung des dico tibi nach propter hoc (gegen VS und Peš). Der Kommentar übergeht dann hier vor allem auch die nachfolgende Begründung: quia dilexit multum und gibt nur das anschließende: nam cui paululum dimissum est, exiguum amat.

Folgende Textvarianten seien gesondert hervorgehoben. Zuerst zu Luc. 7,45: für das *w-hī (men d-ʿellat)* des Kommentars hat Peš: *hâdē dēn hâ*, die VS mehr wie der Kommentar ein: *hī dēn*. Bei Luc. 7,47 beginnt der Kommentar mit: *meṭul hânâ*. Ebenso auch die VS, nur ohne das einleitende *wĕ*. Die Peš weicht davon ab mit ihrem: *ḥlâf hâdē*.

In Luc. 7,47 geht es vor allem um die Übersetzung des griech. *apheōntai* (Perfekt Passiv) in »ihre vielen Sünden sind ihr vergeben« und des nachfolgenden iterativen Präsens *aphietai* in »wem wenig vergeben wird«. Hier haben alle, Kommentar, VS und Peš, für das *apheōntai* das die Vollendung einer Handlung ausdrückende Partizip Passiv Peal: *šbīq(īn)*, prädikativ gebraucht. Anders bei *aphietai* des Schlußsatzes. Ich gebe seine drei syrischen Formen:

Kommentar: *l-haw gēr d-qalīl šbīq leh, zʿōr maḥeb.*
Peš: *haw dēn d-qalīl meštbeq leh, qalīl maḥeb.*
VS: *man d-qalīl gēr eštbeq leh, qalīl hū maḥeb.*

Man sieht die Eigenheiten der einzelnen Texte. Zunächst sei hervorgehoben, daß in den ersten drei Wörtern der Kommentar mehr auf seiten der Peš steht und die VS stark davon abweicht, ganz im Gegensatz zu der Übereinstimmung zwischen Kommentar und VS in den beiden vorangegangenen Fällen. Interessant ist vor allem der Wechsel in der Wiederegabe des griech. Präsens *aphietai*. Der Kommentar beachtet nicht den Unterschied zu dem vorangegangen Perfekt *apheōntai* und behält auch hier sein prädikatives Partizip *šbīq* bei. VS hat anscheinend das korrigieren wollen, indem sie statt des Partizips eine Verbalform, das Ethpeel von *šbaq* setzte, merkwürdigerweise aber das Perfekt. Da scheint die Peš korrigierend eingegriffen zu haben mit ihrem Partizip des Ethpeel: *meštbeq*. Zuletzt sei noch eine Stelle angeführt, wo der Kommentar allein gegen Peš und VS eine sehr auffällige Variante hat. In dem Satz: »wem wenig (griech.: *oligon*; Vulg.: minus) vergeben wird, liebt wenig (*oligon*; minus)«, scheint auch die Wiederholung des *qalīl* (*oligon*) in VS und Peš das Gegebene zu sein. Daß hier der Kommentar in seinem Zitat statt des zweiten *qalīl* das synonyme *z'ōr* hat, ist sehr auffällig.

Luc. 7,47 spielt eine große Rolle in der umstrittenen Erklärung unserer Perikope. Die altkirchliche geht von den Worten des Herrn aus: »ihr (bzw. dir) sind die (vielen) Sünden vergeben«, die er in Luc. 7,47 dem Pharisäer gegenüber und im folgenden Vers 48 zu der Sünderin selber spricht, und sieht darin den Akt der Vergebung. Auf diese Weise werden die vorangehenden Tränen und Küsse der Sünderin zu Zeichen der Reue und Buße, die der Vergebung vorangehen. So hat auch der Kommentar im Vorangehenden gesagt, daß der Herr auf das Abwischen des Staubes seiner Füße durch die Tränen der Sünderin mit seinen sündentilgenden Worten geantwortet habe. Und hier, in unsrer Zitatengruppe, läßt er auf Luc. 7,45 mit der Erwähnung der Küsse der Sünderin unmittelbar das: »deshalb sind ihr ihre vielen Sünden vergeben« von Luc. 7,47, folgen. Genau so verbindet auch Ephräm im Sermo de Dom. N. auf S. 15,13f. mit dem Zitat von Luc. 7,44: »Diese aber netzte meine Füße mit Tränen« unmittelbar das gleiche: »Deshalb sind ihr ihre vielen Sünden vergeben«. Nun fügt aber der Kommentar in seinem Zitat daran noch den Schluß von Luc. 7,47, nämlich: »Wem aber wenig verziehen ist, liebt wenig«. Das greift aber auf die Parabel zurück. Und nach der Parabel — so sagen die neuzeitlichen Vertreter der anderen Interpretation unsrer Perikope — geht das Schenken der Schuld voran und die Tränen und Küsse der Sünderin sind nur Ausdruck ihrer liebevollen Dankbarkeit.

Ganz merkwürdig ist, was der Kommentar als Erklärung an das zusammengestückelte Zitat kurz anfügt mit den Worten: »Zusammen mit diesem (angeführten Zitat?): er läßt wissen und bekräftigt von seinen Gliedern, daß sie die eines Körpers waren und körperlich; denn »sie benetzte (*ṣabb'at* wie Peš und VS) und trocknete (*šawwyat* wie Peš und VS) und salbte (*w-mešḥat*).« Offenbar ist hier aus dem Anfang des Zitats: »sie küßte (*naššqat*)« zu ergänzen. Der Kommentar gibt damit eine zweite, kurze christologische Aussage, die völlig isoliert bleibt. Anders bei Ephräm, wo die gleiche Aussage in dem zu erwartenden Zusammenhang erscheint. Sein Hymnus 47 contra haereses polemisiert nämlich gegen die Leugnung der Körperlichkeit des Herrn durch die Markioniten, und hier heißt es in der Schlußstrophe (8): »Wenn sie (die Markioniten) bei der Eucharistie ein wirkliches Brot brechen und nicht bildhaft, *pagrâ hū šarīrâ geššat ḥaṭṭâytâ da-l-Mâran qerbat* = dann hat einen wirklichen Körper die Sünderin betastet, die unsern Herrn berührt hat«. Das *ḥattâytâ da-l-Mâran qerbat* ist das *ḥaṭṭâytâ d-qerbat leh* aus unsrer Perikope, Luc. 7,39 (VS).

5) X 9b (S. 44,17-20)

Text: *nebkōn hâkēl tayyâbē wa-ntūbūn masklânē da-kbar nadrkūn tar'â ptīḥâ l-me'al w-râḥmay ḥayyē netgarghūn d-tar'â aḥīdâ etmlek la-d-medem b-taktūšhōn lâ s'ar(ū) w-ḥublâ ṭâbâ 'al nafšhōn lâ armīw.*

Übersetzung: Weinen sollen daher die Büßer, und die Sünder sollen Buße tun, damit sie vielleicht die Tür geöffnet zum Eintritt erreichen. Und die das Leben lieben, mögen sich (demütig) zu Boden werfen. Denn die verschlossene Tür ist denen angedroht, die nichts in eignem Bemühen getan und sich nicht ein gutes Unterpfand aufgeladen haben.

Erklärung: Von hier an bis zum Schluß spricht der Kommentar von den Büßern und belehrt sie durch das Beispiel der Sünderin. Das zeigt ganz klar, daß hier die altkirchliche Deutung der Perikope herrscht. Die Büßer sollen weinen wie die Sünderin zu den Füßen des Herrn und die Sünder sollen in ihrer Nachahmung Büßer werden. Für »Sünder« sagt hier der Kommentar *masklânē*. Ephräm gebraucht das Verb *askel* in Hy. contra haer. 26,7 für die Sünde Adams in dem Satz: »Auf die Erde der Disteln und der Verfluchungen verstieß er Adam: *kad askel hwâ*«. Und die Verbindung mit der Buße erscheint in Hy. de eccl. 5,4, wo Ephräm sagt, daß die Einsichtigen »*kad yâd'īn d-aynâ d-askel mṣē tâ'eb, lâ masklīn henōn* = obwohl sie wissen, daß, wer gesündigt hat, Buße tun kann, nicht sündigen«.

Der Kommentar fordert die Sünder auf, Buße zu tun, damit sie »vielleicht« (*kbar*) die Tür geöffnet erreichen. Das »vielleicht« klingt hart und soll wohl die Gefahr der Lage für die Sünder unterstreichen. Man vergleiche zu der gegebenen Situation des (letzten) Gerichtes die folgenden Stellen aus Sermones I 5,553ff., wo hier doch wohl ein Pseudoephräm in einem übersteigerten Sündhaftigkeitsbewußtsein sich schon verdammt sieht und dem zuletzt die Buße als Retterin erscheint. Diese spricht zunächst sehr zurückhaltend: »Ich werde für dich die (göttliche) Güte wegen deiner Schuld bitten und mit Tränen werde ich ihr schmeicheln, daß sie die (göttliche) Gerechtigkeit gewinne... Ich vertraue, daß die Güte meine Bitten für dich erhört.« Erst später heißt es dann bestimmter in den Lobpreisungen von Z. 600ff: »Gepriesen sei der Gütige und Milde, der sich über uns freut, wenn wir Buße tun, und der uns freudig aufnimmt aus Liebe, ohne uns zu tadeln. Gepriesen sei der Gütige, dessen Tür offen steht, jene große, für alle Büßer, und nicht verschließt er vor den Bösen die Tür seiner Güte, wenn sie umkehren.« Wie man sieht, erscheint hier die offene Tür der Güte Gottes zum (Himmel)reich (*malkūtâ*), zu der die geschlossene Tür der göttlichen Gerechtigkeit unschwer zu ergänzen ist.

Aus Furcht vor der verschloßnen Tür mögen sich, wie der Kommentar sagt, »die das Leben lieben (*râḥmay ḥayyē*) zu Boden werfen«. Das Subjekt dieses Satzes geht offenbar auf Ps. 33,13 in seiner Zitierung bei 1 Petr. 3,10 zurück, wo der Text der Peš lautet: *man d-ṣâbē hâkēl ḥayyē w-râḥem yawmâtâ ṭâbē l-meḥzâ*, in der Vulg.: qui enim vult vitam diligere et dies videre bonos. Diese, das Leben Liebende, werden aufgefordert *netgargḥūn*. Dieses *etgargaḥ* erscheint bei Ephräm als Akt der Buße in Sermones II 1,458, wo in bewundernden Ausrufen von den büßenden Niniviten gesagt wird: »Wer hat (je) so gebetet, so gefleht, *manū d-hâkan etmakkak man hū d-hâkan etgargaḥ* = wer hat sich so erniedrigt, wer hat sich so zu Boden geworfen!« Man sieht, wie hier *etgargaḥ* parallel zu *etmakkak* steht!

Eine kurze sprachliche Bemerkung zu dem *mlak* in dem *tar'â aḥīdâ etmlek* des Kommentars, das hier nicht die gewöhnliche Bedeutung von promittere hat, sondern die von »androhen«, die Brockelmann, Lexicon nur für die Verbindung mit der Praep. *'al* angibt. Man sieht, diese Verbindung ist nicht notwendig. Als weiteren Beleg dafür kann ich aus Ephräm Hy. de fide 61,1 anführen, wo es heißt: »Wer sollte sich nicht fürchten *d-raḥyâ mlak Mâran l-ṣawreh d-man akšel* = da unser Herr einen Mühlstein angedroht hat dem Hals dessen, der Ärgernis gab.«

Die verschlossene Tür ist nach dem Kommentar zunächst den Büßern angedroht, die hier nichts in eignem Bemühen (*taktūšhōn*) getan haben. Das Nomen *taktūšâ* gehört zum Verb *etkattaš* = laboravit, operam dedit. Und dieses erscheint in unserem Zusammenhang schon in der Schrift, in Luc. 13,24f., in der Aufforderung der Herrn contendite (*etkattašū* in Peš und VS) intrare per angustam portam!

Die Büßer, denen nach dem Kommentar die verschlossene Tür angedroht ist, werden neben der allgemeinen Aussage ihrer Untätigkeit auch noch konkret gekennzeichnet durch den Satz, sie hätten sich kein gutes Unterpfand (*ḥublâ*) aufgeladen. Ich gebe das schwer genau zu fassende und zu übersetzende syr. *ḥublâ* mit »Pfand« wieder, wobei das »gute Pfand« etwas angibt, das dem Inhaber des Pfandes für etwas zu Empfangendes Sicherheit gibt. Beim deutschen Unterpfand ist das »gut« schon von selbst mitgegeben und wird daher rein pleonastisch. Das gute Pfand, das nach dem Zusammenhang die untätigen Büßer sich nicht aufgeladen haben, ist offenbar ein tätiges Büßerleben mit den Werken der Buße, von denen im Vorangehenden schon genannt worden sind die Tränen, Gebete und Akte der Demut. Diese garantieren den Büßern, daß sie (beim Gericht) die Tür (des Reiches) geöffnet antreffen werden.

6) X 10a (S. 44,21-46,2)

Text: *dem'ēh gēr d-ḥaṭṭâytâ nḥet w-ašīg dukkyâtâ da-ršīmīn hwaw b-hēn ḥamešm(')â dīnârīn d-ḥawbâtâh. hâdâ (h)ī d-amredtâh snīqūtâh 'al behttâ meṭul da-ḥzâteh l-haw d-lâ 'âdel la-snīqē kad maḥṣfīn ellâ šâ(')eṭ l-'atīrē 'al d-meṣṭam'rīn. meṭul haw arīm qâleh ba-ḥnânâ la-ḥnīnē wa-ftaḥ pūmeh b-šubqânâ la-snīqē wa-qalles la-myaqqrânaw ba-bṭīlūt ḥubbhōn d-ṣē(')daw wa-ka(')ar la-mzamm(')nânaw b-besyân reḥmathōn da-lwâteh.*

Übersetzung: Denn die Tränen der Sünderin flossen herab und wuschen ab die Stellen, in denen die fünfhundert Denare ihrer Schulden aufgezeichnet waren. Das heißt: ihre Bedürftigkeit ließ sie sich der Scham widersetzen; sah sie doch jenen, der die Bedürftigen nicht tadelt, wenn sie kühn sind, der vielmehr die Reichen verachtet, weil sie sich schämen. Deswegen hat er (der Herr) seine Stimme erhoben in Mitleid mit den Bemitleidenswerten und hat seinen Mund mit (Worten der) Verzeihung für die Bedürftigen geöffnet und er hat die ihn Ehrenden gelobt wegen des Eifers ihrer Liebe zu ihm und er hat die ihn Einladenden getadelt wegen der Nachlässigkeit ihrer Liebe für ihn.

Erklärung: Der Kommentar fährt fort (bis zum Schluß), die Sünderin als Beispiel für die Büßer hinzustellen. Hier ist es ihre Kühnheit. Die Höhe ihrer Schulden läßt sie in ihrem Benehmen »die Scham« d.h. jedes ängstliche Denken an die Regeln des normalen Anstands verachten, da hier der Herr selber Kühnheit nicht getadelt hat. Als gegensätzliche Haltung führt der Kommentar zunächst allgemein die Reichen an, »die sich schämen«. Doch ist schon hier vor allem an den Pharisäer zu denken. Der Kommentar fährt zwar allgemein weiter; aber in dem Plural »die Einladenden« wird er schon indirekt genannt. Der auf unseren Abschnitt folgende Schluß wird offen noch einmal die Sünderin und den Pharisäer gegenüberstellen.

Nun zu Einzelheiten. Für das *dukkyâtâ* in der Bedeutung von Stellen im Schuldbrief kenne ich aus Ephräm kein Beispiel. Aber aus Brockelmann, Lexicon gewinnt man Luc. 4,17, wo der Herr in der Synagoge von Nazareth beim Öffnen des ihm dargereichten Buches des Isaias die Stelle (*dukktâ*) fand, wo geschrieben stand: der Geist des Herrn ist über mir.

Daß Tränen der Buße Schuldverschreibungen tilgen, sagt auch Ephräm in Hy. de ecclesia 5,16 mit den Worten: »Wenn einer Buße tut, *ḥdâ nuṭptâ d-dem'ē 'âṭyâ šṭâr ḥawbaw* = tilgt ein Tropfen von Tränen seinen Schuldschein«. Und in Hy. de virginitate 46,12 fordert Ephräm zur Buße auf, indem er sagt: »Solange noch Tränen in den Augen sind, *ne'ṭē b-dem'ayn eštâr ḥawbâtan* = laßt uns mit unseren Tränen unseren Schuldbrief tilgen«! Auch in der Verbindung mit unserer Sünderin sagt Ephräm im Sermo de Dom. N. S. 13,1: *'ṭât hây b-dem'ēh z'ōrâtâ šṭârē rawrbē d-ḥawbâtâh* = mit kleinen Tränen tilgte jene (Sünderin) ihre großen Schuldbriefe«.

Das *snīqūtâ* und *snīqē*, mit »Bedürftigkeit« und die »Bedürftigen« übersetzt, tritt in Gegensatz zu den *ʿatīrē*, den »Reichen« und nähert sich so der Bedeutung »die Armen«, syrisch: *meskēnē*. So stehen bei Ephräm in Hy. de nativitate 1,84 *snīqē* und *meskēnē* völlig parallel. Und der Gegensatz zu »reich« kommt in Hy. de ecclesia 14,3 zum Ausdruck, wo Ephräm betet: *teʿtar snīqūt(ī)* = »meine Bedürftigkeit möge reich werden (durch das Kapital deiner Betrachtung)«.

Von der Bedürftigkeit heißt es im Kommentar: *amredtâh ʿal behttâ* = sie ließ (die Sünderin) rebellieren gegen die Scham (als Herrscherin). Für das *amred* sei aus Ephräm Hy. contra haer. 9,9 zitiert, wo es heißt: *man amrdan ʿal nahīrē* = »wer hat uns zu Rebellen gemacht gegen die Sterne (d.h. das Sternenschicksal)«. Die Sünderin wurde zur Rebellin gegen *behttâ*, gegen die Scham. Das *behttâ* personifiziert hat man bei Ephräm in einem etwas anderen Zusammenhang in Hy. de paradiso 7,30. Hier bittet Ephräm zunächst, daß am Tag des Gerichts seine Schulden (Sünden) nicht den Mitmenschen kundgetan werden mögen, fügt aber sofort hinzu: »obwohl wir hierin sehr verächtlich sind. Denn wenn dir unsere Schulden offen liegen, vor wem sollen wir (sie) dann verbergen? *ptakrâ ʿbadteh lī l-behttâ* = zu einem Götzen hab ich mir die Scham gemacht.«

Nach dem Kommentar macht hier die Bedürftigkeit die Büßer kühn (*kad mahṣfīn*). Die Kühnheit, syr. *ḥuṣpâ*, erscheint auch in einer Erklärung Ephräms zu unsrer Perikope in Hy. de virginitate 35,5, aber mit einer Begründung, die näher liegt. Hier heißt es, daß die Sünderin sich nicht geschämt hat (*lâ behtat*), in das Gastmahl der Reinen einzutreten. Dazu die Frage: *b-aynâ kay ḥuṣpâ* = mit welcher Kühnheit? mit der Antwort: »Statt des Weines hat die Liebe sie trunken gemacht«. Also: nicht die Bedürftigkeit, sondern die Liebe.

Für das gegensätzliche Verhalten der Reichen heißt es im Kommentar nur kurz, daß der Herr sie verachtet *ʿal d-meṣṭamʿrīn* = weil sie sich schämen. Das seltene Verb *eṣṭamʿar* habe ich bei Ephräm nicht angetroffen. Es erscheint aber im Kommentar ein zweites Mal in XII 16 zu Beginn des Abschnittes über die Samariterin am Brunnen, wo es auf S. 88,21 zu der Bitte des Herrn »gib mir zu trinken« heißt: *lâ eṣṭamʿar ʿatīrâ d-neš(ʾ)al a(y)k snīqâ* = »es schämte sich der Reiche nicht, wie ein Bedürftiger zu bitten«.

Der Kommentar fährt fort, indem er immer noch die Rolle der Sünderin und des Pharisäers erweitert. So läßt er den Herrn Vergebung (der Sünden) den Bedürftigen verkünden und zuvor, mit einem Wortspiel, »Mitleid für die Bemitleideten« syr. *ḥnânâ la-ḥnīnē*. Dieses Wortspiel habe ich bei Ephräm nicht angetroffen. Im Kommentar erscheint das seltene *ḥnīnâ* noch zweimal in XXII 6, in der am Schluß angefügten Exhortatio. Hier heißt es von Christus (S. 238,13ff.): »Er liebt die Gerechten und erbarmt sich (*ḥâʾen*) der Sünder, das heißt: die Guten rechtfertigt er (*mzakkē*) und für die Schlechten tritt er ein (*snegar ḥšē*), er, der gegen Gerechte für Büßer sich eingesetzt hat.« Es folgt als ein etwas gewaltsames Beispiel die Behandlung der Arbeiter im Weinberg von Matth. 20,10-15. Hier werden die Arbeiter von nur einer Stunde, die trotzdem den ganzen Tageslohn erhielten, in S. 238,16 »*ḥnīnē*« d.h. Bemitleidete, Begnadete, Bevorzugte genannt. Von den andern, den Murrenden, heißt es: *lâ etḥnen(ū) ellâ âf lâ etṭlem(ū)* = sie haben kein Mitleid, aber auch kein Unrecht erfahren. Die den ganzen Tag gearbeitet haben, werden anschließend *prī'ay kēnūtâ* (nach Gerechtigkeit Bezahlte) genannt und die mit nur einer Arbeitsstunde *ḥnīnay ṭaybūtâ* (von der Güte Begnadete).

Stilistisch sehr auffällig ist der Schlußsatz unseres Abschnittes. Zuerst die Gegenüberstellung der Partizipien: *qalles la-myaqqrânaw* (die ihn Ehrenden, wie die Sünderin) und *ka(')ar la-mzammĕnânaw* (die ihn Einladenden, wie der Pharisäer). Und dann der Gegensatz von *ba-bṭīlūt ḥubbhōn* zu dem *b-besyân reḥmathōn*, wo dann an die synonymen Nomina *ḥubbâ* und *reḥmtâ* der gleiche attributive Relativsatz tritt mit dem Wechsel der synonymen Präpositionen *ṣēd* und *lwât*. Für letzteres kann ich ein Beispiel aus Ephräm anführen aus Sermones II 1,411f., aus dem Sermo de Ninivitis, wo die Eltern ihre Kinder angesichts des drohenden Untergangs in einer langen Rede zu trösten suchen und dabei auch sagen: *z'ōr ḥubban ṣēdaykōn men haw ḥubbeh da-lwâtan* = »kleiner ist unsere Liebe zu euch als jene seine (Gottes) Liebe zu uns«.

7) X 10b (S. 46,3-5)

Text: *w-appeq haymânūtâh d-hây l-gelyâ b-tešboḥtâ; w-parsī ḥuššâbaw d-haw b-zu'âmâ. wa-hwâ âsyâ l-hây d-haymnat d-hūyū m(')asē kul; wa-hwâ dâ(')en kasyâtâ l-haw d-âflâ yâda' galyâtâ ḥašbeh hwâ.*

Übersetzung: Und er brachte den Glauben jener (Sünderin) ans Licht mit Lob, und er enthüllte die Gedanken jenes (Pharisäers) mit Tadel. Und er wurde Arzt für jene, die glaubte, daß er der Arzt aller ist, und er wurde zum Richter über geheime (Gedanken) bei jenem, der von ihm dachte, er kenne Offenkundiges nicht.

Erklärung: Der Kommentar geht hier im ersten Satz vom Schlußvers der Perikope aus, von dem Wort des Herrn an die Sünderin: *haymânūtek(ī) aḥyatek(ī)* (Peš und VS) = »dein Glaube hat dich gerettet (das Leben geschenkt)«. Damit hat der Herr, nach dem Kommentar, die geheime seelische Disposition der Sünderin bei ihrem äußeren Auftreten kundgetan, »zu ihrem Lob«. Der Kommentar setzt sein Spiel mit Gegensätzen fort, indem er dem Aufdecken des Glaubens der Sünderin die Enthüllung der (schlechten) Gedanken des Pharisäers entgegensetzt, »zu seinem Tadel«. Was mit dieser

Enthüllung gemeint ist, wird nicht offen gesagt. Sie ist aber zweifellos mit dem Gedanken des Pharisäers zu verbinden, den der Kommentar zu Beginn zitiert hat: Wenn dieser ein Prophet wäre, wüßte er. Die Enthüllung dieses schlechten Gedankens erklärt der Kommentar nicht weiter, sie kann aus Ephräm nachgetragen werden. Dieser sagt zu dem Wort des Herrn in Luc. 7,47, daß der Sünderin »ihre vielen Sünden verziehen sind«; »Der Pharisäer wurde sehr beschämt, wie er hörte, daß der Herr ihre Sünden zahlreich nannte, wegen seines großen Irrtums, da er geglaubt hatte, daß unser Herr nicht einmal, daß sie eine Sünderin sei, wisse«. (Sermo de Dom. N. S. 17,1ff.). Der Kommentar spricht anschließend noch einmal von diesem Gedanken des Pharisäers in einer letzten Gegenüberstellung zu der Sünderin. Auch hier sind seine Geheimnisse seine geheimen Gedanken, über die der Herr richtet. Diesem Herrn als Richter wird im vorangehenden Satz der Herr als Arzt entgegengestellt, an den die Sünderin als Arzt aller (Sünder) geglaubt hat. Das Bild von Christus als Arzt erscheint im Kommentar nur ganz kurz, bei Ephräm dagegen in seinen Erklärungen zu unsrer Perikope im Sermo de Dom. N. zweimal ausführlicher. So sagt er auf S. 38,13ff.: »Deswegen, weil die Propheten Sünder nicht heilen konnten, stieg der Herr der Propheten herab, um die zu heilen, die in einem ganz schlimmen Zustand sich befinden. »Welches wäre nun der Arzt, der einen mit Geschwüren Bedeckten hindern würde, zu ihm zu kommen, o blinder Pharisäer, der du unsern Arzt (mit den Worten) geschmäht hast: Warum hat ihn die mit Geschwüren Bedeckte berührt«? Etwas weiter wird das Bild in der zweiten Stelle ausgeführt, in Sermo de Dom. N. S. 41,15ff. Hier läßt Ephräm die Tränen und Küsse der Sünderin Arzneien (*sammânē*) sein, die sie Christus, ihrem Arzt (*l-âsyâh*), darreicht, »damit er mit ihren Tränen ihre Makel weißwasche und mit ihren Küssen ihre Wunden (*ḥbârâtâh*) heile«. Das dabei Ungewöhnliche an der Tätigkeit des Herrn als Arzt hebt Ephräm anschließend selber hervor mit den Worten: »Das ist der Arzt, der mit den Arzneien, die einer ihm bringt, mit eben diesen ihn heilt«. Hierin unterscheidet sich Christus als Arzt von den menschlichen Ärzten, die Ephräm in Carm. Nis. 34,10 *âsawâtâ b-sammânayhōn* = »Ärzte mit ihren Arzneien« nennt und denen er Christus gegenüberstellt als *âsyâ da-l-kul sâfeq* = als »Arzt, der alles vermag«.

Nun erscheint in den Schlußbetrachtungen des Kommentars, in XXII 5, in einem Satz kurz noch einmal die Sünderin von Luc. 7. Der Satz lautet: *a(y)k hây ḥaṭṭâytâ da-hwât âsītâ la-ḥbârâtâh b-sammânē d-šeqlat w-ez(l)at lwât haw da-pšīq leh da-b-kul medem n(ĕ)mazzeg šubqâneh maḥlem kul kē(')bīn* = »wie jene Sünderin, die zur Ärztin wurde für ihre Wunden mit den Arzneien; sie trug (sie) und ging zu jenem, für den es leicht ist, in alles sein Verzeihen, das alle Leiden heilt, zu mischen«. (S. 238,10f.). Man staunt, wie hier die Sünderin mit ihren Arzneien nach dem Muster menschlicher Ärzte selber zu einer

Ärztin gemacht wird und wie gezwungen dann doch noch die alle Leiden (= Sünden) heilende (*maḥlem*) Vergebung des Herrn damit verbunden wird. Eine sinnlose Zerstörung des Bildes von Christus als Arzt, die Ephräm völlig fremd ist und der daher als Verfasser der Schlußbetrachtungen des Kommentars ausscheidet. Dafür hat auch schon Leloir in: Doctrines et Méthodes de S. Efrem (CSCO subs. 18, S. 15) Argumente erbracht. Er hält aber den Kommentar selbst im großen und ganzen mit der Tradition für ein Werk Ephräms.

Ich habe dagegen vor allem in dem Artikel über die Perikope von der Samariterin am Brunnen (OrChr 74/1990) gezeigt, daß der Kommentar zwar Ephräm kennt und benützt, aber in wesentlichen Dingen von ihm abweicht. Die vorangehende Abhandlung über die Sünderin von Luc. 7 bringt zu dieser Frage nichts von Bedeutung. Dafür sei hier zum Schluß aus einem anderen Zusammenhang eine Stelle besprochen, wo eine Strophe aus einem echten Hymnus Ephräms erscheint, ohne irgendwie als Zitat gekennzeichnet zu werden. Das geschieht inmitten einer Reihe von kurzen Erklärungen zu dem Zerreißen des Tempelvorhanges beim Tode Jesu im Kommentar XXI 5-6 (S. 210,14-20). Hier heißt es:

»Ferner: der Vorhang zerriß ihre verschlossenen Ohren und gab den Lobpreis, den sie versagt hatten. Oder: weil der Geist den Sohn entblößt (am Kreuze) hängen sah, ergriff und zerriß er das Kleid seines Schmuckes. Oder: es sahen die Symbole das Lamm der Symbole. Sie zerrissen den Vorhang und gingen heraus ihm entgegen. Oder: im Tempel hatte der Geist der Prophetie gewohnt, der herabgestiegen war, um den Menschen sein (Christi) Kommen zu verkünden. Zur (selben) Stunde flog er fort, um den Himmlischen die Botschaft von seiner (bevorstehenden) Himmelfahrt zu bringen«.

Die dritte dieser mit *aw (dĕ)* aneinander gereihten Erklärungen (»es sahen die Symbole ... heraus ihm entgegen«) ist nun zweifellos die Strophe eines echten ephrämischen Hymnus, nämlich Hy. de azymis VI 12 aus der Hymnengruppe de azym. III-XXI mit Strophen von zwei Zeilen zu je fünf plus vier Silben. Ich gebe Hy. de azym. VI 12 zusammen mit der vorangehenden Strophe nach dem von mir in CSCO 248, syr. 108, S. 14 edierten, auf zwei alten Handschriften beruhenden Text:

11) *kulhōn gēr ṭupsē * ba-qduš qudšē*
*šrēn hwaw wa-mqawwēn * l-haw gâmar kul*
12) *ḥza(ʾ)ū(h)y dēn râzē * l-emar quštâ*
*ṣraw appay tarʿa * wa-nfaq(ū) l-urʿeh.*

Übersetzung: »Alle Typen hatten im Allerheiligsten gewohnt und gewartet auf jenen Allvollender. (12) Es sahen nun die Symbole das wahre Lamm. Sie zerrissen den Türvorhang und traten heraus, ihm entgegen.« Der Kommentar bringt Str. 12, und zwar die zweite Zeile in voller Übereinstimmung mit meinem Text. Anders in der ersten Zeile. Die Auslassung der Partikel *dēn* stört die Fünfzahl des Gliedes, ist aber sachlich ohne Bedeutung. Sehr auffällig ist dagegen, daß der Kommentar hier statt des *l-emar quštâ* = »das wahre Lamm« ein *l-emar râzē* = »das Lamm der Symbole« hat. Ist hier »Lamm der Symbole« als »Lamm, auf das die alttestamentlichen Symbole gingen« zu verstehen, was wohl sprachlich möglich ist, dann würde es dem Sinne nach von dem »wahren Lamm« meines Textes nicht abweichen. Nun aber erscheint bei Ephräm in der Nähe unsrer Strophen, in Hy. de azym. V 19, ein *emrâ d-râzē*, also sachlich der gleiche Ausdruck wie das *emar râzē* des Kommentars, und von ihm wird gesagt: »Jenes Lamm der Symbole verging, da die Vollendung kam und die Symbole verstummten«. Ephräm hat also den Ausdruck »Lamm der Symbole« ganz anders verstanden, nämlich als das alttestamentliche Paschalamm mit seinen Symbolen, also das Gegenstück des »wahren Lammes«. Ephräm konnte somit unmöglich seine Strophe de azym. 6,12 in der Form des Kommentars zitieren. Nun ist aber auch die Möglichkeit gegeben, daß im Urtext des Kommentars das ephrämische *l-emar quštâ* stand und *l-emar râzē* erst später fehlerhafter Weise eindrang. In diesem Fall könnte das Zitat, das so unvermittelt dem Verfasser des Kommentars in die Feder floß, für Ephräm als Autor geltend gemacht werden. Doch ebenso gut möglich wäre auch anzunehmen, daß hier einer am Werk war, der die Hymnen Ephräms gut kannte, vielleicht einer seiner Schüler.

ANDREW PALMER

The History of the Syrian Orthodox in Jerusalem

Contents of Part One: 1. Introduction. 2. The phenomenon of pilgrimage. 3. Evidence for the use of coastal ferries (illustrated by Fig. 1). 4. The property of the Jacobites in Jerusalem (illustrated by Fig. 2). 5. The Syrian Orthodox at the Holy Sepulchre. 6. The bishops of Jerusalem and relations with the Roman Church. Bibliography.

1. *Introduction*

The subject of this paper has been addressed before by Dōlabānī (1928), Meinardus (1964) and Karkenny (1976). Dōlabānī begins with a survey of the history of the Syrians in Palestine, then lists "the monasteries and the churches which we call after Mary Magdalene and Simon the Pharisee and the site of the Magdalene monastery". The kernel of his article is devoted to this monastery, which Dōlabānī identifies with the convent attested for the mid-eighth century (see note 40, below). He quotes MSS from St Mark's Library by number. Meinardus uses, amongst other literature and sources, "an unpublished study by Behnam Heggawi al-Musoli, secretary of St. Mark's Monastery in Jerusalem, 1955" (= Ǧaǧǧāwī 1955), on which Karkenny clearly relied extensively[1]. Ǧaǧǧāwī had the advantage of access to the library of St Mark's, but information based at one remove on his researches is of uncertain status, because it is not clear where evidence ends and interpretation begins. Moreover, we are not in a position to check all the evidence. Karkenny's work, though unscholarly, is worth reading in parts[2], and it contains photographs of a number of official orders or firmans from the Ottoman period, which are kept in the library of St Mark's at Jerusalem.

1 "Das Buch von Koriah [Karkenny (1976)] beruht offenbar weitgehend auf Vorarbeiten von Metropolit Dionysios Behnam Ǧaǧǧāwī, wie ein Vergleich mit Meinardus zeigt (ich glaube, mich auch an eine entsprechende Äußerung des Bischofs zu erinnern)." (Hubert Kaufhold, personal communication, 18 ii 1990).

2 O. F. A. Meinardus wrote a review of Karkenny (Koriah), which appeared both in *Bibliotheca Orientalis* 36 (1979), 117-18 and in *Bulletin de la société d'archéologie copte* 27 (1982), 143-47. He compares the book to his own about the Copts (1960), to Hintlian (1976) and to a book on "The Rights of the Abyssinian Church in the Holy Places" by Anbā Philippus (1959) and sees them all as responses to the competing claims of the rival anti-Chalcedonian churches. The present article attempts to establish historical fact, regardless of sectarian claims.

Unfortunately it remains difficult to gain access to this library. I stayed in Jerusalem for three months and visited the monastery with great regularity; but it was only during the last three days of my stay that I was permitted to see some books and these the bishop selected for me. My notes on these manuscripts will appear in a coming volume of *Oriens Christianus*. Thus the present article cannot be regarded as definitive, but it does represent an advance on what others have done[3].

The term "Syrian Orthodox" in the title connotes those Syrian Christians, especially from Northern Mesopotamia, whose ancestors opposed the Council of the Church in Chalcedon AD 451. As a result of the conflict which ensued, they adhered to Bishop Jacob of Edessa following his consecration in 543 and rejected the "official" bishop consecrated simultaneously for that see. This brought about a schism which has never been fully healed. From the point of view of the Chalcedonians, the "Jacobites" were the schismatics who broke away from the "Orthodox" Church; from the point of view of the "Jacobites" themselves, the "Chalcedonians" were the ones who had broken with Orthodoxy. Nevertheless the name "Jacobite", like other terms originally intended as derogatory, was defiantly adopted by the Syrian Orthodox themselves, who, until quite recently, were proud of it[4]. In Jerusalem, where all Churches came together, it was necessary to make distinctions plain. The Crusaders initially distinguished Greeks, Armenians, Syrians (meaning the Malkite, or non-Jacobite Syrians) and Jacobites (including Copts, Nubians and Ethiopians)[5].

3 I am grateful to Bernard Hamilton, Jan-Kees de Geus and Geert Jan van Gelder for reading and commenting on an early draft. Hubert Kaufhold contributed substantially to the completeness of my references. I visited Jerusalem with a research grant from the Alexander von Humboldt-Stiftung, Bonn, in the winter of 1985-86. To Metropolitan Dionysius Bahnām Ǧaǧǧāwī are due both thanks for his hospitality and apologies for descending upon him at such a busy time of the year. Though my hope meticulously to examine his library proved vain, he compensated me with abundant opportunities to witness the Syriac Liturgy in the Holy Places, an activity, unlike scholarship, from which eternal merit accrues. For the altars at which the Jacobites celebrate, see Meinardus (1964), pp. 72-81. Everyone at St Mark's, and especially Father Simeon, made our family feel welcome; but our home was the Ecumenical Research Institute at Ṭanṭūr, which we remember with great warmth and gratitude. Kevork Hintlian of the Armenian Patriarchate and David Shulman and Meir Kister of the Hebrew University were most active in making my stay a useful one.

4 The greatest historian whom the Syrian Orthodox can claim, Dionysius of Tellmaḥrē, was proud to use the name "Jacobite" in the ninth century (Chabot 1920, vol. 1, p. 224, A.G. 922); nor can this precedent be dismissed as too antiquated: as recently as 1903 a Syrian Orthodox scribe at Jerusalem, whose manuscript will be described in a sequel to this article, referred to "the blessed Fathers of the enviable nation of the Syrian Jacobites". Fiey (1969) uses the term "Jacobite" for convenience, though with an apology (p. 113), because it is "considered offensive" by those to whom it is applied.

5 Hagenmeyer (1901), p. 164, a letter to Pope Urban II, dated 1098: "Nos enim Turcos et paganos expugnavimus, haereticos autem, Graecos et Armenos, Syros Jacobitasque expugnare nequivimus".

These were perhaps the four main administrative entities, although there were of course many other theological schools and linguistic shadings. Meinardus (1964: 68) has already pointed out the difficulty created by the "highly ambiguous usage of the terms 'Syrian' and 'Jacobite' by the Western pilgrims". For these reasons I do not here eschew the term "Jacobite".

2. *The phenomenon of pilgrimage*

According to a text composed at the Abbey of Qartmīn in Ṭūr 'Abdīn, Philoxenus of Mabbūġ wrote in a letter that seven visits to Qartmīn accumulated merit equal to that of a pilgrimage to Jerusalem, because that monastery was built on the model of the Holy City[6]. This indicates that the Jerusalem pilgrimage was considered by Syrian Orthodox Christians around 500 to be beneficial to the soul; indeed, it was the standard against which other pilgrimages were measured. That pilgrimage still has significance for the Syrian Orthodox can be seen from the status accorded in their communities to those who have been to Jerusalem and have acquired the honorific of 'pilgrim to the Holy City'[7]. These pilgrims are held in honour (*cf.* Fiey 1969: 125); they are also expected to be more devout than the others and to be above any kind of ethical reproach. Younger people who go to St Mark's, but do not yet feel equal to such a responsibility, do not aspire to the honorific title, with all that that entails in the way of ritual performances and assiduous pilgrim-tours[8]. More could be said about Syrian Orthodox pilgrimage as a contemporary phenomenon; but our concern here is its history[9].

The most famous of Syrian Orthodox pilgrims is also the first recorded: Barṣawmō of Claudia. This man lived through the formative period which culminated in the ill-starred Council of Chalcedon and died one year before that universally famous Syrian saint, Symeon Stylites, in AD 458. While Symeon was claimed in retrospect by both sides in the Chalcedonian conflict as a supporter, Barṣawmō was the undisputed hero of the dissenters. One can

6 Palmer (1990), microfiche supplement, *Qartmin Trilogy*, XVIII.8-11.

7 The Ṭūrōyō title *Muqsī* is a contraction of the Arabic *maqdisī*. See Kaufhold (1991).

8 Whether a traveller to Jerusalem is "*maqdisī*" or not can be seen by the presence or absence of a representation of the risen Christ tattooed in blue on his skin. The Syrian Orthodox Church distributes a little booklet in which are set out the conditions under which a journey to Jerusalem can be considered as a valid pilgrimage. These are based on the nine injunctions (ideals rather than conditions: see notes 12 and 32 and the comments in the text a little below note 32 on mounted pilgrims) made by Gregory Barhebraeus (d. 1286) in chapter 9 of the first book of his *Ethicon* (Bedjan 1898), translated by Fiey (1969), pp. 117-20.

9 Fiey (1969) is excellent on the nature and characteristics of (Nestorian and) Jacobite pilgrimage; he treats in turn: 1) the arguments for and against pilgrimage to Jerusalem; 2) the preparations; 3) the journey; 4) the rituals performed; 5) the practice of settling in the Holy Land; 6) the pilgrim's return and 7) his death.

read his Life in Syriac, in Arabic and in Ethiopic; and there must surely be an Armenian version, too[10]. His achievements as "the Principal of the Extreme Ascetics" (*rīšō d-āvīlē*) are there zealously catalogued and jealously enumerated. They include four pilgrimages to Jerusalem.

On his first journey, Barṣawmō established his custom of going barefoot, without satchel, purse or stick, neither carrying provisions with him nor entering human settlements on the way. Coins he would not accept as alms. Since Barṣawmō was like Walter Bonatti, who always went one further than other mountaineers, climbing solo if they had climbed in company or scaling a face in the winter which had already been scaled in the summer, we can read this passage as the negative image of the normal pilgrim's equipment and habits. What Barṣawmō did not do was what every pilgrim, even the most devout, normally did.

From this first pilgrimage we learn nothing about the routes from Mesopotamia to the Holy Land. But Barṣawmō's second journey is described in more detail. From Jerusalem he took "the desert route" towards Sinaï, which obliged him to pass through a pagan city called Reqem d-Gaya. This has been understood to mean Nabataean Petra; but "Reqem D-Geyʿa", if that is the same place, is elsewhere identified with the biblical Kadesh-Barnea[11]. Barṣawmō's passage was accompanied by a torrential rainfall, which only stopped when the pagans were converted. On his way back from Mount Sinaï, Barṣawmō went to Rabbat Moab, where there was a great synagogue of the Jews. As at Reqem d-Gaya, the pre-Christian cult did not survive the passage of the saint[12]. The last point mentioned on his journey north (or "back to the east", as the hagiographer puts it) is Telanissus, near Antioch, where he visited Symeon Stylites. Symeon's appearance in the hagiography serves the transparent purpose of attributing to the Stylite himself (and through him to God) the statement that Barṣawmō was the holiest man of his time. Telanissus, therefore, need not have been a point on a genuine journey, though that is not in itself improbable. Reqem d-Gaya and Rabbat Moab also serve a symbolic purpose, the one standing for paganism, the other for Judaism, while the desert route is probably symbolic of the unchristianized regions of the world. Nevertheless, it was conceivable to the intended audience of this story that a party of pilgrims (Barṣawmō was accompanied on this occasion by "forty" monks) might reach Jerusalem and Sinaï by an

10 Grébaut (1908-9); the contents are summarised in Nau (1913), pp. 272-6, 379-89 and (1914a), pp. 113-34, 278-89; the historicity of the text was investigated by Honigmann (1954), chapter 2; I am preparing an edition.

11 Honigmann (1954), p. 17 note 1; Höhne and Wahle (1981).

12 Nau (1927a and b). The indignant Barṣawmō and his loutish disciples clearly did not know the injunction: "Let [the pilgrim's] speech be friendly and his attitude to all and sundry gentle." (Fiey 1969: 118, citing Barhebraeus.)

inland route. We must remember here again that Barṣawmō was no ordinary pilgrim and that this desert route was probably not the one most frequently taken.

On his third and fourth journeys Barṣawmō took to the sea. The first time he embarked at Laodicaea with one hundred disciples and sailed to Cyprus, whence the company crossed back to Palestine in two boats, weathering a storm which seemed to blow them onto the Outer Ocean, so long were they out of sight of land. Back on dry land he passed Sebaste, which is Samaria; now it was the turn of some Samaritans to be converted, this time without any violence. At Jerusalem he visited Golgotha and the Holy Sepulchre, then lodged on Mount Sion in a certain large monastery near the basilica. This must be the "monastery of Photinus on Mount Sion", where he stayed during his fourth and last pilgrimage[13]. On this occasion he also had a large company with him; they had taken the road to Antioch by way of Cyrrhus, where Jacob, another saint made famous by the Chalcedonian Theodoret, provided a glowing testimonial to Barṣawmō's sanctity. From the port of Antioch (Seleucia) they had sailed along the coast to the Holy Land. Was this last not the most obvious way to go? Since Wilkinson, who has studied ancient travel in Palestine, does not mention the coastal ferries, it seems worth arguing the point that they were available, especially since much of the evidence is in unpublished Syriac texts[14].

3. *Evidence for the use of coastal ferries*

The first relevant text is a Latin one. Egeria, the fourth-century pilgrim, describes the length of the journey from Jerusalem to Edessa as twenty-five *mansiones*, meaning that one spent twenty-five nights in different places along the way. Between Jerusalem and Antioch she mentions no place, which would be odd in so detailed a narrative, unless she went by sea. By contrast, between Antioch and Edessa she made notes on the journey through Coele Syria to Euphratensis, on Hierapolis (Mabbūġ), on the Euphrates crossing, and on

13 Nau (1914a), pp. 115 and 122; Milik (1960-61), pp. 164-6, identified this monastery with the church of the Samaritan Woman, citing evidence that her name may have been preserved as Photina. If he is right, a corruption must have crept into the manuscript tradition at an early stage: by the omission of one dot the feminine possessive suffix could have been transformed into the masculine found in all the witnesses (DYRH D-PWṬYN'). But in fact, the very presence of the possessive suffix and the absence of an honorific suggest that the reference is not to the dedicate of a church within the monastery, but to the founder of the monastery.

14 Wilkinson (1977), pp. 15-32. It was noted above that Barṣawmō's hagiographer envisaged his journey from Jerusalem back to Claudia, south of Melitene (Malatya), as a journey from west to east rather than from south to north. If one was accustomed to the coastal route to Jerusalem, one would know that every morning's journey began with the sun in one's back and would therefore conclude instinctively that Jerusalem lay to the west of Antioch.

Batanis (Baṭnōn da-Srūġ). If she did not go by sea, she must have made a special detour to see Antioch, knowing that she would pass through it again on her way from Edessa to Tarsus[15]. Besides, the fifth-century Syriac version of the legend of Abgar tells how the king of Edessa sent a messenger to Jerusalem, who left Edessa on 14 March and arrived in Jerusalem on 12 April, a period of exactly thirty days[16]. This messenger would have been mounted on a horse and intent on speed, but anxious to avoid the possible delay of waiting for a fair wind or being blown off course. If thirty days was a fast riding speed overland, twenty-five days was probably the normal journey-time for those who went by boat with a favourable wind and continued by donkey or on foot. As we shall see, some fifteenth-century pilgrims managed to reach Ṭūr ʿAbdīn from Jerusalem in under a month and this was impressive.

The so-called *Chronicle of Joshua the Stylite*, composed in Syriac at Edessa in or shortly after 506[17], contains the following passage relevant to our enquiry: "We received a letter from certain acquaintances of ours, who were travelling to Jerusalem, in which it was stated that, on the same night in which that great blazing fire appeared, the city of Ptolemais or ʿAkkō (= Acre) was overturned, and nothing in it left standing"[18]. The *Life of Aḥḥō of Rīš ʿAynō*, which is more in the nature of a folk-tale than a biography of the sixth-century saint, is more explicit because of the role played in the story by the ferry-crew, who turn out to be Aḥḥō's brothers. Aḥḥō stayed for one and a half years in Palestine, then set off home; but when he reached Acre "he felt so weary from the toil of the road, that he decided to board ship for Antioch". The text continues: "when they had sailed as far as Tiberias, a heavy gale struck their ship and it was obliged to stay out at sea for three days before entering harbour"[19]. Clearly it was normal to dock every night. The reference to Tiberias suggests that one spoke of the ports not by their own names, but by the names of the important inland cities which they served.

The most interesting description of all is the fifteenth-century source already referred to. The priest Addai of Bēṯ Səvīrīnō in Ṭūr ʿAbdīn made the journey in 1491/2. He writes of it in such an unpolished and inconsistent style (one cannot help improving it in translation) that he can hardly even have written a preparatory draft[20]. The passage omitted from the middle concerns

15 Francheschini and Weber (1965) and Wilkinson (1981), sections 17-19 of the *Itinerarium*.
16 Philips (1876), p. 3; Howard (1981), p. 7.
17 For the true authorship see Palmer (1990b).
18 Wright (1882), chapter xlvii; Chabot (1927), 274: 4-9.
19 *Cf.* Vööbus (1956); Baumstark (1922); I am preparing an edition.
20 Budge (1932), vol. 2, pp. L-LII (Syriac text, fol. 200a-201a); the translation given in this article is my own.

matters of politics, which need not concern us here. I append my comments in the form of footnotes:

> The priest Addai [...] was accompanied by his son, the priest Qawmē, the monk Rabbān Šābō of Ṣālaḥ, two priests of Bēṯ Səvīrīnō, Gabriel and Reuben, and many laymen from the same village. They went with Ḫwāğa Ḥasan[21] of Mardīn, the emir, who had undertaken a diplomatic mission to Egypt bearing splendid gifts and letters of peaceful intent from Sulaymān Bağ. His son, Muḥammad, accompanied him, as did a long caravan of merchants. [...]
>
> Ḫwāğa Ḥasan showed tokens of great respect to the priest Addai and to his fellow-pilgrims and they did not have to give a farthing to anyone throughout the journey. They enjoyed great comfort, thanks to the ambassador and his servants, as far as the town of Ramla[22]; there they encountered the emir of Jerusalem, on his way to the Holy City. After consulting with us, the ambassador said, "I am going to commit you to the protection of this man; I will give him instructions about you". We unpacked two fine coats as a present for the governor of Jerusalem and we entered the city in his company. Many hostile eyes followed us on our way, but they were unable to do us any harm[23].
>
> On his way back from Egypt[24] the ambassador said to us, "Will you not go back with me to our own country?" But it was the middle of January when he returned and not yet time for us to head for home. We stayed to receive the Holy Light[25] and to get a blessing from the Holy Sepulchre and from the Holy Places, then we left the Holy City and went back home, the priest Addai and his companions. Two of them, however, Rabbān Šābō the monk, from Ṣālaḥ, and the priest Gabriel from Bēṯ Səvīrīnō, died in Damascus; the priest Addai and his

21 "Ḫwāğa was a title particularly of great merchants; it was not appropriate for the clerisy": communication from Michael Rogers of the British Museum, 31 vii 1984.

22 From the fact that Ramla lay on Addai's route to Jerusalem we can infer that he came by sea, probably having embarked at Seleucia by Antioch; and from the fact that Addai does not tell us this, though he goes into some detail about the return journey by way of Damascus and Ḥama, we understand that this was the normal route (see below).

23 This is a graphic expression of the fears which were felt by pilgrims, even on the well-trodden highway between Jaffa and Jerusalem; it also shows that even after giving two fine coats to the governor of Jerusalem, Addai and his companions had possessions with them which made them acutely conscious of potential robbers (*cf.* note 32).

24 This seems to imply that the ambassador decided to visit Jerusalem after all on his way back home, surely because of his Muslim faith, whereas his urgent business had made it advisable to avoid the delay on the way to Egypt, since he saw an opportunity of transferring his duty of protection to another powerful man. This inference, if valid, gives some indication of how seriously the duty of protecting Christians could be taken by a Muslim, since the ambassador would apparently have made the detour to Jerusalem, however urgent his international mission, if he had not met the governor of that city at Ramla.

25 This is a reference to the ritual commemorating Christ's Resurrection on Easter Sunday, whereby a light "appeared" out of the Holy Sepulchre, which was used to distribute the flame to each pilgrim present. Meinardus (1964:79), in the section of his article devoted to "The Syrian Jacobite Sites of the 20th Century", gives a time-table for the Jacobite activities in the Church of the Resurrection during Holy Week: "At 1.00 p.m., the Syrian Jacobite representatives take the Holy Fire from the *Kouvouklion* to the Chapel of St. Nicodemus. Simultaneously, Syrian Jacobite laymen take the Holy Fire from the southern oval window of the Chapel of the Angel and proceed via the southern portion of the Rotunda to the Chapel of St. Nicodemus". On the descent of the Holy Light, or Holy Fire, see Fiey (1969), pp. 119-20. Barhebraeus (cited *ibid.*, p. 118) enjoins the pilgrim to be at Jerusalem for the whole of Holy Week (see note 8).

son the priest Qawmē, and the two priests Ṣəlīvō and Reuben, Addai's disciples, were there to prepare them for burial. For when we had come ashore off the Sea of Cyprus, some of us had gone to Damascus, while others continued as far as Tripolis and travelled to Ḥama from there. When we ourselves reached Ḥama, Rabbān Joshua the monk, of Bēṯ Səvīrīnō, the son of the priest Moses, became ill and died and was given a funeral and buried by the aforementioned priests.

In Damascus, the priest Qawmē fell seriously ill, but God — glory to His Grace! — made him well again. His father, in Ḥama, was waiting for his return[26]. The priest Addai waited for forty days, then went to Damascus with great sorrow[27] and so they came back (eventually) to Ḥama. However, their departure from Damascus was delayed until after Pentecost, because the entire land of Šām, together with Egypt and Romania, was in the grip of a fatal epidemic[28]. Moreover, the roads had been blocked by certain persons. Meanwhile some of their companions were safe at home after a month on the road, having escaped the contagion altogether[29].

From Ḥama they came to Aleppo. But the roads were closed to merchants and to travellers in both directions because of the horrible disease which infected the whole of the land of Šām. Besides, strife had broken out with the kingdom of the Mongols. Since they[30] were in an uncomfortable situation and certain friends not previously mentioned, whom we had expected to be making the journey by way of Edessa, did not arrive, they went with a commercial convoy of certain Muslim rebels, which took a path through the difficult mountain-country to Gargar, following the course of the Euphrates[31]. After eight days they entered Gargar, where the laird of Gargar seized and abused them and imprisoned them in his castle for eight days, until the feast of St Thomas Apostle (3 July), having deprived them of their girdles, their crosses and their provisions. Afterwards he released them and they crossed over the Euphrates. Bishop Bahnām of Gargar — the Lord have mercy on him! — who had been the disciple of the patriarch, John the Gargarite (*Gargarī*) — God have mercy on both of them! — was very kind to them indeed[32]. From there they came to Ḥaṣram castle

26 Addai himself, it would appear, probably accompanied by his disciples, Səlīvō and Reuben, sailed on to Tripolis and went to Ḥama direct. His son, with the monk Šābō and the priest Gabriel, disembarked, probably at Beirut, and crossed the mountains to Damascus, where the disease caught up with them.

27 Addai waited at Ḥama for forty days (which may perhaps be a way of saying "for a long time", considering there are only fifty days between Easter and Pentecost), then travelled south to Damascus to find out what had happened, fearing the worst for his son.

28 "Šām" designates virtually the whole area between Egypt and Anatolia; the latter is here referred to as "Romania".

29 Addai can only have learned this after his return; for discussion of the journey-time, see above.

30 Addai and his son, with their remaining companions.

31 This convoy was a poor substitute for a friendly caravan, which would have taken the normal route through Edessa; yet clearly the pilgrims did not dare to take even that route without an escort, at least not in the unstable situation described by Addai. On the route between Damascus and Aleppo, however, it must have been easy to find a party to go with, since Addai speaks of these journeys without any comment. Addai's route up the Euphrates is likely to have been the old Roman road from Zeugma (present-day Belkis, near Nizip) to Rumkale, Samosata and Gargar, parts of which had to be tunnelled in the walls of the river-gorge. See Wagner (1976).

32 It is interesting to note that Addai and his companions had at least two fine coats in their baggage on the way to Jerusalem, although they cannot have known they would have to find a present for the governor of Jerusalem (*cf.* note 23), whereas the laird of Gargar could find

and the laird of that castle seized them and stripped and plundered them of what remained in their possession. He gave them their fill of pain and misfortune; and if God — praise to His Goodness! — had not come to their aid, all of them would have been killed. From there they reached the town of Čarmūk[33] and found some small relief; and so they came to Amida[34]. But they found all the gates of the city cemented up with masonry and Nūr ʿAlī Baġ pitilessly sacking and plundering all the territory of Ḥasan Baġ.

Since Addai's friends probably had to get back to Bēṯ Səvīrīnō they must have embarked at Jaffa or at Caesarea and have sailed in very good time to Seleucia, where they must have hired mounts for the journey to Edessa in a caravan which was leaving the same day with that destination. They must have been equally fortunate in finding a convoy with which to ride to Nisibis, from which they could perhaps reach home in one long day's riding. Of course, they must have ridden, in spite of Barhebraeus's injunction to the pilgrim to go on foot "if possible" (see note 8). They cannot have been exaggerating their speed to impress the unfortunate Addai, because everyone knew when they arrived and the date of Easter was fixed as the eve of their departure. In fact, their good fortune may be linked to the large-scale rhythm of pilgrimage: travelling from Jerusalem to a Christian area immediately after Easter, one was riding on the crest of a wave. There was every chance of finding large numbers of people making the same journey, having perhaps combined their business interests with a pilgrimage to Jerusalem (*cf.* note 32).

My sketch map (Fig. 1) gives an idea of the routes which could have been taken by the North-Mesopotamian pilgrims going to Jerusalem. It can be used to follow the routes of Egeria, Barṣawmō, Aḥḥō, Theodotus, Addai and his companions. Theodotus (see note 38, below) visited Sinai first, presumably making the journey largely be sea (since no places on the way are named), and walked from there to Jerusalem, which was, in terms of the

nothing of value on them when they returned except for girdles, crosses and provisions. Perhaps they took saleable articles with them to pay for their journey home. Commerce may also be the explanation of the choice not to go with the multitude on the return journey, especially since Addai nowhere says *why* he and his son and their friends needed to go to Damascus and Ḥama. It would have been all too easy for a moralist to put their bad luck down to their worldly concerns. That insinuation may be present, for example, in the *Chronicle of Joshua the Stylite* (Wright 1882, chapters xxxiv-xxxv; Chabot 1927, 260:5-262:6), where an evil fate befalls pilgrims at Arsamosata, many of whom have commercial reasons for attending the feast of the martyrs; and Barhebraeus discouraged pilgrims from trying to combine material with spiritual profit (see note 8). The kindness of the Bishop of Gargar may have consisted in mediating with the laird of Gargar and in giving the pilgrims new belts and enough money (as they thought) to reach home. John, the son of Qūphar, of ʿAynwardo, was called *Gargarī*, "the Gargarite". He was one of two patriarchs in Ṭūr ʿAbdīn and he died at Ḥāḥ in the early part of AD 1493. This information is to be found in Abbeloos and Lamy (1872-77), cols. 841-44, part of the continuation of the *Ecclesiastical History* of Barhebraeus. The author of this continuation was none other than the priest Addai of Bēṯ Səvīrīnō.

33 Modern Çermük.

34 Modern Diyarbakır, on the Tigris.

"History of Salvation", the right order in which to do things. That he took first to the sea is suggested more specifically by his encounter with a rich Antiochene on the first leg of his journey: Antioch was otherwise very much out of his way from the monastery of Qennešrē opposite Ǧerablūs.

FIG. 1: ROUTES FROM MESOPOTAMIA TO JERUSALEM AND SINAI

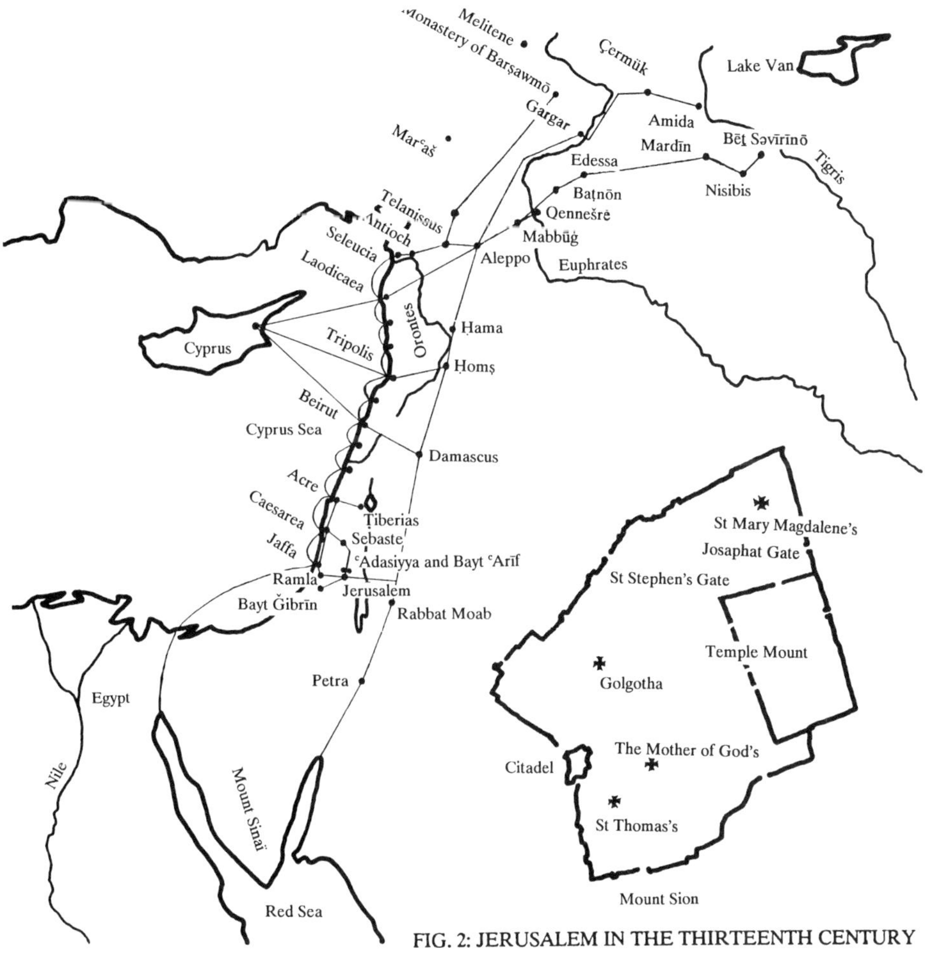

FIG. 2: JERUSALEM IN THE THIRTEENTH CENTURY

4. *The property of the Jacobites in Jerusalem* (Fig. 2)

Barṣawmō had stayed in a monastery on Mount Sion. The Life does not mention the fact that the Upper Room was usually thought to have been on that mountain[35]. Later tradition (from the sixteenth century) would situate the Upper Room in the monastery of St Mark. The location of the Upper Room on Mount Sion, which is widely favoured by non-Syrians, is attested in at least one Syriac source, although that is not Syrian Orthodox, but Chalcedonian: the *Inauguration Anthem of Hagia Sophia at Edessa*, written in the 540s[36].

Who gave lodging to Jacobite pilgrims after the destruction of the monastery of Photinus on Mount Sion[37] and before the first recorded construction of a Jacobite church in Jerusalem is uncertain; as we shall see, they probably had their own church there by the Arab conquest, although there is no record of its construction. One example of a pilgrim from the early Islamic period is Theodotus of Amida († 698). He caused illnesses to be healed by scattering dust from the Holy Sepulchre. But nothing is recorded about where he stayed[38]. Around 800, during the lifetime of Charlemagne, there were 29 recluses on the Mount of Olives, eleven speakers of Greek, four Georgians, six Syrians, two Armenians, five Latins, and "one who chants in the Saracen tongue" (a lonely solitary indeed!). There was a Syrian recluse at the bottom and another at the top of the steps leading up onto the hill, along with a couple of Greek hermits and one Georgian[39]. It is not stated whether these Syrian hermits were Jacobites; but, given such detail, it would be surprising if a sizeable Syrian *monastic establishment* had been overlooked in this description of Jerusalem.

Yet a *church* belonging to the Jacobites there certainly was at the time of Charlemagne; and the context in which it is mentioned suggests that they considered it to be older than the establishment of Islam[40]. For when the

35 O'Connor (1980), p. 75; Tobler (1874), pp. 134-6, 197-9, 242.

36 Palmer (1988), pp. 133 and 156.

37 This probably occurred when Mount Sion was burned by the Persians in 614.

38 For this text, of which I am preparing an edition, see Palmer (1987a, 1989, forthcoming) and Vööbus (1976).

39 Tobler (1874), p. 79.

40 If the monastery of Photinus on Mount Sion was the resort of Jacobites in the early period, as the Life of Barṣawmō suggests, then the early seventh century, after the Persian sack of 614 and before the Arab conquest of Jerusalem in 638, is the most likely date for the construction of the church destroyed by Hārūn. Dōlabānī (1928), pp. 438-40 cites from St Mark's MS 123 the following two colophons: 1) "This book was given to our Jacobite church in Jerusalem by Ḥannah, the mother superior, and her fellow-nun and spiritual friend ʿAzīzto. May God pardon them and their departed ones and write their names in the heavenly Jerusalem! The gift was made in the reign of me, the least of all exiles, Jeremy, in name the metropolitan of the same see; and I have decreed by the living word of the Lord that no one shall have authority to remove it from the said place or to rub out this record. The year is 1061 (AD 749/50)". 2) "Michael, by the limitless grace of almighty God patriarch of the apostolic see of Antioch (= Michael I, 1166-1199)... Let no one [remove] this book from our monastery... which is named after St Mary Magdalene". From these two colophons Dōlabānī concludes that the monastery of Mary Magdalene was inhabited by Jacobite nuns in the eighth century; equally, the nunnery having ceased to exist, the ninth-century foundation

caliph Hārūn al-Rashīd ordered the destruction of Jacobite churches in 806/7, his pretext must have been that they had been built after Muḥammad, something which Muslim law forbade; yet "he tore down ancient churches, too, and our church in Jerusalem"[41]. This explains the construction in the early ninth century of a new Jacobite church, on which more below.

Appended to the chronicle just cited, which was written by the twelfth-century Jacobite patriarch Michael, is a list of the bishops of Jerusalem, beginning with James, the brother of Jesus[42]. The Syrian Orthodox possess no register of episcopal ordinations going back before 793, but they claim a certain Theodosius, bishop of Jerusalem, a contemporary of Chalcedon (451), and Severus (590-635) as opponents of the Council[43]. From 793 until the reign of Michael himself (1106-99) the bishops listed there also appear in the Jacobite *Register of Episcopal Ordinations*[44]. These metropolitan bishops cannot have been without a church and a residence in Jerusalem and, since they were all monks, there must have been a Jacobite monastic establishment of kinds in the Holy City from the beginning of this period at least. This may at first have been the nunnery attested by St Mark's MS 123 (see note 40). From that colophon it seems that the establishment may have been limited to two nuns and the metropolitan. The absence from the *Register* of explicit references to bishops who had received their monastic training in Jerusalem before the early twelfth century suggests that the "monastery" there was at first little more than the establishment of the bishop. The first reference to a bishop who had received his training at "our monastery in Jerusalem" shortly precedes the consecration of Ignatius Ḥesnūn, who found the existing episcopal residence at Jerusalem unworthy of the dignity of his office[45].

In the first quarter of the twelfth century this Ignatius Ḥesnūn (d. 1124/5) rebuilt the church and monastery of St Mary Magdalene on the site of the previous church, which had been founded by an Egyptian called Macarius of Nabrūwah in the early ninth century, apparently to replace the church destroyed in 806/7[46]. This establishment was probably ruined like many of

of Mary Magdalene may have inherited its books. These colophons do not prove, as Dōlabānī claims, that St Mary Magdalene's was the residence of the Jacobite metropolitans from the time of the Arab Conquest onwards.

41 Chabot (1899-1910) XII.5, vol. 3, p. 21 (Syriac text, p. 490). The word 'and' here means 'including'.

42 Chabot (1899-1910), Appendix IV.

43 See Fedalto (1983), p. 24; the bishop Samuel does not belong in this list, since he was a Malkite ("Syrus").

44 Chabot (1899-1910), Appendix III, hereinafter referred to as *Register*.

45 *Register*, XLI.30,32; Martin (1889), pp. 52, 73.

46 Ḥesnūn: Martin (1889), pp. 52, 73, translated below; a record of the death of this bishop has survived in epigraphic form on the chancel-screen of the present main church at St Mark's = No. 2 in Appendix II, following Part 2. On Macarius see Evetts (1915), p. 461.

the other Christian shrines of Jerusalem by the Caliph al-Ḥākim in 1009[47]. For more than eighty years after that no Jacobite church is known to have existed at Jerusalem. But in 1092 Manṣūr, a Jacobite from Tilbāna in Egypt, built a church there, which is not to be confused with the church built by Macarius. Abū 'l-Makārim, who wrote between the two periods of Crusader rule in the city, clearly distinguishes St Mary Magdalene's from the church built by Manṣūr[48]. If the two churches have nevertheless been confounded, that is because the latter is described as "the" church of the Orthodox Jacobites in Jerusalem. This could, however, be because St Mary Magdalene's, which Ignatius Ḥesnūn rebuilt from its ruins, was out of use in 1092. Alternatively, Abū 'l-Makārim was referring to his own time, when St Mary Magdalene's had been converted into a Muslim school.

The church and monastery of St Mary Magdalene, to which was added the title "and of Simon the Pharisee" (Simon is sometimes named first and once the name of Mary Magdalene is omitted: see Appendix I following Part 2 of this article), was near St Anne's in the north-west quarter of Jerusalem, by a postern gate which gave access to the space between the two walls without forming an entrance to the city[49]. This situation can be reconstructed on the basis of the topographical sketch in a manuscript of Cambrai, where the church is drawn as if standing on an elevation, though on the Cambrai plan the inner wall with the postern gate is not represented[50]. In the twelfth century the monks claimed to possess a hair of the Magdalene, which had been discovered on the spot, "proving" that this was where she had anointed

47 Bernard Hamilton, personal communication, 2 vii 1990.

48 Renaudot (1713), p. 466, quoted by Cerulli (1943), p. 13 (who verified the text in the Vatican MSS) and Meinardus (1960), pp. 12-13 and p. 16 (Abū 'l-Makārim).

49 There were not two monasteries, one of Simon and one of the Magdalene, as is supposed by Meinardus (1931), p. 63; as for the "church of St Peter", of which Karkenny (1976), p. 62 states that "Almost every time the Church of St Mary Magdalene is mentioned, this church is referred to as a church in the neighbourhood", this must, I think, be a similar error, compounded by the confusion of Simon with Peter. Karkenny, *loc. cit.*, further mentions the "church of Mary Kar'a" and the "church of al-Bashoura" as Syrian, but cites no evidence. Tobler (1874), pp. 164-5, 219-20; Taylor (1931), p. 121. The postern gate plays a romantic role in the tale reported in *L'Estoire de Eracles Empereur et la Conqueste de la terre d'Outremer*, in *Historiens des Croisades: Historiens Occidentaux*, II, p. 27: In 1185 or 1186 the Jacobite abbot is supposed to have aided a spy of the Count of Tripolis by letting him in through the postern and disguising him as a monk. The story-teller conveniently forgot that the postern did not give access from outside the city. The north-west quarter was called the Jewry, yet in the twelfth century it was inhabited by the Syrians (the Malkites had a church of St Chariton near St Stephen's Gate); Prawer (1980), pp. 93ff., suggests that the Jewry was depopulated by the Crusader massacre of 1099 and that the Syrians, displaced by the Europeans from the area around Golgotha, moved into the empty houses of the unfortunate Jews.

50 The Cambrai Plan is published Röhricht (1891), pp. 139-40, plate IV; it is reproduced photographically in Boase (1971), fig. 2, and in Vincent and Abel (1922), p. 944; for a modern plan of Crusader Jerusalem see Prag (1989), p. 39.

Jesus's feet[51]. The Gospels are unanimous that this anointing occurred at Simon's house in Bethany, but evidently pilgrims were not generally familiar with the exact text of the Bible (Matthew 26:6-13; Mark 14:3-9; John 12:1-8), nor did the monks trouble to disillusion them. Other relics were the head of St James and an arm of St Stephen[52]. Opposite the entrance to St Mary Magdalene's was built a hostel around a courtyard, with three rain-water cisterns under it. This was done by Ignatius, son of Busayr of Ǧādina, the successor of Ignatius Ḥesnūn, shortly after 1125[53].

According to various manuscript colophons of the twelfth century the monastery attached to this church could prove its legal claim to the villages of Bayt ʿArīf and ʿAdasiyya, as well as to that of Dayr Ḏakariyya[54]. The estates of Bayt ʿArīf and ʿAdasiyya straddled the Nablūs road to the north of Jerusalem at a few miles' distance[55]. Dayr Ḏakariyya has not been located[56]; like the other two it was abandoned when the Jacobites fled to Egypt in 1098 before the Crusader assault on Jerusalem and it was subsequently claimed by the Frankish conquerors. Bayt ʿArīf and ʿAdasiyya were claimed by the knight Geoffrey of the Tower of David. All these estates were restored to the Jacobites in the twelfth century, after lengthy and expensive legal battles. In ʿAdasiyya they built a defensive tower containing a chapel on the fourth storey. There were two rain-water cisterns at the foot of the tower. Next to this tower was built a small monastery, which was regarded as a dependency of St Mary Magdalene's. It was called the Monastery of the Tower or the Monastery of ʿAdasa[57]. In Dayr Ḏakariyya they built a tower for defence, a church and a number of rooms around the tower[58].

51 Tobler (1874), pp. 132-3; Meinardus (1960), p. 15: some hair of St Mary Magdalene preserved in a feretory in the Monastery of the Syrians in Wādī al-Naṭrūn, Egypt (*cf.* Meinardus 1964: 64); an anonymous pilgrim of 1140, translated in *P.P.T.S.*, VI, 12, quoted by Meinardus, *ibid.*, also saw the Magdalene's hair.

52 See the anonymous pilgrim of 1140 (note 51).

53 Martin (1889), pp. 54, 75, 76, translated below.

54 Martin (1888, 1889); Taylor (1931) with Appendix I, following Part 2 of this article. The name "Ḏakariyya" has not been satisfactorily explained.

55 Prawer (1980), p. 132.

56 Taylor (1931), p. 124, translates this passage wrongly: the village "had belonged to the monastery formerly, in the time of the Muslims"; it was not taken by the Muslims. This and other mistakes make him say on p. 121 falsely (a) that the refugees' demands for food and clothing were *violent*, (b) that Dayr Ḏakariyya had been alienated from the monastery since the *Muslim* conquest and (c) that Ignatius had to be defended against a *charge* of wrongful confiscation. The inaccuracy of Taylor's translation is such that only a new translation can make this colophon useful. My translation, made from the copy published by Taylor, forms Appendix I of this article.

57 Martin (1889), pp. 50-3, 54, 71, 73, 76.

58 Taylor (1931), p. 124; for a better translation, see Appendix I. The fact that the text there translated refers to "our monasteries", in the plural, at Jerusalem shows that the Monastery of the Tower at ʿAdasiyya was in operation in 1148, so that the same writer's claim that the

In the interval of Muslim rule which followed Saladin's capture of the city in 1187 St Mary Magdalene's was converted into a Muslim school named al-Maymūniyya, after Saladin's treasurer, who founded it[59]. This gave the Muslims a claim to it when they returned, which seems to have meant that the Syrian Orthodox were obliged to abandon the church, although they certainly occupied it again from 1229 to 1244. The ruins of the "New Maymūniyya" survived into the mid-nineteenth century and were planned and drawn then. The reconstruction of the church of St Mary Magdalene by De Vogüé is impressive[60]. One can well believe that it was accounted the fourth in importance among the churches of Jerusalem[61].

When the Jacobites had to leave St Mary Magdalene's, they probably moved directly to St Thomas's[62]. This was originally a German church and so is likely to have been vacated at the end of second period of Crusader rule[63]. This tiny Crusader building near the citadel was given to the Muslims by the incumbent Jacobite monk when he was converted to Islam in 1451/2[64]. The Syriac inscriptions by the entrance in the south wall were deleted and that entrance was walled up to make a simple miḥrāb[65]. The conversion of the building into a mosque made it impossible for the Syrian Orthodox to reclaim it[66]; but evidence from seventeenth-century pilgrims and later writers suggests that the Muslims did not use it[67].

monasteries did not have estates and villages to provide for more than their subsistence in bread and pulses should not be read as a denial that they possessed ʿAdasiyya and Bayt ʿArīf at that time. The apologetic tenor of this text requires that estates other than Dayr Ḏakariyya be kept as far as possible out of the picture in order to deprive an opponent of the argument that the Jacobites did not need Dayr Ḏakariyya in addition to their other estates.

59 Abū 'l-Yumn al-ʿUlaymī, *Kitāb al-ins al-ğalīl bi-ta'rīḫ al-Quds wa-l-Ḫalīl* (Cairo, A.H. 1283), p. 399, cited by Cerulli (1943), vol. I, p. 14.

60 Vincent and Abel (1922), p. 992; Vogüé (1860), pp. 292-5 and Plate XXI, reproduced by Cerulli (1943), fig. 2.

61 Meinardus (1960), p. 21.

62 Meinardus (1964), p. 67, refers to Ǧaǧǧāwī (1955) for the information that the Jacobites were in possession of St Thomas's in 1354 and that Basil III, Jacobite patriarch of Antioch, resided in that monastery and was buried there in 1444. This tallies with the following MS evidence for the monastery of St Thomas supplied to me by Hubert Kaufhold: "1353: Paris Syr. 213 and Paris Syr. 245 (s. Zotenberg); 1417/8: Jerusalem, Markuskloster 96 [Baumstark (1911), p. 108, No. 10]; 1430: Vermerk in der Hs. Damaskus 5/23 (olim Jerusalem 117): Stiftung für das Thomaskloster in Jerusalem durch den Patriarchen Ignatios Hadaya".

63 Vincent and Abel (1922), p. 950 note 2.

64 Abbeloos and Lamy (1872-77), pt. 2, cols. 835-42; Cambridge, University Library, MS Dd. 3.8/1 s. XV, foll. 82-87; *cf.* Wright (1901), pp. 979-85, and Barṣawm (1943), p. 450. I am preparing an edition.

65 Vincent and Abel (1922), pp. 950-53, with a plan, elevations, drawings and two photographs.

66 The Cambridge MS (note 64), fol. 86a-b: "Then he (John Bar Šay Allāh) took the trouble to go up to Egypt to rescue Saint Thomas, but he was unable to do so, because he (*sic*) *had been made by them into a place for their worship (bēṯ masgəḏhūn)*".

67 Moore (1961), pp. 84, 89, 97; O'Connor (1980), p. 52; Prag (1989), p. 213; the Armenian claim to the chapel, asserted by O'Connor, is not mentioned by Hintlian (1976).

For twenty years after 1452 the Jacobites were without a church in the Holy City. Then they acquired the monastery of the Mother of God, Mary. This monastery had originally belonged to the Copts, but it was bought from them by the patriarch Ḫalaf in the 1470s and extended through the incorporation of adjacent properties by his successor, John. This sale was ratified by the Mamluk and Muslim religious authorities in Egypt[68]. The monastery of the Mother of God is identical with the present St Mark's, which also bears the dedication to her[69]. This monastery was endowed with a hostel by George of Bēṯ Səvīrīnō, bishop of Qartmīn Abbey, in 1489/90. Next to the monastery, in the vicinity of the hostel, was the house of Mary, the mother of John Mark, which had been recently acquired by the Syrians at the time of the priest Addai's visit in 1491/2[70]. That was the house to which the apostle Peter ran when he escaped from prison (Acts 12:12).

In telling the story of this escape, Addai calls the house Peter's house, and describes the maid Rhoda as Peter's daughter[71]. This shows that the association with St Peter, not that with St Mark, was uppermost in his mind. Later, by a process we can imaginatively reconstruct, the house came to be identified with the location of the Last Supper. Mark 14:51-2 tells of a young man who escaped naked after Jesus's arrest in the garden of Gethsemane, leaving the soldiers with nothing but a sheet in their hands. Who else could known this but "Mark" himself? And how did he come to be there, wrapped only in a sheet, unless he had been sleeping in the house where Jesus ate the Passover meal[72]? The church of the Mother of God contains a Syriac inscription, possibly made about 1500, to judge by the letter-forms, which claims that the church was rebuilt after the destruction of Jerusalem by Titus in AD 73 (*sic*), and that the previous structure on the site, though proclaimed a church by

68 For the information in these four sentences, see note 64.

69 Bahnām (1962). "Der Name 'Muttergotteskirche' bleibt eigentlich immer erhalten. In Ordinationslisten erscheint häufig 'Markuskloster und Muttergotteskirche'." (Hubert Kaufhold, personal communication, 18 ii 1990). One example, pointed out to me by Hubert Kaufhold, is in the seventeenth century MS Egerton 704 in the British Library: see Wright (1870), p. 2.

70 Palmer (1990a), microfiche supplement, *Book of Life*, H. 18 and H. 24, Syriac text, fol. L, pp. 81-2. This is also the source for the information in the previous sentence.

71 Palmer (1990a), microfiche supplement, *Book of Life*, H. 18, Syriac text, fol. L, p. 82; on authorship, see E3.

72 The name of "St Mark's" seems first to appear in the two-volume Syriac Old Testament in Milan, according to Galbiati (1963), p. 192: "lavoro compiuto a Gerusalemme nel monastero di San Marco ... nel 1613" (*cf.* note 69). Sandys (1632) uses the name and calls it "an obscure church in the custody of the Syrians". Doubdan (1652) has the following description of St Mark's: "The entrance is very dark and leads to a long wooden slope at the foot of about twenty steps, at the top of which there is a little courtyard from which one enters the church". A little further on he mentions the ruins of a chapel said to be the Cenacle. The Swedish pilgrim, Hasselquist (1751), says that the House of St Mark is a Syrian church with an old stone font. These travellers are known to me from Moore (1961), pp. 85, 89, 97.

the apostles, had originally been the house of Mary, the mother of John Mark[73]. Some bishop of the monastery appears to have considered this inscription fraudulent and to have covered it with plaster, for it was only rediscovered in 1940, when the church was restored. Persons without sufficient knowledge of Syriac epigraphy have pronounced it to be of the fifth or sixth century.

Shortly after Addai's visit, the Syrian Orthodox appear to have regained the monastery attached to the former church of St Thomas, though not the church itself. Karkenny (1976: 59-60) translates a firman dated AH 987 (AD 1579/80), which confirms the rights of the Jacobites to St Mark's and St Thomas's "churches", for which we should read "monasteries". Just before this, Karkenny had translated another document dated AH 1030 (AD 1620/21) confirming the identity of a press "situated within St Thomas's Convent, owned by the Syrian Jacobites, located in the Zion Street to the West of the Victorious Fortress"; and on p. 58 he distinguishes between the erstwhile church of St Thomas, which exists as a mosque "up to this day and is taken care of by the sons of Al-Deisi", and a monastery of the same name, the ruins of which were sold to the Anglicans by the Muslims in 1838, enabling them to build Christ Church there. The Vatican Syriac MS 259 was bought for the monastery of St Thomas at Jerusalem in 1515[74].

Karkenny (1976), pp. 52-6, provides information not to be found elsewhere, except in the library of St Mark's, about the so-called Monastery of the Lentils (Dayr al-ʿAdas). We have seen that the Monastery of the Tower at ʿAdasiyya was also called the Monastery of ʿAdasa. But at a later date there was a monastery called Dayr al-ʿAdas in the city of Jerusalem itself. This monastery came into Syrian Orthodox hands in 1532, when it was bought by "Bishop Gregorius Yousef Al Korrji" from "a muslim called Yousef Ben Marei" for the sum of 4,000 dirhams. (According to Meinardus 1964: 68-9,

73 Bahnām (1962); O'Connor (1980), p. 52; Prag (1989), pp. 212-3. The inscription is published as No. 1 in Appendix II, after Part 2 of this article.

74 Mai (1825-38), vol. 5, p. 2. I owe this reference to Hubert Kaufhold, who adds the following: "Es müßte 1479 in Jerusalem auch noch eine syrische Kirche des heiligen Georg gegeben haben, s. die Weiheliste der Hs. Paris Syr. 110 [Nau (1915), pp. 512-15]: 'Le Saint Esprit a ordonné Michel prêtre pour la sainte église de Mar Georges à Jérusalem et pour toutes les églises de Dieu'. Oder war es die Weihe eines Kopten für das koptische Georgkloster, das aber erstmals 1720 belegt ist [Meinardus (1960), pp. 66-9]? Vielleicht hatten die Kopten zu dieser Zeit keinen Bischof in Jerusalem. In der Liste der koptischen Bischöfe bei Meinardus [(1960), p. 81] sind für die Zeit von 1362-1575 keine vermerkt. Oder ist die Georgkirche in Damaskus gemeint (die in Paris Syr. 110 ein paarmal erscheint)? 1585 wurde in Jerusalem noch die Hs. Leningrad 236 (Evangelien, jakobitisch, karschuni) geschrieben 'au monastère vénéré nommé "La Prison du Messie" (ḥabs al-masīḥ) qui est à Sion, auprès du Cénacle, le 12 jour du jeune de la Vierge, l'an 1896 de l'ère des Grecs' (s. D. Günzbourg u.a., Les Mss. Arabes ... de l'Institut des Langues Orientales, St. Petersbourg 1891, 94f.). Auch ein Kloster der Jakobiten? Wohl kaum".

who refers to Ǧaǧǧāwī 1955, the date of acquisition was 1527; Nau 1915: 518-9 seems to show that Gregory Kurǧī — "the Georgian" — was succeeded in or before September 1527 by Gregory Bahnām). The acquisition was confirmed by an "official document" numbered 95-96-97, which is "preserved in the monastery of St. Mark". Karkenny does not fulfil his promise to translate this document; but he refers to the journal *Al-Ḥikma*, Jerusalem 1933, p. 149. He does translate an Ottoman order dated AH 979 (AD 1571/2), which proves Syrian Jacobite possession of a monastery of this name in Jerusalem. This document is also cited by Dōlabānī (1928) 437, who says it is numbered 100 in the library of St Mark's.

According to B. Meistermann d'Alsace, *Nouveau Guide de la Terre Sainte* (Paris, 1907), p. 150, quoted by Karkenny: "After you go out of the Church of the Flagellation heading towards the Jebusite valley, about forty paces from there, you can see a small chapel in the name of al-ʿAdas which was rebuilt and repaired at the beginning of the twelfth century and very recently on the site of an old building. Nearby is an ancient monastery, an enormous building which goes back to the twelfth century. It survived until the sixteenth century. All the pilgrims link it with the house of Herod Antipas". From this it is clear that the monastery acquired in 1532 or 1527 was artfully identified, perhaps for the purpose of supporting a Syrian Orthodox claim, with the monastery at the village of ʿAdasiyya on the Nablus road, the location of which had by that time generally been forgotten.

"In AG 1897 (= AD 1585/6) Gregory (bishop) of Jerusalem, that is John of Gargar, the man who restored Dayr al-ʿAdasī, was martyred". This record, included in inscription No. 2 (see Appendix II), must refer to the monastery in the city. According to Meinardus (1964: 69) this John of Gargar was ordained in 1575 and Nau (1915), p. 519, confirms that the date was between 1574 and 1579; it was he who transferred the archepiscopal see "from the Monastery of St Mark to the Monastery of St Thomas"[75]. Karkenny (1976: 54-5) describes the martyrdom of this Gregory. A sacristan with a grudge against the bishop presented him with a pair of ritual slippers for the celebration of the Liturgy. He did not tell him that the name of the Prophet

75 Meinardus adds in the same place the following: "Other Syrian Jacobite sites in the 16th century included two nunneries which were maintained by a certain Michael, a monk, and the Adass Monastery, north of the Ecce Homo Arch (Via Dolorosa), the site of which commemorated the imprisonment of St Peter (Acts XII:4ff.)"; his source is again Ǧaǧǧāwī (1955). For the eighth-century "nunnery" see note 40, above. The connection with a monk called Michael suggests that the reference here is to a twelfth-century colophon written by a monk of that name (Lyons, municipal library, MS 1, on which see below). He refers to "the nuns of the two monasteries", whereby we should understand that nuns were attached to the two male monasteries of St Mary Magdalene and of the Tower in ʿAdasiyya. On Dayr al-ʿAdas, see also Vincent and Abel (1922), p. 952 note 3.

Muḥammad was written underneath them. Then he informed the Muslims that trampling on the name of the Prophet was part of the ritual performed by the bishop in his church. On this pretext Gregory was hanged outside the gate of his monastery[76].

5. *The Syrian Orthodox at the Holy Sepulchre*

In May, 966, (not 965, as Fiey 1969: 124 writes) a tornado of violence left the Holy City in ruins. Even the dome of the Holy Sepulchre was destroyed. A rich Jacobite from Iraq donated the money necessary for repairing it, but died before the work was finished. His name was ʿAlī b. Suwār, but he was known as Ibn al-Ḥammār, "the son of the donkey-man". We know about him from a reliable chronicler, the eleventh-century historian Yaḥyā b. Saʿīd of Antioch (see Kratchkovsky and Vasiliev 1924: 803-4).

However that may be, the Jacobites do not seem to have possessed a chapel at the Holy Sepulchre before Easter 1168, for in that year their patriarch Michael was still obliged to celebrate the Feast of the Resurrection at St Mary Magdalene's[77]. John of Würzburg, who visited Jerusalem *c.* 1165, shows considerable interest in the Jacobite monastery, yet he mentions no chapel of the Jacobites near Golgotha. However, the bishop to whom John dedicated his book, Theodoric of Würzburg, includes the Jacobites and the Nubians (who belonged to the Jacobite communion) among the communities he saw celebrating the liturgy in the Church of the Resurrection at some time between 1169 and 1173[78]. The *Citez de Iherusalem*, which appears to have been begun before and finished after 1187, tells us that there was a chapel ("mostier") to the left of the main door of the Holy Sepulchre, which was called "St Jake des Jacobins"[79]. In these circumstances it seems likely that the patriarch Michael's friendly reception by the Latin patriarch Amalric on the eve of Easter Sunday, 1168, may have led to the concession of the chapel of St James to the Jacobites.

To this may have been added that of the Mother of God, Mary, which Abū 'l-Makārim (before 1208) says the Copts had at the Sepulchre; for although they were in full communion with the Syrian Jacobites, they celebrated the

76 Karkenny gives the following references for the martyrdom: "The German historian Hamire, p. 157 [not in Karkenny's bibliography]. Cambridge library No. Dd 3082. Ottoman History by Ahmad Rasim, vol. 1, p. 433. Patriarchal Magazine, Jerusalem, vol. 1, p. 150".

77 Abbeloos and Lamy (1872-77), vol. 2, cols. 545-6; French translation: Chabot (1899-1910), vol. 3, p. 332.

78 Tobler (1865), cited by Cerulli (1943), pp. 29-30, who warns against possible interpolations in this unique MS of the fifteenth century.

79 Tobler (1874), pp. 202-3; *cf.* Michelant and Raynard (1882), pp. 35 and 174, cited by Meinardus (1960), p. 16.

liturgy in a different language[80]. The anonymous pilgrim from Loos in 1419 says that the Abyssinians, the Jacobites (*i.e.* Copts?) and the Syrians had two chapels in the Church of the Resurrection, one of which was situated behind the Holy Sepulchre; the chapel of the Jacobites behind the Holy Sepulchre was also noticed by another anonymous pilgrim in 1445[81]. By this is probably meant the Chapel of Nicodemus, in which the Syrian Orthodox are now to be found. At present, on the basis of the "Status Quo"[82], the Jacobites celebrate facing the Sepulchre in the western niche of the rotunda. It is incumbent upon them to exercize this and their other rights with regularity[83].

As for the identity of the other chapel, the evidence is confusing. A pilgrim's guide-book of 1350 describes a chapel of John the Evangelist as belonging to the Jacobites[84]. In John Poloner's *Descriptio Terrae Sanctae* of 1422 we read of four chapels encircling the Station of the Cross at the entrance to the Temple of the Sepulchre, of which the second from the left, in the corner, was dedicated to All Angels and held by the Jacobites[85]. By the (later?) fifteenth century, according to Prag (1989), "the Jacobites owned the Chapel of Helena", which the Armenians took over from them *c.* 1719.

Churches of the Syrian Orthodox in the Holy Land not directly connected with the Holy City are beyond the scope of this article, in spite of the fact that the title of Metropolitan of Jerusalem was often combined with the words "and of the sea-coast"[86].

80 Meinardus (1960), p. 16; Moravillé (1905), pp. 83-4, cited by Meinardus (1960), p. 21, where however reference is made to "one service in two languages". Bernard Hamilton suggests that the Coptic chapel in the Holy Sepulchre may have been a gift of Saladin after 1187. "He was Sultan of Egypt and Coptic power in Jerusalem seems to date from that time": personal communication, 2 vii 1990.

81 Meinardus (1960), pp. 21-22.

82 Cust (1929).

83 Information supplied by Mōr Dionysius Bahnām Ǧaǧǧāwī, Syrian Orthodox metropolitan of Jerusalem in 1986.

84 *P.P.T.S.* VI.9.

85 Tobler (1874), pp. 228-9.

86 One example is in the British Library MS 14,695, fol. 1a; see Wright (1870), p. 286. Another is in the text translated in Appendix I, below; Taylor (1931) interprets it as meaning "of Jerusalem and of all Palestine". But the MS in question was written for a church of St Mary Magdalene in Tyre (Taylor misunderstood this as a reference to the wall — reading *šūrō* for *ṣūr* — near the monastery of St Mary Magdalene in Jerusalem), which suggests that the Jacobites had churches in the harbour-towns to serve the pilgrims from Mesopotamia, most of whom came, as we have seen, by the sea-route. Note 97 (in Part 2 of this article) is an example of the title "metropolitan of Jerusalem and of the cities of the sea-coast". From Nau (1915), pp. 511-20, we learn of three Jacobite churches in and around Tripolis in the fifteenth century and of the addition of Damascus and Tripolis to the metropolitan title of Jerusalem in the sixteenth century. Dōlabānī (1928), pp. 436-37 refers to: 1. the church in Tyre; 2. a church to the south of the dome of the Ascension, said to be "the grave of the sinner, Mary, and the house of Simon the Pharisee" (report by the monk Sergius of Ṭūr ʿAbdīn of his pilgrimage to

6. *The bishops of Jerusalem and relations with the Roman Church*

Reference has already been made to Appendix IV of the *Chronicle of Michael*, in which the metropolitans of Jerusalem up to Michael's time (or rather those recognized as such by the Syrian Orthodox) are listed. For the period after that research needs to be done in manuscript collections in order to supplement and correct the sparse and unreliable[87] data in Meinardus (1964: 81-2), Karkenny (1976: 79) and Fedalto (1983: 25). For the present it will have to suffice to list the bishops of Jerusalem from the *Register*, which was begun in the late eighth century, giving the approximate date of their ordination; the numbering takes account of the undated names preceding these bishops in Appendix IV. In the last column, the figure in Roman numerals represents the ordaining patriarch, while the slash between the two figures in Arabic numerals represents the words "out of" in the formula "*n*th out of *x*", where *x* is the total number of bishops ordained by that patriarch:

NAME	POST	ANTE	MONASTERY OF ORIGIN	IN REGISTER
Timothy I	792	818	James, Cyrrhus	XVII 28th / 86
Job	816	845	–	XVIII 13th / 99
Ignatius I	816	846	Bīzūnō [Raqqa]	XVIII 37th / 99
Joseph III	816	846	Bīzūnō [Raqqa]	XVIII 67th / 99
John II	845	875	Tell ʿĒda [Antioch]	XIX 41th / 85
Cyril III Noah	845	875	–	XIX 66th / 85
Severus	877	884	Zūqnīn [Amida]	XX 26th / 26
Joseph IV	909	924	–, Damascus	XXIII 7th / 41
Theodore	909	924	Aṯūnōs [Rīš ʿAynō]	XXIII 21st / 41
Cyril IV	922	936	–, Edessa	XXIV 16th / 32
Jeremy II	935	954	–, Edessa	XXV 47th / 48
Thomas II	964	986	Tarʿēl, Marʿaš	XXIX 27th / 48
John III	1006	1031	Of the Cliff, Antioch	XXXI 28th / 48
Philoxenus II	1003	1031	Bar Gōgī [Melitene]	XXXI 39th / 48
Zacharias	1041	1058	Barīḏ [Melitene]	XXXIII 4th / 30
Thomas III	1041	1058	Qartmīn, Ṭūr ʿAbdīn	XXXIII 13th / 30
Timothy II	1062	1074	–, Amida	XXXV 12th / 17
John IV	1079	1083	Barīḏ [Melitene]	XXXIX 1st / 5
Cyril V[88]	1090	1130	Barṣawmō [Melitene]	XLI 1st / 61

Jerusalem in the mid-fifteenth century, MS 291 in the monastery of St Mark at Jerusalem); 3. the monastery of Mary Magdalene and Simon the Pharisee in the Holy City, which he distinguishes firmly from the monastery al-ʿAdas. At certain dates there were Jacobite bishops at Acre and at Tripolis: Hamilton (1980), pp. 347.

87 "Die Liste der Bischöfe bei Meinardus ist übrigens äußerst unzuverlässig (so werden A.Gr. teilweise als A.D. ausgegeben)": (Hubert Kaufhold, personal communication, 18 ii 1990.) Nau (1915), pp. 115-20, is an example of the kind of research needed to supplement the "maigres notices recueillis par Le Quien dans son vieil *Oriens christianus*".

88 After Cyril V, Fedalto (1983: 24) intrudes "Samuel 'Syrorum ep.'", giving as his source a

NAME	POST	ANTE	MONASTERY OF ORIGIN	IN REGISTER
David	1090	1130	Of the Valley of Elijah	XLI 17th / 61
Ignatius II Ḥesnūn	1090	1130	–	XLI 32nd / 61
Ignatius III Ğādina	1123	1140	Of the patriarchate	[see Part 2]
Ignatius IV Romanus	1138	1167	Of Jerusalem	XLIII 2nd / 34
Athanasius	1167	1200	– [Melitene]	XLIV 26th / 55
Ignatius V[89]	1167	1200	Of Jerusalem	XLIV 52nd / 55

It will be noticed that these bishops are all known to come from Syrian monasteries or towns, except for three whose origin is not stated. The Jacobite metropolitan episcopate of Jerusalem fell under the patriarchal jurisdiction of Antioch, not of Alexandria (see Hamilton 1980: 350). That makes it improbable that Cyril II of Alexandria consecrated the church built by Manṣūr al-Tilbānī in 1092, as Cerulli and Meinardus assume; it seems their source has simply "the Patriarch"[90]. At any rate, when Alexandria did interfere by consecrating a metropolitan for Jerusalem in 1235 or 1236, this caused a crisis in the relationship between the two patriarchates. The patriarch of Antioch travelled to the Holy City and lodged in St Mary Magdalene's, which had at that time a sizeable community of seventy monks. The schism which ensued in 1237 was triggered by the Coptic refusal to regard St Mary Magdalene's any longer as the Jacobite cathedral of Jerusalem. Antioch at the same time interfered in the jurisdiction of Alexandria by consecrating for the first time a native *abuna* for Ethiopia, where the Copts had always insisted on appointing one of themselves[91]. Barhebraeus represents this as a retaliatory measure; but he does not explain Alexandria's reason for provoking the crisis. Bernard Hamilton's discussion of Latin relations with the Jacobites, excellent as it is, also leaves this vital question insufficiently explained. In 1236 the Jacobite patriarch Ignatius II (1222-1252) swore a solemn oath of obedience to the Roman see and received the Dominican habit from the 'frères prêcheurs'. While this was technically an act of individual rather than corporate submission, it seems possible that it gave

certain "monachus anon. Scaphusensis", in RHC *Hist. occ.*, V, pp. 337-339". This Samuel should not be seen as a Jacobite.

89 "Der Bischof Thomas (ordin. zwischen 964 und 986) ist vermutlich identisch mit dem Metropoliten Thomas von Jerusalem, der für 1006 und 1007 in den Hss. Brit. Libr. 12149 und 12148 belegt ist [see Wright (1870), pp. 267f. and 264f.], so daß der folgende Johannes frühestens 1007 geweiht wurde. Genauere Ordinationsdaten finden sich für die drei letzten Bischöfe bei Honigmann [(1954), p. 110f.] (natürlich nur aufgrund von Michael bzw. Barhebraeus): Ignatius 1139, Athanasius 1185, Ignatius 1193": (Hubert Kaufhold, personal communication, 18 ii 1990.)

90 See note 48.

91 Abbeloos and Lamy (1872-77), vol. 2, pp. 654-64.

Alexandria the pretext for consecrating a bishop in the jurisdiction of Antioch. However, more study is needed before this question can be resolved[92].

With hindsight it is possible to see symptoms of the tendency to Union with Rome in the relations between the Jacobites and the Franks during the twelfth century. The colophons which will be quoted in Part 2 call King Fulk and King Baldwin III "victorious", an epithet traditionally reserved for rulers regarded by the writer as having correct beliefs and thus pleasing God, who "gives victory" in war. More explicitly, the colophon translated in Appendix I endorses the propaganda of the Second Crusade entirely: it was launched "in the name of Christ and for the sake of the Christian nation and in order to avenge Edessa and the rest of the Christians who had perished and to keep those countries that remained in Christian hands; above all, however, for the sake of that Holy Sepulchre of Christ and the rest of the holy places in Jerusalem". The same text reproduces the Crusaders' anti-Byzantine propaganda, calling the Byzantines "Greeks" as opposed to the true "Romans" from the West and stressing (against the universal claim of the Byzantine throne) that the emperor of Rome was the "king of kings". On the other side, the twelfth-century Latin Patriarch of Jerusalem and Bishop of Acre, Jacques de Vitry, devotes many pages of his "History of Jerusalem" to the doctrines and the practices of the Jacobites. Close study of this text should reveal how the Franks of the first Crusader century assessed the Jacobite "heresy"; this in turn might suggest the kind of concessions which must have been made by the Jacobites in the thirteenth century to open the way for Union[93]. [To be continued.]

92 Cahen (1940), pp. 681-4; Hamilton (1980), pp. 347-55. If Hamilton is right in identifying the "Jacobite archbishop of Egypt", whose profession of faith was received by the Dominicans at the same time as that of Ignatius II, with the metropolitan of Jerusalem appointed by Alexandria, then this appointment must have preceded the patriarch's profession of faith. But the identification is uncertain; and if Alexandria was genuinely interested in union with Rome, why did it allow a schism with Antioch to occur and to continue? Hamilton himself points out (p. 354) that "the hostility of the Mamluk authorities towards the Christian powers" made union between Rome and Alexandria impossible.

93 *P.P.T.S.* XI, pp. 67-76, cited by Meinardus (1964), p. 66. I have not seen this, but in a letter of Jacques, besides the passage cited in note 128, we read the following (Huygens 1960: 83f.; my translation): "There were Jacobites there with their bishop, who circumcised their little boys like the Jews and revealed their sins to none but God in confession. Others of them did not practise circumcision and confessed their sins to priests, but both groups made the sign of the Cross with a single finger". He goes on to relate how he spoke to them through an Arabic-speaker in their church and explained their errors to them: "When they heard this Word of God, which they had not been accustomed to hear, they were so moved to compunction by the Grace of God that they solemnly promised me not to practise circumcision in future and to make their confession to priests". Jacques allowed, concealing his true opinion, that the sign of the Cross, made with one finger, would admit of an orthodox interpretation, as a symbol of the unity of the Holy Trinity. We can see in this conversation the kind of manœuvres that would be necessary to bring about a Union between the Churches. Contrast

BIBLIOGRAPHY

Abbeloos and Lamy (1872-77) = J.-B. Abbeloos and T. J. Lamy, ed., *Gregorii Barhebraei chronicon ecclesiasticum*, 2 pts. in 3 fascicles (Louvain);

Anschütz (1984) = H. Anschütz, *Die syrisch-orthodoxen Christen vom Ṭūr 'Abdīn: eine altchristliche Bevölkerungsgruppe zwischen Beharrung, Stagnation und Auflösung* (Würzburg) = *Das östliche Christentum*, N.F. 34;

Bahnām (1962) = G. P. Bahnām, *Bayt Marqus fī Ūrišalīm aw Dayr Mār Marqus li-'l-Suryān* (Jerusalem) [in Arabic; I am indebted to Geert Jan van Gelder for a translation];

Barṣawm (1943) = I. A. Barṣawm, *Al-lu'lu' al-manṯūr fī ta'rīḫ al-'ulūm wa-'l-ādāb al-suryāniyya* = *Histoire des sciences et de la littérature syriaque* (reprinted: Aleppo, 1956; Baghdad, 1976; Glane, 1987) [in Arabic], occasional references in the footnotes to MSS at St Mark's;

[Barṣawm, *Catalogue* = I. A. Barṣawm, a catalogue of St Mark's library in the series "Syriac manuscripts throughout the world", known in MS form to Bahnām (1962);]

Baumstark (1911, 1912, 1913) = A. Baumstark, "Die liturgischen Handschriften des jakobitischen Markusklosters in Jerusalem", *Oriens Christianus*, N.S. 1 (1911), pp. 103-15, 286-314; N.S. 2 (1912), p. 120 ("Nachtrag"); *id.*, with the assistance of G. Graf and A. Rücker, "Die literarischen Handschriften des jakobitischen Markusklosters in Jerusalem", *Oriens Christianus*, N.S. 2 (1912), pp. 120-37, 317-33; *Oriens Christianus*, N.S. 3 (1913), pp. 128-34, 311-27;

Baumstark (1922) = A. Baumstark, *Geschichte der syrischen Literatur mit Ausschluß der christlich-palästinensischen Texte* (Berlin);

Bedjan (1898) = P. Bedjan, ed., *Ethicon, seu Moralia Gregorii Barhebraei. Liber Columbae, seu Directorium Monachorum* (Paris);

Beugnot (1843) = Beugnot, ed., *Livre des Assises de la Cour des Bourgeois* = *Historiens des Croisades: Lois*, vol. 2 (Paris);

Boase (1971) = T. S. R. Boase, *Kingdoms and Strongholds of the Crusaders* (London);

Bresc-Bautier (1984) = G. Bresc-Bautier, ed., *Le Cartulaire du Chapître du Saint-Sépulcre de Jérusalem. Académie des Inscriptions et des Belles-Lettres, Documents relatifs à l'Histoire des Croisades 15* (Paris);

Budge (1932) = E. A. Wallis Budge, *The Chronography of Gregory Abū'l-Faraj, 1225-1286, the Son of Aaron, the Hebrew Physician, Commonly Known as Bar Hebraeus, Being the First Part of his Political History of the World*, 2 vols. (London; reprint: Amsterdam, 1976);

Cahen (1940) = C. Cahen, *La Syrie de Nord à l'époque des Croisades* (Paris);

Catalogue Départements XXX, 1 (1900) = *Catalogue général des manuscrits des bibliothèques publiques de France, Départements*, t. XXX, 1 (Paris);

Cerulli (1943) = E. Cerulli, *Etiopi in Palestina: Storia della comunità etiopica di Gerusalemme*, 2 vols. (Rome);

Chabot (1899-1910) = J.-B. Chabot, *Chronique de Michel le Syrien, patriarche jacobite d'Antioche 1166-1199*, 4 vols. the last of which contains the Syriac text (Paris; reprint Brussels, 1963, including the introduction and the general index, which were originally published separately);

Jacques's attitude to the Syrian Christians of the Byzantine Rite (Huygens 1960: 84f.), whom he regards as "traitors, utterly corrupt, [...] divulgers of the secrets of Christianity to the Saracens"; they refused to bow at the Latin consecration, because the bread was unleavened, not leavened as in the Byzantine rite, nor would they use Latin altars without prior ablution. Nevertheless, he managed to extract a promise of better life from a group of them by preaching them a sermon. On the close relations between Syrian Jacobites and Franks, compare Kawerau (1955), p. 73f.

Chabot (1920-74) = I.-B. Chabot, ed., *Anonymi auctoris chronicon ad annum Christi 1234 pertinens*, 4 vols., 2 of text and 2 of translation = CSCO 81, 82, 109, 354 (Paris, 1920, 1916, 1937; Louvain 1974);

Chabot (1927) = I.-B. Chabot, *Incerti auctoris chronicon Pseudo-Dionysianum vulgo dictum*, vol. 1, *textus* CSCO 91 (Paris); Latin translation in vol. 1, *versio*, CSCO 121 (Paris, 1949);

Cobham (1908) = C. D. Cobham, *Excerpta Cypria* (Cambridge);

Conder (1897) = C. R. Conder, *The Latin Kingdom of Jerusalem (1099-1291)* (London);

Cust (1929) = L. G. A. Cust, *The Status Quo in the Holy Places* (Printed for the Government of Palestine by His Majesty's Stationery Office);

Dagron (1976) = G. Dagron, "Minorités ethniques et religieuses dans l'Orient byzantin à la fin du Xe et au XIe siècle: l'immigration syrienne", *Travaux et Mémoires* 6 (1976), pp. 177-216, reprinted in G. Dagron, *La Romanité chrétienne en Orient: héritages et mutations* (London, 1984);

Dōlabānī (1928) = H. Dōlabānī, "Al-Suryān fī Filastīn", *Al-Ḥikma* 2 (1928), pp. 434-443 [in Arabic; I am indebted to Adrie Drint for a translation];

Evetts (1915) = B. Evetts, ed., *The History of the Coptic Patriarchs of Alexandria*, Part IV, *Patrologia Orientalis* 10 (Paris), p. 461;

Fedalto (1983) = G. Fedalto, "Liste vescovili del patriarcato di Gerusalemme: I. Gerusalemme e Palestina prima", *Orientalia Christiana Periodica* 49 (1983), pp. 5-41;

Fiey (1969) = J. M. Fiey, "Le Pélerinage des Nestoriens et Jacobites à Jérusalem", *Cahiers de civilisation médiévale. X^e-XIIe siècles*, 12 (1969), pp. 113-26;

Francheschini and Weber (1965) = E. Francheschini and R. Weber, *Itinerarium Egeriae*, in *Corpus Christianorum, Series Latina*, vol. 175 (Turnhout);

[Ğaǧǧāwī (1955) = B. Ğaǧǧāwī, unpublished study on the subject of this article, the existence of which is attested by Meinardus (1964)];

Galbiati (1963) = E. Galbiati, "I fondi orientali minori (siriaco, etiopico, armeno) dell'Ambrosiana", *Istituto Lombardo, Accademia di Scienze e Lettere, Atti del Convegno di Studi su la Lombardia e l'Oriente, Milano, 11-15 Giugno, 1962* (Milan), pp. 190-99;

Grandclaude (1923) = M. Grandclaude, *Étude critique sur les Assises de Jérusalem* (Paris);

Grébaut (1908-9) = S. Grébaut, "Vie (éthiopienne) de Barṣauma le Syrien", *Revue de l'Orient Chrétien* 13 (1908), pp. 337-45; 14 (1909), pp. 135-42, 264-75, with an appendix on pp. 401-16 on "Barṣauma le Syrien d'après le Synaxaire éthiopien";

Gülcan (1977) = E. Gülcan, with H. Hughes-Brock, "The Life of Nuns in Ṭur 'Abdīn", *Sobornost* 7:4 (1977), pp. 288-98;

Hagenmeyer (1901) = H. Hagenmeyer, ed., *Epistulae et chartae ad historiam primi belli sacri spectantes quae superstunt* (Innsbruck);

Hamilton (1980) = B. Hamilton, *The Latin Church in the Crusader States: The Secular Church* (London);

Hatch (1946) = W. H. P. Hatch, *An Album of Dated Syriac Manuscripts. Monumenta palaeographica vetera, 2nd series* (Boston);

Hintlian (1976) = K. Hintlian, *History of the Armenians in the Holy Land* (Jerusalem);

Höhne and Wahle (1981) = E. Höhne and H. Wahle, *Palästina: Historisch-archäologische Karte* (Göttingen), separate publication of B. Reicke and L. Rost, *Biblisch-historisches Handwörterbuch* (Göttingen, 1981), pp. 161-284;

Honigmann (1954) = E. Honigmann, *Le Couvent de Barṣaumā et le patriarcat jacobite d'Antioche et de Syrie* (Louvain);

Howard (1981) = G. Howard, *The Teaching of Addai* (Chico, California);

Huygens (1960) = R. B. C. Huygens, ed., *Lettres de Jacques de Vitry (1160/1170-1240), évêque de Saint-Jean-d'Acre* (Leiden);

Jarry (1972) = J. Jarry, "Inscriptions syriaques et arabes inédites du Ṭour ʿAbdīn", *Annales Islamologiques* 10 (1972), pp. 207-250;

Karkenny (1976) = Y. Koriah Karkenny, *The Syrian Orthodox Church in the Holy Land* (Jerusalem);

Kaufhold (1991) = H. Kaufhold, "Der Ehrentitel 'Jerusalempilger'", *OC* 75 (1991), pp. 44-61;

Kawerau (1955) = P. Kawerau, *Die jakobitische Kirche im Zeitalter der syrischen Renaissance* (Berlin); I was unable to consult the second edition (Berlin, 1960);

Kratchkovsky (1924) = I. Kratchkovsky and A. Vasiliev, ed. and trans., *Histoire de Yahya-ibn-Saʿïd d'Antioche*, fasc. 1, *Patrologia orientalis* 18 (1924), pp. 701-833;

Macler (1901) = F. Macler, *Notice des manuscrits syriaques conservés dans la Bibliothèque du Couvent des Syriens jacobites de Jérusalem, etc.* (Paris [date supplied by Bahnām (1962)]);

Mai (1825-38) = A. Mai, *Scriptorum veterum nova collectio*, 10 vols. (Rome);

Martin (1888, 1889) = F. Martin, "Les premiers Princes croisés et les syriens jacobites de Jérusalem", *Journal Asiatique*, série 8, vol. 12 (1888), pp. 471-90; vol. 13 (1889), pp. 33-79;

Mayer (1977) = H. E. Mayer, *Bistümer, Klöster und Stifte im Königreich Jerusalem* (Stuttgart) = *Monumenta Germaniae Historica, Schriften*, 26;

Mayer (1988) = H. E. Mayer, *The Crusades*, second edition (Oxford);

Meinardus (1960) = O. A. Meinardus, *The Copts in Jerusalem* (Cairo);

Meinardus (1964) = O. A. Meinardus, "The Syrian Jacobites in the Holy City", *Orientalia Suecana* 12 for the year 1963 (Uppsala, 1964), pp. 60-82;

Michelant and Raynard (1882) = H. Michelant and G. Raynard, *Itinéraires à Jérusalem et descriptions de la Terre Sainte rédigés en français aux XI., XII., et XIII. siècles* (Geneva);

Milik (1960-61) = J. T. Milik, "La Topographie de Jérusalem vers la fin de l'époque byzantine", *Mélanges de l'Université Saint-Joseph* 37 (1960-61), pp. 127-89;

Moore (1961) = E. A. Moore, *The Ancient Churches of Old Jerusalem: The Evidence of the Pilgrims* (Beirut);

Moravillé (1905) = H. Moravillé, "Un Pèlerinage en Terre Sainte et au Sinaï au XVe siècle", *Bibliothèque de l'École des Chartes* 66 (1905);

Nau (1899) = F. Nau, "Le Croisé lorrain Godefroy de Ascha, d'après deux documents syriaques du XIIe siècle", *Journal Asiatique*, série 9, vol. 14 (1899), pp. 421-31;

Nau (1900) = F. Nau, "Les Croisés Henry et Godefroy du château de Ascha (Assche, Asch, Esch ou Aix), d'après les historiens occidentaux et deux notices syriaques du XIIe siècle", *L'Ancien pays de Looz*, 4 (1900), pp. 21-25, also published separately with virtually the same title, adding: "Note suivie de quelques considérations par le Dr. C. Bamps, 2e édition" (Hasselt, 1900);

Nau (1913, 1914a, 1920) = F. Nau, "Résumé de monographies syriaques", *Revue de l'Orient Chrétien* 18 (1913), pp. 272-6, 379-89; 19 (1914), pp. 113-34, 278-89; 15 (1920), pp. 113-34;

Nau (1914b) = F. Nau, "Sur quelques Autographes de Michel le Syrien, patriarche d'Antioche de 1166 à 1199", *Revue de l'Orient Chrétien* 19 (1914), pp. 379-80;

Nau (1915) = "Corrections et additions au catalogue des manuscrits syriaques de Paris", *Journal Asiatique* 11.5 (1915), pp. 487-536;

Nau (1927a) = F. Nau, "Deux Épisodes d'histoire juive sous Théodose II — 423 et 438 — d'après la Vie de Barṣauma le Syrien", *Revue des Études Juives* 93 (1927), pp. 184-206;

Nau (1927b) = F. Nau, "Sur la Synagogue de Rabbat Moab (422) et un mouvement sioniste favorisé par l'impératrice Eudocie (438) d'après la Vie de Barṣauma le Syrien", *Journal Asiatique* 210 (1927), pp. 189-92;

O'Connor (1980) = J. Murphy O'Connor, *The Holy Land: An Archaeological Guide from Earliest Times to 1700* (Oxford);

P.P.T.S. = *Palestine Pilgrims Text Society*, 13 vols. (London, 1896-1907);

Palmer (1986) = A. N. Palmer, "Charting Undercurrents in the History of the West-Syrian People: The Resettlement of Byzantine Melitene After 934", *Oriens Christianus* 70 (1986), pp. 37-68;

Palmer (1987a) = A. N. Palmer, "Saints" Lives with a Difference: Elijah on John of Tella (d. 538) and Joseph on Theodotos of Amida (d. 698)", *IV Symposium Syriacum 1984: Literary Genres in Syriac Literature*, ed. H. J. W. Drijvers etc. (Rome, 1987) = *Orientalia Christiana Analecta* 229, pp. 202-16;

Palmer (1987b) = A. N. Palmer, "A Corpus of Inscriptions from Ṭūr 'Abdīn and Environs", *Oriens Christianus* 71 (1987), pp. 53-139;

Palmer (1988) = A. N. Palmer, "The Inauguration Anthem of Hagia Sophia in Edessa: A New Edition and Translation with Historical and Architectural Notes and a Comparison with a Contemporary Constantinopolitan Kontakion", *Byzantine and Modern Greek Studies* 12 (1988), pp. 117-67;

Palmer (1989) = A. N. Palmer, "*Semper vagus*: The Anatomy of a Mobile Monk", *Studia Patristica* XVIII, 2 (Kalamazoo and Louvain), pp. 255-60;

Palmer (1990a) = A. N. Palmer, *Monk and Mason on the Tigris Frontier: The Early History of Ṭūr 'Abdīn* (Cambridge);

Palmer (1990b) = A.N. Palmer, "Who Wrote the Chronicle of Joshua the Stylite?", in R. Schulz and M. Görg, eds., *Lingua restituta orientalis: Festgabe für Julius Aßfalg = Ägypten und Altes Testament* 20 (Wiesbaden), pp. 272-84;

Palmer (forthcoming) = A. N. Palmer, "The Garšūnī Version of the Life of Theodotus of Amida", forthcoming in the *Acta of the third Conference on Christian Arabic Studies, Louvain-la-Neuve, 1988*;

Pedersen (1983) = K. Pedersen, *The History of the Ethiopian Community in the Holy Land from the Time of Emperor Tewodros II till 1974* (Jerusalem);

Phillips (1876) = G. Phillips, ed., *The Doctrine of Addai the Apostle* (London);

Prag (1989) = K. Prag, *Jerusalem* (London);

Prawer (1980) = J. Prawer, *Crusader Institutions* (Oxford);

Recoura (1924/5) = G. Recoura, "*Les Assises de Jérusalem* à propos d'un livre récent [*sc.* Grandclaude 1923]", *Le Moyen Âge*, 2.26 (1924/5), p. 158;

Renaudot (1713) = E. Renaudot, *Historia Patriarcharum Alexandrinorum Iacobitarum* (Paris);

Röhricht (1891) = R. Röhricht, "Karten und Pläne zur Palästinakunde aus dem VII. bis XVI. Jahrhundert", *Zeitschrift des Deutschen Palästina-Vereins* 14 (1891);

Röhricht (1893, 1904) = R. Röhricht, *Regesta Regni Hierosolymitani* (Innsbruck, 1893) and *Additamentum* (Innsbruck, 1904);

Rozière (1849) = E. de Rozière, *Cartulaire de l'église du Saint-Sépulcre de Jérusalem* (Paris);

Taylor (1931) = W. R. Taylor, "A New Syriac Fragment Dealing With Incidents in the Second Crusade", *Annual of the American School of Oriental Research* 11 (1931), pp. 120-30;

Tinnefeld (1975) = F. Tinnefeld, "Die Stadt Melitene in ihrer späteren byzantinischen Epoche (934-1101)", *Actes du XIVe congrès international des études byzantines, Bucarest 6-12 Sept. 1971*, vol. 2 (Bucarest, 1975), pp. 435-43;

Tobler (1865) = T. Tobler, *Theodorici libellus de locis editus circa A.D. 1172, cui accedunt breviores aliquot descriptiones* (St Gallen);

Tobler (1874) = T. Tobler, ed., *Descriptiones Terrae Sanctae ex saeculo VIII. IX. XII. et XV.* (Leipzig; reprint: Hildesheim and New York, 1974);

Vincent and Abel (1922) = H. Vincent and F.-M. Abel, *Jérusalem: Recherches de topographie, d'archéologie et d'histoire*, vol. 2: *Jérusalem nouvelle* (Paris);

Vogüé (1860) = M. de Vogüé, *Les Églises de la Terre Sainte* (Paris);

Vööbus (1956) = A. Vööbus, *Quelques Observations littéraires et historiques sur la Vie syriaque inédite de Mar Aḥa* (Stockholm);

Vööbus (1976) = A. Vööbus, "Découverte de la biographie de Théodote d'Amid par Šemʿōn de Samosate", *Le Muséon* 89 (1976), pp. 39-42.

Wagner (1976) = J. Wagner, *Seleukeia am Euphrat / Zeugma. Beihefte zum Tübinger Atlas des Vorderen Orients, Reihe B. Nummer 10* (Wiesbaden);

Wilkinson (1977) = J. Wilkinson, *Jerusalem Pilgrims Before the Crusades* (Warminster);

Wilkinson (1981) = J. Wilkinson, *Egeria's Travels to the Holy Land*, revised edition (Jerusalem and Warminster);

Wright (1870) = W. Wright, *Catalogue of Syriac Manuscripts in the British Museum Acquired Since the Year 1838*, vol. 1 (London);

Wright (1882) = W. Wright, ed., *The Chronicle of Joshua the Stylite* (Cambridge);

Wright (1901) = W. Wright, *A Catalogue of the Syriac Manuscripts in the Library of the University of Cambridge* (Cambridge);

Zotenberg (1874) = H. Zotenberg, *Catalogue des manuscrits syriaques et sabéens [mandaïtes] de la Bibliothèque Nationale* (Paris);

HUBERT KAUFHOLD

Der Ehrentitel »Jerusalempilger«

(syrisch *maqdšāyā*, arabisch *maqdisī*, armenisch *mahtesi*)

1. Allgemeines

Der verbreitete, dem Personennamen meist voran-, aber auch nachgestellte syrische Titel *maqdšāyā* für christliche Jerusalempilger leitet sich von einer Bezeichnung für die Stadt Jerusalem ab. Dabei dürfte das Arabische Pate gestanden haben.

Im Arabischen kommt der Name »Jerusalem« (*Ūrušalīm*) zwar vor, doch gebräuchlicher als Bezeichnung der Stadt ist *Bait al-maqdis*, eine Verkürzung des ursprünglichen *Īliyā madīnat bait al-maqdis* »Aelia, die Stadt des Heiligtums (Tempels)«[1]. Die davon abgeleitete Nisbe ist *maqdisī*, die in zahlreichen Namen vorkommt[2]. Sie bezeichnet jemanden, der zu Jerusalem gehört, also von dort stammt oder dort wohnt. Im christlichen Bereich kommt später — teilweise mit etwas abweichender, in der Schrift aber gewöhnlich nicht feststellbarer Vokalisation — die gängige Bedeutung »Jerusalempilger" hinzu[3].

Dem arabischen *Bait al-maqdis* entspricht im Syrischen *Bēṯ maqdšā*. Allerdings wird damit die Heilige Stadt nur selten bezeichnet. Ganz üblich ist vielmehr der Name *Ōrišlem* »Jerusalem«[4], dem allenfalls noch ein *mḏīnaṯ quḏšā* »Stadt der Heiligkeit« vorausgeht oder nachgestellt wird[5]. Trotzdem

1 Auch *Bait al-muqaddas*. Später wird die Kurzform *al-Quds* üblich. Vgl. S. D. Goitein, EI² s.v. al-Ḳuds A.2.

2 Vgl. etwa EI², Index to volume I-V, S. 193 s.v. al-Maḳdisī.

3 G. Graf, Verzeichnis arabischer kirchlicher Termini, 2. Aufl., Louvain 1954, 88 s.v. *qds* »Jerusalempilger«: *maqdasī* und *muqdusī*. J. G. Hava, al-Faraid. Arabic-English Dictionary, Beirut, Nachdruck 1964, 592, differenziert: *maqdisī* »relating to Jerusalem« und als Dialektform Syriens: *muqdasī* (plur. *maqādisa*) »Pilgrim to Jerusalem«; ebenso J. B. Belot, Vocabulaire arabe-français, 16. Aufl., Beirut 1951, 621. R. Dozy, Supplement aux dictionnaires arabes, Band 2, Leiden 1879, 315: »*maqdasī*, pl. *maqādisa*, et *muqaddasī* pèlerin de Jerusalem. M: c'est *maqdisī* ou *muqaddasī*, mais le vulgaire dit en ce sens *muqdusī*, pl. *maqādisa*«. A. Jaba - F. Justi, Dictionnaire kurde-français, St.-Petersbourg 1879, 403: »mok'dasi, pèlerin chrétien allant a Jérusalem«. Im folgenden schreibe ich immer *maqdisī*. Die Übersetzung »sacristain« für *maqdisī* von S. Scheil (ROC 1, 1896, 45 n. 1) ist unzutreffend.

4 Thesaurus Syriacus I 101, 489.

5 Ebenda I 844, II 3502.

dürfte das syrische *maqdšāyā* nach dem Muster des arabischen *maqdisī* gebildet worden sein. Es ist eine von *maqdšā* »Heiligtum« abgeleitete Adjektivbildung[6] — wie arabisch *maqdisī* von *maqdis* — und geht nicht unmittelbar auf die Wurzel *qdš* »heilig« zurück. *maqdšāyā* bedeutet insbesondere nicht, daß der Pilger »geheiligt« sei, auch wenn später die Grundbedeutung der Wurzel *qdš* dabei mitgeklungen haben mag (vgl. etwa unten die Erklärung von Audo). Wenn J. M. Fiey in seinem Aufsatz über die Wallfahrt der Syrer nach Jerusalem[7] bei der Erwähnung des Pilgertitels auf die in der frühchristlichen Literatur bezeugte Klasse der »Geheiligten« verweist, ist dem entgegenzuhalten, daß der syrische Ausdruck dafür *mqaddšē* lautet, also das Passivpartizip des Pa‘‘el verwendet wird[8]. Ein Zusammenhang mit dem Pilgertitel besteht demnach nicht. Der geistliche Nutzen einer Wallfahrt wird im Syrischen häufig durch das Eṯpa‘‘al von *brk* ausgedrückt: »gesegnet durch die heiligen Stätten" (vgl. Thesaurus Syriacus I 612); *qdš* gebraucht man dafür — wenn ich recht sehe — nicht.

Syrische Lexika verzeichnen für *maqdšāyā* folgendes:

a) Thesaurus Syriacus, t. II, fasc. IX, Oxford 1893, 3503f.: »Hierosolymitanus«.

b) J. P. Margoliouth, Supplement to the Thesaurus Syriacus, Oxford 1927, 293b: »Not *a native of Jerusalem* but *a pilgrim* who had visited *the holy city*«, mit Verweis auf Th. Nöldeke, Syrische Inschriften, ZA 21, 1908, 160f. [= Rezension zu H. Pognon, Inscriptions sémitiques, Paris 1907; vgl. unten Fußn. 40]. Nöldeke schreibt: »Mit Recht nimmt aber Pognon das Wort als Bezeichnung des Pilgers, der in Jerusalem ... gewesen ist. Das bedeutet ܡܩܕܫܝܐ auch in allen Stellen bei P[ayne] Sm[ith, Thesaurus II] 3503«. Nöldeke verweist noch auf die arabische Form ܡܩܕܣܝ »Heutzutage muqdusī oder ähnlich«. Im Supplement wird ferner die falsche Vokalisierung *mqadšāyā*[9] vermerkt (mit Hinweis auf Gottheil, JAOS 20, 1897, 188). Unter dem Stichwort *maqdisī* hatte der Thesaurus Syriacus (II 2198b) bereits die richtige Bedeutung angegeben: »Forte *qui peregrinationem ad Hierosolyma ... fecerit*«.

6 Vgl. Th. Nöldeke, Kurzgefaßte syrische Grammatik, 2. Aufl., Leipzig 1898, § 135.

7 Le pèlerinage des Nestoriens et Jacobites à Jerusalem, in: Cahiers de civilisation médiévale Xᵉ-XIIᵉ Siècles, tome 10, Poitiers 1969, 113-126 (hier: 124).

8 So in den von Fiey zitierten Stellen: Acta Martyrum et Sanctorum (Ed. P. Bedjan) II 241, Z. 9 (fem. sing.); 254, Z. 3 v.u.; Kanon 8 der Synode des Isaak, s. J. B. Chabot, Synodicon Orientale, Paris 1902, 25/265.

9 *mqadšāyā* wäre auch gar keine übliche Nominalform; belegt ist nur *mqadšānā* »consecrans« vom part. act. masc. Pa‘‘el (vgl. Nöldeke aaO § 130). Die Bedeutung »peregrinator Hierosolymitanus« für *mqadšānā* bei C. Brockelmann, Lexicon Syriacum, 2. Aufl., Halle 1928, 650a, beruht auf der falschen, von Nöldeke richtiggestellten Lesung bei Pognon.

c) J. Payne Smith, A Compendious Syriac Dictionary, Oxford 1903, gibt für *maqdšāyā* noch allein an: »an inhabitant of Jerusalem« (S. 296).

d) Carl Brockelmann, Lexicon Syriacum, 2. Aufl., Halle an der Saale 1928, verzeichnet beide Wörter nicht (s. aber Fußnote 9).

e) Thomas Audo, Dictionnaire de la langue chaldéenne, Mosul 1897 (Nachdruck Losser/Holland 1985 unter dem Titel: Treasure of the Syriac Language), 405: *maqdšāyā. maqdšāitā. hau da-s'ar dukkyāṯā qaddīšāṯā ḏa-ḇ-Ōrišlem* (»... der, welcher die heiligen Stätten in Jerusalem besucht hat«).

f) J. E. Manna, Vocabulaire chaldéen-arabe, Mosul 1900 (Nachdruck Beirut 1975 unter dem Titel: Chaldean-Arabic Dictionary), erklärt ܡܩܕܫܝܐ auf S. 660 arabisch mit »maqdisī, ḥāǧǧ«.

Das Wort wird gelegentlich auch bei Frauen verwendet, und zwar — wie bei Audo angegeben — in der weiblichen Form *maqdšāitā*[10].

Der Titel scheint erst seit dem Ende des 13. Jhdts. vorzukommen. Ich kann nicht den Anspruch erheben, das Material vollständig zu überblicken, habe aber insbesondere eine Vielzahl von Kolophonen, die sich für eine solche Untersuchung vor allem anbieten, durchgesehen, so daß ich glaube, ein im wesentlichen zutreffendes Bild zu geben. Es ist freilich nicht auszuschließen, daß weitere und möglicherweise frühere Belege in der syrischen Literatur vorhanden sind. Es kommt hinzu, daß viele derartige Schreibervermerke im Laufe der Zeit verlorengegangen sind, daß der Titel in den Handschriftenkatalogen häufig nicht vermerkt ist und daß er wohl schon verwendet wurde, bevor er in Kolophonen seinen Niederschlag fand. Für eine Entstehung nach dem Ende des 13. Jhdts. spricht auch folgendes: Barhebraeus (gestorben 1286 A.D.) befaßt sich in seinem »Ethikon« mit der Wallfahrt nach Jerusalem und gibt Anweisungen dafür[11]. Man hätte erwarten können, daß er den Titel *maqdšāyā* erwähnt. Das ist jedoch nicht der Fall, ein Hinweis darauf, daß er zu seiner Zeit noch nicht üblich war.

Barhebraeus bestimmt (Abschnitt 1, Kapitel 3, Kanon 5), den Besuch in Jerusalem zeitlich so zu legen, daß der Pilger in der Karwoche in Jerusalem ist und das Osterfest dort feiern kann. Das ist so sehr *die* Zeit für Pilgerfahrten geworden, daß das syrisch-türkische Wörterbuch von Simon Atto[12] das Wort *maqdšāyā* erklärt als: 1) Einwohner von Jerusalem und 2) Christ, der *zu*

10 S. etwa Oxford Syr. 55: *maqdšāitā Lu'lu'* (J. P. Smith, Cat. S. 199/200).

11 Abschnitt 1, Kapitel 9. Text: P. Bedjan, Ethicon seu moralia, Paris 1898, 111-120; sowie Ausgabe des St. Ephrem the Syrian Monastery, Losser/Holland 1985: Ethicon. Christian Ethics (Morals), 60-64. Teilweise übersetzt von Fiey aaO 116ff. Es dürfte sich lohnen, diese christlichen Anweisungen mit den islamischen Vorschriften für die Wallfahrt nach Mekka zu vergleichen. Vermutlich hat Barhebraeus dort Anleihen gemacht.

12 Süryanice-Türkçe Sözlük, 1989, 129.

Ostern eine Wallfahrt nach Jerusalem gemacht hat. Ob diese Einschränkung von jeher galt, läßt sich schwer sagen[13].

Ein Titel für Jerusalempilger ist weder in der griechischen noch in der abendländischen Kirche bekannt[14]. Wahrscheinlich sollte *maqdisī* oder *maqdšāyā* eine christlich-orientalische Entsprechung für das islamische *ḥāǧǧ* »Mekkapilger« sein. Ich habe nicht feststellen können, ab wann im Islam *ḥāǧǧ* nicht mehr nur eine einfache — wenn auch achtungsvolle — Bezeichnung für einen Pilger war, sondern als Ehrentitel mit dessen Namen verbunden wurde[15]. Diese Verwendung ist möglicherweise ebenfalls erst um die Wende vom 13. zum 14. Jhdt. entstanden[16]. Für einen Zusammenhang des christlichen mit dem islamischen Brauch spricht vielleicht auch, daß die arabische Form *maqdisī*, wie bereits ausgeführt, anscheinend die ältere ist und daß das syrische *maqdšāyā* erst nach diesem Muster gebildet wurde. Auch im Ṭūrōyō findet sich übrigens eine Form, die auf das Arabische zurückgeht: *meqsī*[17]/ *miqsī*[18]/*muqsī* (fem. *muqsīye*).

2. Belege für den Pilgertitel vor dem 13. Jhdt.?

a) In einer arabischen Handschrift aus dem Besitz von Karl Vollers, die nach dessen Angaben aus dem 10. Jhdt. stammt, findet sich ein Text über eine Religionsdisputation in Jerusalem zwischen Muslimen und einen christlichen

13 Immerhin ergibt sich aus dem Bericht über die Pilgerreise mehrerer Einwohner von Bēṯ Sḇīrīnā im Jahre 1495/96, daß die Pilger Wert darauf legten, nicht schon im Januar zurückzureisen, sondern erst, nachdem sie das Heilige Feuer empfangen hatten, also nach Ostern (E. A. W. Budge, The Chronography of Gregory Abū'l-Faraj, vol. II, London 1932, S. LI; A. Barsaum, Maḵtḇānūṯā ḏ-ʿal aṯrā ḏ-Ṭūr ʿAbdīn, 1964, 113). Im Kolophon der Hs. Jerusalem 12* (1515) heißt es: »als wir ... nach Jerusalem kamen und das [Heilige] Feuer und die heiligen Wallfahrten vollendet hatten, ...« (A. Baumstark, Die literarischen Hss. des jakobitischen Markusklosters in Jerusalem, in: OrChr 10, 1912, 133. Vgl. auch unten im Text die Äußerung von J. Schiltberger.

14 Ich habe jedenfalls in dieser Richtung nichts gefunden, etwa in dem umfassenden Werk von B. Kötting, Peregrinatio religiosa, Münster 1950, oder bei L. Kriss-Rettenbeck u.a. (Hrsg.), Wallfahrt hat keine Grenzen. Themen zu einer Ausstellung des Bayerischen Nationalmuseums, München-Zürich 1984, insbesondere S. 308-315: E. Egenter, Jerusalem — Ziel der Pilger damals und heute; S. 316-330: P. S. Cowe, Pilgrimage to Jerusalem by the Eastern Churches. Das von Cowe aaO 323 erwähnte griech. προσκυνητής meint allgemein »Pilger«, nicht unbedingt »Jerusalempilger«, auch ist es kein Titel.

15 Die einschlägigen Werke geben dazu nichts her, z.B. M. Gaudefroy-Demombynes, Le pèlerinage à la Mekke, Paris 1923, oder EI s.v. Ḥadjdj, Ism.

16 Die in der EI angegebenen Personen mit der türkischen Form Ḥādjdjī ... (s. den Indexband s.v.) gehen zeitlich jedenfalls nicht weiter zurück.

17 Vgl. K. Jacob - A. Elkhoury, The Guide. The First Literary-Colloquial Syriac Dictionary, o.O. (Schweden) 1985, 197.

18 Vgl. etwa H. Aydin, Die syrisch-orthodoxe Kirche von Antiochien, Glane 1990, 108ff. (gemeint ist wohl die Aussprache des türkischen ı).

Mönch, der *al-Maqdisī* (oder — in der Schrift ja nicht zu unterscheiden — *Muqaddasī*) genannt wird[19]. Der Mönch gibt an, in Tiberias geboren zu sein, sich in einem Kloster in oder bei Edessa aufgehalten zu haben und als Pilger nach Jerusalem gekommen zu sein. Vollers versteht *maqdisī* als »Jerusalimit« und deutet den Namen in der sicherlich fiktiven Disputation als typisch: der Mönch aus Edessa, dem »Muttersitz des syrischen Christentums«, repräsentiere die christliche Weisheit, Tiberias sei der Sitz jüdischer, heidnischer und christlicher Gelehrsamkeit und Jerusalem sei die den drei Religionen heilige Stadt; einer der muslimischen Vertreter heiße dementsprechend *al-Baṣrī*, also »aus Baṣra stammend, womit die islamische Gelehrsamkeit gemeint« sei[20]. In anderen Handschriften fehlt die Bezeichnung *Maqdisī*, dafür erscheint der Name Ibrahīm. Graf spricht davon, daß Ibrahīm »ein zur Pilgerfahrt nach Jerusalem (bait al-maqdis, bait al-muqaddas) gekommener, darum al-Maqdisī oder al-Muqaddasī beibenamter Mönch namens Abraham« gewesen sei[21]. Es sieht so aus, als ob Graf damit auf den Pilgertitel anspielen wollte und nicht nur auf die übliche Bezeichnung für jemanden, der in Jerusalem wohnte oder von dort stammte. Der Verfasser des Textes wird aber Letzteres meinen. Es ist ja anzunehmen, daß Pilger sich erst dann als *maqdisī* bezeichneten, wenn sie von der Reise nach Jerusalem wieder zurückgekehrt waren. Da sich unser Mönch noch in Jerusalem aufhält, wird die Bezeichnung »Jerusalemit« im Sinne von »Einwohner von Jerusalem« gemeint sein. Die Quelle stellt damit noch keinen Beleg für den Pilgertitel dar. Die beiden Bedeutungen hängen natürlich eng zusammen und eine Abgrenzung ist deshalb wohl nicht immer einfach. Man wird sich die Entstehung des Titels so vorzustellen haben, daß im Laufe der Zeit nicht nur Leute, die aus Jerusalem stammten oder ständig dort lebten, als *maqdisī* bezeichnet wurden, sondern auch solche, die sich nur kurze Zeit als Pilger in der heiligen Stadt aufgehalten hatten.

b) 1174 A.D. schrieb der Mönch Basileios bar Saʿīd Sāḇā Maqdisī aus Edessa die beiden Handschriften Paris Syr. 67 und Cambridge Ll 2.4. Nach H. Zotenberg, der die Pariser Handschrift beschrieb, wird er »Mouqaddesi (le pèlerin)«[22] genannt. In der Cambridger Handschrift heißt es aber ausdrücklich *d-meṯīḏaʿ b-ḡensā ḏ-maqdisī*[23] »der unter dem Familiennamen Maqdisī bekannt ist« (im Hinblick auf die syrische Schreibung ܡܩܕܣܝ wohl nicht: Muqaddasī).

19 Karl Vollers, Das Religionsgespräch von Jerusalem (um 800 D) aus dem Arabischen übersetzt, in: ZKG 29, Gotha 1908, 29-71, 197-221.

20 Ebda. 30f.

21 Graf II 29. Die Ausgabe von G. B. Marcuzzo, Le dialogue d'Abraham de Tibèriade, Rom 1986 (vgl. OCP 53, 1987, 444f.) war mir nicht zugänglich.

22 Catalogue des mss. syriaques, Paris 1874, 35.

23 A. Barsaum, Min ta'rīḫ al-abrašiyāt as-suryanīya, in: Maǧallat al-baṭriyarkīya 7, Jerusalem 1940, 134. Im Katalog von Wright ist der Kolophon nicht zitiert.

Er war also kein »Pilger«. Das Wort ist demnach auch hier in der ursprünglichen Bedeutung »zu Jerusalem gehörend« zu verstehen.

3. Westsyrische Belege

Der älteste mir bekannte syrische Beleg für den Pilgertitel stammt vom Anfang des 14. Jhdts. In der Hs. Brit. Libr. 18,714, einem 1214 A.D. geschriebenen Evangeliar, finden sich fliegende Blätter mit Vermerken, darunter einem aus dem Jahre 1305 A.D. Darin werden unter den Mönchen des Klosters Mār Malkē im Ṭūr ʿAḇdīn ein *maqdisī* Gabriel und ein Rabban Yešūʿ *maqdisī* aufgezählt[24]. Hier kann — zumindest bei ersterem — nichts anderes als »Jerusalempilger« gemeint sein. Bemerkenswert ist, daß der Vermerk in syrischer Sprache verfaßt ist, jedoch der arabische Pilgertitel verwendet wird, ein weiterer Hinweis darauf, daß das syrische *maqdšāyā* erst später aufkam.

Danach klafft wieder ein Lücke von etwa 165 Jahren. Das Vorkommen des Titels hängt aber sicherlich nicht zuletzt damit zusammen, ob überhaupt eine Möglichkeit zu Pilgerfahrten nach Jerusalem bestand. Dafür waren die politische Lage, der Wohnort, also die Länge des Reiseweges, und gewiß auch die finanziellen Mittel der Gläubigen von Bedeutung. Fiey weist zutreffend auf die großen Schwierigkeiten hin, schreibt aber gleichwohl: »Malgré tout les dangers réels, le flot des pélerins orientaux semble avoir été pratiquement ininterrompu«. Durch Fakten läßt sich diese Behauptung allerdings nicht belegen, im Gegenteil, Fiey zitiert selbst eine widersprechende Äußerung des nestorianischen Katholikos Denḥā I. aus der Zeit um 1280: »Ce n'est pas le moment d'aller à Jérusalem, les routes sont troublées, les chemins sont coupés«[25]. Andererseits berichtet Johann Schiltberger, der sich von 1394 bis 1427 im Orient aufhielt und auch Jerusalem besuchte, daß zu Ostern (!) viel Volk aus Armenien, aus Syrien und aus Priester Johanns Land komme, um das Heilige Feuer zu sehen[26]. Auf die armenischen Pilger gehe ich unten noch ein. Jedenfalls war aber das 14. und die erste Hälfte des 15. Jhdt. — die Zeit der Mongolenstürme und danach — Pilgerfahrten sicherlich besonders ungünstig. Danach folgen die syrischen Belege aber Schlag auf Schlag, wobei die Jahreszahlen (= A.D.) natürlich meist nicht das Datum der Reise meinen, sondern später liegen[27]:

24 W. Wright, Catalogue I, S. 164b.

25 AaO 114.

26 Vgl. U. Schlemmer (Hrsg.), Johannes Schiltberger. Als Sklave im Osmanischen Reich, Stuttgart 1983, 151.

27 Bei den folgenden Handschriften werden die gängigen Kataloge der großen Sammlungen nicht eigens in Fußnoten angegeben: J. S. Assemani (Rom), W. Wright (London und Cambridge), R. P. Smith (Oxford), A. Mingana (Birmingham), H. Zotenberg (Paris), E. Sachau (Berlin), I. Armalet (Scharfeh).

1470 schrieb der Priestermönch Qūpār die Hs. Amsterdam 184 für den Archidiakon Barṣaumā, Sohn des *maqdšāyā* Amīrōs aus ʿUrbīš bei Gargar (nördlich von Edessa am Euphrat)[28]. Hier handelt es sich eindeutig nicht um eine Familienbezeichnung, sondern der Vater des Bestellers war nach Jerusalem gepilgert.

Die Hs. Göttingen Syr. 5 wurde im Jahre 1481 geschrieben vom Mönchspriester Yešūʿ, Sohn des Mönchspriesters Johannes, Sohn des *maqdšāyā* Ḥasan, Sohn des Ṣaumeh (usw.) aus Qasṭrā Qilliṯ (im Ṭūr ʿAbdīn)[29].

1501: Kaufvermerk in der Hs. Paris Syr. 62. Verkäufer ist der »Priester David, Sohn des *maqdšāyā* Mubarak aus Mardin«[30].

1515: Schreiber der Hs. Jerusalem 12* ist der Mönch Johannes aus Mardin, Sohn des *maqdisī* Simeon[31]. Aus dem Kolophon ergibt sich, daß auch er in Jerusalem war. Er legt sich den Pilgertitel aber nicht selbst bei.

1518 schrieb der Hegumenos Saʿdallāh, Sohn des *maqdšāyā* ʿAbdallāh in Homs die Hs. Oxford Syr. 9.

1528 verkaufte der »Maphrian Ḥabīb, Sohn des verstorbenen Diakons Malkē, Sohn des *maqdisī* Simeon« die Hs. Mardin Orth. 310 (so ein Vermerk in arabischer Schrift in der Hs.[32]; in Karšūnī wiedergegeben in der Abschrift Ming. Syr. 8). Der Maphrian Basileios Ḥabīb stammte aus Manṣūrīya bei Mardin. Er war vorher als Metropolit (mit dem Namen Athanasios Ḥabīb) mit seinem Onkel, dem Mönch Johannes (identisch mit dem des Vermerkes von 1515), selbst in Jerusalem gewesen (vgl. die Hss. Jerusalem 12*[33]; Paris Syr. 74; Brit. Libr. Arund. Or. 11[34]), doch fehlt auch bei ihm der Titel.

Im Kolophon der 1549 im Kreuzkloster im Ṭūr ʿAbdīn geschriebenen Hs. Jerusalem 34[35] berichtet der Schreiber Qaumē, daß er und sein Mitbruder Abraham in Jerusalem waren. Der Pilgertitel fehlt bei beiden. Am Schluß heißt es: »Betet für die Gläubigen, die in Jerusalem wohnen«, und dann zählt der Schreiber einige Namen auf, darunter auch einen *maqdisī* Elias und seine

28 J. Th. Beelen, S. Clementis Romani Epistulae binae de Virginitate, syriace, Löwen 1856, S. xv.

29 A. Rahlfs, Syrische Hss., in: Verzeichnis der Hss. im preuss. Staate. I. Hannover, 3. Göttingen, Band 3, Berlin 1894, 466.

30 F. Nau, Litterature canonique syriaque inédite, in: ROC 14, 1909, 2.

31 A. Baumstark, Die literarischen Hss. des jakobitischen Markusklosters in Jerusalem, in: OrChr 10, 1912, 133.

32 Die Handschriften der syrisch-orthodoxen Metropolie in Mardin sind bisher nicht katalogisiert.

33 Baumstark aaO 133.

34 F. Rosen - J. Forshall, Catalogue codd. mss. qui in Museo Britannico asservantur. Pars prima, London 1838, 60f. (Nr. 38).

35 A. Baumstark, Die liturgischen Hss. des jakobitischen Markusklosters in Jerusalem, in: OrChr 9, 1911, 294 (mit nur kurzen und teilweise unrichtigen Angaben aus dem interessanten Kolophon). Bei meinem Besuch 1986 befand sich die Hs. zum gottesdienstlichen Gebrauch in der Kirche des Markusklosters.

Söhne Diakon ʿĪsā und Diakon Joseph. Es hat hier den Anschein, als ob ein Bewohner von Jerusalem den Pilgertitel trug. Der genannte ʿĪsā ist wahrscheinlich identisch mit dem »diacre ʿĪsā ibn Maqdisī... ibn al-Qarīʿ«, der einen Besitzervermerk in der Hs. Paris Arab. 190 anbrachte und sie 1589 in Jerusalem(!) an einen Bischof verkaufte[36]; der in der Handschrift offenbar unleserliche Vatersname wäre danach Īlīyā.

1553 und 1554 schreibt der Metropolit Dionysios Isaak von Zypern und Ḥisn Ziyād (= Ḫarpūṭ), Sohn des *maqdisī* Ibrahīmšāh, aus Aleppo stammend, die Hss. Scharfeh Syr. 3/2 und 3/15.

Der Partriarch Ignatios Niʿmatallāh regierte von 1557 bis 1576. Er war Sohn des *maqdisī* Johannes (Ḥannā) aus der Familie Nūraddīn aus Mardin[37].

Zwischen 1577 und 1592 kopierte der »Mönchpriester Johannes, Sohn des *maqdšāyā* Mardiros, Sohn des *maqdšāyā* Barṣaumā (Armēnāyā)« u.a. die Hss. Scharfeh Syr. 5/3, Oxford Syr. 15 und Berlin Syr. 139. Er unternahm selbst zwei Pilgerreisen nach Jerusalem, eine davon 1585, bezeichnete sich aber auch danach nicht als *maqdšāyā*. Johannes war, wie schon der Vatersname zeigt, armenischer Herkunft, stammte aus Wank bei Gargar und wurde später Metropolit von Kappadokien und Edessa[38]. Zu der armenischen Form des Pilgertitels siehe unten Abschnitt 6.

In der bereits genannten Hs. Brit. Libr. 18,714 steht auch ein 1578 entstandener Vermerk in arabischer Sprache. Darin räumt ein *maqdisī* Sulaimān aus dem Dorf Manʿar(?) der syrischen Gemeinde in Jerusalem das Recht ein, an einem bestimmten Ort Holz zu schlagen. Es könnte sich um eine Stiftung anläßlich einer Pilgerfahrt handeln.

1581 schrieb der Diakon Ḥasan, Sohn des Ḥaḏbšabbā, Sohn des *maqdšāyā* Jakob (usw.) aus Quṣūr (bei Mardin) die Hs. Scharfeh Syr. 15/4[39].

Der Mönchpriester Sāhdā, Sohn des *maqdšāyā* oder *maqdisī* Johannes (ܒܪ ܡܩܕܣܝܣ ܐܘܗܢܢܣ), aus Gargar (nach der Schreibung des Vatersnamens und der Herkunft offenbar armenischer Abstammung) schrieb u.a. die Hss. Mardin Orth. 121 (1588) und Oxford Syr. 199 (1594). Sein Vater ist sicher der Johannes aus Gargar, der 1580 in Jerusalem(!) und dann — vermutlich auf der Rückreise — in Homs die Hs. Oxford Syr. 30 kopierte (sich aber selbst den Titel nicht beilegte).

In einer Bauinschrift in ʿArnas (im Ṭūr ʿAbdīn) aus dem Jahre 1592 wird der *maqdšāyā* Joseph, Sohn des Emanuel, erwähnt[40].

36 G. Troupeau, Catalogue des mss. arabes, tome 1, Paris 1972, 161.

37 Barsaum, Histoire 459; G. Levi della Vida, Documenti intorno alle relazioni della chiese orientali con la S. Sede, Vatikanstadt 1948, 4.

38 Barsaum, Histoire 460f., 494 Nr. 241.

39 S. auch Barsaum, Histoire 494 Nr. 245.

40 H. Pognon, Inscriptions sémitiques 99: fälschlich *mqadšānā*, richtiggestellt von Nöldeke aaO; zutreffend auch A. Barsaum, Makṯbānūṯā ḏ-ʿal aṯrā ḏ-Ṭūr ʿAbdīn, 1964, 137.

Im Kolophon der 1593 im Kloster az-Zaʿfarān geschriebenen Hs. Mardin Orth. 71 erscheint der Priester Georg, Sohn des *maqdšāyā* Abraham.

1594 wird im Haus des *maqdisī* Ibrāhīm al-Ḥabbāz in Hama die Hs. Paris Syr. 65 vollendet.

1595 wird die Hs. Scharfeh Syr. 5/16 für den Diakon Ṭaibūtallāh, Sohn des *maqdšāyā* Malkē aus Kalibīn (bei Mardin) restauriert.

Um 1600 schrieb in Jerusalem der Mönch Abraham, Sohn des verstorbenen *maqdšāyā* Yešūʿ, genannt Ġazwī (ܓܙܘܝ), aus dem Dorf Quṣūr im Gebiet von Mardin, die Hs. Brit. Libr. Egerton 704. Wright nimmt im Katalog als Entstehungszeit das 17. Jhdt. an, doch läßt sich die Datierung weiter eingrenzen. Barṣaum[41] gibt nämlich die Jahre 1579 bis 1607 an, aus denen er offenbar Kolophone Abrahams kannte.

1603, 1631: ʿAbdalmasīḥ, Sohn des *maqdšāyā* Ǧumʿā in Bēṯ Ḥudaidā (d.i. Qaraqōš): Hss. Ming. Syr. 565 und 225.

1613: Priester ʿAbdalaḥad, Sohn des *maqdšāyā* Yūsufšāh, aus Aleppo: Borg. Syr. 168[42].

1623, 1624: Priester Ġarīb, Sohn des verstorbenen *maqdisī* Isaias, aus Manṣūrīya bei Mardin: Hss. Oxford Syr. 66 und Bagdad, Chaldäisches Kloster 75[43].

1632: ʿAbdallāh ibn *m(u)qsī* ʿAbdalḥaiy aus Gazarta: Scharfeh Syr. 11/10.

1634: Safar, Sohn des *maqdisī* Joseph: Scharfeh Syr. 19/10.

1642: Diakon Joseph, Sohn des *maqdisī* Ḥabībšāh: Scharfeh Syr. 11/11.

Ich breche ab. Weitere Beispiele lassen sich durchgehend bis zum 20. Jhdt. finden. Wie mir Herr Archidiakon Hanna Aydin, Glane/Holland, bestätigte, ist der Titel auch heute noch in der syrisch-orthodoxen Kirche durchaus gebräuchlich.

Eine Wallfahrt nach Jerusalem verschaffte dem Pilger zweifellos soziale Achtung in seiner Gemeinde[44]. Die Bezeichnung als *maqdisī* oder *maqdšāyā* stellt nicht einfach die sachliche Feststellung dar, daß der Betreffende Jerusalem besucht hat, sondern ist ein Ehrentitel, auf den man Wert legte, denn er wird in den Kolophonen offensichtlich sorgfältig vermerkt, etwa bei einzelnen Vorfahren in einer Abstammungskette oder bei einzelnen von mehreren Zeitgenossen. Die Schreiber bezeichnen sich, wenn ich recht sehe, selbst aber nicht so, auch wenn sie eine Pilgerfahrt nach Jerusalem gemacht haben (vgl. die obigen Angaben zu den Jahren 1515, 1549, 1577/1592, 1588). Eben weil es ein ehrenvoller Zusatz zum Namen ist, wurde er nur bei anderen verwendet.

41 Histoire 494 Nr. 242.

42 R. Duval, Lexicon syriacum auctore Hassan Bar Bahlul, Band 3, Paris 1886, S. XXXVII.

43 P. Haddad - J. Isaac, Syriac and Arabic Manuscripts in the Library of the Chaldean Monastery Baghdad, part 1: Syriac Mss., Bagdad 1988, 46.

44 Fiey aaO 124f.

Bischöfe führten den Titel anscheinend auch nicht (vgl. oben zu 1528). Ich habe jedenfalls keinen Beleg dafür gefunden.

Bei den oben vermerkten Pilgertiteln überwiegt die syrische Form *maqdšāyā*, aber auch das arabische *maqdisī* kommt in syrisch abgefaßten Kolophonen nicht selten vor; einmal erscheint auch die aus dem Ṭūrōyō bekannte Form *muqsī*.

Die genannten Träger des Titels stammten — soweit eine Herkunft angegeben ist — fast ausschließlich aus dem nordsyrisch-mesopotamischen Gebiet: aus Aleppo (2 Belege), aus Mardin (2) und den umliegenden Ortschaften Manṣūrīya (2), Quṣūr (2), Kalībīn (1), aus dem Ṭūr ʿAbdīn (Kloster Mār Malkē, Qilliṯ und ʿArnas: je 1) sowie aus Gargar (1) und Dörfern in der Umgebung (Wank und ʿUrbīš: je 1). Der erste Beleg für einen Pilger aus dem heutigen Iraq stammt erst aus dem Jahre 1603, der erste Wallfahrer mit dem Titel aus dem ebenfalls weiter entfernten Gāzartā (heute: Cisre/Türkei) ist für 1632 belegt.

4. Ostsyrische Belege

Bei den Ostsyrern kann ich den Titel *maqdšāyā/maqdisī* erst seit der zweiten Hälfte des 16. Jhdts. belegen, also erheblich später als bei den Westsyrern. Vielleicht liegt das daran, daß wegen der Umstände und des weiteren Weges Pilgerfahrten für sie erst später in Frage kamen. Damit läßt sich die folgende Feststellung Fieys für Jerusalem gut in Einklang bringen: »1283 a été la dernière date historique rencontrée; on n'entendra plus parler de Nestoriens à Jérusalem pendant près de trois cents ans«[45].

1567 schreibt der in Gāzartā lebende Priester Yahḇallāhā, Sohn des Priesters Farağ *maqdšāyā*, Sohn des Diakons Markos aus Alqōš, die Hs. Mosul Chald. 55[46]. Er ist identisch mit dem bekannten Priester ʿAṭāya (d.i. die arabische Übersetzung von Yahḇallāhā), von dem zahlreiche Handschriften aus der Zeit zwischen 1536 und 1594 erhalten sind; er starb 1596[47].

1593 kaufte der *maqdisī* Yūsufšāh an-Nasṭūrī (!) ibn Darwīš drei Bände des Lexikons des Bar Bahlūl: Hs. Halle, DMG, Syr. 1[48].

45 Fiey aaO 122.

46 Addai Scher läßt, wie bei allen seinen Handschriftenbeschreibungen, den Pilgertitel bei den Namen weg. Eine Abschrift der Mosuler Handschrift ist die Hs. Vat. Syr. 624, die den Kolophon der Vorlage samt Pilgertitel enthält, s. A. van Lantschoot, Inventaire des mss. syriaques des fonds Vatican, Vatikanstadt 1965, 156.

47 In den anderen Handschriften dürfte der Pilgertitel überall stehen, doch wird er teilweise in den Katalogen nicht vermerkt. In einigen Beschreibungen sieht es so aus, als ob der Schreiber den Titel selbst führt, doch scheint es sich dabei um Fehler der Kataloge zu handeln.

48 J. Aßfalg, Syrische Handschriften, Wiesbaden 1963, 115 (Nr. 50).

1594 stiftet der *maqdisī* Daniel aus Mosul die Hs. Mosul, Chald. 16 (= Bagdad, Chald. Patriarchat 1210) dem Eliaskloster bei Mosul[49]. In der Handschrift findet sich noch ein Vermerk aus dem Jahre 1672, in dem ein *maqdisī* ʿAbdalḥay und ein *maqdisī* ʿAbdalǧalīl erwähnt werden[50].

Besteller der 1601 geschriebenen Hs. Ming. Syr. 542 und ihr Stifter für eine Kirche in Rustāqā ist ein Darwīš *maqdšāyā* vom Stamme der Boḫṭināyē (nördlich von Gāzartā).

Die Liste ließe sich leicht fortsetzen. Auch bei den Ostsyrern finden sich zahlreiche weitere Beispiele aus späterer Zeit. Erwähnt sei noch der Priester Georg, Sohn des Priesters Daniel, welcher der bekannten Kopistenfamilie Hōmō in Alqōš angehörte. Er war 1724/25 Sakristan des nestorianischen Klosters in Jerusalem[51] und bezeichnete sich in den nach seiner Rückkehr kopierten Handschriften selbst als *maqdšāyā*: Tellkeph 42 (1730)[52]; Bagdad, Chald. Kloster 48 (1730)[53]; Notre-Dame des Semences 139[54] = Bagdad, Chald. Kloster 248 (1731)[55].

5. Melkiten und Maroniten

Für Angehörige der melkitischen und maronitischen Kirche kenne ich nur wenige Belege für den Titel *maqdisī*, keinen für *maqdšāyā*.

In einer Reihe von Fällen legt die Namensformen eher eine Herkunft des Betreffenden aus Jerusalem oder einen Familiennamen nahe, nicht den Pilgertitel. Einige solche Beispiele für die Melkiten:
Nuṣair ibn al-qass Ṣāliḥ al-Maqdisī (1285)[56].
Sulaimān ibn Dawūd al-Maqdisī (1465) (Paris Arab. 268).
Šukrallāh ibn Maqdisī (1688) (Paris Arab. 258).

Bei den beiden folgenden Namen ist aber eher vom Pilgertitel auszugehen:
»nicolas, fils du *maqdessi* Francis Pharʿaun« aus Damaskus (1766)[57].
ʿAbdallāh Ṭarrād ibn al-Maqdisī Michael aus Beirut (19. Jhdt.)[58].

49 Der Titel ist aus den Beschreibungen von Addai Scher nicht ersichtlich, vgl. aber J. M. Fiey, Assyrie chrétienne, Band 2, Beirut 1965, 654, n. 1.
50 Ebda. 654f.
51 J. B. Chabot, Notice sur les mss. syriaques conservés dans la bibliothèque du patriarcat grec orthodoxe de Jérusalem, in: Journal Asiatique, 9. sér., Bd. 3, Paris 1894, Nr. 7 und 27.
52 J. Habbi, in: Catalogue of the Syriac mss. in Iraq, vol. I, Bagdad 1977, 34.
53 Haddad-Isaac aaO 116.
54 J. Vosté, Catalogue de la bibliothèque Syro-chaldéenne du couvent de Notre-Dame des Sémences, Rome-Paris 1929, 52.
55 Haddad-Isaac aaO 34.
56 J. Nasrallah, Histoire du mouvement littéraire dans l'église Melchite, Band III, 2, Louvain-Paris 1981, 204.
57 J. Nasrallah, Catalogue des manuscrits du Liban, Band 1, Harissa 1958, 94 (Nr. 62).
58 Graf III 165.

Bei dem maronitischen Bischof Dawūd ibn Ḥanna al-Maqdisī (1452, 1463 A.D.)[59] ist schwer zu sagen, ob al-Maqdisī als Pilgertitel oder als normaler Namensbestandteil verwendet wird.

Bei den Melchiten und Maroniten scheint eher der arabische Titel *ḥāğğ*, den die Muslime im Zusammenhang mit einer Wallfahrt nach Mekka verwenden, auf Jerusalempilger angewandt worden zu sein. Der Maronit Butros Dau schreibt: »To the descendents of Michael… [15./16. Jhdt.] was applied, as is the custom in the Orient, the surname 'Hajj' (pilgrim) when the said Michael visited the Holy Land«[60]. Daraus wurde dann offenbar ein Familienname. Aber *ḥāğğ* findet sich auch sonst in einer Form, die als Pilgertitel verstanden werden muß, so etwa bei den Melchiten:
al-ḥāğğ Ṯalğa ibn al-ḫūrī Ḥaurān aus Hama (16./17. Jhdt.)[61].
Yūsuf al-Mūṣauwir ibn al-ḥāğğ Antonios (16./17. Jhdt.)[62].
Elias ibn al-ḥāğğ Masarra ibn al-ḥāğğ Saʿāda, gebürtig aus Qāra (17. Jhdt.)[63].
Šukrallāh ibn al-ḥāğğ Elias al-Qārī (17./18. Jhdt.)64.
Michael ibn al-ḥāğğ Ibrahīm ibn al-Mubaiyad (1720)[65].
Yuwāṣaf ibn al-ḥāğğ Niʿma (18. Jhdt.)[66].

oder bei den Maroniten
Yūḥannā ibn al-ḥāğğ Ḥasan (1478 A.D.)[67].
Elias ibn al-ḥāğğ Ḥannā (17. Jhdt.)[68].
Heute scheint ein solcher Titel aber nicht mehr üblich zu sein.

6. Armenier

Von zwei Angehörigen der westsyrischen Kirche armenischer Herkunft, die 1577/1592 bzw. 1588/1594 den syrischen Titel *maqdšāyā* trugen, war oben schon die Rede.

Herr Professor Aßfalg machte mich freundlicherweise auf eine armenische Entsprechung aufmerksam, die vielfach belegt und auch in Wörterbüchern verzeichnet ist. Die anscheinend heute gebräuchliche Form, die im »Erklärenden

59 M. Breydy, Geschichte der Syro-Arabischen Literatur der Maroniten vom VII. bis XVI. Jahrhundert, Opladen 1985, 224.
60 Religious, Cultural and Political History of the Maronites, o.O., o.J. (etwa 1983), 391.
61 Nasrallah, Histoire du mouvement, Band IV, 1, Louvain-Paris 1979, 214-217.
62 Ebda. 302.
63 Ebda. 212-214; Nasrallah, Catalogue des mss. du Liban, Band 3, Beirut 1961, 208 (Nr. 283).
64 Nasrallah, Histoire du mouvement, Band IV, 1, 301f. Auch aus Qāra stammend, es könnte sich um den Sohn des Elias (zu Fußn. 63) handeln, der dann ebenfalls nach Jerusalem gepilgert wäre.
65 Nasrallah, Catalogue. Band 1, 182 (Nr. 12).
66 Nasrallah, Histoire du mouvement, Band IV, 1, S. 306.
67 Breydy, Geschichte 225.
68 J. Raphael, Le rôle du college maronite romain, Beirut 1950, 116 (vgl. Graf III 335).

Wörterbuch der zeitgenössischen armenischen Sprache« (*Žamanakakicʻ hayocʻ lezvi bacʻatrakan bararan*), Band 3, Erewan 1974, 467b, sowie bei E. B. Agayan, *Ardi hayereni bacʻatrakan bararan* [»Neues armenisches erklärendes Wörterbuch«], Band 2, Erewan 1976, 959b, verzeichnet ist, lautet *mahtesi* und wird dort zutreffend erklärt als »Christ, der die Pilgerfahrt nach Jerusalem gemacht hat«.

Hr. Ačaryan, *Hayeren armatakan bararan* [»Armenisches etymologisches Wörterbuch«], Band 3, Erewan 1977, 236a gibt verschiedene Schreibungen an: *մահտեսի* (*mahtesi*), *մահդեսի* (*mahdesi*), *մուղտեսի* (*muġtesi*), *մուղդսի* (*mugdsi*), *մղտեսի* (*mġtesi*), *մղդըսի* (*mġdᵉsi*), *մղդէսի* (*mġdēsi*), *մըղտէսի* (*mᵉġtēsi*), *մղդըսի* (*mġdᵉsi*), *մագտիսի* (*magtisi*). Er erklärt das Wort ebenso (»einer, der die Pilgerfahrt nach Jerusalem gemacht hat«) und führt es zu Recht auf das arabische *maqdisī*/*muqdisī* zurück[69].

Der arabische Laut *q*, der in unserem Wort vorkommt, wird im Mittelarmenischen gewöhnlich mit *կ* (*k*) wiedergegeben, aber auch mit *ղ* (*ġ*)[70]. Die von Ačaryan vermerkten Formen mit *ġ* sind somit nicht auffällig. Eine Schreibung mit *k* scheint nicht vorzukommen. Viel häufiger erscheint anstelle des *ġ* jedoch ein *հ* (*h*), das lautlich nicht zu erklären ist[71]. Auch wenn man annimmt, daß das *q* in *maqdisī* in Syrien mundartlich zu ʼ (Hamza) geworden ist, wäre es im Armenischen vermutlich gar nicht ausgedrückt, jedenfalls kaum durch *h* wiedergegeben worden. Die Form mit *g*, die Ačaryan angibt, habe ich sonst nirgends belegt gefunden (s. unten die Tabelle).

Der Unterschied beim ersten Konsonanten der zweiten Silbe, nämlich der Wechsel der ursprünglichen *d* zu *t* erklärt sich ohne weiteres aus der westarmenischen Aussprache, in der wohl seit dem 11. Jhdt. *t* zu *d* und *d* zu *t* verschoben wurde, so daß für die Wiedergabe des arabischen *d* ein *t* geschrieben werden mußte.

Für die sehr unterschiedliche Vokalisation der ersten Silbe im Armenischen (*a, e, u* und *ᵉ* [mit und ohne besonderes Zeichen]) läßt sich die arabische Grundlage schwer ermitteln. Wie bereits Karst feststellte, zeigen sich zwischen arabischen Originalwörtern und den entsprechenden armenischen Lehnwörtern im Vokalismus auffällige Unterschiede. Karst schreibt zu Recht: »Die Differenzen beruhen teils auf Vokalreduktion, teils auf ungenauer, nachlässiger Wiedergabe, teils wohl auch darauf, dass bereits das Originalwort jenen

69 So auch Cowe aaO (oben Fußn. 14).

70 J. Karst, Historische Grammatik des Kilikisch-Armenischen, Strassbourg 1901, 38f. Es finden sich in aus dem Arabischen stammenden Wörtern für *q* aber auch *խ* (*ḫ*) und *ք* (*kʻ*), vgl. H. Hübschmann, Armenische Grammatik. Erster Teil, Leipzig 1897, 271 (Nr. 97), 274 (Nr. 129).

71 Man könnte jedoch auf die Schreibung »Urumhala« für die armenische Stadt Rūm Qalʻa (Hromkla) bei Schiltberger (Schlemmer aaO 81) hinweisen.

scheinbar abnormen Vokalismus zeigte, indem es der (arabischen, resp. persischen) Volkssprache, nicht der Schriftsprache angehörte, so dass in diesem Falle nur scheinbar unregelmäßige Wiedergabe vorläge«[72]. Die Vokalisierung mit *u* geht wohl auf das oben erwähnte volkssprachliche *muqdusī* oder *muqdasī* zurück, das *a* eher auf die klassische Form *maqdisī*. Der Murmelvokal im Armenischen könnte auf *u* und *a* beruhen. Entsprechendes gilt für die Vokalisation der zweiten Silbe. Den armenischen Schreibern war die Etymologie wahrscheinlich nicht geläufig und sie schrieben so, wie sie oder ihre Gewährsleute das Wort hörten. Die Vielfalt ist beträchtlich und es läßt sich auch kaum eine Entwicklung feststellen.

Eine besondere Femininform des Wortes gibt es nicht, wäre auch im Armenischen, das im allgemeinen keine unterschiedlichen Formen für die Genera kennt, nicht zu erwarten. Es finden sich aber zahlreiche Belege, in denen Frauen den Pilgertitel tragen.

Er wird — in den jeweiligen Schreibweisen — teils nach der o-Deklination behandelt (Gen. *mahdasoy*), teils nach der u-Deklination (Gen. *mahdasu*). Abgeleitet davon ist das Abstractum *mahtesutʿiwn* »Pilgerfahrt, Pilgereigenschaft«.

Daneben gibt es im Armenischen das islamische *hāǧǧī* (s. oben Fußn. 16), für Mekkapilger, aber — wie bei Melkiten und Maroniten — auch für christliche Jerusalemwallfahrer, und zwar in der Schreibung *hači* oder *hadži*: »Erklärendes Wörterbuch« aaO 264a und 301b; Aġayan aaO, Band 1, 797b und 827a; Ačaryan verzeichnet das Wort in seinem etymologischen Wörterbuch nicht.

Um den verschiedenen armenischen Schreibungen des christlichen Pilgertitels näher nachzugehen, habe ich die für diesen Zweck bequem benutzbaren umfangreichen Namensregister in den Sammelbänden für die armenischen Kolophone durchgesehen. Soweit ich sehe, erscheint der Titel seit dem Ende des 13. Jhdts.[73]. Der erste mir bekannte Beleg stammt aus dem Jahre 1297 und erwähnt einen *մահ[դ/տաս]ի Դմլոճ*[74], der zweite von 1307 (*մուղտեսի*), dann von 1351 (*մղտսի*), 1357 (*մահդասի*), 1370, 1386, 1391, 1393, 1394, 1398. Die beiden einzigen Belege für einen christlichen *hāǧǧī*, die ich kenne, finden sich in Kolophonen aus den Jahren 1358 und 1622; in letzterem erscheint

72 Ebda. 39f.

73 In dem Band des Katholikos Garegin I. über die Kolophone bis zum Jahre 1250 (Antilias 1951) habe ich keinen Beleg gefunden (abgesehen von einem aus dem Jahre 1628, S. 815f.). A. K. Sanjian, Colophons of Armenian Manuscripts 1301-1480, Cambridge/Mass. 1969, bietet den ersten für 1441.

74 A. S. Matʿevosyan, Hayeri dzeragreri hišatakaranner XIII dar, Erevan 1984, 795 (Nr. 632). Da der Titel in der betreffenden Handschrift offenbar abgekürzt ist, läßt sich nicht feststellen, ob eine Schreibung mit *d* oder *t* dahintersteht.

gleichzeitig der Titel *mahtasi*[75]. Die Ausgaben armenischer Inschriften, die ich durchgesehen habe[76], waren wenig ergiebig. Die Belege für den Pilgertitel stammen, soweit überhaupt datiert, aus späterer Zeit. Auch hier treten verschiedene Schreibungen auf. Besonderheiten gegenüber den Kolophonen lassen sich nicht feststellen.

Bei der nachstehenden Tabelle habe ich mich auf die Kolophone beschränkt. In der linken Spalte sind die verschiedenen Schreibweisen für den Pilgertitel aufgeführt. Die ost- bzw. westarmenischen Formen, die sich nur durch den Wechsel von *d* zu *t* unterscheiden, stehen — falls beide vorkommen — jeweils untereinander. Den Anfang machen die Formen mit *h* in der ersten Silbe, die viel uneinheitlicheren mit *ġ* (mit Vokal *a, u, ō, e* und *ᵉ* in der ersten Silbe) schließen sich an. Am Ende folgt die völlig alleinstehende Schreibung mit *t'* am Anfang der zweiten Silbe. Ich habe die Formen aus den Sammelbänden mit Kolophonen[77] übernommen und nicht überprüfen können. In einigen wenigen Fällen mag man zweifeln, ob sie so wirklich in den Handschriften stehen oder nur ein Druckfehler vorliegt. Die folgenden Ausführungen beruhen auf der Annahme, daß die Lesungen richtig sind. Leider fehlen noch die Bände für das 16. Jhdt., so daß insofern eine Lücke bleibt. Der Titel scheint auch noch später sehr verbreitet gewesen zu sein, denn E. Dulaurier bezeichnet ihn 1859 als »très-fréquent aujourd'hui chez les Arméniens«[78].

75 L. S. Ḫačikyan, XIV dari hayeren dzeragreri hišatakaranner, Erewan 1950. *mahtesī*: S. 52 (Nr. 66), 391 (470), 425 (508), 491 (601), 562 (702a), 587f. (734a), 604 (751a), 608 (759a), 623 (779a). *hači*: ebda. S. 436 (Nr. 523); V. Hakobyan - A. Hovhannisyan, Hayeren dzeragreri XVII dari hišatakaranner. Hator II (1621-1640), Erevan 1978, 79.

76 Corpus Inscriptionum Armeniacarum, Bd. 1ff., Erevan 1960ff. (Belege aus dem 17. Jhdt.); P. M. Muradjan, Armjanskaja epigrafika Gruzii, Tbilisi 1988 (18. Jhdt.); M. E. Stone, Epigraphica Armeniaca Hierosolymitana, I-IV, in: Annual of Armenian Linguistics 1 (1980) 51-68; 2 (1981) 71-83; REA 18 (1985) 559-581; 20 (1986-1987) 463-479 (meist 18. Jhdt.).

77 Außer den schon genannten: L. S. Ḫačikyan, XV dari hayeren dzeragreri hišatakaranner. Masn I. (1401-1450), Erevan 1955; Masn II. (1451-1480 tt.), Erevan 1958; Masn III. (1481-1500 tt.), Erevan 1967; V. Hakobyan - A. Hovhannisyan, Hayeren dzeragreri XVII dari hišatakaranner. Hator 1 (1601-1620 tt.), Erevan 1974. Nicht mehr verwendet habe ich V. Hakobyan, Hator III (1641-1660), Erevan 1984, weil im Personenregister dieses Bandes der Pilgertitel leider nicht vermerkt ist.

78 Recherches sur la chronologie arménienne. T. 1, Paris 1859, 160.

	1301-1400	1401-1450	1451-1480	1481-1500	16. Jh.	1601-1620	1621-1640[79]
մահդասի	4	12	22	2	?	6	2
մահտասի	1	1	1			3	3
մահդեսի		1				1	1
մահտեսի		2				6	5
մաղդասի		2	3	1		1	
մուղդասի		1	3	1			
մուղտասի			1				
մուղդեսի						1	
մուղտեսի	1						
մուղ[տ?]էսի						1	
մօղդասի				1			
մեղտեսի		1					
մղդասի			1				
մղտասի		1	1				
մղտեսի	2	3	5			3	1
մղդէսի				1			
մղտէսի			1				
մղտիսի			1				
մղդսի			1				
մղտսի	1	2				1	
մղտեսցի						1	
մղտեցի		1				1	
մղխտեսի			1				
մաղթասի			1				
	9	27	42	6	?	24	12

Die bei weitem häufigste Form, zum Teil mehr als die Hälfte, ist *mahdasi*, und das von Anfang an. Dieser Befund ist umso auffallender, als — wie oben bereits erwähnt — das *h* lautlich nicht zu erklären ist. Man hätte meinen können, daß für die Schreibung mit *h* und den in diesen Fällen entschieden einheitlicheren Vokalbestand die bei Ačaryan angegebene eigenartige volkstümliche Deutung des Pilgertitels als *մահ(ը) տեսի* (*mah*^{e}*tesi*) »ich habe den Tod gesehen« maßgeblich war. Das ist aber schwer möglich, denn die am Anfang weit überwiegende Form ist eben *mahdasi* und nicht *mahtesi*. Letztere holt erst im 17. Jhdt. auf (oder vielleicht schon im 16. Jhdt.?). Diese spätere Entwicklung mag wohl auf die Volksetymologie zurückgehen, und sie wird auch dazu geführt haben, daß sich in den angegebenen modernen Wörterbüchern die Form *mahtesi* schließlich als einzige durchgesetzt hat. Gleichzeitig wurden

79 Für die Jahre 1621-1640 ist der Titel im Register offenbar nicht überall vermerkt (s. auch Fußn. 77 a. E.). Die Zahlen sind deshalb nicht vollständig. Es erschien mir für den Zweck dieses Aufsatzes jedoch nicht erforderlich, die Texte sämtlicher Kolophone durchzusehen.

die Formen mit *ġ* weniger. Es gibt aber keine Anhaltspunkte dafür, daß sie älter sind als die mit *h*, wie Ačaryan aaO meint.

Das Verhältnis der westarmenischen Schreibung zur ostarmenischen kehrt sich im Laufe der Zeit um. Während anfangs bei den wenigen Beispielen aus dem 14. Jhdt. das Verhältnis ungefähr ausgeglichen ist, überwiegt dann die Schreibung mit *d*, später ist die mit *t* in der Mehrzahl:

	1301-1400	1401-1450	1451-1480	1481-1500	–	1601-1620	1621-1640
ostarmen. (*d*)	4	16	30	6		8	3
westarmen. (*t*)	5	11	11	0		15	9

Angesichts des geringen statistischen Materials und anderer Unsicherheiten kann man daraus aber wohl nicht unbedingt schließen, daß die Zahl der Pilger aus Ostarmenien verhältnismäßig abnahm; hier müßten auch die Kolophone selbst untersucht werden.

Es fällt auf, daß im 14. und 15. Jhdt. keineswegs — wie bei den syrischen Belegen — eine Lücke klafft, sondern daß es auch in diesen für die orientalischen Christen dunklen Jahrhunderten offenbar immer eine nicht unbeträchtliche Zahl armenischer Jerusalempilger gab, und zwar nicht nur aus dem näher gelegenen Kilikien, sondern auch aus Ostarmenien. Während der syrische Titel erstmals 1470 wieder auftritt (da ihn der Vater des Schreibers trägt, wird die Wallfahrt wohl einige Jahre früher gewesen sein), bieten die armenischen Kolophone bereits ab der Mitte des 14. Jhdts. eine ununterbrochene Reihe von Belegen. Für diesen Unterschied kann ich keine befriedigende Erklärung geben. An syrischen Handschriften aus der betreffenden Zeit fehlt es jedenfalls nicht. Es kann natürlich sein, daß die Benennung mit dem Ehrentitel auch etwas von einer Mode an sich hatte, die sich bei den Syrern erst später richtig durchsetzte. Möglicherweise war aber auch die Zahl der syrischen Pilger tatsächlich geringer.

Auf den ersten Blick erstaunlich ist ferner, daß der Pilgertitel erstmals ungefähr gleichzeitig in der westsyrischen und armenischen Kirche auftritt, nämlich um die Wende vom 13. zum 14. Jhdt., ja, daß der früheste mir bekannte armenische Beleg sogar zehn Jahre älter ist als der erste syrische. Es muß also nicht so sein, daß die Armenier die Gewohnheit, Pilger mit einem Ehrentitel auszuzeichnen, von ihren benachbarten westsyrischen Glaubensbrüdern übernommen haben, auch wenn man sonst gewöhnt ist, die Syrer als Gebende und die Armenier als Nehmende anzusehen (z.B. bei der Übersetzungsliteratur). Die armenische Form ist ja auch von einem arabischen Wort abgeleitet, nicht von einem syrischen. Dies deutet nochmals darauf hin, daß das arabische *maqdisī* offenbar die Grundlage war, sowohl für die syrische wie für die armenische Form, außerdem auch, daß der Titel nicht im syrischen Sprachgebiet entstanden ist (vielleicht in Jerusalem?). Allerdings war das Arabische zu dieser Zeit bereits in einigen Gebieten Umgangssprache der westsyrischen Christen. Wenn es stimmt, daß die Christen damit dem islamischen Titel *ḥāǧǧ* »Mekkapilger« einen eigenen entgegensetzen wollten, ist es merkwürdig, daß wir bei Griechen, Georgiern, Kopten und Äthiopiern[80], die ebenfalls nach Jerusalem pilgerten, nichts Entsprechendes finden. Vielleicht sahen sie keinen Anlaß, muslimische Sitten zu übernehmen, weil die Angehörigen dieser Konfessionen — freilich mit Ausnahme der Kopten — nicht in einem Ausmaß wie Syrer und Armenier unter islamischer Herrschaft und neben Muslimen leben mußten.

80 Die äthiopische Gemeinschaft der "Pilger" (*naggādyān*) in Jerusalem und Ägypten, von der E. Cerulli berichtet (Etiopi in Palestina, Band 2, Rom 1947, 353ff.), hat mit unserem Pilgertitel nichts zu tun, auch wenn einige der Angehörigen "Heilige" (*qeddusān*) genannt werden. "'Pellegrini' sono quelli che partecipano alla communità per il periodo del loro pellegrinaggio in Terra Santa ... 'Santi', invece, sono quelli che si sono vincolati con voto a restare a Gerusalemme (o nelle communità egiziane collegate) vita natural durante" (ebda. 355).

OMERT J. SCHRIER

Chronological Problems Concerning the Lives of Severus bar Mašqā, Athanasius of Balad, Julianus Romāyā, Yoḥannān Sābā, George of the Arabs and Jacob of Edessa

1.0 A mist of mystery is spread over the history of the West-Syrian Church at the end of the viiith centuries[1]. In modern literature uncertainty prevails concerning the chronology of some of the major events in the lives of the men who dominated Monophysite life between 680 and 710 A.D. No special study seems to have ever been devoted to this period. The lists of patriarchs in Spuler (1964) and Hage (1966) are at variance with each other[2]. Hage, whose dissertation remains the most informative study on the history of the West-Syrian Church in the viith and viiith centuries, dit not make use of all the material available. It did not fit into his plan, moreover, to discuss statements in the sources that are deviant from those of his main authority, Michael the Syrian. Brock (1976) has gathered essential information about all the regular sources that refer to the viith century, but it was not his intention to discuss their contents. Nor could he pay attention to the casual remarks that can be found in some manuscripts. There is reason, therefore, to find out whether it is possible to clear up the chronology of this period, in the hope that in this way a basis is laid for a study that will do justice to all the aspects of its history. That study will not be written by me.

It may be helpful to begin with a survey of the patriarchs and "maphrians"[3] involved and of the initial and final dates of their pontificates, as given by Michael the Syrian (MS) and Barhebraeus (BH). All dates in this section are given according to the Seleucid era. More details will be provided below.

1 I am much indebted to Professor L. Van Rompay and Mrs. drs. Peri Bearman, who kindly commented on argument and style of this paper. For the remaining errors I am responsible. Dr. J. J. S. Weitenberg was willing to discuss with me the Armenian translation of Michael the Syrian. It proved to have no bearing on our subject.
The abbreviations used will be explained at the end of this article. Where Syriac sources are quoted, references to modern translations have been added.

2 Spuler (1964) 213, Hage (1966) Table A.

3 For this time the term "maphrian" is an anachronism; see Hage (1966) 25 n. 214 and Fiey (1974) 139-140.

Some obvious conclusions are drawn in § 2. The real problems are mustered in § 3. We will have a look at our resources in § 4. In § 5 an attempt is made to solve some chronological problems. Our conclusions are to be found in § 6.

1.1. *Patriarchs*:

Severus bar Mašqā — ord. 978 (MS?), 979 (BH), died 991 (BH), 995 (MS), having held his post 12 years (MS, BH);

Athanasius of Balad — ord. 991 (BH), 995 (MS, BH), died in September 998 (MS, BH), having held his post 3 years (MS, BH);

Julianus Romāyā — ord. November 999 (MS, BH), died 1019 (MS, BH), having held his post 20 years (MS), 21 years (MS, BH).

"*Maphrians*": (only BH)

Bar 'Išoʿ — ord. 980, died 17 December 995, having held his post 15 years;

Abraham — died after a short time;

David — died after 6 months;

interregnum — 6 years;

Yoḥannān Sābā — died January (999), having held his post 1 year and 6 months;

Denḥā II — ord. March 999, died October 1039, having held his post 40 years.

2.0. The Seleucid year ran from 1 October to 30 September. In order to find the corresponding dates in the Christian era, one has to substract the number 312 (for the period 1 October - 31 December) or 311 (for the other months) from the number of the Seleucid year.

Some simple conclusions can be drawn immediately.

2.1. Patriarch Athanasius of Balad died on 11 September 998 Sel., according to MS IV 446[a]-447[a] [4] (II 474); the same month and the same year were meant by Barhebraeus, as appears from BH I 293-6 [5]. The date corresponds to 11 September 687, not to 11 September 686, as e.g. Baumstark, Spuler, Ortiz de Urbina and Vööbus state[6].

4 As is well known, Michael presented his material in either one, two or three columns. The terms *gawrā 'ellāytā*, 'the superior column', and *gawrā taḥtāytā*, 'the inferior column' (MS IV 377), do not refer to the right and left columns of the page respectively, as Chabot in his Introduction to MS (I xxiv) says, but to the exterior and interior columns respectively. On the odd pages (= the recto side of the folios), therefore, the *gawrā 'ellāytā* is the left column, on the even pages it is the right one.
In the following, I will use the symbol [a] to refer to the outside column of Michael's text, and [b] (and [c]) to denote the following one(s).

5 See further below, § 5.4.3.

6 Baumstark (1922) 256, Spuler (1964) 213, Ortiz de Urbina (1965) 183, Vööbus (1970) 202. Hage (1966) Table A has the correct dating. On Athanasius' dates see below, § 5.4.

2.2. Two months after the death of Athanasius, George of the Arabs was ordained bishop, in November (MS IV 447ᵃ-II 474) 687, therefore. We find the same data in the text of BH I 293 (294)[7]. The consecration did not take place, therefore, in November 686, as was thought by Abbeloos-Lamy, Ryssel, Baumstark, Ortiz de Urbina and Vööbus[8], but in November 687, as Hage and de Halleux saw[9].

2.3. In the same month, MS IV 447ᵃ (II 474) continues, Julianus Romāyā was consecrated patriarch, that is to say in November 687, which corresponds to *Tešrin* II 999 Sel., the date mentioned in Michael's Appendix III (MS IV 752 - III 449). The same year is named by BH I 295 (296). It is clear that Hage is correct in placing Julianus' ordination in November 687, whereas Spuler's date (688) is based on an error[10].

Julianus died, according to MS IV 448ᵃ (II 476), BH I 295 (296) and all the other sources, in 1019 Sel., i.e. in 707/8. In his Appendix III Michael holds that his pontificate lasted 20 years (MS IV 752 - III 449). This is correct. In his main text, however, Michael says that Julianus reigned 21 years (MS IV 448ᵃ - II 476). The source of this error is obvious. In the latter passage Michael subtracted 998, the last date he had mentioned (MS IV 447ᵃ - II 474) from 1019 (MS IV 448ᵃ - II 476), without realizing that by November the new year 999 had already started. Barhebraeus, who is wholly dependent on Michael here, simply copied this error (BH I 295-296).

We may now already conclude that the year of Julianus' death is correctly rendered by Hage. Spuler's date (708) is a little too exact[11].

3.0. The real problems arise from the fact that MS and BH sometimes provide contradictory or inconsistent information, as a glance at our § 1.1. proves. Evidence that can be gathered from other sources makes the mist still denser. The problems involved have been noticed in the secondary literature, though they have never been discussed in relation with each other, as far as I know. In the following subsections they are presented more or less in the form modern scholars have left them.

7 See further below, § 5.4.3.

8 Abbeloos-Lamy in BH I 304 n. 4, Ryssel (1891) xv, Baumstark (1922) 257 (the specification that the consecration took place on 11 November is due to a misunderstanding of Chabot's "teshrin II (nov.)" in MS II 474), Ortiz de Urbina (1965) 183. Vööbus (1970) 219, who bases himself on Ryssel (= November 686), erroneously speaks of Barhebraeus as representing "Another tradition" (= November 687).

9 Hage (1966) 96, de Halleux in *Le Muséon* 94 (1981) 208. For another, incorrect, dating see below, § 5.3.

10 Hage (1966) Table A, Spuler (1964) 213.

11 Hage (1966) Table A, Spuler (1964) 213. See below, § 5.2.

3.1. According to Spuler, Severus bar Mašqā died in "680 (683/4?)"[12]. Hage states that his death fell in 683/4. In a note he adds, without discussion, that BH mentions the year 679/80[13].

3.2. Abbeloos-Lamy point out[14] that, according to BH I 285 (286), Severus bar Mašqā wrote a letter to *Yoḥannān mapryānā d-madnḥā*, whereas it is said in the second part of the *Chronicon ecclesiasticum* that Yoḥannān had been "maphrian" for only one year and a half when he died in January 688 (BH II 145-146)[15].

The letter of Mar Severus makes up part of a collection of six letters that document the end of a conflict between the patriarchate of Antioch and some bishops. The letters have been preserved in MS IV 438-444 - II 458-468[16]. Fiey correctly observed that, whereas Severus addressed Yoḥannān in his letter as *mēṭrō d-purnāsā madnḥāyā d-Bēt Parsāyē* (MS IV 438ª - II 458), the formerly rebellious bishops gave him the title of *mēṭrō d-ʿumrā d-Mār(y) Mattay* (MS IV 438ᵇ - II 458) and Yoḥannān spoke of himself as *mēṭrop̄ d-ʿumrā d-Mār(y) Mattay wa-d-Bēt Parsāyē* (MS IV 439ᵇ - II 460). Possibly, Fiey writes, there were some doubts whether the see of Tagrit was occupied legitimately at that time[17]. Hage puts it in this way: "der Metropolit Johannes Saḇā, dem dieser Titel offiziell nur für die Provinz Aṯōr und Nineve zustand, (ließ sich) ... vom Patriarchen als 'Metropolit Persiens' anreden"[18], but this formulation leaves the responsibility of the patriarch himself for this address out of account. In any case, the designations referred to do not contribute to an immediate understanding of the function Yoḥannān held at the time these letters were written[19].

3.3. Abbeloos-Lamy make clear, furthermore, that Barhebraeus' datings in BH II, referring to "maphrians", are inconsistent with those in BH I, which relate to patriarchs[20]. According to BH II 133 (134), "maphrian" Abraham[21] was ordained by patriarch Athanasius (of Balad), but died after a short time. His death was approximately coincident with that of the patriarch (BH II 141-2), who died in September 687 (BH I 293-294)[22]. The pontificate of Abraham's successor, David, lasted only six months, after which the see of

12 Spuler (1964) 213.
13 Hage (1966) Table A with n. 27. See below, § 5.5.
14 Abbeloos-Lamy in BH II 146 n. 2.
15 For the year see below, § 3.3. and 5.6.1.
16 For these letters see below, § 4.1.1.
17 Fiey (1974) 378.
18 Hage (1966) 38.
19 See below, § 5.7.
20 Abbeloos-Lamy in BH II 146 n. 2 and cf. R. Abramowski (1940) 91 n. 1.
21 See above, § 1.1.
22 See above, § 2.1.

Tagrit remained empty for six years (BH II 141-142), which brings us to at least the year 693. The next "maphrian" was Yoḥannān Sābā, who died, after a reign of one year and a half, in January of an unspecified year (BH II 145-146). By then we are in, say, the year 695. His successor, however, Denḥā II, was consecrated in March 688 (BH II 145-146). Hage notes the problem also[23].

3.4. According to Vööbus (1970), no certainty can be reached about the year in which Jacob of Edessa was ordained bishop and the date of his death. In his view, the first event can have taken place in 675/6 or 680, as well as in 684, whereas Jacob's death can be placed in either 704, 708 or 710. Moreover, he held that our sources give rise to uncertainty as to the circumstances under which Jacob died[24]. In 1977 he was ready to accept the generally adopted view that Jacob died in 708, but he remained sceptic about the other issues[25].

3.5. It is clear that the exact chronological setting of some events that took place around 700 A.D. is still problematic. Considered separately, none of the questions involved can be solved with the available evidence. The only way out is to discuss them in their mutual relationship.

4.0. Before treating the problems themselves, we have to inspect the instruments at our disposal. These are:

1) documents, preserved either independently or within the *Chronicle* of Michael the Syrian,
2) statements made by Michael the Syrian in his main text or in his Appendix III,
3) statements made by Barhebraeus in BH II,
4) data found in other Syriac or Arabic sources,
5) sound reasoning.

The first three items deserve a separate treatment.

4.1.1. An important part in our discussions will be played by a corpus of six letters, which has been preserved in MS IV 438-444 (II 458-468). The letters relate to the end of a conflict between a number of the most prominent Monophysite bishops and the patriarchate of Antioch. Peace was signed at the Synod of Reš‘ayna[26]. The first of these letters is directed by patriarch

23 Hage (1966) Table B, n. 144. See below, § 5.6.
24 Vööbus (1970) 207-8 and 211-2; Vööbus bases his views on material that is assembled by Baumstark (1922) 248 n. 3.
25 Vööbus (1977). See below, § 5.1.
26 About this conflict see MS IV 436ª-437ª (II 456-457), IV 444ª (II 470) and IV 469ª (II 513-514), *Chron. ad ann. 1234* II 262-263 (197-198), BH I 283-288 and Hage (1966) 33.

Severus bar Mašqā to Yoḥannān Sābā, at that moment, as we will see, metropolitan of Mar Mattay[27]. Severus writes that his end is near and asks Yoḥannān to prevent the rebellious bishops from taking advantage of his death. One of his supporters, Severus makes clear, is Mar Gabriel (MS IV 438ª-440ª - II 458-462)[28]. The five other letters are written after Severus' death. In two of them the rebellious bishops express their wish to restore peace. They are willing to name Severus again in the diptychs and, though they object to the activities of Mar Gabriel of Reš'ayna, who was making arrangements outside his own diocese, they are ready to accept the latter's decisions. They ask him to come to them in Edessa and join them in the pursuit of peace (MS IV 440ª-442ª - II 462-465 and IV 442ª-444ª - II 564-468). Apparently, the bishops had struck the right note, for we find Mar Gabriel subscribing, together with his former opponents, to a fourth letter, directed to Yoḥannān Sābā, in which the bishops formally renounce their decision to depose patriarch Severus (MS IV 438ᵇ - II 458-459)[29]. The fifth and sixth letters, written by Yoḥannān Sābā and the joint bishops respectively[30], announce to the whole Church and its worldly lords that peace has definitely returned.

From this survey it appears that, if we want to read these letters in a chronological order, we must first read the exterior columns of MS IV 438-444 and then the interior ones (corresponding to the left and right columns respectively of II 458-468)[31], in this way:

1.	MS IV 438ª-440ª - II 458-462	left c.	Severus
2.	MS IV 440ª-442ª - II 462-465	left c.	bishops (− Gabriel)
3.	MS IV 442ª-444ª - II 465-468	left c.	bishops (− Gabriel)
4.	MS IV 438ᵇ - II 458	right c.	bishops (+ Gabriel)
5.	MS IV 439ᵇ-441ᵇ - II 459-464	right c.	Yoḥannān Sābā
6.	MS IV 441ᵇ-444ᵇ - II 464-468	right c.	bishops (+ Gabriel)

27 See below, § 5.7.

28 The *Chronicon ad annum 1234* II 262-263 (197-198) erroneously makes Gabriel an opponent of Severus. So does, in his wake, Hage (1966) 33 n. 305. The *Chronicon ad annum 1234* is dependent on the lost *Chronicle* of (the real) Dionysius of Tellmahre, cf. Fiey in the Introduction to the translation of *Chron. ad ann. 1234* II, p. ix.
Part of the letter is quoted in BH I 285 (286).

29 The fact that Gabriel subscribed to this letter together with the former rebels will have misled (Dionysius of Tellmahre and) the author of the *Chronicon ad annum 1234* (see above n. 28). Gabriel's signature meant no more than that the solidarity between the bishops was restored. Part of this letter is quoted in BH I 285-8.

30 The last letter is not quoted in its entirety by Michael. In the form we have it, it does not speak of the ordination of patriarch Athanasius, though the superscription announces that the subject will be treated (MS IV 441ᵇ - II 464), cf. below, n. 114. For other extracts in MS see MS IV 413ª (II 417) and Chabot in MS I 255 n. 1.

31 The survey in Baumstark (1922) 256 needs correction.

This means that the remarks inserted by Michael himself between some of these letters should be read in the same order. The most interesting of them, for our purposes, are those after letters 3 and 4. After letter 3, Michael declares that this letter and the preceding one were copied (or published), with the bishops' permission, by Jacob of Edessa, when he resided in Edessa before being ordained bishop of that city: *hālēn tartēn 'eggrātā Ya'qob 'Urhāyā 'aṣṣaḥ 'enēn men mappsānutā d-'epis(qopē) kad 'āmar (h)wā b-'Urhāy qdām d-nettasraḥ lāh 'epis(qopā)*[32]. Thereupon (*bātar hālēn*), Michael continues, the bishops went to Reš'ayna and held a synod there under the presidency of Yoḥannān Sābā (MS IV 444ª - II 468). From the latter part of this note it appears that Gabriel had not accepted the bishops' invitation to come to Edessa. The bishops had to go to Reš'ayna, the see of their most prominent opponent. Letter 4, therefore, was written in Reš'ayna, 'at the request of Yoḥannān' (MS IV 438ᵇ - 458). It must have been this letter, in which the bishops formally renounced their rebellion, that persuaded Yoḥannān to make the long journey from Mar Mattay to Reš'ayna (MS IV 439ᵇ - II 460-461). After letter 4, Michael notes: *hālēn hway ba-šnat ṣ̄ṣ̄h̄ d-Yawnāyē* (MS IV 439ᵇ - II 459), which means that, according to Michael, the formal submission of the bishops, which led to the Synod of Reš'ayna, took place in 683/4 A.D. In the narrative part of his work Michael holds the same view: the Synod of Reš'ayna, in which peace was restored, was held in 683/4, after the death of Severus (MS IV 444ª - II 470).

On this point Michael's communications are of special interest, as becomes clear when they are considered in the light of one of the Syriac texts we just quoted. According to that note, Jacob of Edessa copied (or published) some of the letters the rebellious bishops had written. Within the context of the attempt to reconcile the two conflicting parties this remark was utterly irrelevant. It is improbable, therefore, that Michael borrowed it, directly or indirectly, from any historian other than Jacob himself. The structure of Jacob's historical work, his *Chronicle*, forbids us to assume that Michael took the letters from that work[33]. Presumably, therefore, they stem from a private collection of Jacob, as Abramowski already supposed[34]. It cannot be proven that the notes which accompany the letters in Michael's text were copied from

32 Versions like 'à la demande des évêques' (Chabot) and 'im Auftrag der Bischöfe redigiert' (Baumstark [1922] 256) do not do justice to the Syriac text. By some error Tisserant (1947) holds that Jacob acted as the secretary of a synod in Edessa that was convoked by patriarch Severus. According to him, Jacob himself was at that time a priest. In reality, Jacob was a monk, by then, for all we know (cf. MS IV 445ª - II 471). The bishops wrote the letters on their own initiative, when Severus was already dead, cf. MS IV 440ª (II 468).

33 Michael extensively used Jacob's *Chronicle*, see below, § 4.2.1.

34 R. Abramowski (1940) 91. Michael was certainly interested in Jacob's literary legacy, see *Chron. ad ann. 1234* II 314 (235).

remarks by Jacob, but Michael can hardly have written them down if he had found evidence in Jacob's *Chronicle* or his collection of letters that ran counter to their contents. Presumably, therefore, the Synod of Reš'ayna was dated in 683/4 by Jacob himself. We will see below that there is other evidence which supports and specifies this dating[35].

4.1.2. Michael has preserved still another document, an anonymous *Vita* of Jacob of Edessa. We will discuss this text below[36].

4.2.0. To assess the historical value of the statements made by Michael himself in his narrative, we have to look at his sources. Fortunately, for our period Michael partly based himself on data that were provided, again, by Jacob of Edessa. Jacob himself took part in the events we are discussing here. It seems worthwhile to examine to what extent Michael depends on Jacob's historical work.

4.2.1. Michael himself asserts that he has incorporated into his work the whole of Jacob's *Chronicle* (MS IV 450 - II 482). The *Chronicle* of Jacob of Edessa is to be divided into an introductory part, which treats of the chronology of Eusebius' *Chronicle*, and the so-called 'Canons'. The 'Canons' started where Eusebius' *Chronicle* ended, i.e. in 326 A.D. (JE 263 [200] and 288 [215]). They consisted of a central column, in which Jacob gave a synchronic survey, in tabular form, of the regnal years of the leaders of the most important empires, and two margins, in which he noted the major events that occurred in their years. These remarks were written in a very succinct style, if only because of lack of space. Brooks hesitantly assumed, on the basis of a note by Elias of Nisibis, that Jacob's *Chronicle* ended in 692 A.D.[37]. In this case there was no need for Brooks to be so cautious, for Elias' statement is confirmed by a remark made by Michael himself, who writes that Jacob's *Chronicle* covered the period from Adam to the reign of (the anti-)caliph Abdallah (MS IV 128ᵇ - I 255). Abdallah died in 692 A.D.[38]. A note by Theodosius of Edessa, preserved in MS *l.c.*, gives the same information[39]. It is beyond doubt, therefore, that the *Chronicle* of Jacob of Edessa ran to the year 692 A.D. Elsewhere, however, Michael states that Jacob's *Chronicle* extended to the year 709/10 (MS IV 450 - II 483). We have to assume, therefore, with Brooks[40], that one of Jacob's disciples continued

35 See below, § 5.1.3., 5.4.1., 5.5.1. and 5.6.1.

36 See below, § 5.1.

37 Brooks in the Introduction to his translation of JE, p. 197, and p. 255 n. 1; see Elias II 99 (111 Chabot, 304 Delaporte); cf. Baumstark (1922) 254.

38 Cf. H. A. R. Gibb in *EI* I 54-55 s.v. 'Abd Allāh b. al-Zubayr.

39 According to Theodosius, Jacob's *Chronicle* ended with the reign of the Byzantine emperor Justinian (II; 685-695 A.D.) and that of Abdallah. The caliph's name is here abbreviated to a simple *'Abd*, but see Chabot in MS I 255 n. 2.

40 See above, n. 37.

his master's 'Canons' for eighteen years. Michael himself had reached a similar conclusion[41]. We may conclude that Michael had at his disposal an exemplar of the *Chronicle* of Jacob of Edessa, in which the author had come to the year 692 and a continuator to 709/10.

As we said just now, Michael writes that he has inserted the whole of Jacob's *Chronicle* into his own work. We can control this statement only partly, since the fragments of Jacob's *Chronicle* we have at our disposal do not go beyond the year 631 A.D.[42]. As for the introductory part, Michael's claim is on the whole justified[43], though it is clear that he has abbreviated and omitted passages[44]. On the other hand, in MS IV 42ᵇ-44ᵇ (I 71-73) he quotes a passage from Jacob's *Chronicle* that cannot be found back in Brooks' edition of JE. This fact seems to have escaped the notice of Brooks, but it lends weight to his contention that ms. *London Br. Libr. Add.* 14,685, the sole source for his edition of JE, only gives "a series of extracts" from Jacob's *Chronicle*[45]. As regards the 'Canons', Michael could not simply reproduce them, in view of the different plan of his own work. He placed Jacob's central column at the bottom of the page, and the notes in Jacob's margins in suitable places in his own text, retaining the characteristic short notice style which distinguishes them from their context[46]. Chabot holds that in this way Michael succeeded indeed in integrating the complete text of the 'Canons' into his own work[47]. There is not much reason to question his view[48].

41 In MS IV 450 (II 483) Michael holds, assuming that Jacob had kept working on his *Chronicle* until his death in 708, that a pupil of Jacob prolonged the 'Canons' for two years. As an alternative explanation he is willing to assume that Jacob died only in 709/10, a proposal that will prove to be superfluous, see also below, § 5.1.2. Michael seems not to have observed that his remarks here (Jacob's *Chronicle* ended in 709/10) and those in MS IV 128ᵇ - I 255 (it reached the reign of Abdallah, i.e. till 692) are incompatible.

42 JE 327 (251). In his translation, pp. 252-255, Brooks has supplemented, borrowing from Michael's *Chronicle*, the 'Canons' up to 709/10.

43 Compare JE 261-264 (199-201) with MS IV 127ᵃᵇ-128ᵃᵇ (I 253-255), JE 278-283 (209-212) with MS IV 76-78 (I 118-120). Jacob's notes in JE 283-287 (212-214) are to be found back, *sparsim*, in MS IV 140 sqq. (I 278 sqq.) and in MS IV 129-130 (I 256-257).

44 See the remark of Chabot in MS I 255 n. 1 and the marginal note in MS IV 129 - I 256, which refers to JE 265-278 (201-209). Michael omitted in MS IV 130 (I 257) the last lines of JE 287 (214).

45 Brooks in *ZDMG* 53 (1899) 263; he did not repeat this statement in his edition and translation of JE.

46 See R. Abramowski (1940) 16.

47 Chabot in the Introduction to MS, I xxvi.

48 One could remark that Jacob's statement, according to which Constantine the Great wrote a letter to bishop Macarius of Jerusalem (JE 288 [215]), does not recur in MS. There may be other slight omissions, but they do not inflict serious doubt as to the correctness of Chabot's view.

From the fragments of Jacob's *Chronicle* that have been preserved it is clear that he used to note, in the right margin, the changes on the Monophysite thrones of Antioch and Edessa[49] as well as those in other prominent sees. We may conclude, therefore, that Michael, when dating the reigns of the successive patriarchs of Antioch in the period 680-692, utilized the notes Jacob of Edessa had made in his *Chronicle*. For the period between 693 and 710, he had at this disposal the notes of a man who had been tutored in the school of Jacob. In view of these facts, it is clear that, with respect to the sees of Antioch and Edessa, the chronology of Michael deserves much respect, at least for the period mentioned.

4.2.2. The foregoing makes clear that Jacob of Edessa was not Michael's only source for our period. On the contrary, apart from the short-style notes that are due to Jacob of Edessa, Michael's narrative about the events that took place between 582 and 842 is wholly dependent on the *Chronicle* of a ixth-century author, Dionysius of Tellmahre[50]. This circumstance compels us to be on our guard. We will see, however, that wherever we can verify him, Michael's statements are in harmony with evidence that can be gathered from independent sources[51].

4.2.3. For the period between 680 and 710, our conclusion must be that the chronological data Michael supplies about the sees of Antioch and Edessa can hardly be wrong (§ 4.2.1.), and that in the narrative part of his work he is also to be considered a very reliable source indeed (§ 4.2.2.).

4.3. About the sources of the second book of Barhebraeus' *Chronicon ecclesiasticum* we have no information. As far as I know, nobody has yet discussed the question. Barhebraeus himself writes that he found much material in the libraries in Marga[52]. That could very well be true, but it is improbable that he found there any information about the succession of "maphrians" in the years 680-710. One may suppose that for that subject Barhebraeus made use of what he could find in the archives in Tagrit, Mosul and Mar Mattay, the successive residences of the "maphrians"[53]. The lists of "maphrians" that were preserved in these libraries contained at least, one

49 See e.g., JE 322-323 (244-245) and 324 (248, read *Athanasium* instead of *Anastasium*). In Hage's extremely rich 'Anhang' one finds a complete (?) list of bishops of Edessa who sat between 600 and 800, cf. Hage (1966) 98-99. Bishop Daniel is also attested to in ms. *Br. Libr. Add.* 12,181, cf. Wright, catal. Brit. Museum 564, in 668/9 A.D.

50 See R. Abramowski (1940) 16, 27-28.

51 In one case, Michael is right over against the *Vita* of Jacob of Edessa (see below, § 5.1.2.); another time he has drawn a wrong conclusion from a letter by Severus bar Mašqā (see below, § 5.7.).

52 Barhebraeus, *Chron. syr.* 2 (2).

53 The "maphrians" resided in Tagrit till 1089 A.D., then in Mosul, and from 1155 A.D. in Mar Mattay, see e.g. Kawerau (1955) 21.

may presume, the names of these prelates in a chronological order, and some indications about the dates of their ordination and death or the length of their pontificate. It seems reasonable, then, to assume that on these points the data in BH II can be trusted. The following, especially § 5.5.2. and § 5.6., will prove this surmise to be correct.

5.0. Now that we have seen something of the problems (§ 3.) and the means at our disposal (§ 4.), we can try to look for solutions. It seems best to work first in a retrograde way and to begin with Jacob of Edessa.

5.1.1. In the case of Jacob we have to do with two chronological problems: the year in which he was ordained bishop and the date of his death. An excellent discussion of the biographical data is to be found in Tisserant (1947)[54].

An anonymous *Vita*, preserved in MS IV 445ª-446ª - II 471-472, supplies us with a rather detailed account of Jacob's life. The *Vita* does not speak of Jacob's birth date. It does not mention either the names of his parents nor his baptismal name. We will see that it dates Jacob's death incorrectly. Clearly the *Vita* was not written by one of Jacob's pupils. It must be dated some generations later. Vööbus did not think much of its historical value[55], but for Tisserant (1947) it was an important and reliable document. We will have to discuss it in some detail.

According to the *Vita*, Jacob was ordained bishop of Edessa by patriarch Athanasius. At that moment, the author writes, he had already lived for some time in Edessa. Jacob remained in office for four years only, for he came into conflict with part of his clergy, whom he reproached with a too lax understanding of their duties. Because he did not receive sufficient support from the side of the patriarch, he placed his see at the disposal of Athanasius' successor, Julianus and withdrew to the monastery of Qayšum. In his place a kind old man, Ḥabib, was consecrated bishop[56]. At the request of the monks of Eusebona, Jacob moved over to that monastery, where he remained for eleven years. As a consequence of a new conflict, he parted again and took residence in Tellʿadda. There he stayed for nine years, working on his revision of the Peshitta. When the old Ḥabib died, the citizens of Edessa wanted Jacob to be their bishop again. Thus Jacob ascended again the throne of Edessa,

54 The biography of Jacob of Edessa in K.-E. Rignell, *A Letter from Jacob of Edessa to John the Stylite of Litarab Concerning Ecclesiastical Canons* (Lund 1979) 15-21, is dependent on secondary literature and refers, where it does make use of primary sources, to BH instead of MS.

55 Vööbus (1970) 207.

56 For an edifying story relating to Ḥabib see Ps.-D. 16-19 (15-17) (Chabot 1895), 160-163 (Chabot 1933).

but when he returned to Tell'adda, four months later, in order to recover his books, he died there on 5 June 704. So much for the *Vita*.

5.1.2. Let us begin with the year in which Jacob died. The *Vita* cannot be right in stating that Jacob died in June 704. Two manuscripts written only some years after Jacob's death, in 718/9 and 718/20, and containing Jacob's revision of I-II *Samuel* and *I Kings* and of *Daniel* respectively, inform us that Jacob finished the revision of these books in 1016 Sel., i.e. between 1 October 704 and 30 September 705. The former adds that he was working then in Tell'adda[57]. Jacob cannot have died, therefore, in June 704[58].

There is no reason either to trust the statement in the *Chronicle* of Pseudo-Dionysius, according to which Jacob died in 709/10[59]. The chronology of this work is notoriously unreliable[60]. In this case the author makes things even worse than usual by having Jacob succeeded in 709/10 by Ḥabib. In reality Jacob was succeeded after his death by his disciple Constantine[61]. The cause of the dating error in Pseudo-Dionysius is rather obvious, as Baumstark and Tisserant pointed out[62]. After the *Chronicle* of Jacob had been prolonged till 709/10, it was a plausible inference that Jacob himself had lived up to that year[63].

There is still a third tradition. According to MS IV 448ª (II 476), Jacob died 5 June 708[64]. This statement is made in the succinct style that is characteristic of borrowings from Jacob's *Chronicle*. Presumably, therefore, this testimony directly originates from a contemporary, one of Jacob's own pupils[65]. The statement is confirmed, moreover, by two independent witnesses, Elias of Nisibis, and the *Chronicon ad annum 819*[66]. It is repeated by the latter's descendent, the *Chronicon ad annum 846*[67], and by Barhebraeus in BH I 293 (294). Its accuracy can hardly be doubted.

57 Mss *London Br. Libr. Add.* 14,429, cf. catal. Wright 37-39, and *Paris. syr.* 27, cf. catal. Zotenberg 11-12.
58 Elsewhere Michael states that Jacob died in 708, see below in this section. Michael does not discuss the contradiction. See below, § 5.1.3.
59 Ps.-D. 12 (11) (Chabot 1895), 155-6 (Chabot 1933).
60 See Chabot (1895) xxxiii and the lists on pp. xxxvi and xxxviii, and Witakowski (1987) 28, 171-172.
61 *Pace* Chabot (1895) 11 n. 5 and Vööbus (1970) 212 n. 74, see MS IV 450ª (II 480) and IV 769 (III 494). Constantine was in function in 726, whereas Ps.-Dionysius holds that Ḥabib was bishop from 710 till 728/9, cf. Hage (1966) 98-9 with nn. 70 and 72.
62 Baumstark (1922) 249 n. 1, Tisserant (1947) 288.
63 See above, § 4.2.1. with n. 41.
64 Cf. also MS IV 450 - II 480 and IV 450 *ad finem* (II 483).
65 See above, § 4.2.1. One may presume that Jacob's continuator noted changes on the throne of Edessa, as Jacob did himself (see above, n. 49), especially in the case of the see being occupied by his own master.
66 Elias I 158 (76 Chabot, 98 Delaporte), *Chron. ad ann. 819* 14 (10).
67 *Chron. ad ann. 846* 233 (176; Brook's supplements prove to have been correct). This *Chronicon* does not mention the year 707/8, but places Jacob's death between the events related to the years 706/7 and 708/9.

5.1.3. Let us return now to the *Vita*. It held, incorrectly, as we have seen just now, that Jacob died in June 704. This error, together with the omissions mentioned above[68], might lead one to the conclusion that the *Vita* cannot be relied on. This inference would be wrong, however. The testimony of the *Vita* proves to be in complete harmony with the information we can gather from other sources, if only one takes into account that Jacob died in June 708. Five arguments can be adduced for this thesis.

First, according to the *Vita*, Jacob was working on his revision of the Peshitta during a nine years' sojourn in Tellʿadda and left this monastery only four months before his death. This means that, if Jacob died on 5 June 708, he must have lived in Tellʿadda from 699 till about 5 February 708. This conclusion is in agreement with the fact that he was working on *Samuel*, *Kings* and *Daniel* in Tellʿadda in 704/5, as two nearly contemporaneous manuscripts have taught us[69].

Second, going backwards we read in the *Vita* that, prior to his stay in Tellʿadda, Jacob had lived for eleven years in Eusebona and for an unspecified time (which I take to have lasted some weeks or months) in Qaysum. His conflict with patriarch Julianus and retirement as bishop of Edessa must be placed, then, in about 688, which is in accordance with the datum that Julianus was consecrated patriarch in November 687[70].

Third, the first time Jacob was bishop of Edessa, he held the post for four years. His ordination, then, took place in about 684. This conclusion is in harmony with two notes, presumably originating, as we have seen, from Jacob himself, according to which he was not yet bishop when he copied the two letters that led to the Synod of Rešʿayna (683/4)[71]. It is also in agreement with a note that is written in the original hand in the margin of the words *l-Yaʿqob ʾepisqopā d-ʾUrhāy* in ms. *Par. syr.* 62, fol. 273r (ixth cent., Letter of Jacob of Edessa on canonical questions): *d-hānā da-šnat ṣṣḥ d-Yawnāyē*. The most natural interpretation of these words is, of course, that Jacob wrote this letter (and was bishop, therefore) in 686/7[72].

Fourth, a small detail, according to one of the notes after letter 3, Jacob was already resident in Edessa when he copied these letters[73]. The same information is provided by the *Vita*, which says that, when Jacob was consecrated bishop of Edessa, he had already lived there for some time.

Fifth, the *Vita* says that Jacob was consecrated bishop by patriarch

68 See above, § 5.1.1.
69 See above, § 5.1.2.
70 See above, § 2.3. and below, § 5.2.
71 See above, § 4.1.1.
72 See Renaudot (1847) II 380 and Lamy (1859) 214; cf. Vööbus (1970) 208.
73 See above, § 4.1.1.

Athanasius, which is in agreement with the fact that Athanasius was elected patriarch at the Synod of Rešʿayna, and was in function, thus, in 684[74].

The above confrontation of data provided by the *Vita* and those originating from other sources proves that wherever the *Vita* can be controlled it is in accordance with external evidence, except for the fact that it dates Jacob's death four years too early, in June 704. That date is at variance with information we gathered from other sources[75]. It is also incompatible with controllable data furnished by the *Vita* itself. It would imply that the conflict with patriarch Julianus, which broke out, according to the *Vita*, some twenty years before Jacob's death, had to be placed in about 684, and his consecration by patriarch Athanasius, four years earlier, in about 680. Both dates are impossible[76]. Everything fits, however, if the chronological data we find in the *Vita* are tied in with 5 June 708, the date at which Jacob really died. It is clear, therefore, that the *Vita* provides a reliable and coherent picture of the main events in Jacob's life. The biographical details it contains are completely in accordance with the other evidence which we have at our disposal. We have only to correct the date it gives for Jacob's death. The date 704 in the *Vita* may be due to a scribal error of a copyist, of Michael, or of the author himself[77]. We will offer another suggestion below[78].

5.1.4. The date at which Jacob was ordained bishop of Edessa[79] needs to be discussed more in detail. The material assembled in § 5.1.3. taught us that Jacob received the consecration in 683/4 from the hands of patriarch Athanasius, who was elected in that year by the Synod of Rešʿayna.

Baumstark registered two contra-indications[80]. The first of these is the information provided by a liturgical manuscript (now lost), which, according to Assemani, had been consulted by Antonius Marsilius Columna. This manuscript had Jacob ordained in 641 and his friend George of the Arabs in 647[81]. Since the latter was ordained in fact, according to Baumstark, in 686[82], Baumstark concluded that the manuscript had Jacob be ordained

74 See below, § 5.4.

75 See above, § 5.1.2.

76 See above, § 2.3., and below, § 5.2. and 5.4.2.

77 The whole tradition of Michael's *Chronicle* depends on a single Syriac manuscript, according to Chabot in the Introduction to MS, I xxxviii-li. The Arab translation also reads 704, cf. Chabot in MS II 472 n. 9.
Baumstark (1922) 249 n. 1 too hastily blames a copyist: Barhebraeus could find the correct dating elsewhere in MS, see above, § 5.1.2.

78 See below, § 5.5.2.

79 In reality the man we are used to calling Jacob of Edessa was given the name of Jacob only when he was ordained bishop. We do not know his baptismal name.

80 Baumstark (1922) 248 n. 3.

81 *BO* I 469.

82 In reality, George was consecrated bishop in 687 (see above, § 2.2. and below, § 5.3.), but the difference is unimportant for the reasoning in our main text.

bishop six years earlier, i.e. in 680. Here Baumstark applies a reasoning that is incorrect. We simply to not know whether the year 647 of the manuscript is equivalent with the year 686 of the Christian era. In the same way one could contend that the year 641 in the manuscript corresponds to, say, 584 A.D. and that George was, therefore, consecrated in 690, according to the codex. Moreover, there is no era known to us in which the year 647 corresponds to 686 (or 687[83]) A.D., as Baumstark himself admits. If Assemani's communication is correct, we can only conclude that, according to this manuscript, six years passed between both ordinations. The dates given prove that the author did not have a clear view of viith-century chronology.

Baumstark's statement that, according to Pseudo-Dionysius, Jacob was consecrated bishop in 676/7 is not correct either. We have not to do with a communication by Pseudo-Dionysius, who is himself a far from trustworthy witness[84], but with a note that is introduced by an unexperienced hand in the margin of the manuscript[85]. Such a notice carries little weight, especially if it is contradicted by witnesses as reliable as ours have proved to be.

5.1.5. It will be clear that we do not share the views of Vööbus (1970) and (1977)[86]. The scepticism he displays proves to be unfounded. One point remains to be discussed. It relates to Jacob's last days. According to Vööbus, Barhebraeus holds, in contravention of what is said by other sources, that Jacob's second term of office also ended in a conflict. Moreover, Vööbus feels, Michael is causing confusion by stating that Jacob was succeeded, after his death, by Ḥabib[87]. In reality, Barhebraeus does not speak, either in the passage Vööbus refers to or elsewhere, about a conflict during Jacob's second time of office, and where Michael speaks of Jacob's successor he calls him Constantine[88]. Even in these cases there is no ground for Vööbus' scepticism.

5.1.6. We may conclude, with Tisserant (1947), that Jacob died on 5 June 708 and that he was consecrated bishop by patriarch Athanasius of Balad in 683/4, after the Synod of Rešʿayna. We will see below that the latter

83 Cf. above, n. 82.

84 See above, § 5.1.2 with nn. 60 and 61.

85 Ps.-D. 9 (9) (Chabot 1895), 153 (Chabot 1933). Chabot prints the note at the year 664/5, in both editions. According to Assemani *BO* I 425-6, Baumstark (1922) 248 n. 3 and Tisserant (1947), it belongs to the year 676/7. Chabot (1933) 153 n. 2 refers to a quite different Jacob. Assemani *BO* I 426 sub XXIV erroneously reports that, according to (Pseudo-)Dionysius, Jacob was ordained in 650/1. It was one of Jacob's predecessors, Cyriacus, who was consecrated in that year, according to Pseudo-Dionysius. Assemani's statement is at variance with the manuscript evidence, as reported by Chabot in both his editions and Assemani's own saying in *BO* I 425 sub XXIII.

86 See above, § 3.4. and 5.1.1.

87 Vööbus (1970) 211-212 and (1977). He refers to BH I 293 (294) and MS IV 446ᵃ (II 472), resp.

88 It is Pseudo-Dionysius who states that Jacob was succeeded, after his death, by Ḥabib, see above, § 5.1.2.

conclusion is supported from quite different angles[89]. It will even prove possible to date the ceremony rather exactly[90].

5.2. Patriarch Julianus Romāyā died in the same year as Jacob of Edessa, in 707/8. The coincidence is noted by the *Chronicum ad annum 819*, Elias of Nisibis, Michael and Barhebraeus[91]. The date itself is uncontested. Even Pseudo-Dionysius mentions his death under the lemma 1019 Sel.[92]. According to Elias, Julianus died in 89 Hegira[93], that is to say, between 1 December 707 and 20 November 708. If we combine the Moslem and Seleucid data, we find that Julianus died between 1 December 707 and 30 September 708.

We have already collected some testimonies according to which Julianus ascended the throne of Antioch in November 687[94]. The same year is mentioned by the *Chronica ad annum 819* and *ad annum 846*[95]. This dating is confirmed by the *Vita* of Jacob of Edessa, which holds that four years after Jacob's consecration as bishop (683/4), i.e. in 687/8, he came into conflict with patriarch Julianus[96]. Over against these witnesses, there is no reason to pay attention to Pseudo-Dionysius, who places Julianus' consecration only in 703/4[97].

5.3. In November 687, in the same year and the same month in which Julianus was ordained patriarch of Antioche, the old Sergius Zkunāyā[98] consecrated George bishop of the Arabs, executing in this way the last will of Julianus' predecessor, Athanasius of Balad[99]. The event is placed in the same year by the *Chronica ad annum 819* and *ad annum 846*[100]. A liturgical manuscript, now lost, dated George's consecration in 647, according to

89 See below, § 5.4.1. and 5.5.1.

90 See below, § 5.6.4.

91 *Chron. ad ann. 819* 14 (10), Elias I 158 (76 Brooks, 98 Delaporte), MS IV 448ᵃ (II 476), BH I 295 (296).

92 Ps.-D. 11 (11) (Chabot 1895), 155 (Chabot 1933).

93 See above, n. 91.

94 See above, § 2.3.

95 *Chron. ad ann. 819* 13 (8), *Chron. ad ann. 846* 232 (175).

96 MS 445ᵃ-446ᵃ (II 471-2), BH I 289 (290). See above, § 5.1.

97 Ps.-D. 11 (10) (Chabot 1895), 155 (Chabot 1933). See also below, § 5.3. and 5.4.

98 Sergius Zkunāya was one of the chief opponents of patriarch Severus bar Mašqā, cf. MS IV 436ᵃ-438ᵃ (II 456-458), and for that reason became one of the *bêtes noires* of Dionysius of Tellmahre, cf. MS IV 516ᵇ (III 64-5) and *Chron. ad ann. 1234* II 264 (198). It is remarkable, however, that he was held in high esteem by Severus' successor Athanasius of Balad, who appointed him *rēšā d-'epis(qopē)* (MS IV 447ᵃ - II 474), and by George of the Arabs, cf. Ryssel (1891) 109. Sergius was never "maphrian" nor bishop of Antioch, of course, *pace* Ryssel (1891) XV.

99 For the testimonies see above, § 2.2. See also below, § 5.4.3.

100 *Chron. ad ann. 819* 13 (8-9), *Chron. ad ann. 846* 232 (175).

Assemani. We have seen that this testimony has no value[101]. The date itself is impossible, since George was still active in the years 713/4-717/8[102] and died in February 724[103].

5.4.1. Two months before the consecration of George and of Julianus, on 11 September 687 A.D., the latter's predecessor, patriarch Athanasius of Balad, expired[104]. His pontificate had lasted only three years, Michael informs us, both in his main text and in his Appendix III. Michael's statement is repeated by Barhebraeus[105]. His consecration must have taken place, then, in 683/4 A.D. This is, in fact, exactly the year in which he was elected patriarch by the Synod of Reš'ayna, according to the *Chronicon ad annum 846*, Michael[106] and Barhebraeus in BH I 289 (290). Independent information confirms this dating. We have already learned from the *Vita* of Jacob of Edessa that Jacob was ordained bishop by patriarch Athanasius. The ceremony took place in 683/4[107]. Secondly, a marginal note in many manuscripts that contain canonical decisions of a patriarch Athanasius says *d-hānā d-ba-šnat tša'm'ā wa-teš'in w-ḥammeš d-Yawnāyē*. The oldest of these codices dates from the viiith century. The only patriarch Athanasius the author of this note can have had in mind is Athanasius of Balad[108]. At the end, therefore, of 995 Sel., that is to say, before 1 October 684 A.D., Athanasius was sitting on the throne of Antioch.

These date enable us to refute two divergent statements. Pseudo-Dionysius makes Athanasius patriarch from 687/8 till 703/4[109]. A Nestorian source, the *Liber turris*, written in Arabic by Mārī ibn Sulaymān, declares that Athanasius succeeded Severus bar Mašqā during the pontificate of Ḥnānišo'[110], whose accession it places, correctly, in the year 67 H. (July 686 - July 687)[111].

101 See above, § 5.1.4.
102 See Wright, catal. Brit. Museum 986-8, Ryssel (1891) XV.
103 MS IV 457a (II 491), BH I 303 (304).
104 For references see above, § 2.1.
105 See MS IV 447ª (II 474), IV 752 (III 449), BH I 293 (294).
106 *Chron. ad ann. 846* 231 (175), MS IV 444ª (II 470-1) and IV 446ª-447ª (II 474).
107 See above, § 5.1.
108 See Vööbus (1970) 200-1 and Zotenberg, catal. Bibl. Nat. 28.
109 Ps.-D. 10 and 11 resp. (10) (Chabot 1895), 154 and 155 resp. (Chabot 1933).
110 Mari fol. 180ʳ (56-7).
111 Ḥnānišo' ascended the throne of Seleucia/Ctesiphon in 67 H. (28 July 686 - 17 July 687), according to Mari fol. 178ᵛ (55), Elias I 149 (72 Brooks, 93 Delaporte) and BH II 135 (136). 'Amr and Ṣalība place his accession in 997 Sel. (= 685/6, see Amr-Sliba 59* [34]; not in 995 Sel., as Gismondi translates; see also the text published by Ebied-Young (1974) 98). These data imply that Ḥnānišo' was consecrated catholicus between 28 July and 30 September 686. He died after a pontificate of fourteen years (BH II 139 [140]) and nine months (Mari fol. 180ʳ [57] and Amr-Sliba 60* [35]; not *cum mensibus septem* or *decem*, as Gismondi writes), in May or June 701, therefore. This date is in accordance with Elias I 55 (31 Brooks, 44 Delaporte) and 155 (74 Brooks, 96 Delaporte), according to whom Ḥnānišo' died in the

Both dates are impossible. Athanasius was already patriarch at the end of the year 683/4. Mārī's error is already corrected by Ṣalība[112].

5.4.2. In one tradition Athanasius' accession is placed earlier than 683/4. This tradition is to be found in Barhebraeus. We have seen that in BH I 289 (290) Barhebraeus holds, in accordance with Michael, that Athanasius was elected patriarch in 683/4 by the Synod of Rešʿayna[113]. Some lines earlier, however, in BH I 287 (288), Barhebraeus writes that the Synod of Rešʿayna chose Athanasius in 679/80. To understand Barhebraeus' rather puzzling behaviour in this matter, we have to turn to his source, Michael's *Chronicle*. Michael starts his short biography of Athanasius by saying that *bāh* (sc. *ša(n)tā*) *ʾetkannšat sunodos ... da-hwāt b-Rešʿaynā* (MS IV 444ª - II 470). In this text the word *bāh* (*ša(n)tā*) refers to the year in which, according to Michael, Athanasius' predecessor Severus bar Mašqā died, 995 Sel. = 683/4 A.D. It was in the Synod of Rešʿayna that Athanasius was elccted patriarch, Michael continues[114]. He then gives a short survey of Athanasius' life before his election, after which he repeats that Athanasius was called to the primacy in 683/4. Barhebraeus copied Michael's note almost exactly, BH I 287-289 (288-290). With him, however, the word *bāh* (*ša(n)tā*) refers to another year, namely 991 Sel. = 679/80 A.D., for in the foregoing sentence he had stated that Athanasius' predecessor died in that year. But at the end of his note Barhebraeus repeats Michael's saying that Athanasius was ordained in 995 Sel. = 683/4 A.D. at the Synod of Rešʿayna[115]. In this way the resulting text states within a few lines that Athanasius was consecrated patriarch at the Synod of Rešʿayna in 679/80 and in 683/4. Barhebraeus leaves the inconsistency undiscussed. It is not difficult to see that it from an attempt to combine Michael's data with the view that Athanasius' predecessor Severus bar Mašqā died in 679/80. We will discuss the latter tradition below, in § 5.5.2. It will prove to be wrong. Both the death of Severus and the ordination of Athanasius at the Synod of Rešʿayna took place in the year 683/4. In § 5.6. we will see that it is possible to establish a more detailed chronology of that turbulent year.

year 82 H. (Febr. 701 - Febr. 702). Tisserant (1931) 262 (= Hage [1966] 94) and Spuler (1964) 209, who rely too much on the result of a calculation error of Ṣalība (see Amr-Sliba 60* [35]), should be corrected. The excellent biography in Sachau (1908) VI-XVII could have been a trifle more exact in chronological matters.

112 Ṣalība does not speak of Athanasius, but has Severus die in 995 Sel. (= 683/4). See below, § 5.5.1.

113 See above, § 5.4.1.

114 This is confirmed by the superscription of letter 6 in MS IV 441ᵇ (II 464). The letter itself does not speak of Athanasius' election, see above, n. 30.

115 Barhebraeus adds some details (the monastery in which the ceremony took place, the bishop who laid hands on the new patriarch), which he borrowed from Michael's Appendix III (MS IV 752 - III 449), see also below, n. 130.

5.4.3. Barhebraeus ends his survey of Athanasius' pontificate by reporting that he died after a reign of three years. In the text as it is edited by Abbeloos-Lamy, he continues by reporting that in November, two months after the death of Athanasius, George of the Arabs was consecrated bishop and that Athanasius' successor was ordained in 687/8 (BH I 293-296). If this is the correct reading, it is clear that Barhebraeus dated the death of Athanasius, correctly, in 686/7. The oldest manuscript of Barhebraeus' *Chronicon ecclesiasticum*, however, ms. *Vaticanus syr.* 166[116], has a different text. After the words *w-'asraḥu(h)y* (sc. George) *b-tešrin (')ḥrāy bātar trēn yarḥin d-'undāneh d-paṭriyar̄* (= Athanasius), it adds *ba-šnat tša' mā' w-teš'in wa-tmānē*. It seems reasonable to suppose that this is what Barhebraeus really wrote. The text is somewhat ambiguous. It is unclear whether the dating relates to the death of Athanasius or to the consecration of George. There can be no doubt, however, that Barhebraeus is wholly dependent here on Michael's *Chronicle*, esp. MS IV 447 (II 474). If the year refers to the death of Athanasius, Barhebraeus is in line with Michael (Athanasius died in September 687). If it relates to the ordination of George, we have to do with a simple error of Barhebraeus, who did not realize, then, that between the death of Athanasius (dated by Michael reports), a new Seleucid year had started. Even in the latter interpretation, this text cannot be adduced to support the view of those scholars who placed Athanasius' death and the consecration of George in 686 (see above, § 2.1 and § 2.2.). Since the publication of Michael's *Chronicle*, it is clear that Barhebraeus merely repeats what he read (or thought he read) in Michael.

5.5.1. Athanasius' predecessor on the throne of Antioch was Severus bar Mašqā. According to Michael, Severus died in 683/4 (MS IV 444ª - II 470). This statement is supported, as we have seen, by a remark of, presumably, Jacob of Edessa, who was contemporaneous with the event[117]. Ṣalība, too, places Severus' death in 683/4, during the pontificate of catholicus Yoḥannān bar Martā[118].

116 Comp. Abbeloos-Lamy *ad* BH I 294. They refer to *BO* II 335. It was ms. *Vat. syr.* 166 (written before 1356/7) that was epitomized by Assemani, cf. Assemanus-Assemanus, catal. Bibl. Vat. III 340, 341. Unfortunately, Abbeloos-Lamy left the manuscript out of consideration.

117 See above, § 4.1.1. and 5.1.3.

118 Amr-Sliba 58* (34; for "Sajuri" read "Sīwirā" [Arabic *Sywry*] or, in Latin, "Severus"). Yoḥannān was catholicus from 681/2 till 683/4, *pace* Tisserant (1931) 262 (= Hage [1966] 94) and Spuler (1964) 209, cf. BH II 133 (134), Amr-Sliba 58* (34) and the text edited by Ebied-Young (1974) 98 (Elias I 54 [31 Brooks, 43 Delaporte] is obviously an error). His predecessor Georgius still wrote a letter in the year 60 H. (October 679 - September 680), cf. Chabot (1902) 237 (490), and died in 680/1, cf. Ṣalība in Amr-Sliba 57* (33). Modern scholars agree. See below, § 5.5.3.

Documentary evidence even allows us to be a little more exact. It is to be found in a letter that has been preserved by Michael in the collection we have discussed already[119]. In the first letter, written by Severus shortly before his death, the patriarch addresses Yoḥannān Sābā as *mēṭrō d-purnāsā madnḥāyā d-Bēt Parsāyē*[120]. Head of the Eastern diocese was, of course, the "maphrian"[121]. Severus cannot have written this letter, therefore, before the death of Bar 'Išoʿ, who was "maphrian" from 668/9 till his death on 17 December 683[122]. We will return to this letter below[123], but we can conclude already now that Severus cannot have died before 17 December 683. We know, on the other hand, that Severus' successor was in office on 30 September 684[124]. These facts enable us to conclude that Severus died between 17 December 683 and 30 September 684, that is to say in the year 683/4, just as Michael said. A more exact dating will be given below[125].

5.5.2. In our texts we can find several divergent opinions. The most prominent of these is the one we have already met above[126]. According to Barhebraeus, Severus died in 679/80, after a pontificate of 12 years (BH I 287-288)[127]. Severus' accession is dated by Barhebraeus in 667/8, the year following that in which his predecessor Theodorus died (BH I 281-284). Presumably that is correct. Michael and the *Chronicon ad annum 1234* report that Theodorus died in 666/7, after which Michael continues by saying *w-'ettasraḥ Sēwērā d-men dayrā d-Pāgimtā d-metkannē bar Mašqā*. Nearly the same text is to be found in the *Chronicon* mentioned[128]. It is most probably here that both Michael and the *Chronicon ad annum 1234* omit a small detail that Barhebraeus chose to transmit, viz. that between the death of Theodorus and the consecration of his successor a new Seleucid year had begun. There is no reason to doubt, therefore, that, according to both Michael and Barhebraeus, Severus was ordained patriarch in 667/8. The difference between both authors consists in that Barhebraeus has Severus reign 12 years and die in 679/80,

119 See above, §4.1.1.
120 See MS IV 438ᵃ (II 458).
121 See e.g. Kawerau (1955) 21 and Hage (1966) 25.
122 See BH II 131-134.
123 See §5.7.
124 See above, §5.4.
125 See §5.6.
126 See §5.4.2.
127 Barhebraeus' remark led to uncertainty with Spuler (1964) 213. It is the only deviant opinion mentioned by Hage (1966) 141 n. 27.
128 MS IV 435ᵃ (II 453), *Chron. ad ann. 1234* II 262 (197; unfortunately, the folio is missing in which the death of Severus is mentioned). According to the *Chron. ad ann. 819* 12 (8) and Ps.-D. 9 (9) (Chabot 1895), 153 (Chabot 1933), Theodorus died in 664/5. It is improbable that these *Chronica* are right over against the testimony of Michael and Barhebraeus. Pseudo-Dionysius, in any case, is wrong in his dating of Theodorus' accession, cf. Hage (1966) 140 n. 16 and 142 n. 113. (the *Chron. ad ann. 819* is silent on the latter issue).

creating in this way, as we have seen, a hopeless muddle as to the dating of the Synod of Reš'ayna and the accession of Severus' successor Athanasius[129], whereas Michael holds that Severus died in 683/4, i.e. after a pontificate of 16 (or 17) years. Barhebraeus' testimony proved to be untrue, but his opinion was not unfounded. Michael himself says, not in his main text, but in his Appendix III, that Severus' pontificate lasted 12 years (MS IV 752 - III 449). Barhebraeus knew and used Michael's Appendix, as Chabot has already noted[130]. It appears by now that the inconsistency we found in Barhebraeus goes back to a discrepancy between Michael's main text and his Appendix III. Michael does not discuss the difference between his two statements. The discrepancy can be explained, however, if we are right in assuming, with Barhebraeus, that Severus ascended the patriarchal throne in 667/8[131]. In that case the difference between the two traditions amounts to four years. Perhaps there is a relationship between these four years and the fact that, during the last four years of his life, i.e., from 679/80 till 683/4, Severus was embroiled in a serious conflict with an important part of his Church, both in the East and in the West. During those years Severus' opponents did not acknowledge him as patriarch of Antioch and even went as far as to anathematize him[132]. In my view it is not a wild guess to suppose that the source of Michael's Appendix III, taking Severus' deposition seriously, did not consider him patriarch during the last four years of his life, thus reducing the length of his pontificate to twelve years[133]. Barhebraeus, then, interpreted this note incorrectly and assumed that Severus died after a pontificate of twelve years, i.e. in 679/80, and was succeeded in the same year by Athanasius. The same error may have been made by the author of the *Vita* of Jacob of Edessa. Placing Athanasius' accession in 679/80, he had to have Jacob die twenty-four years later, in 704 in stead of in 708[134].

5.5.3. There exist two other traditions about the year of Severus' death.

According to the *Chronica ad annum 819* and *annum 846*, Severus died in 682/3. The same statement occurs in Pseudo-Dionysius[135]. The mistake

129 See above, § 5.4.2.

130 Chabot in MS III 450 n. 13. In his Appendix Michael gives details which he omits in his main text, but which recur in Barhebraeus' text, comp., e.g., MS 752 (III 449) with BH I 279-282 (Theodorus), 281-284 (Severus), 289-290 (Athanasius), 295-296 (Julianus) and above, n. 115.

131 See earlier in this section.

132 See MS IV 437ª (II 457) and cf. BH I 285 (286) (read with C *s'aw w-'aḥrmu(h)y, (eum) anathematizare ausi sunt*, cf. *Lectiones variae* in BH II 879 and MS IV 437ª. See above, § 4.1.1.

133 Possibly the source of the remark in Michael's Appendix III reflects the views of the monastery of Mar Gabriel in Qartamin. One of Severus' chief opponents, Ḥnānyā was bishop of Qartamin, cf. MS IV 436ª (II 456) and BH I 283 (284).

134 See above, § 5.1.3., and below, § 5.6.3.

135 *Chron. ad ann. 819* 12 (8), *Chron. ad ann. 846* 231 (175), Ps.-D. 10 (10) (Chabot 1895), 154 (Chabot 1933). The *Chronicon ad annum 819* and Pseudo-Dionysius also agree in dating the

may be due to a calculation error. The *Chronicon ad annum 819* and its descendent, the *Chronicon ad annum 846*[136], have Severus die in the same year (994 Sel.) as caliph Yazid b. Muʿāwiya. We know for sure that Yazīd died on 11 November 683[137], in the year 995 Sel. therefore. The chroniclers noted that he had reigned three years and five (or six) months after the death of his father[138], which they correctly placed in 991 Sel.[139], for Muʿāwiya died in April/May 680[140]. Adding three years and five (or six) months to the year 991, the authors of the *Chronica* assumed that Yazīd still died in 994, without realizing that when Yazīd died a new Seleucid year had started. The misdating of the death of Yazīd will have brought about the misdating of Severus' death.

The other divergent tradition is to be found in the *Liber turris*. It states that Severus died during the pontificate of the catholicus Ḥnānišoʿ. We have discussed this view above[141]. Mārī has been corrected already by Ṣalība[142].

5.5.4. We have stated our provisional conclusions in § 5.5.1.

5.6.0.. Thus far we have mainly occupied ourselves with the lives of men who lived in the western provinces of the Syrian Monophysite Church. It now seems opportune to discuss the problems that relate to the chronology of those who were entrusted with the administration of the eastern provinces, the so-called "maphrians". We will see that our discussions will enable us to be somewhat more detailed about events that occurred in the West in the year 683/4. Our sole source in this respect is the second part of Barhebraeus' *Chronicon ecclesiasticum*. In the following we will summarize Barhebraeus' narrative from a chronological point of view. Only here and there will we indicate by the symbol (...) that we are omitting a detail. These remarks will be treated in § 5.6.2.

5.6.1. We will begin with "maphrian" Bar Išoʿ, who was ordained in 668/9 and died on 17 December 683[143]. After him, patriarch (...) ordained Abraham, who lived only a short time (*zabnā zʿorā*) after his election[144]. When Abraham died, and the patriarch, too, the Oriental bishops did not await the

death of patriarch Theodorus in 664/5, see above n. 128. The *Chronicon ad annum 846* is deficient here.

136 See Chabot in the Praefatio of his translation of the *Chronicon ad annum 819*, p. I.

137 See H. Lammens in *EI* IV 1162.

138 Five months: *Chron. ad ann. 819* 12 (8); six: *Chron. ad ann. 846* 231 (175).

139 *Chron. ad ann. 819* 12 (8), *Chron. ad ann. 846* 231 (175).

140 See H. Lammens in *EI* III 618.

141 See § 5.4.1. with n. 110.

142 See above, § 5.5.1. with n. 118.

143 BH II 131-134. There is no reason to doubt Barhebraeus' chronology here, see above, § 4.3. The synchronisms Barhebraeus establishes between the pontificate of Bar Išoʿ and the reigns of caliphs and Nestorian catholici are correct.

144 BH II 133 (134).

election of a new patriarch, but themselves ordained David "maphrian". Six months later the western bishops invited David to take part in the election of a new patriarch: *w-kad 'ezal 'nad tammān*[145]. After his death, the see of Tagrit remained vacant for (...) years. During that time (*hāydēn*) the monks of Mar Mattay urged their metropolitan Yoḥannān Sābā to appoint bishops for the dioceses that had become vacant in the East. Yoḥannān refused to do so, because it had been the privilege of the "maphrian" since 628/9 to ordain bishops in the East. The monks, disappointed, reported to the newly installed patriarch that, in view of his great age, Yoḥannān had retired from his post. They asked for a new metropolitan. The patriarch did not see what the monks were up to and sent a new metropolitan. Outraged, Yoḥannān left Mar Mattay for a monastery near Tagrit. A plague brought the monks to their senses again and drove the new metropolitan from the monastery. Yoḥannān forgave the monks, but refused to return to Mar Mattay. After that (*bātar hālēn*) he was elected "maphrian" by six bishops. Having held his post for one year and a half, Yoḥannān died on 2 January[146], his successor, Denḥā, being ordained in March 688[147].

The chronology of this passage is wholly clear. After the death of Bar Išoʿ (17 December 683), the patriarch consecrated Abraham "maphrian". The patriarch at that time was Severus bar Mašqā. Severus, therefore, was still alive in, say, January 684. After a short time, however, both he and Abraham died, in about February. Thereupon the Oriental bishops ordained David "maphrian", without waiting for the consent of the new patriarch. This made David's consecration, strictly speaking, illegal[148]. Nevertheless, the occidental bishops asked him to be present at the election of Severus' successor. This event took place, as we have seen, in the Synod of Rešʿayna (683/4)[149]. There (*tamman*) he died, however. That is why his name is missing in the documents we have discussed above[150]. Barhebraeus says that he had filled his post for only six months. The Synod of Rešʿayna must have taken place, then, in one of the last months of the year 683/4, in August or September of that year. This conclusion is in accordance with what we would expect. The letters preserved in MS IV 438-444 (II 458-468) make clear that the discussions which ensued from the death of Severus (683/4) and led to the Synod of

145 BH II 141 (142).

146 *b-yom trēn b-kānon 'ḥrāy*, according to ms. *Vat. syr.* 166, cf. Abbeloos-Lamy *ad* BH II 145 and n. 7 above. The later codices add *ȳd* after *trēn*: 'on the second day (of the week), 14 January', which is in itself impossible, since 14 January 688 fell on a Tuesday.

147 BH II 141-146.

148 See Hage (1966) 27-28 and 143 n. 121. Hage is rather laconic about the canonical aspect of the matter.

149 See above, § 5.4.1.

150 See above, § 4.1.1.

Reš'ayna (also 683/4)[151] must have taken some time. David, therefore, died in August or September 684. Since David's successor as metropolitan of Tagrit, Yoḥannān Sābā, died on 2 January 688 after a pontificate of one year and six months, he must have been appointed in June or July 686. The throne of Tagrit was vacant, therefore, from August/September 684 till June/July 686, that is to say for nearly two years. It was during that time that the metropolitan of Mosul/Nineveh, Yoḥannān Sābā, defended the rights of the "maphrian", and, indirectly, those of the patriarch, against the monks of Mar Mattay, his own residence. The patriarch the monks appealed to, and who naively granted their request to send a new metropolitan, was Athanasius (684-687)[152].

5.6.2. We have seen by now that all of the details furnished by Barhebraeus in his narrative easily fit into the chronological scheme we have sketched in § 5.1., 5.4. and 5.5. The two remarks we have passed over in silence thus far, marking them with (...), and which have yielded so many problems to modern scholars[153] can easily be explained now. We have seen that Barhebraeus, misled by a remark in Michael's Appendix III, supposed that patriarch Severus bar Mašqā died in 679/80, and was succeeded in that year by Athanasius (BH I 287-288)[154]. No wonder, then, that he assumed that it was Athanasius who consecrated, after the death of Bar Išo' (December 683), the new "maphrian" Abraham (BH II 133-134). In reality, the ordination of Abraham must have been one of the last deeds of Severus bar Mašqā.

The other place is not difficult either. We have seen, again, that after the death of David the post of metropolitan of Tagrit was not filled for a period of two years, from August/September 684 (beginning of the Synod of Reš'ayna) till June/July 686[155]. According to Barhebraeus, the throne of

151 See above, § 4.1.1.

152 It was not Julianus, as Abbeloos-Lamy *ad* BH II 144 and Hage (1966) on several places, esp. p. 38, assume. When Julian became patriarch (November 687). Yoḥannān was already metropolitan of Tagrit. The fact that the Oriental bishops omitted to ask Julian for his approval of the election of "maphrian" Denḥā II *b-'ellat hāy d-bel'ād šalmuthon šaddar mēṭrō l-'umrā 'al melltā d-dayrāyē ḥaššānē balḥud* (BH II 147-148) does not oblige us to assume that it was Julianus who had sent a metropolitan so rashly. The Tagritans had simply lost their confidence in the patriarchate and feared that the interference of Athanasius with the affairs of Mar Mattay would prove to be the beginning of an attack on the relative independence of the Oriental part of the church. The position of their metropolitan could be forced into line with that of the western bishops, who had had to acknowledge, at the Synod of Reš'ayna, that they were not entitled to ordain bishops (comp. MS IV 436^{a}-437^{a} - II 457 and their submission, later, MS IV 438^{b} - II 458-459). The sources on this conflict are MS IV 448^{a} (II 475-476), IV 469^{a}-470^{a} (II 514), BH I 295 (296) and II 147-150, see also the note of Dionysius of Tellmahre in MS IV 517^{b} (III 65) and *Chron. ad ann. 1234* II 264 (198). For another view see Hage (1966) 30 n. 268 and 38 n. 374.

153 See above, § 3.2. and 3.3.

154 See above, § 5.5.2.

155 See above, § 5.6.1.

Tagrit was vacant for six years (BH II 141-142). That need not amaze us, since we know that Barhebraeus had placed the Synod of Reš'ayna in 679/80 (BH I 287-288). The difference amounts to four years, the same number that separates the real date of the Synod of Reš'ayna from the one adopted by Barhebraeus.

5.6.3. It appears by now that Barhebraeus' decision to opt for the tradition according to which Severus' pontificate lasted 12 years brought him into difficulties at least two times. In BH I 287-290 he was obliged to state within a few lines that the Synod of Reš'ayna took place in 679/80 and in 683/4[156]. Here, in BH II 133-146, he had to squeeze the reigns of Abraham (a short time) and David (six months), an interregnum (six years) and the pontificate of Yoḥannān Sābā (one year and six months) between two fixed points of time, the death of Bar Išo' (December 683) and the enthronement of Denḥā II (March 688), a hopeless enterprise, of course[157]. He could have avoided the error by keeping to the data furnished by MS IV 444ª (II 470), but he had to choose between Michael's main text and his Appendix III, without having an incontrovertible criterion. He chose wrong. The same error seems to have tricked the author of the *Vita* of Jacob of Edessa. It seems that some of the most intriguing problems we have discussed in this paper originate from a single source, a tradition that was hostile to Severus bar Mašqā[158].

5.6.4. Now that we know that the Synod of Reš'ayna was held in August/September 684, we can also be slightly more exact in dating some of Athanasius' decisions. It must have been in the last weeks of 683/4 that he proceeded to ordain for the important see of Edessa a monk who was living there already, who had been tutored in Qennešrin, as he had been himself,

156 See above, § 5.4.2. and 5.5.2.

157 Hage (1966). esp. Table B, tried to make the best of it, but came into conflict with other hard facts, see his n. 144 on p. 143. There can be no doubt as to the dates of Denḥā II. He was consecrated in March 688 (BH II 145-146) and died in October 727, after a pontificate of 40 years (999 Sel. - 1039 Sel.; BH II 149-150). The dates of the "maphrians" in BH II have a solid base, comp. above, § 4.3. In this case, moreover, Barhebraeus is supported by MS IV 462ª (II 503; the scribal error in the Syriac text is rightly corrected by Chabot, see MS II 503 n. 9, as the context and the Arabic translation prove; his suggestion in MS III 450 n. 4 is to be rejected, therefore). In BH I, it is true, Barhebraeus says that Denḥā died in 1051 Sel. (= 739/40), in the same year as patriarch Athanasius III (BH I 303-306; in BH I 306 *septemdecim* is to be corrected in *quindecim*). But here he is following Michael, except for the dating year. Michael held, *l.c.*, that Denḥā and Athanasius both died in 727/8. Michael (or his source) must have made a mistake here, for Athanasius was still in office in 735/6, see *Chron. ad ann. 819* 17 (12), *Chron. ad ann. 846* 235 (178), and is even mentioned in 739/40, see the inscription published by Palmer (1987) 60-61. He certainly died in the latter year, as the consensus between Elias I 168 (80 Brooks, 103 Delaporte) and BH I 303-306 proves. According to Michael's Appendix III, MS IV 752 (III 450), Athanasius died in 1055 Sel. (743/4). In my view we have to do with a scribal error: read *'n'* (= 1051) in stead of *'nh* (1055).

158 See above, § 5.1.3. and 5.5.2.

and who shared his penchant for Greek studies and strict views in canonical matters. He gave him the name of Jacob[159].

In the same period he must have issued his canons, providing the marginal note we quoted is to be interpreted in the same way as the one that accompanies a canonical letter of Jacob of Edessa[160].

5.7. Finally, the riddle of the titles applied to Yoḥannān Sābā in the famous letters of 683/4[161]. In the first letter, written by Severus bar Mašqā shortly before his death, the patriarch addresses Yoḥannān as *mēṭrō d-purnāsā madnḥāyā d-Bēt Parsāyē* (MS IV 438ᵃ - II 458). This title is normally reserved to the "maphrian" and Severus cannot have used it when there was a metropolitan of Tagrit in office[162]. It is improbable that Severus wrote the letter between the death of Bar Išoʿ (December 683) and the consecration of Abraham. The see of Tagrit ranked second only to that of Antioch, and one cannot see why Severus would have applied to the metropolitan of Mar Mattay for help in his struggle against the dangerous rebellion, when he could hope that the post of Tagrit would be filled with a loyal supporter. It is only when his hopes were deceived by the death of Abraham that Severus, feeling that his end was near, asked Yoḥannān to defend the rights of the patriarch when he would no longer be able to do so himself. By giving him the title of *mēṭrō d-purnāsā madnḥāyā* he made clear that he considered him the factual head of the eastern province. Officially, however, Yoḥannān was no more than the metropolitan of Mar Mattay, and thus is he called by the bishops assembled in Rešʿayna in letter four: *mēṭrō d-ʿumrā d-Mār(y) Mattay* (MS IV 438ᵇ - II 458). Moreover, a new "maphriam" had been elected, David. After the death of the latter, however, in Rešʿayna itself[163], Yoḥannān was fully entitled to assume that he was again entrusted with the supervision of the eastern dioceses. That is why he could introduce himself in letter 5 as *meṭrōp̄ d-ʿumrā d-Mār(y) Mattay wa-d-Bēt Parsāyē* (MS IV 439ᵇ - II 460). The eastern bishops may well have been content with the factual situation, for Yoḥannān was a much respected man[164]. That would explain why they did not elect a successor for Tagrit. It would also make clear why the monks of Mar Mattay had some reason to expect that Yoḥannān would use his prerogative more amply by appointing new bishops. It was only after the outbreak of an open conflict between Yoḥannān and the monks of Mar

159 See above, § 5.1. For the views of Athanasius see Vööbus (1970) 200-202, for those of Jacob of Edessa Tisserant (1947).
160 See above, § 5.4.1. and 5.1.3. resp.
161 See above, § 3.2. and, for the letters, § 4.1.1.
162 See above, § 5.5.1.
163 See above, § 5.6.1.
164 See letter 6, in MS IV 443ᵇ-446ᵇ (II 464-468).

Mattay that six bishops decided to clear up the situation and elect Yoḥannān officially "maphrian"[165]. However that may be, the titles Yoḥannān is addressed with in the letters preserved in MS IV 438-444 (II 458-468) need not amaze us, providing we are ready to look at them in their historical context.

We can also understand now why Michael and Barhebraeus assumed that Yoḥannān was already *mēṭrō d-Tagrit* or *mapryānā* in 684 (MS IV 444^{a}-II 468, BH I 285-286). Severus and Yoḥannān had not made it easy for later historians to interpret their letters correctly.

6. The chronological results of our inquiry can be summarized in the following table (Roman figures refer to the months according to the modern calendar; b. = bishop, c. = East-Syrian catholicus, m. = "maphrian", p. = West-Syrian patriarch):

679/80		p. Severus bar Mašqā deposed by prominent bishops (§ 5.5.)
680/1		Death of c. Georgius (n. 118)
681/2		Ordination of c. Yoḥannān bar Martā (n. 118)
683	17 XII	Death of m. Bar Išoʿ (§ 5.6.)
683/4		Death of c. Yoḥannān bar Martā (n. 118)
684	ca. I	Ordination of m. Abraham (§ 5.6.)
	ca. II	Death of m. Abraham (§ 5.6.)
		Letter (1) of p. Severus bar Mašqā to Yoḥannān Sābā (§ 4.1.1., 5.7)
		Death of p. Severus bar Mašqā (§ 5.5.)
	II-III	Uncanonical ordination of m. David (§ 5.6.)
	?	Conciliatory letters (2, 3) of the rebellious bishops (§ 4.1.1.), copied by Jacob of Edessa (§ 5.1.3.)
	VIII-IX	Bishops in Rešʿayna (§ 4.1.1.)
		Death of m. David (§ 5.6.)
		Letter (4) of the Rešʿayna bishops to Yoḥannān Sābā (§ 4.1.1., 5.7.)
		Yoḥannān Sābā in Rešʿayna, Synod (§ 4.1.1.)
		Peace letter (5) by Yoḥannān Sābā (§ 4.1.1., 5.7)
		Ordination of p. Athanasius of Balad (§ 5.4.)
		Letter (6) of Synod of Rešʿayna (§ 4.1.1.)
		Ordination of Jacob as b. of Edessa (§ 5.1., 5.6.4.)
		Issue of canons by p. Athanasius (?) (§ 5.6.4.)
684/6		Conflict Yoḥannān Sābā - Mar Mattay (§ 5.6.)

165 See above, § 5.6.1.

686	VI-VII	Election of m. Yoḥannān Sābā (§ 5.6.)
	28 VII - 30 IX	Ordination of c. Ḥnānišoʿ (n. 111)
686/7		Canonical letter by Jacob of Edessa (§ 5.1.3.)
687	11 IX	Death of p. Athanasius of Balad (§ 5.4.)
	XI	Ordination of George as b. of the Arabs (§ 5.3.)
		Ordination of p. Julianus Romāya (§ 5.2.)
688	2 I	Death of m. Yoḥannān Sābā (§ 5.6.)
	?	Retirement of Jacob as bishop of Edessa; Jacob in Qayšum and in Eusebona (§ 5.1.)
	III	Uncanonical ordination of m. Denḥa II; beginning of conflict p. Julianus - m. Denḥa (nn. 152 and 157)
692		Jacob completes his *Chronicle* (§ 4.2.1.)
699		Jacob moves to Tellʿadda (§ 5.1.)
701	V-VI	Death of c. Ḥnānišoʿ (n. 111)
704/5		Jacob working on *Samuel, Kings* and *Daniel* (§ 5.1.)
707/8	1 XII - 30 IX	Death of p. Julianus Romāyā (§ 5.2.)
708	ca. 5 II	Jacob again bishop of Edessa (§ 5.1.)
	5 VI	Death of b. Jacob of Edessa (§ 5.1.)

ABBREVIATIONS PECULIAR TO THIS PAPER

R. Abramowski (1940) — R. Abramowski, *Dionysius von Tellmahre, jakobitischer Patriarch von 818-845* (Abhandlungen für die Kunde des Morgenlandes XXV 2, Leipzig 1940).

Amr-Sliba — *Maris Amri et Slibae De Patriarchis Nestorianorum commentaria* II 1-2, ed. and tr. H. Gismondi (Romae 1896-1897).

Barhebraeus, *Chron. syr.* — see Bedjan (1890) (text) and Budge (1932) (transl.).

Bedjan (1890) — *Gregorii Barhebraei Chronicon Syriacum*, ed. P. Bedjan (Parisiis 1890).

BH — *Gregorii Barhebraei Chronicon ecclesiasticum*, edd. and trr. J. B. Abbeloos - Th. J. Lamy (Parisiis-Lovanii 1872-1877).

BO — J. S. Assemanus, *Bibliotheca Orientalis Clementino-Vaticana* (Romae 1719-1728).

Brock (1976) — S. P. Brock, "Syriac Sources for Seventh-Century History", in *Byzantine and Modern Greek Studies* 2 (1976) 17-36.

Budge (1932) — E. A. W. Budge, *The Chronography of ... Bar Hebraeus* I (Oxford-London 1932).

Chabot (1895) — *Chronique de Denys de Tell-Mahré*. Quatrième partie, publiée et traduite par J.-B. Chabot (Bibliothèque des Hautes Études. Sciences philosophiques et historiques 112, Paris 1895).

Chabot (1902) — J. B. Chabot, *Synodicon Orientale, ou recueil de synodes nestoriens* (= Notices et extraits des manuscrits de la Bibliothèque Nationale et autres bibliothèques 37, Paris 1902).

Chron. ad ann. 819 — *Chronicon anonymum ad A.D. 819 pertinens*, ed. A. Barsaum in CSCO 81/Syr. 36 (1920), tr. I.-B. Chabot in CSCO 109/Syr. 56 (1937, repr. 1952).

Chron. ad ann. 846 — *Chronicon anonymum ad annum A.D. 846 pertinens*, ed. E.-W. Brooks in CSCO 3/Syr. 3 (1904), tr. I.-B. Chabot in CSCO 4/Syr. 4 (1904).

Chron. ad ann. 1234 — *Anonymi auctoris Chronicon ad annum Christi 1234 pertinens* I, ed. I.-B. Chabot in CSCO 81/Syr. 36 (1920), tr. I.-B. Chabot in CSCO 109/Syr. 56 (1937, repr. 1952); II, ed. I.-B. Chabot in CSCO 82/Syr. 37 (1947), tr. A. Abouna, with an Introduction by J.-M. Fiey, in CSCO 354/Syr. 154 (1974).

Delaporte (1910) — *La Chronographie d'Élie Bar-Šinaya métropolitain de Nisibe*, traduite par L. J. Delaporte (Bibliothèque des Hautes Études 180, Paris 1910).

Ebied-Young (1974) — R. Y. Ebied - M. J. L. Young, "A Treatise in Arabic on the Nestorian Patriarchs", in *Le Muséon* 87 (1974) 87-113.

Elias — *Eliae metropolitae Nisibeni opus chronologicum* I, ed. E. W. Brooks in CSCO 62*/Syr. 21 (1910), tr. E. W. Brooks in CSCO 63*/Syr. 23 (1910); II, ed. I.-B. Chabot in CSCO 62**/ Syr. 22 (1909), tr. I.-B. Chabot in CSCO 63**/Syr. 24 (1910); see also Delaporte (1910).

Fiey (1974) — "Les diocèses du 'maphrianat' syrien 629-1860" I, in *Parole de l'Orient* 5 (1974) 133-164.

Hage (1966) — W. Hage, *Die syrisch-jakobitische Kirche in frühislamischer Zeit nach orientalischen Quellen* (Wiesbaden 1966).

Honigmann (1954) — E. Honigmann, *Le couvent de Barṣaumā et le patriarcat jacobite d'Antioche et de Syrie* (CSCO 146, Subsidia 7, Louvain 1954).

JE — *Chronicon Jacobi Edesseni*, ed. E.-W. Brooks in CSCO 5/Syr. 5 (1905), tr. E.-W. Brooks in CSCO 6/Syr. 6 (1907).

Kawerau (1955) — P. Kawerau, *Die Jakobitische Kirche im Zeitalter der syrischen Renaissance. Idee und Wirklichkeit* (Berliner byzantinische Arbeiten 3, Berlin 1955).

Lamy (1859) — Th. J. Lamy, *Dissertatio de Syrorum fide et disciplina in re eucharistica* (Lovanii 1859).

Mari — *Maris Amri et Slibae De Patriarchis Nestorianorum commentaria* I 1-2, ed. and tr. H. Gismondi (Romae 1899).

MS — *Chronique de Michel le Syrien, patriarche jacobite d'Antioche 1166-1199*, ed. and tr. J.-B. Chabot (Paris 1899-1924).

Ortiz de Urbina (1965) — I. Ortiz de Urbina, *Patrologia Syriaca (Romae 1965²)*.

Palmer (1987) — A. Palmer, "A Corpus of Inscriptions from Ṭūr ʿAbdīn and Environs", in *OrChr* 71 (1987) 53-139.

Ps.-D. — *Incerti auctoris Chronicon Pseudo-Dionysianum vulgo dictum* II, ed. I.-B. Chabot in CSCO 104/Syr. 53 (1933); see also Chabot (1895).

Renaudot (1847) — E. Renaudot, *Liturgiarum orientalium collectio* (Francofurti-Londini 1847²).

Ryssel (1891) — V. Ryssel, *Georgs des Araberbischofs Gedichte und Briefe* (Leipzig 1891).

Sachau (1908) — E. Sachau, *Syrische Rechtsbücher* II (Berlin 1908).

Spuler (1964) — B. Spuler, *Die morgenländischen Kirchen* (augm. repr. of *HO* I 8, 2 [Leiden etc. 1952], Leiden 1964).

Tisserant (1931) — E. Tisserant, "L'église nestorienne", in *Dictionnaire de théologie catholique* XI (Paris 1931) col. 157-238.

Tisserant (1947) — E. Tisserant, "Jacques d'Édesse", in *Dictionnaire de théologie catholique* VIII (Paris 1947) col. 286-291.

Vööbus (1970) — A. Vööbus, *Syrische Kanonessammlungen. Ein Beitrag zur Quellenkunde. I. Westsyrische Originalurkunden.* 1.A. (CSCO 307/Subsidia 35, Louvain 1970).

Vööbus (1977) — A. Vööbus, "Giacomo di Edessa", in *Dizionario degli Istituti di perfezioni* IV (1977) col. 1155-1156.

Witakowski (1987) — W. Witakowski, *The Syriac Chronicle of Pseudo-Dionysius of Tel-Mahrē. A Study in the History of Historiography* (Studia Semitica Upsaliensia 9, Uppsala 1987).

JOSEPH HABBI

Synodalité de l'Église d'Orient de Séleucie-Ctésiphon

On admait bien discuter si l'Église est synodale par sa constitution, ou si c'est l'influence des systèmes politiques qui l'ont accordé cette forme du gouvernement. Facilement admetterait-on cette prérogative à l'Église Orientale, étant l'Occidentale plutôt monarchique.

Le Concile Vatican II a révalué la marque collégiale; la *Lumen Gentium* parle du Collège Apostolique et du Collège Episcopal (LG 22). Le Concile renouvela aussi la doctrine théologique et juridique concernante le Concile Œcuménique (CD 4). Mais tous ceux qui connaissent la genèse des Actes du Concile, savent que pour arriver à ces résultats, surtout de la communion, collégialité et pluralisme, on a dû lutter beaucoup, et que faute d'une Ecclésiologie tardivement élaborée, les Pères du Vatican II hésitaient d'accorder à la collégialité, et donc à la synodalité, le rôle qu'elles devraient avoir, et pour y atténuer la poussée, ils ont trop insisté sur la place du Romain Pontife.

Nous voudrions dans cet essai éclairer la synodalité de l'Église comme caractéristique spécifique et fondamentale, émanante de sa structure constitutive essentielle, grâce aux donnés bibliques et historiques, notamment de l'Église d'Orient Mésopotamien de Séleucie-Ctésiphon.

Le Collège Episcopal dans l'Église du NT

La Constitution Dogmatique sur l'Église du Vatican II dit:

> De même que saint Pierre et les autres apôtres constituent, de par l'institution du Seigneur, un seul collège apostolique, semblablement le Pontife romain, successeur de Pierre et les Évêques successeurs des Apôtres, forment entre eux un tout. Déjà la plus antique discipline en vertu de laquelle les évêques établis dans le monde entier vivaient en communion entre eux et avec l'évêque de Rome par le lien de l'unité, de la charité et de la paix, et de même la réunion de Conciles, où l'on décidait en commun de toutes les questions les plus importantes, par une décision que l'avis de l'ensemble permettait d'équilibrer, tout cela signifiait le caractère et la nature collégiale de l'ordre épiscopal; elle se trouve manifestement confirmée par le fait des Conciles œcuméniques tenus tout le long des siècles (LG 22; cfr aussi CD 4).

Cette collégialité des évêqyues, et leur formation d'un seul collège, qui succède au Collège Apostolique, leur accordent une charge universelle:

Comme membre du collège épiscopal et légitime successeur des Apôtres chacun d'entre eux (chaque évêque) est tenu, à l'égard de l'Église universelle, de par l'institution et le précepte du Christ, à cette sollicitude qui est, pour l'Église universelle, éminement profitable, même si elle ne s'exerce pas par un acte de juridiction (LG 23; cfr AG 38).

Le Concile a évité exprès le terme *corps*, utilisant celui du *collège* pour désigner le regroupement et la communion des évêques, pour une raison claire. Toute l'Église est le Corps du Christ, dont tous les croyants sont membres d'un seul corps (1 Co 12,12), et membres les uns des autres (Rm 12,5). Les principes constitutionnels de cette incorporation est le Baptême et l'Eucharistie (1 Co 12,13; 10,17). Ce Corps a pour tête le Christ lui-même (Col 1,18); le Christ est aussi le sauveur du Corps, qui est l'Église (Ep 5,23-28), et l'unité des membres du Corps est assurée par le Christ (Col 2,19), car nous sommes tous reconciliés par le sang du Christ pour devenir un seule peuple et un seul homme nouveau (Ep 2,14-16)[1].

Théorétiquement, un membre n'agit pas sans le corps; il est mort ou inerte en dehors du corps; agissant seul, le membre exerce son action dans le corps, et son influence s'étend à tous les membres du corps. Il n'y a pas un membre important et un autre inutile, même s'il y a des membres en plus honneur et d'autres de moins (cfr 1 Co 12).

Historiquement, les Apôtres et les premiers Disciples ont senti le besoin d'assumer la charge non seulement d'annoncer la Bonne Nouvelle (Evangelion), mais aussi de servir les frères; le service - la diaconie (*diakonia* en grec, *tešmešta* en langues araméennes) est la mission chrétienne par excellence; du service est né le ministère, *mešaret* en hébreu (Ex 24,13) qui est le prêtre du culte; Mattias a été appelé à remplir le ministère avec les Onze (Ac 1,17.25); la vocation de Paul est aussi un appel au ministère (1 Tm 1,12). Le ministère est ministre de Dieu et du Christ (2 Co 6,3; 11,23), mais aussi de l'Évangile, du Corps du Christ, de l'Église (Col 1,23; Ep 3,7; Col 1,25).

Le ministère dans l'Église naissante a été lié à l'apostolat. Jésus a enseigné à ses Apôtres à regarder leur fonction comme un service de Lui, des autres, de tous (Jn 12,26; Mc 10,42-44; Ac 1,17-25; Rm 1,1). Le ministère est d'une grandeur supérieure à celle de Moïse, parce qu'il est un service de la Nouvelle Alliance, de Dieu, du Christ, de l'Esprit, de l'Évangile, de la justice, de l'amour (2 Co 6,3-4; 5,18; 11,23; Col 1,23-25; Ep 3,7 etc.), qu'il faut remplir dignement (Ac 20,24).

Ce ministère déborde l'exercise de l'apostolat proprement dit, car il s'applique à des services matériels nécessaires à la communauté, comme le service des tables, qui est à l'origine du service, et la collecte pour les pauvres

1 François Amiot, *Corps du Christ*, dans: Vocabulaire de Théologie Biblique (= VTB), Ed. du Cerf, §9, Paris 1971, 215-216.

(Ac 6,1; 11,29; 12,25; Rm 15,31). Mais le ministère est confié à des personnes, qui sont des Apôtres, Disciples et Diacres, ce qu'il montre qu'il y a dans l'Église diversité de ministères (Ep 4,12): apostolat, prophétie, enseignement, évangélisation, charges pastorales.

Tout service est comme un mandat reçu de Dieu (1 P 4,11), à effectuer sous l'impulsion de l'Esprit (1 Co 12,7).

On irait contre l'histoire sainte et ecclésiastique, si on nie le caractère hiérarchique du ministère. Dès le temps des Apôtres on assiste à la naissance d'une hiérarchie du gouvernement qui prolonge leur action[2]. Paul et Barnabé établirent partout, dans les communautés chrétiennes, des Anciens (presbyteroi) (Ac 14,23) pour présider dans les assemblés et exercer leur mission; il y en a plusieurs dans une même église (Ac 20,17); leur agir est collégial, sous la direction des Apôtres (Ac 15,2-6; 16,4; Tt 1,5). Le collège présbyterial est soumis à des règles précises; c'est l'imposition des mains qui établit les presbytres dans leurs fonctions; il s'agit d'un charisme particulier de l'Esprit-Saint (1 Tm 5,17-22).

Les évêques (episkopoi ou surveillants) sont préposés pour veiller sur les communautés-églises, comme pasteurs des troupeaux, à l'image du Christ (1 P 5,2-4; Jn 10). Les Epîtres pastorales montrent qu'il y a dans chaque communauté (diocèse) un seul évêque; il doit être choisi avec soin parmi les presbytres pour gouverner (administrer, servir, présider) les presbytres, diacres, et fidèles, avec autorité, en matière de rites liturgiques, d'enseignement doctrinal et de surveillance (Ac 20,28-29; 1 Tm 2,1-15; 4,13-16; Tt 1,9). On assiste ainsi à une évolution dans l'organisation de l'Église.

Le différend surgi parmi les judéo-chrétiens et les chrétiens convertis du gentilisme, nous éclaire davantage dans cette marque spécifique de la collégialité et de la synodalité; au Synode de Jérusalem, les Apôtres sont un collège; leur action avec les presbytres et la communauté est synodale (Ac 15). Il est vrai qu'on ne peut pas encore bien distinguer les Apôtres des Anciens, dans les Actes de ce Synode, mais le rôle des Apôtres est bien plus spécifique et déterminant que celui de tous les autres. Nous avons évité le mot sacerdoce, car notre recherche est à propos de la manière d'agir des pasteurs-pères-chefs de l'Église.

Le développement du Collège Apostolique dans l'Église

Nous ne pouvons pas aborder ce sujet sans évoquer le problème concentré dans la double conception de l'Église: celle d'une église-communauté-communion, et l'autre d'une église-société-institution. La collégialité et la

2 Pierre Grelot, *Ministère*, dans VTB, 754.

synodalité résultent bien différentes dans l'une ou dans l'autre. N'oublions pas aussi que les divergeances catholiques, orthodoxes et protestantes sont principalement à la base de la conception de l'Église, ce sont surtout des différends ecclésiologiques.

L'Église s'est efformée dans un *procès* normal, selon des catégories culturelles et historiques existantes, sans s'éloigner, tant que lui était possible, de sa réalité originelle; toutefois, on sait bien qu'il y a des influences qui poussent très loin certains aspects de façon que des éléments originaux restent en ombre. Les disputes théologiques, les persécutions et l'interférence politique romaine et byzantine ont obligé l'Église à s'organiser en société, incarnant son événement dans des systèmes institutionnels adéquats; et grâce à l'idée d'un dieu absolu, d'une paternité tribale, des monarchies et des régimes solitaires, elle préféra la forme monarchique; le droit romain la marquera par des empreintes très fortes. Il suffit d'évoquer la doctrine commune synthétisée par Ch. Journet.

Le titre du Premier Livre est: «La Hiérarchie Apostolique ou la cause efficiente immédiate de l'Église et son Apostolicité». Journet distingue trois phases des régimes divins du peuple de Dieu et de l'Église, l'antérieur qui diffère des régimes postérieurs à la chute, avec lesquelles commencera l'Église proprement dite; le premier qui est le régime de rédemption (1 Tm 2,5-6); le troisième est le régime actuel de l'Église de médiation visible de l'incarnation et de la hiérarchie. L'A. explique la médiation de la hiérarchie par privilèges de l'action par contact, qui était exercée directement par le Christ pendant sa vie terrestre, et après l'Ascension, elle est possible grâce aux hommes revêtus de pouvoirs divins et hiérarchiques, par lesquels l'action qu'on exerce du haut du ciel, pourrait être conduite sensiblement jusqu'à chacun de nous; c'est la vertu hiérarchique, ou apostolique, qui aura pour effet propre la formation de l'Église[3].

Fondements du collège hiérarchique

Mais l'Église est un mystère; elle n'est pas une réalité de ce monde, qui se présenterait à toutes les mensurations et à toutes les analyses; elle est le lieu de tous les mystères. Le mystère de l'Église est inscrit dans le plus populaire de nos symboles de foi: nous croyons en l'Église Une, Sainte, Catholique et Apostolique. Elle est l'Église de Dieu, son Épouse, sa Maison, son Temple, son Sanctuaire. Elle n'est pas seulement la première des œuvres de l'Esprit sanctificateur, mais celle qui comprend, conditionne et absorbe toutes les

3 Charles Journet, L'Église du Verbe Incarné, I. La Hiérarchie Apostolique, Desclée de Brouwer, 3ᵉ éd., 1962, p. 1-16.

autres; tout le processus du salut s'accomplit en elle; il s'identifie à elle[4], De Lubac ne méconnait pas l'autre aspect de l'Église, visible, temporelle, sociale, hiérarchique; il voulait, à l'époque d'avant le Concile, en 1952 et 1953, date de la première et de la seconde édition de son ouvrage, relever l'aspect invisible, intérieur, spirituel et communautaire. L'Encyclique *Mystici Corporis* de Pie XII parle de la structure sociale de la communauté chrétienne comme d'un ordre inférieur aux dons spirituels. De Lubac affirme que les lignes essentielles sont tout de même d'institution divine, car la communauté universelle est aussi une communauté visible; elle se rend visible par la communauté particulière. L'A. conclut:

> Ce serait là encore faire «de la spéculation platonicienne» au lieu d'écouter Jésus Christ (Il cite Karl Barth, L'Église et les Églises, trad. Moobs, dans *Œcumenica*, t. III, p. 141). «Dès le lendemain de la mort de Jésus», une Église existait, vivait, telle que Jésus l'avait faite (a). Or l'Église actuelle doit être en continuité vérifiable avec cette communauté des premiers disciples, qui fut depuis le premier jour un groupe bien déterminé, social, organisé, avec ses chefs, ses rites, ses usages, et bientôt sa législation. Elle doit, par une succession réelle et ininterrompue, tenir à «la racine de la société chrétienne» (Il cite Saint Augustin, Epist. 232, n. 3: «Videtis certe multos praecisos a radice christianae societatis, quae per Sedes Apostolorum et successiones episcoporum certa per orbem propagatione diffunditur»). Ce n'est pas en traitant cette succession de «profane», de «mécanique ou de juridique», qu'on en éliminera l'exigence. Qu'on mette, si l'on y parvient, un sens précis sous le terme d'apostolicité 'pneumatique' en l'opposant à toute idée de succession 'historique' (b). Jamais, en tout cas, depuis la première origine, on n'a compris ainsi les choses. Nous en croirons plutôt saint Irénée, montrant les Apôtres confiant aux évêques les Églises dont ils avaient la charge (c). Si l'Église visible d'aujourd'hui n'est pas l'Église 'apostolique', elle ne continue pas réellement la mission du Christ et elle n'est pas son Église»[5].

De Lubac refuse la dissociation du visible et de l'invisible, des charismes et de la hiérarchie, de l'esprit et de l'autorité, dans l'Église, visible et Corps «mystique» du Christ; et le Concile confirma l'unité de la réalité complexe de l'Église:

> Cette société organisée hiérarchiquement d'une part et le Corps mystique d'autre part, l'ensemble discernable aux yeux et la communauté spirituelle, l'Église terrestre et l'Église enrichie des biens célestes ne doivent pas être considérées comme deux choses, elles constituent au contraire une seule réalité complexe, faite d'un double élément humain et divin (LG 8).

Tout chrétien est prêtre; mais au sein du sacerdoce général ou commun, il y a le sacerdoce spécial ou ministériel, fruit du sacrement de l'ordre, et c'est justement l'ordre qui est à l'origine de la hiérarchie ecclésiastique, qui joue d'un triple pouvoir, en raison du triple rôle: de gouvernement, d'enseignement et de sanctification, trois éléments qui découlent de l'unique mission[6].

4 Henri de Lubac, Méditation sur l'Église, Paris, Aubier, 1953, p. 9-36.
5 H. de Lubac, Méditation sur l'Église, p. 73-74.
6 De Lubac, p. 113-123.

L'Église est bien une communauté (Ac 1-2), communion d'amour (1 Jn 1,3-7), non formelle; vie communautaire d'expérience du Christ en rapports interpersonnels pour la réalisation du salut réciproque, dont le contenu est concret. Les mots, les rites, les faits et les institutions sont d'actualisation concrète de la communion ecclésiastique; tout cela exige une hiérarchie sur le plan visible, qui ne peut s'exprimer qu'en esprit de service, car l'amour est la *lex fundamentalis* (1 Co 13). L'élément de l'objectivité est à l'origine de l'autorité ecclésiastique.

La première incarnation de l'autorité dans l'Église est l'annonce de la Parole, par l'Écriture Sainte et la prédication des ministres de la Parole de Dieu, qui sont bien choisis, sacrés et destinés à cette diaconie. Le sacre, grâce à l'imposition des mains et l'effusion de l'Esprit, accorde la faculté d'administrer les sacrements, signes du salut; et la consécration d'individus mûnis de pouvoir, donne une garantie pour une coordination de la communauté vers une but commun pour le bien de tous; le corps en est le symbole (1 Co 12).

C'est de l'Église événement qu'une structure fondamentale dérive sans aucun efforcement; elle n'est pas juridique, ni civile, ni matérielle; elle est communion interpersonnelle dans le temps et les lieux; elle est sociale, ayant son passé, présent et futur, diverse de la prospective intérieure qui est le règne de Dieu; elle est nécessairement apostolique, et grâce à l'apostolicité, l'Église est l'événement du Christ actualisé dans le temps et les pays; elle s'incarne dans les situations concrètes tout en conservant la Tradition Apostolique; elle est toujours neuve et fidèle aux débuts dans un sens dynamique; chaque moment de la vie de l'Église a sa proportion, règne, apostolicité, grâce à la présence de l'Esprit[7].

Le NT utilise le mot *Ecclesia* — Église pour indiquer les réunis au nom de Jésus-Christ; *ʿEdta* donne encore le sens de la réunion liturgique de caractère de fête[8]; l'église est aussi la communauté délimitée géographiquement et historiquement, comme participation de la plénitude (plèrôma) du Christ (Mt 18,20; 1 Ts 1,1; 1 Co 1,1; Rm 16,5; Eph 1,22s); elle est aussi la forme corporelle d'un dessein cosmique d'unité, de paix et d'amour, grâce à la rencontre intime des personnes dans la communication de l'expérience du Christ. L'incarnation de l'événement de l'annonce produit la structure de l'universalité, qui exige une œuvre missionnaire permanente, et la création des liens de communication. Partant de l'unité essentielle, on peut expliquer la diversité concrète, comme on peut partir des églises-communautés particulières pour monter à l'unité souhaitée dans le Christ Tête du Corps; dans les deux

7 S. Dianich, *Communità*, Nuovo Dizionario di Teologia (= NDT), EP, Roma 1979, p. 151-158.
8 ʿAbdišoʿ Sobensis, Ordo Iudiciorum Ecclesiasticorum, ed. J. M. Vosté, Fonti, CCO, ser. II, fasc. XV, Vatican 1940, p. 113.

cas, la communion est la note explicative; des biens de tout genre sont bien nécessaires pour la réaliser; un de ces liens est la hiérarchie.

On pourrait comprendre la Hiérarchie ecclésiastique différemment. L'histoire de l'Église nous offre plusieurs modalités; mais nous pensons qu'une conception juridique a joué un rôle très remarquable dans la vie des églises; il faut revaluer la conception pastorale de caractère paternel, qui est plus biblique et culturel[9]. Notre but ici est d'examiner plutôt l'agir de la Hiérarchie ecclésiastique. Nous verrons qu'une *synodalité* dans la vie et l'action est plus consonne avec le concept des pasteurs-pères-ministres, qu'à celui des hiérarques-chefs-supérieurs.

Examinons cette conception théorétiquement, historiquement, et d'après les donnés de l'histoire de l'Église d'Orient de Séleucie-Ctésiphon.

Synodalité théorétique

Le pouvoir du Christ est service (*diakonia, tešmešta*) pour le salut de tout l'homme et de tous les hommes, qui lui coûte sa vie (Mt 11,4-5; 20,20-28; Mc 9,35; Lc 7,18-23; 4,16-21; 6,20). L'ennemi du service est la domination; le serviteur est possédé par son maître (*dominus*); son service n'est pas un emploi, devoir, obligation, infligé par un contract à ademplir en raison de la possession que le maître a de droit sur la personne du serviteur, et de conséquence, sur son activité toute entière. Qui moralement devient serviteur d'un autre, il se donne totalement, sans rien exiger ou demander; seul le maître peut lui bénéficier, s'il est bon et fidèle, mais sans aucun mérite de sa part (Lc 17,10).

Le serviteur dans la Bible n'est pas l'esclave; il peut devenir l'homme de confiance et l'héritier (Gn 24,2). Servir Dieu est un honneur; il implique une fidélité qui renouvelle l'alliance. Ceux qui détiennent le pouvoir dans l'Église, sont des serviteurs pour leurs frères, tous les hommes. Leur service doit être inspiré par un amour intégral, envers Dieu et les hommes; le vrai serviteur est un sauveur[10].

Le mot *hiérarchie* (*hierarchia*) n'a jamais été employé dans les textes bibliques; mais celui de *Principatus, Ordo, Dignitas* en se référant au Christ, non à l'Église. L'*exousia* (autorité) est plutôt une force et capacité pour chasser les démons; le pouvoir est *dynamis* ou force dynamique. Ainsi, on serait obligé de dire que le concept de hiérarchie-autorité-pouvoir est

9 Cfr communication au V. Symposium Syriacum de Leuven-Louvain, 28-31 août 1988: Typologie du 'père' dans les sources canoniques syro-orientales; et mon étude: La structure patriarcale de l'Église, qui apparaîtra dans *la Parole de l'Orient* (Melto); tandis que la communication apparaîtra dans les Actes du V. Symposium Syriacum, éd. OCA, Rome.

10 Charles Augrain & Marc-François Lacan, *Servir & Serviteur de Dieu*, dans VTB, 1218-1224.

introduit dans l'Ecclésiologie par des influences étrangères, notamment civiles. A-t-on bien fait d'insérer une terminologie profane dans la structure ecclésiastique?

Certes, le Christ était revêtu d'un pouvoir clairement exercé au cours de sa vie (Mt 8,8). Il l'a conféré solenellement à ses Apôtres avant son Ascension au Ciel (Mt 28.19). C'est justement le texte de Mt 28,19 qui est la pierre angulaire de toute la spéculation traditionnelle. À y ajouter le pouvoir de lier et délier sur la terre, comme au ciel (Mt 16,19; 18,8). Malgré les discussions et les difficultés, il ne faut pas diminuer la force de ces textes matthéens. Il faut les comprendre comme fin du conflit entre Dieu et l'homme, en ce sens que Dieu communique son pouvoir à l'homme pour libérer la création, déformée et morte, quand l'homme s'est crue capable de dérober à Dieu son pouvoir, tandis que c'est la puissance de Dieu qui est le fondement de la foi des disciples (1 Co 2,5); sans la force divine, l'homme n'est pas seulement faible, mais sans force; sans la paternité divine, l'homme n'est pas père; sans la supériorité divine, l'homme reste dans l'esclavage; la principauté du Christ est unique (1 Co 12,4-7) et la victoire de Jésus-Christ sur la mort, le monde et les ténèbres, abolit la domination de l'homme sur ses semblables.

Toute autre autorité n'a pas valeur en soi, mais uniquement comme témoignage de l'annonce évangélique que les Apôtres reçoivent par l'Esprit (Jn 1,34; 3,11; Ac 4,33). La légitimité de l'autorité est fondée grâce à l'authenticité du témoignage (Ac 15,28). Tout genre d'autorité, n'a sens que *dans* la communauté et *pour* elle (2 Co 4,5; 1 Tm 5,17s)[11].

Les Douze apparaissent comme un *collège*; ce ne sont pas comme des individus isolés que Jésus a rencontrés au cours de ses voyages et laissés sur place; il les a réunis comme disciples. Les disciples d'un maître formaient à ces époques là une communauté bien délinée. Jésus le Maître et le Messie, envoya ses disciples, deux à deux, prêcher dans les villages; il a choisi, parmi ses disciples, des Apôtres, de nombre douze, témoins de lui, et leur a confié la continuation de sa mission, mûnis de son pouvoir; c'est au Collège des Douze rassemblés, représentants le reste du peuple de Dieu, racheté par le Sang de l'Agneau, Jésus-Christ que l'Esprit Saint est donné (Ac 2)[12].

Pour accepter la collégialité, et donc la synodalité, il faut d'abord admettre que l'Église est vraiment fondée sur les Apôtres, et que le Collège des Évêques succède au Collège Apostolique. Une remarque à faire ici à propos de la personnification très poussée du pouvoir ecclésiastique; les Sources parlent

11 G. Alberigo, *Autorità e potere*, dans NDT, p. 53-54.

12 Dom Bernard Botte, *La Collégialité dans le Nouveau Testament et chez les Pères apostoliques*, dans: Le Concile et les Conciles, ouvrage en collaboration, Ed. de Chevetogne & Ed. du Cerf, 1960, p. 5-6.

plutôt de la Tradition Apostolique vivante dans l'autorité transmise par l'imposition des mains aux personnes choisies pour servir les communautés[13], et fait des évêques successeurs des Apôtres[14] dans la mesure où les fonctions du Collège Apostolique sont transmissables. Le Concile le dit clairement:

> C'est en vertu de la consécration sacramentelle et par la communion hiérarchique avec le chef du collège et ses membres que quelqu'un est fait membre du corps épiscopal (LG 22).
> Les évêques, en vertu de leur consécration sacramentelle, et par leur communion hiérarchique avec le chef et les membres du collège, sont établis membres du corps épiscopal. «L'ordre des évêques, qui succède au collège apostolique pour le magistère et le gouvernement pastoral, bien mieux dans lequel se perpétue le corps apostolique constitue, lui aussi, en union avec le Pontife romain, son chef, et jamais en dehors de ce chef, le sujet d'un pouvoir suprême et plénier sur l'Église universelle (CD 4).
> Tous les évêques en tant que membres du corps épiscopal qui succède au collège des Apôtres, ont été consacrés non seulement pour un diocèse, mais pour le salut du monde entier (AG 38).

Il n'y a pas une constitution juridique qui subordonne un évêque à un autre; pour les Catholiques il y a la primauté du Chef-Tête du Corps; pour tous, il y a la communion entre tous les Évêques-Pères; le sens commun d'une solidalité humaine et chrétienne, et les exigences surtout d'une unité ecclésiale, souhaitée par le Christ lui-même et à construire dans la foi, l'amour et l'espérance, pour assurer la sussistance et la perfection du Corps du Christ, animé par l'Esprit, sont à la base de la communion ecclésiastique et hiérarchique; telle communion est plus profonde de la conformité extérieure et des liens sociaux et juridiques.

Sur le plan de la foi, l'Église est menacée par le syncrétisme; sur le plan de l'amour, par l'isolement et l'égoïsme; et sur le plan de l'unique corps et même esprit, par les divisions. Le seul fait d'être multitude, diverse et pluraliste, ne contrarie pas son unité intérieure, profonde et essentielle. L'unité de l'Église n'est réalisable que grâce à l'Esprit; mais l'Esprit-Saint n'agit pas mécaniquement; il a besoin de nous; et c'est justement grâce à la communion que l'unité est assurée.

D'autre part, la Tradition Apostolique vivante a été transmise à des hommes chargés de la garder et transmettre, en vertu surtout de l'autorité reçue pour guider les communautés des croyants. Les évêques doivent se soumettre à la Tradition pour la porter aux membres; ils doivent agir et vivre en communion avec tous les membres de l'unique Collège[15].

13 Cfr I Lettr. Clem., 44,1-3.

14 Lettr. d'Ignace d'Antioche, Philadel., 4,1.

15 Voir les Écrits des Pères, notamment Hippolyte, Irénée, Cyprien etc. Cfr C.H. Turner, *Apostolic succession*, dans: Essays on the Early History of the Church and the Ministry, ed. H.B. Swete, London 1919, p. 93-214.

Par sa composition multiple, ce collège exprime la variété et l'universalité du peuple de Dieu; il exprime par son rassemblement sous un seul chef, l'unité du troupeau du Christ. Dans ce collège, les évêques fidèles à observer le primat et l'autorité de leur chef jouissent, pour le bien de leurs fidèles et même de toute l'Église, d'un pouvoir propre, l'Esprit-Saint assurant par l'action continue de sa force, la structure et la concorde dans l'organisme. Le pouvoir suprême dont jouit ce collège à l'égard de l'Église universelle s'exerce solennellement dans le Concile œcuménique (LG 22).

C'est au sein de chaque Église locale qu'on trouve la Tradition Apostolique, incarnée dans le Symbole ou la Règle de la Foi, qui résume les données de la Sainte Écriture; sa transmission est par la voie de la Succession Apostolique incarnée dans les Évêques locaux. Soit par nécessité, soit par utilité, les évêques devaient échanger de vues entre eux synodalement assemblés en divers lieux, ou par correspondance[16]. Saint Cyprien reporte ce que le presbytérat romain écrit au nom de l'Église Romaine, durant la vacance du siège:

C'est en effet une charge facilement impopulaire et un lourd fardeau que d'avoir, sans être en nombre, à examiner la faute d'un grand nombre et d'être seul à prononcer la sentence quand beaucoup de personnes ont commis le crime. D'ailleurs une décision ne peut avoir grande force qui ne semblerait pas avoir reçu les suffrages d'un grand nombre de délibérants. Considérez que le monde presque entier a été ravagé (*totum orbem paene vastatum*), que l'on voit partout à terre des débris et des ruines et qu'ainsi la situation réclame pour le jugement des assises aussi considérables que la propagation du délit[17].

Nous avons par saint Cyprien que cette lettre a été expédiée à toutes les Églises du monde, et Cyprien lui fait écho par ces paroles:

Ce n'est pas là l'affaire d'un petit nombre ou d'une seule Église ou d'une seule province, mais du monde entier (*totius orbis*)[18].

À distinguer la *communio ecclesiastica* de la *communio hierarchica*, comme nous l'avons dit (cfr LG 23); c'est la seconde qui nous interesse particulièrement. La communion ecclésiastique est assurée dans le *protos*, pasteur et père de son église particulière, parce que chaque église possède la plénitude venante du Père dans le Christ et par lui, agissante dans le Corps, qui est l'Église une et identique dans n'importe quel temps et lieu; peuple de Dieu assemblé pour annoncer la Bonne Nouvelle, et communauté des frères d'un père visible mûni de tous les charismes nécessaires; l'évêque, le patriarche ou le primat est en même temps fils de l'Église et frère des frères; tandis que la communion hiérarchique se manifeste par l'échange des lettres entre les évêques-chefs-pères des églises, et surtout dans les synodes ou conciles qui

16 Socrate, Hist. Eccl., I,6.

17 Dom Hilaire Marot, *Conciles anténicéens et conciles œcuméniques*, dans: Le Concile et les Conciles, p. 29.

18 Cyprien, Lettre XIX.

expriment solennellement leur collégialité. Dans la communion hiérarchique, l'évêque, au sein d'un patriarcat ou d'une Église particulière, et le protos-père dans les Églises patriarcales, résume sa portion d'église, en manière qu'il puisse représenter tous les membres de son propre église, décider en leur nom et actualiser la communion ecclésiastique, sans méconnaître les droits des plus petits.

Synodalité historique

À partir de la moitié du IIe siècle, on a commencé à reconnaître à un individu la responsabilité de guider la communauté; c'est la volonté de donner l'esprit unc incarnation visible, qu'on a donné, sur le plan social, la naissance des évêques (episkopoi), comme lien d'unité dans la charité, avec une marque de transcendance, exprimée dans les Lettres d'Ignace d'Antioche, puis par d'autres, faisant de la soumission à l'évêque la soumission à Dieu[19].

Après une dizaine d'annés, vers 115-120, la synodalité connut son apparition; un synode ou concile qui réunit plusieurs évêques se réunissant pour discuter des problèmes diocésains; leurs décisions ont un caractère législatif et judiciaire. Mais les premiers synodes, proprement dits, sonst ceux qui ont été célébré en Asie Mineure entre 160 et 175 pour faire front au Montanisme; il ne s'agit plus désormais de constater la simple Règle de Foi à opposer aux déviations, mais de se mettre au clair sur certaines précisions et élaborations doctrinales, ou sur certaines règles disciplinaires de la vie chrétienne. Vingt ans plus tard, vers 195, c'est l'affaire de Pâque; et vers l'an 250 on est devant une seconde ondée de synodes: à Rome, en Afrique du Nord, à Antioche etc. pour traiter le problème des *Lapsi* et le baptême des hérétiques; 10 ans plus tard, les premières disputes christologiques. Le premier Concile œcuménique est celui de Nicée de l'an 325. Les choses sont assez claires après cette date[20].

Du point de vue structurelle et doctrinale l'image des assemblées synodales change selon le moment historique et les régions. En Asie Mineure, l'intérêt doctrinal prévalait; en Égypte et en Occident l'aspect disciplinaire; en Afrique, une rigidité collégiale est remarquable; mais, il n'y a pas une diversité essentielle dans la structure synodale[21]. L'autorité de chaque synode, particulier ou régional, ne fut jamais limité au milieu du propre territoire, ni par les évêques. Pourquoi?

19 Lettre d'Ignace d'Antioche, Magn., III,1-2; VI,1; Trall., II,1.

20 Marot, Conciles anténicéens et conciles œcuméniques, p. 23-37. Cfr Hubert Jedin, Kleine Konziliengeschichte, Herder, Freiburg i. Br. 1959.

21 E. Corecco, Sinodalità, dans NDT, p. 1467.

L'institution conciliaire a son lien théologique dans la synodalité de la constitution de l'Église, manifestée désormais dans le Concile de Jérusalem (Ac 15); mais les synodes et les conciles qui se sont développés à partir de la moitié du IIe s., ne dérivent pas directement du premier fait apostolique de Jérusalem. Il ne faut pas non plus se limiter à la seule critique historico-positive pour expliquer l'origine des conciles; une raison à admettre est le besoin de se consulter pour des problèmes urgents, et l'autoconscience de la solidalité et de leur efformation comme collège, membres distincts d'une Église unique; l'Église particulière n'est pas une entité isolée du reste du corps ecclésial; l'élection d'un évêque ne se limitait pas à la communauté diocésaine, or exigeait 2 ou 3 évêques au minimum, pour assurer justement la communion entre les églises[22]. On ne doit pas donc conditionner le fait conciliaire par l'impulsion des Empereurs Romains, comme s'il s'était un phénomène nait de l'influence du Sénat et du Droit Romain; l'expérience de l'Église de Séleucie-Ctésiphon, lointaine de cette atmosphère, vient à confirmer l'analyse qui accorde au sens communautaire du corps, sans toutefois exclure que dans l'unité on expérimente la force.

Il ne faut pas penser à une rupture entre l'Église Apostolique et l'Église ou les Églises du second siècle, et forcément les Églises des siècles suivants. Une élaboration progressive de l'ecclésialité après la diffusion du Christianisme dans plusieurs régions et pays, et l'institution et constitution des communautés-églises, n'était point une opération facile. Une fois le caractère eschatologique très poussé venait à être modéré par celui charismatique, il fallait du temps pour que le caractère communautaire et sociale prenne une configuration théologico-juridique. Des influences extérieures ne pouvaient pas manquer; elles furent très violentes avant que le Christianisme aie pris ses conceptions et ses structures fondamentales, telles le légalisme juif, l'intellectualisme grec, le ritualisme païen et le juridisme romain; ils furent bien des aides, mais aussi des dangers auxquels l'Église devait faire face[23].

L'affaire du montanisme révèle les premières excommunications prises collégialement. Ex-communication signifie se détacher et se séparer de la communion. Les premiers donnés historiques laissent percevoir que ce sont les individus irréguliers qui s'écartent eux-mêmes de la vie commune avec les autres; ce n'est pas un acte coercitif de la part de la Hiérarchie; c'est l'hérétique ou le pêcheur qui s'excommunie[24].

22 Voir la Tradition Apostolique d'Hippolyte a. 215; Concile d'Arles a. 314; Concile de Nicée a. 325.

23 Botte, La collégialité ..., p. 2-3.

24 Cfr p.ex. Corpus Scriptorum Ecclesiasticorum Latinorum, ed. W. Hartel, III,810-827; J. Lebreton, Saint Cyprien, dans: Fliche et Martin, Histoire de l'Église, II, p. 203; L. Bayard, St. Cyprien, Corresp., Lett. de Firmilianos.

Une autre remarque à faire à propos des premières réunions ecclésiastiques, est le rôle important et normal des laïcs, qui sera restreint par la suite, notamment dans les conciles plus généraux, probablement à cause du nombre, et pour des difficultés pratiques, tout en considérant le phénomène de la représentation officielle des évêques, chefs et pères des communautés. Eusèbe de Césarée, père de l'Histoire Ecclésiastique dit:

> Les fidèles d'Asie se réunirent souvent à cette fin en de nombreux endroits de l'Asie; ils examinèrent les discours récents et montrèrent qu'ils étaient profanes et, après avoir condamné l'hérésie, ils chassèrent de l'Église les sectateurs et les retranchèrent de la communion (Hist. Eccl. V,XVI,10).

Eusèbe, comme les Actes des synodes et conciles préfèrent plutôt un langage juridique, qui dominera progressivement dans l'Église.

Aux premiers synodes et conciles convoqués en Orient et en Occident, comme aussi aux premiers Conciles Œcuméniques, le nombre des évêques présents fut assez élevé, les décisions des participants à l'unanimité. Eusèbe l'atteste clairement[25]. Saint Cyprien dit:

> Omnes uno consensu, de consensu et auctoritate communi, quod decrevimus communi consilio universi judicamus (Epistul. LXVII,6).

On est immédiatement devant des ruptures et des divisions une fois que le consensus unanime est affaibli, comme dans les cas des Conciles d'Ephèse et de Calcédoine. Seule la convinction d'être avec la Tradition Apostolique reste enracinée dans les esprits, malgré la diversité des vues sur le plan doctrinal ou disciplinaire; comme signe visible de la fidélité à la tradition est la référence de tous aux décisions des conciles antérieurs; les *orthodoxes* comme les *hétérodoxes* disent que leurs décisions ne sont pas nouvelles. Le concile est bien une institution régulière dans l'Église.

C'est dans ce contexte qu'il faut comprendre le rôle des Empereurs dans la convocation des conciles; ils avaient la conscience de remplir un devoir de leur charge; en tant que princes chrétiens, les Empereurs, Constantin, Théodose ou Marcion, devaient veiller à la paix et à l'unité de l'Église dans l'Empire pacifié et unifié; assurer la convocation et procurer les moyens matériels nécessaires étaient une chose secondaire[26].

Nous ne voulons pas entrer dans la problématique de l'œcuménicité des conciles, qui est en dehors de notre but, et parce que nous considérons *apostolique* chaque réunion, assemblée, synode, ou concile des évêques, en vertu justement de l'apostolicité des églises. Il suffit que le collège réuni représente la Foi et la Tradition Apostoliques, pour que le synode ou le

25 Eusèbe, hist. Eccl., VII,28-30.

26 Pierre-Thomas Camelot, *Les Conciles œcuméniques des IVe et Ve siècles*, dans: Le Concile et les Conciles, p. 50-51.

concile soit apostolique[27]. Le synode-concile est l'expression sollennelle de la collégialité.

(La nature collégiale de l'ordre épiscopal) se trouve manifestement confirmée par le fait des Conciles œcuméniques tenus tout le long des siècles (LG 22)
Dès les premiers siècles de l'Église, la communion de la charité fraternelle et le souci de la mission universelle confiée aux Apôtres, ont poussé les Évêques, placés à la tête des Églises particulières, à associer leurs forces et leurs volontés en vue de promouvoir le bien commun de l'ensemble des Églises et de chacune d'elles. Pour cette raison, des Synodes, des Conciles provinciaux et enfin des Conciles pléniers ont été constitués, où les Évêques décrétèrent les normes identiques à observer dans les diverses Églises pour l'enseignement des vérités de la foi et l'organisation de la discipline ecclésiastique (CD 36).

La synodalité dans l'Église de l'Orient de Séleucie-Ctésiphon

L'Église de l'Orient de Séleucie-Ctésiphon est peu connue dans l'Histoire Ecclésiastique, sa Théologie et son Ecclésiologie de moins; pour en avoir du profit, nous partons des termes de l'Église et de la Hiérarchie, pour examiner ensuite la notion de la communion, collégialité et synodalité. Afin de délimiter le sujet, nous nous limitons aux seules sources canoniques, notamment les Actes des Synodes Orientaux[28], c'est la source la plus officielle et sûre.

Le mot utilisé pour désigner l'Église est *ʿedta* ou église[29]; mais il y a aussi celui de *kenša, knušta*: congrégation, communauté, et de *ʿamma, gawa, marʿyṯa*: peuple, masse, troupeau dans le sens de paroisse, diocèse[30]. Des adjectifs bien connus sont fréquents: église de Dieu, peuple des chrétiens, peuple de Dieu, masse ou congrégation ou communauté des croyants, troupeau ou paroisse ou diocèse du Christ, etc. Appellations spécifiques: toutes les églises et les communautés de l'Orient, ou tout le peuple de Dieu dans tous les lieux ou pays de l'Orient, dont le Catholicos (Patriarche) est le chef ou le père[31].

Depuis des annés on est, dans les milieux catholiques et orthodoxes, vis-à-vis d'un ressentiment provoqué par le concept de la Hiérarchie, fruit d'une influence protestante et pour diminuer la poussée des dimensions de l'autorité (exousia) et du pouvoir (dynamis). Il serait toutefois contre l'histoire ecclésiastique nier le caractère hiérarchique; l'exemple de cette Église de l'Orient

27 Camelot, Les Conciles ..., p. 63.
28 Ed. J.-B. Chabot, Synodicon Orientale, ou Recueil de Synodes Nestoriens, Paris 1902. Cfr Oscar Braun, Das Buch der Synhados, oder Synodicon Orientale, Wien 1900 (Philo Press, Amsterdam 1975) = SO.
29 Synode de Mar Isḥaq: SO, texte syr. p. 18, trad. fanc., p. 254; Synode de Mar Yahbalaha, t. p. 37, tr. p. 277.
30 Cfr SO, p. 17, 18, 21, 27, 37, 44-53, 54, 69 etc.
31 SO, 18/255.

Mesopotamien, restée lointaine des influence romaines et byzantines, plus que toutes les autres Églises particulières, vient à dissiper nos doutes[32].

Le terme *rešanuṯa*, supériorité, employée beaucoup dans les Actes synodaux de l'Église de l'orient Mésopotamien, dérive du mot *reša*, tête; il s'applique au chef des évêques (*reša d'appesqope*), le Catholicos, et aux évêques qui sont des chefs ou supérieurs (*rešane*)[33]; tous des administrateurs, économes (*mḏabrane*) de l'Église et du sacerdoce[34], dans le sens du service[35], mais tous doués d'un vrai pouvoir (*šultana*) pour être têtes (chefs) des membres[36], d'une signorité ou domination (*maruṯa*)[37] et d'une primauté ou grandeur (*rabbuṯa*)[38]. Le Catholicos est le plus grand, ou le Primat (*rabba*) et chef-tête (*reša*) de tous les Évêques[39]; il a la grandeur ou la primauté du sacerdoce[40], et le plus haut degré du presbytérat, de l'épiscopat et du diaconat[41]. Son siège apostolique de la grande Église de Koḫe a l'honneur et la primauté sur tous les autres sièges épiscopaux[42]. Mais, il s'agit d'une supériorité paternelle (*rešanuṯa abahayta*)[43]. C'est l'unité du corps qui détermine l'unité de l'autorité, et l'unité du gouvernement-administration (*mḏabranuṯa* = économie) dérive de l'unité de la principauté ou supériorité; personne peut contredire le pouvoir ecclésiastique[44], qui est au service de l'ordre (*tagma*), et pour le soin (*yassipuṯa*) de tous les membres, de la part du Catholicos et du Synode[45].

Il s'agit donc d'une véritable hiérarchie dans la structure constitutionnelle de l'Église de l'Orient Mésopotamien, avec une accentuation du service, de la familiarité patriarcale-paternelle, sans exclure le caractère juridique[46].

ʿAbdišoʿ Métropolite de Nisibe, auteur de la Collection Canonique officielle de l'Église de Séleucie-Ctésiphon, explique dans son *Ordo Iudiciorum Ecclesiasticorum* les degrés ecclésiastiques, qui se divisent en sept, dont le premier est le Patriarche, père des prélats, et le Catholicos ou le général, l'universel[47].

32 Cfr E. Tisserant, *Nestorienne* (Église), DTC, XI,1, 1931, col. 157-323; J. M. Fiey, Jalons pour une Histoire de l'Église en Iraq, CSCO 310, Subs. 36, Louvain 1970; J. Habbi, Kanissat al-Mašriq, 1, Bagdad 1989.
33 SO, 18/253.
34 SO, 37, 40.
35 SO, Synode de Mar Babai, p. 65.
36 SO, 20.
37 SO, Synode de Mar Dadišoʿ, 51.
38 SO, 41.
39 SO, 33.
40 SO, 44.
41 SO, Synode de Mar Aba, 71.
42 SO, Synode de Mar Babai, 63.
43 SO, 63.
44 SO, 20-21.
45 SO, 69 et 71.
46 SO, Synode de Dadišoʿ, t. 43-53, tr. 285-298.
47 ʿAbdišoʿ, Ordo Iudiciorum Ecclesiasticorum, ed. Vosté, p. 109.

Le Traité XI du Nomocanon de ʿAbdišoʿ est consacré à la grande dignité du Patriarcat, sa sublimité et son honneur[48].

La forme naturelle de l'exercise collégial de l'autorité est le synode. Si quelqu'un a une accusation, qu'il la porte devant la congrégation[49]. Mais les synodes ne sont pas en premier lieu pour examiner les accusations et résoudre les problèmes: «Nous tous, évêques de toutes les contrées d'Orient, nous nous sommes réunis pour saluer et vénérer notre Père l'honorable Mar Yahbalaha, évêque, catholicos de l'Orient, et pour visiter son honorable frère Mar Acacius, évêque et ambassadeur»; à la visite et à la vénération, les pères du synode de Mar Yahbalaha de 420 expriment clairement le but de leur réunion: «Il convient que nous recherchions, que nous écrivions, que nous sanctionnions et que nous firmions de notre sceau et de notre signature, les glorieuses constitutions qui furent convenablement établis par la tradition des bienheureux Apôtres, nos pères, pour la direction du sacerdoce, ainsi que les lois stables et les canons établis dans les synodes des évêques qui eurent lieu à diverses reprises en Occident»[50]. Il y a donc toute une continuité de la synodalité dans l'Église.

Les termes employés pour désigner le synode est: congrégation ou communauté (*knušya*), séance ou session des pères (*mawtba*), et le mot grec syrianisé de *sunhados*[51]. Très fréquemment on qualifie le synode par l'adjectif saint, ou grand (*qaddišta, rabbṯa*; le synode en syriaque est féminin)[52].

Les Synodes Orientaux se composent des évêques, qui se réunissent de divers lieux et de toutes les contrées[53], auprès ou avec le Catholicos, chef, tête et père de tous; les Évêques sont ses frères et membres de l'unique corps[54]. Il suffit que les Évêques se réunissent pour que ce soit le synode[55], avec l'intention évidemment de se réunir collégialement pour célébrer un synode. Les évêques réunis en synode sont tous des pères[56], pères saints[57], frères et membres[58], et aussi fils du service du peuple[59]; ils forment un seul corps, le

48 ʿAbdišoʿ, Collectio Canonum Synodicorum, SVNC, ed. A. Mai, X, Rome 1838, p. 154s.
49 SO, 48.
50 SO, 38, 42.
51 SO, 19-20, 44, 53, 64.
52 SO, 21, 38.
53 SO, 20, 47.
54 SO, 20-21.
55 SO, 20, 38, 69.
56 SO, 38.
57 SO, Synode de Mar Aqaq, 55.
58 SO, 50.
59 SO, 39.

Corps du Christ[60], qui est le corps des évêques frères de tout l'Orient[61]; le Patriarche est le père des pères[62].

On dirait qu'on est devant une conception de l'Église-institution, non de l'Église-événement. Pour avoir l'ensemble de l'optique, il faut compléter ces textes par ceux qui insistent sur la communion et la collégialité (*šawtapuṯa*), d'où le rôle du peuple de Dieu, fidèles laïcs et clercs, apparaît clairement[63]; déjà la conception *patriarcale* diminue celle juridique.

L'utilité des synodes est énorme. Les synodes assurent la communion[64]; le ministère ou gouvernement sacerdotal[65], l'établissement juste du service (*diakonia*) de l'Église du Christ[66]; et la promulgation des canons ecclésiastiques, des avertissements, des définitions, des rites véridiques[67], et tout ce qui est nécessaire pour le gouvernement, l'administration[68], et ce qui est juste pour la règle de l'Église[69]. Grâce aux synodes, les disputes, les schismes et les divisions cessent[70]; les éloignés acceptent les définitions synodales[71], et les Constitutions Apostoliques s'établissent et se transmettent convenablement.

Les sanctions à infliger contre ceux qui se mettent contre les synodes et leurs décisions sont fortes et connues. Les Actes des Synodes Orientaux de cette Église insistent sur l'ex-communication; et il y a deux mots pour exprimer cette réalité, antithèse de la marque essentielle de l'Église, la communion; le premier est *ḥerma* dans le sens d'anathème, et le second est *la-meštaḥlap* ou non-communier[72]; il y a aussi la censure (*'issar*), le rejet (*šda*), le mépris (*istli*) etc.[73].

Conséquences de l'excommunication et de l'anathème sont: la perte du pouvoir ecclésiastique[74], la dégradation[75], la colère de Dieu et le mépris de la part de tout le peuple de Dieu[76]; non seulement les évêques, pères du synode,

60 SO, 40.
61 SO, 64.
62 SO, 111.
63 Nous préparons une étude: Communion (*Šawtapuṯa*) et collégialité.
64 SO, 38.
65 SO, 38.
66 SO, 22, 53.
67 SO, 63.
68 SO, 64.
69 SO, 20.
70 SO, 19.
71 SO, 19.
72 SO, 21.
73 SO, 35.
74 SO, 21.
75 SO, 30, 47.
76 SO, 21, 35.

mais tous ceux qui sont avec eux[77]. Il y a parfois des expressions fortes et exagérées, certes pour accentuer la nécessité de la communion, de la collégialité et de la synodalité, comme l'abolition de la mémoire de ceux qui se mettent contre les synodes et les décisions synodales[78]; ils n'auront ni médicament, ni pardon[79]; toutefois, l'Église étant Mère, elle accepte les pénitents; s'ils manifestent des signes de pénitence, c'est alors qu'ils acceptent la grâce (*raḥme*, le contraire du *ḥerma*)[80].

Les étapes d'un synode sont: la notification par des lettres[81], ou par une *saqra* (*sagra*)[82]. La convocation est générale, et la participation de tous est obligatoire, sous peines de déposition, à l'exception des cas prévus dans les canons[83]. Les évêques réunis en synode doivent écouter[84], discuter, décider, et confirmer leur opinion par le serment, et leurs décisions par le sceau et la signature[85]. Chaque évêque doit avoir une copie des délibérations prises et des canons définis[86]; et tous sont obligés à garder avec diligence les décisions synodales[87].

Le nombre des participants n'était pas toujours très élevé; certainement à cause des difficultés de voyage et de l'âge des évêques. Au premier synode officiel de Mar Ishaq de 410, ils étaient 38; seulement 12 dans celui de Mar Yahbalaha de 420; 37 au synode de Mar Dadišoʿ; de 424; 25 au celui de Mar Acacius de 486; 37 au synode de Mar Babai de 497, avec des prêtres et notaires etc. La formule généralement employée pour l'adhésion aux actes était: «Moi, (...), évêque de ..., j'adhère à tout ce qui est écrit ci-dessus, et j'ai signé et scellé», ou: «J'ai confirmé tout ce qui écrit ci-dessus» etc.[88].

La régularité des synodes fut bien exigée. Les réunions synodales ne sont pas facultatives. Il fallait convoquer chaque quatre ans un synode général auprès le Catholicos-Patriarche avec la participation de tous les Métropolites et Évêques. Chaque deux ans, les évêques d'une province ecclésiastique se réunissent chez le Métropolite; et deux fois par ans, le clergé, les moines et les notables chez l'Évêque; le temps prescrit pour la convocation des synodes ne fut pas toujours le même, il varia selon les circonstances[89].

77 SO, 34.
78 SO, 35.
79 SO, 35.
80 SO, 35.
81 SO, 19.
82 SO, 63.
83 SO, 19.
84 SO, 19, 20.
85 Voir Synode de Mar Aqaq: SO, 53-59; la conclusion du Synode de Mar Yahbalaha: SO, 41.
86 SO, 26,53-54, 83.
87 SO, 84.
88 Cfr Synodes de Mar Yahbalaha et de Mar Aqaq.
89 SO, 30, 90-91, 121.

Il faut aussi mentionner les réunions que le Chorévêque ou le Périodeute (*korappesqopa, sa'ora*) devait tenir avec le clergé et les moines; le Prieur avec ses moines; et le Chorévêque avec le clergé et les moines auprès de l'Évêque. Des réunions obligatoires encore se faisaient en présence du Métropolite et des Évêques de la province ecclésiastique, en occasion de l'élection du propre évêque[90].

La synodalité dans la vie de l'Église de l'Orient de Séleucie-Ctésiphon était fort pratiquée, grâce à une conception claire et profonde qui trouve ses racines dans la constitution de l'Église elle-même, et seulement de conséquence, pour combattre l'absolutisme et la dictature des chefs ecclésiastiques. Le Synode de Mar Joseph de 554 le dit en termes précis:

> Il a été dit que des hommes élevés au degré de la paternité suprême, c'est-à-dire du patriarcat, traitent les affaires à eux seuls, les terminent et les signent, et, sans les montrer aux évêques ni les lire en leur présence, exigent impérieusement que ceux-ci les signent. Et s'ils ne les signent pas, ils leur suscitent des ennuis, les anathématisent et les rejettent de l'épiscopat. — C'est pourquoi nous avons défini que: le métropolitain ou le patriarche doit faire tout ce qu'il fait avec le conseil de la communauté. L'affaire qu'il aura réglée aura d'autant plus d'autorité qu'elle aura été soumise à l'examen d'évêques plus nombreux[91].

On pourrait objecter qu'il s'agit d'une autorité morale acquise par la réunion d'un grand nombre des évêques; mais le nombre élevé que nous avons de textes qui exigent la synodalité, offre une certitude que l'Église de l'Orient Mésopotamien l'exigeait nécessairement. Le même canon VII du Synode de Mar Joseph continue:

> Si l'urgence de l'affaire ne donne pas le temps de réunir les évêques, ou si la rapidité de la chose ne laisse pas le temps nécessaire, parce qu'en la laissant subsister jusqu'à l'arrivée des évêques il en résulterait du dommage, que *rien ne soit fait*, dans ces cas d'urgence, sans la présence d'au moins trois évêques; *car l'assemblée de trois* évêques peut être considérée *comme l'assemblée de tous*, selon la parole de Notre-Seigneur qui a dit: «Là où deux ou trois seront réunis en mon nom, je serai au milieu d'eux»[92].

Ceci fait rappeler l'exigence aussi de deux ou trois évêques, comme minimum, et le métropolitain, pour l'élection, le sacre et la confirmation des évêques. Ainsi, l'évêque, collégialement et synodalement élu, sacré et confirmé, collégialement et synodalement il doit agir.

L'évêque est encore libre dans les synodes; personne peut l'obliger à signer, ni peut-il dénier ce qu'on a décrété d'accord avec les autres. Écoutons encore le Synode de Joseph:

90 Cfr J. Habbi, La figure juridique de l'évêque dans l'histoire de l'Église Assyro-Chaldéenne, Kanon VII (1985), p. 195-212.

91 SO, 101.

92 SO, 101.

On a dit encore qu'il se trouve certains évêques qui, dans les assemblées générales, font avec bonne volonté tout ce qui leur est prescrit par leurs supérieurs et leurs directeurs; puis quelque temps après les uns nient (disant): «Nous n'avons pas fait cela», les autres disent: «Nous l'avons fait par contrainte». Il se trouve ainsi qu'autres sont leurs paroles et autres leurs actes ... — Contre ceux-là nous définissons canoniquement: Qu'une sévère réprimande leur sera adressée par les évêques leurs frères[98].

Dans la *Pragmatique* des réformes provinciales de Mar Aba le Grand, a. 544, on trouve des définitions et des règles relatives aux divers degrés du gouvernement ecclésiastique. Le raisonnement de l'Église de l'Orient de Séleucie-Ctésiphon révèle une Ecclésiologie bien délinée, qui, à compléter avec les autres donnés, peut nous fournir les éléments essentiels d'une saine conception ecclésiologique.

Le raisonnement part justement du corps humain, figure paulinienne de l'Église; après avoir condamnée toute dualité, reprenant le symbole de l'unicité dans le mariage, où une femme ne doit pas appartenir à deux maris, ni un corps doit avoir deux têtes, Mar Aba passe au gouvernement de l'Église, but de la réforme. Il s'adresse aux pasteurs vigilants des brebis raisonnables de Notre Seigneur Jésus-Christ, expliquant que le corps humain, aussi longtemps qu'il est dans cette vie transistoire, doit être gouverné par la régularité et la modération des choses nécessaires, de peur que, par leur abondance, il ne soit suffoqué ou ne devienne indomptable, ou que, par leur pénurie, il ne soit épuisé et affaibli, et que, troublé et agité par les désordres, avili et retenu par les vanités, il ne se précipite vers la ruine. Il est nécessaire donc que les pasteurs détiennent les clefs du royaume et appliquent les définitions et les canons de l'Église. Rien qui n'est pas permis, ni convenable à aucun des chrétiens, doit se passer dans les assemblés; car, toutes les fois que le chef est sain, ceux qui sont soumis à sa direction se conservent très facilement indemnes; c'est des directeurs que dépend toute la sollicitude ecclésiastique. C'est pourquoi Notre-Seigneur choisit des Apôtres et il les fait connaître les œuvres qui leur conviennent et la puissance qu'ils ont dans les hauteurs et les profondeurs; et Saint Paul, qui veillait avec sollicitude sur les pasteurs de l'Église, ordonna des métropolitains dans les métropoles et des évêques dans les villes; et les saints Pères qui furent choisis après les Apôtres, marchèrent sur leurs traces.

Mar Aba devait insister sur le pouvoir ecclésiastique et le respect de ses degrés: le patriarche, les métropolitains et les évêques, à cause du désordre qui régnait dans l'Église de Séleucie-Ctésiphon; il confirma la nécessité d'obéir au Patriarche, quand il appelle les métropolitains et les évêques en assemblée, et:

93 SO, 100.

Si les métropolitains ou les évêques se réunissent au siège du patriarche, ou les évêques au siège du métropolitain, et, si, pour quelque motif, le patriarche ou le métropolitain ne se trouve pas dans sa résidence, les métropolitains et les évêques ne peuvent pas même entrer dans la ville où est le siège du patriarche, ou s'il arrive qu'ils y entrent, ils ne peuvent en aucune façon prescrire, agir, rédiger des écrits, relativement au gouvernement ou aux affaires ecclésiastiques, sans lui ou sans sa permission, ni même y accomplir sans lui les fonctions de leur ordre. Il en est de même pour les évêques dans le siège du métropolitain, à moins toutefois qu'ils ne soient avec le patriarche.

Le texte de Mar Aba continue:

Selon la volonté du Christ, les choses paraissent ainsi dans notre région orientale et dans les régions adjacents, selon cette tradition qui est la (tradition) apostolique[94].

Mar Aba rappelle la dualité du régime qui régna pendant quinze ans dans son Église, et l'établissement de la régularité, grâce aux efforts de son prédécesseur Mar Paulus et les siens; les décrets et les décisions pris en assemblée, seront notifiés à tous les évêques, afin d'obtenir le consentement commun, signe du respect de la tradition apostolique et des canons ecclésiastiques.

Chaque fois que les canons synodaux viennent en oubli, les chefs-pasteurs-pères de l'Église doivent les renouveler:

Ces canons, qui malheureusement de nos jours ont été oubliés, nous les avons renouvelés et nous les renouvelons dans ce saint synode de notre assemblée bénie, nous, et vous tous; afin que ces canons qui sont écrits, en ordre, ci-dessous, soient confirmés par nous, par vous, et par toute la communauté, au moyen des signatures et des sceaux, sous la sanction de la parole de Dieu[95].

Le canon XXII du même synode de Mar Joseph dit:

L'assemblée des évêques a aussi voulu que les canons paternels qui ont été renouvelés par le zèle du catholicos Mar Aba, de bonne mémoire, soient observés avec soin, et que quiconque les transgressera reçoive le châtiment de sa faute, selon qu'il paraîtra convenable à l'assemblée générale des évêques[96].

Les métropolitains et les évêques s'assemblent près du patriarche «pour les affaires communes, afin qu'en leur présence mutuelle et par son intermédiaire les choses qui ont besoin d'être corrigées soient corrigées, et que les choses bien réglées soient confirmées et consolidées»[97]. Le canon XVI précise encore que:

Toutes les affaires qu'il convient de traiter en commun, les corrections qui demandent à être faites, seront réglées par leur (évêques, métropolitains et patriarche) intermédiaire de manière à procurer le bien de la communauté. S'il y a une querelle ou une inimitié, elle sera résolue et

94 SO, 69-70, 90-94.
95 SO, Synode de Mar Yausep, 96-98.
96 SO, 108.
97 SO, Synode de Mar Ḥasqiyyel, 380, c. 15.

terminée parmi eux. S'il y a des évêques qui restent et ne viennent pas par négligence, ils seront blâmés par le synode[98].

C'est pour réaliser l'unité spirituelle et visible de l'Église que les synodes se célèbrent en esprit de fidélité à l'enseignement du Christ et de la Tradition apostolique, pour le bien commun de tous. La synodalité étant une marque essentielle de la collégialité dans l'Église, elle est signe de la communion qui unit tous les chrétiens au Christ, et participation réelle au souci de l'Église particulière et universelle.

98 SO, 380, c. 16.

S. A. M. ADSHEAD and K. ADSHEAD

Topography and Sanctity in the North Syrian Corridor

In this paper, systemic topography, as currently being developed especially in France, will be used to cast light on aspects of the sanctity in Theodoret's *Philotheos*. In particular, the notion of a corridor will be used to illumine the diversity in unity of that sanctity, the special role within it of Simeon Stylites, and its possible relationship to an ancient and ongoing Judaeo-Christian ascetic tradition.

Syrian topography and Christian sanctity are, of course, no strangers. Peter Brown, in his famous paper "The Rise and Function of the Holy Man in Late Antiquity" and in his Madrid conference paper "Town, Village and Holy Man: the case of Syria", acknowledges more than once his dependence on Georges Tchalenko's *Villages antiques de la Syrie du Nord.* "Masterly archaeological survey" is his tribute in the former, "inspired evocation of a distinctive area" in the latter. Since Tchalenko and Brown, we have had to see the saints of the Syrian desert as figures in a landscape: the landscape of the lost villages of the limestone massif on the road from Antioch to the imperial frontier, or more widely, from Seleucia on the sea to Seleucia on the Tigris. Yet in his latest book *The Body and Society* Brown has relinquished, where Syria is concerned, the geographical perspective in favour of a more theological tradition in Judaeo-Christian asceticism as his main explanatory theme. It will be argued here that retention of the geographic inspiration, reinvigorated by recent debate, might have served him better. For we feel that in Chapter 16 (the Syrian chapter) something has been forfeited[1].

When Tchalenko wrote, it was against the background of the escape in geography from determinism into "possibilisme": not the milieu making man, but rather the space-time conjuncture offering a range of possibilities. As Lucien Febvre wrote: "Des nécessités, nulle part. Des possibilités, par-

1 P. R. L. Brown, "The Rise and Function of the Holy Man in Late Antiquity" *JRS* 71 (1971) 80-101; "Town, Village and Holy Man: the case of Syria" in D. M. Pippidi, ed. *Assimilation et résistance à la culture gréco-romaine dans le monde ancien* (Paris, 1976); G. Tchalenko, *Villages antiques de la Syrie du Nord* (Paris, 1953): P. R. L. Brown, *The Body and Society* (London, 1988) ch. 16.

tout"[2]. Since the 1960's, however, it has been increasingly recognized that "possibilisme" was not enough: "une philosophie une peu courte" in the words of Pierre Claval, meaning, perhaps, that the field was left too wide open, too little excluded[3]. In particular, possibilisme seemed to shut social and human geography off from the formal systems and theories of systems taken from cybernetics, with which the rest of geography was increasingly preoccupied. Recently therefore the French school has been revitalized by the introduction of a more systemic approach. Since the 1980's there has been an energetic dialogue going on, to which the 1985 *L'Espace géographique* colloque of six papers has made a particularly notable contribution. Other good starting points are the Journal *Le Débat* throughout 1980 and the 1984 Avignon conference *Systèmes et localisations*. Recent developments are conveniently summarized by J.-R. Pitte in "Le Retour de La Géographie" in the revue *Vingtième Siècle* for July-September 1989[4].

What is to be understood by system in this context? Loosely, anything that consists of parts connected together may be called a system. In a system as conceived by human geography, the components will not only be spatio-temporal (the physical landscape of North Syria 360-460 AD, with its orography, climate, flora and fauna), but also cultural: the population, their perceptions and expressions, their interaction with the natural world, their mutual communications. Together these form a whole microcosm which is yet susceptible of formal, even diagrammatic, analysis. In this sense, a system therefore is something to be understood rather than simply observed, as was the case with both the determinist and the possibilist versions of the milieu. A system will have both a history and a geography, its operations will take effect in a variety of time scales, and those effects may be seen as variously determined, probable or only possible in terms of laws, initial conditions, adventitious facts, etc.

The particular system which is relevant to Theodoret's *Philotheos*[5] is that of the North Syrian corridor. A corridor may be defined as a preferred line of movement, whether for war, trade or cultural exchange, between two areas of settled and less restricted circulation. Before Bulliet's revolution of the camel

2 L. Febvre, *La Terre et l'Évolution humaine* (Paris, 1922) p. 234.

3 P. Claval, "Causalité et Géographie" *L'Espace Géographique* 2 (1985) p. 111.

4 *Vingtième Siècle, Revue d'histoire* 23 (juillet-septembre, 1989) 83-90.

5 The translations given are those of R. M. Price in his *A History of the Monks of Syria by Theodoret of Cyrrhus* (Kalamazoo, 1985). For the text we have used P. Canivet and A. Leroy-Molinghen, *Théodoret de Cyr. Histoire des Moines de la Syrie. Sources Chrétiennes 234, 257* (Paris 1979). P. Canivet's *Le Monachisme syrien selon Théodoret de Cyr. Théologie historique 42* has also been indispensable, particularly ch. 7 "Chronologie et Topographie", even though our conclusions differ from those he reached.

against the wheel, North Syria formed such a corridor[6]. It extended, at its widest extent, from one Seleucia to another, at a lesser extent from Antioch to Zeugma, imperial capital to imperial frontier. It was a corridor because to the north lay the escarpment of the Taurus and to the south lay the wilderness of the Desert. Only in the narrow line in between, could waggons and pack animals find the gradients, food, wheelwrights, blacksmiths and other back-up services they required. The only alternative to the road was the river, but it had its problems and Julian's use of it in his attack on Ctesiphon was not encouraging. But the corridor, west to east, was not uninterrupted. Beside the Taurus, there were lesser ranges going north and south: Mt Amanus separating the Antiochid from Cilcia; Mt Silpius, the beginning of the Lebanon, separating the Antiochid from the Upper Orontes, Coele-Syria and the Bekaa; Mt Belus, as Tchalenko called it, the beginning of the Anti-Lebanon, separating Antioch from Beroea, the modern Aleppo. Beyond these, the corridor was interrupted again, north-south, by the gorges of the Euphrates and the Tigris. A corridor, yes, but also a low switchback.

In Theodoret's time, the century between the external schism in northern Syria produced by the rendition of Nisibis in 363 and the internal schism produced by the definition of Chalcedon in 451, the corridor ran most effectively from Antioch to the Roman forts beyond the Euphrates on the upper Khabur. This stretch was divided by its undulations into five sections. First, there was the coastal plain, interrupted by Mt Amanus, but present in Cilicia and extending to the south as far as Latakia. Second, there were the seaword foothills, principally Mt Silpius, focused towards Antioch. Third, there was the limestone massif, skirted to the north by the main road from Antioch to Cyrrhus. Fourth, there were the landward foothills, focussed towards Cyrrhus and the other interior oases such as Edessa. Finally, there was the inland plain, the frontier beyond the Euphrates. It was these five sections which were the habitat of Theodoret's North Syrian sanctity. They provided the opportunities and constraints with which it lived, defining its freedoms of pitch and play. Thus understood as a topographical system, a self-constituting collection of parts, the North Syrian corridor may now be examined as a factor in 3 aspects of the sanctity depicted by Theodoret: its diversity in unity, the specific persona within it of Simeon Stylites, and its relation to earlier forms of Christian spirituality.

6 R. Bulliet, *The Camel and the Wheel* (Harvard, 1975).

The Diversity in Unity of North Syrian Sanctity

Because it was a collection of *parts*, the North Syrian corridor provided Theodoret's holy men with a variety of environments. Consequently a single spirituality was differently schematized as to its base, audience, sphere of activities, and enemies. To bring this out, we will focus on the 3 middle sections of the corridor, the 2 sets of foothills and the massif central, since the coastal and inland plains are more marginal to Theodoret's account.

First, the single spirituality. It was a highly physical spirituality of radical somatization. The body became the expression of the Spirit. Theodoret makes this clear when, having described James of Nisibis' asceticism, he says: "while he thereby wore down his body, he provided his soul unceasingly with spiritual nourishment. Purifying the eye of his thought he prepared a clear mirror for the Holy Spirit and ... he was changed into His Image from glory to glory"[7]. Moreover it was a somatization of a particular kind. Of the three later monastic virtues of poverty, chastity and obedience, the Syrian ascetics most emphasized poverty. Chastity was taken for granted, virginity being only invoked by Theodoret in a passage which dismisses gender differences, and obedience, in a Benedictine or Ignatian sense, was hardly recognized as a virtue[8]. Again, within the category of poverty, of the three basic human needs of food, clothing and shelter, it was the renunciation of shelter which was most emphasized. As Festugière noted, the ascetics of North Syria were characteristically ὑπαίθριοι *hypaithrioi*, out of doors folk[9].

Thus in the case of James of Nisibis, his prototype, Theodoret says: "In spring, summer and autumn he used the thickets with the sky for roof; in the winter season a cave received him and provided scanty shelter"[10]. Peter the Galatian lived in an old tomb as did Zeno of Pontus[11]. Of Maron, the first hermit in the Cyrrhestica, Theodoret tells us that, "Embracing the open air life, he repaired to a hill-top formerly honoured by the impious. Consecrating to God the precinct of demons on it, he lived there pitching a small tent which he seldom used"[12]. Similarly, Eusebius of Asikha: "Repairing to a mountain ridge ῥαχία τις ὄρους and using a mere enclosure θριγκίον whose stones he did not even join together with clay, he continued for the rest of his life to endure the hardship of the open air ... Frozen in winter and burnt in summer, he bore with endurance the contrasting temperatures of the air"[13].

7 Theodoret, p. 13.
8 Theodoret, p. 187.
9 A. J. Festugière, *Antioche Paienne et Chrétienne*, de Boccard, Paris, 1959, pp. 295, 299-306.
10 Theodoret, p. 13.
11 Theodoret, pp. 82, 96.
12 Theodoret, p. 117.
13 Theodoret, p. 126.

Limnaeus lived on a hillside "without a cell or tent or hut" i.e. in another θριγκίον possibly a sheepfold, while his companion John, "Repairing to a jagged ridge, prone to storms and northward facing... has now spent twenty-five years there exposed to the contrasting assaults of the atmosphere"[14]. Even in the case of those ascetics who were not *hypaithrioi* in a strict sense, shelter was kept to a minimum or turned into a form of discipline. Thus Marcianus lived in a cell too small for his body, while Baradatus constructed a chest κιβωτός of similar dimensions[15]. If Francis of Assisi naked followed the naked Christ and Caroline Bynum's holy women saw Christ and themselves as sacred food, the saints of the Syrian desert par excellence proclaimed the homeless Christ, *salus* without *domus*, to use the language of Le Roy Ladurie's *Montaillou*[16], and this holds true whichever section of the corrider they inhabited.

Next, the localized variations, shaped by the parts of the topographical system.

First, there was a variant of the seaward foothills focusing on Antioch. Here Macedonius the Barley Eater may be taken as typical. His base was mobile, in the hills above Antioch; his primary audience was the pious women of the city; his sphere of activity was the imperial capital; and the enemies he confronted were people involved in imperial politics. Theodoret tells us: "He had as his wrestling-ground and stadium παλαίστραν – καὶ στάδιον the tops of the mountains; he did not settle in one place, but now dwelt in this one and then transferred to that. This he did not through dislike of the places but to escape from the crowds of those who visited him... He continued living in this way for forty-five years, using neither tent nor hut, but making his stops in a deep hole"[17]. Among his visitors, Theodoret mentions his own mother who consulted him about her sterility, another patrician lady who suffered from acute *boulimia*, the father of a demoniac girl, and the father of a delirious anoretic. To all these he gave relief, either instantly, or by a house call to the city. In the public sphere, Macedonius was involved in the affairs of the empire. Following the famous riot against the statues in 387, he remonstrated with the generals deputed to punish the city, ordering them to tell the emperor that he could destroy bodies but not recreate them. "He said this in Syriac τῇ σύρᾳ γλώττῃ", Theodoret tells us, "and while the interpreter translated it into Greek, the generals shuddered as

14 Theodoret, pp. 151-152.

15 Theodoret, pp. 38, 178.

16 C.W. Bynum, *Holy Feast and Holy Fast, The Religious significance of Food to Medieval Women* (California, 1987); Emmanuel Le Roy Ladurie, *Montaillou, Village Occitan de 1294 à 1324*, Gallimard, Paris, 1975.

17 Theodoret, p. 100.

they listened, and promised to convey his message to the emperor"[18]. No doubt, if he had lived a generation earlier, he would, like his predecessor Aphrahat the Persian, have taken part in the campaign against Arianism, very much an imperial heresy in the days of emperor Valens[19]. Thus on the seaward foothills, ascetics had a mobile base, their primary audience was pious women, their sphere of activity was the empire, and their enemies were imperial officials and imperial heresies.

Second, there was a variant of the spirituality of massif central, Tchalenko's limestone massif covered with its oil producing villages. Here Simeon Stylites himself may be taken as typical. On his pillar, Simeon was nothing if not conspicious, but his base, unlike Macedonius, was not mobile but static, and static within a coenobitic community. Simeon was not in any true sense a solitary, and contrary to what Gibbon thought, his elevation on the pillar was more evangelical than ascetic. Theodoret comments: "Just as those who have obtained kingship over men alter periodically the images on their coins ... so the universal Sovereign of all things by attaching to piety ... these new and various modes of life τὰς καινὰς ταύτας καὶ παντοδαπὰς πολιτείας, stirs to eulogy the tongues not only of those nurtured in the faith but also of those afflicted by lack of faith"[20]. Simeon's first audience were the faithful of Telanissus, but he soon attracted pilgrims from all over North Syria and eventually from the whole *oikumene*. Because he became a figure in the universal church, his public sphere of activity was its controversies, and his enemies were Nestorianism on the one hand, and Monophysitism on the other. For, again contrary to what Gibbon thought, Simeon was not an extremist. A figure of the universal church, he was well aware of the Catholic *via media*. Thus he reconciled Nestorianizing bishops to Ephesus I, and Monophysitizing monks to Chalcedon. After his death, when his body was peremptorily seized by the patriarch of Antioch, the quadruple pilgrimage basilica of Qalat Seman was built by emperor Zeno as part of his policy of reconciliation between the churches. Theodoret emphasizes the ecclesial character of Simeon's sanctity: "he does not neglect care of the holy churches — now fighting pagan impiety ἑλληνικῇ δυσσεβείᾳ, now defeating the insolence of the Jews, 'Ιουδαίων θρασύτητα, at other times scattering the bands of the heretics, sometimes sending instructions on these matters to the emperor, sometimes rousing the governors to divine zeal, at other times urging the very shepherds of the churches to take still greater care of their flocks"[21].

18 Theodoret, pp. 103-104.

19 Theodoret, p. 74.

20 Theodoret, p. 166. The comparison of Simeon to a dazzling lamp on a lampstand in Theodoret ch. 13 is to the point here but Canivet doubts the authenticity of the passage.

21 Theodoret, p. 177.

Third, there was a variant of the landward foothills focusing on the oases to the south of the Taurus escarpment. Here James of Cyrrhestica may be taken as typical. James was based on the hill of Sheih Khoros, four miles west of Cyrrhus. Like Macedonius the Barley Easter, he was a *hypaithrios*: "this man bidding farewell to all those things, tent and hut and enclosure, has the sky for roof, and lets in all the contrasting assaults of the air, as he is now inundated by torrential rain, now frozen by frost and snow, at other times burnt and consumed by the sun"[22]. But unlike Macedonius and more like Simeon, he was relatively static and public: "Living in this place he is observed by all comers, so that it is unceasingly under the eys of spectators that he serves in combat"[23]. Unlike Simeon, however, James was not associated with any coenobitic community: he was a true eremite. Moreover his audience was only local. When it was throught he was dying, "all the men of the town" οἱ τοῦ ἄστεως ἅπαντες, Theodoret tells us, formed a bodyguard to prevent "the local inhabitants" οἱ περιοίκοι from dismembering him prematurely in search of relics"[24]. His miracles too were local: "Through his blessing many fevers have been quenched, many agues have abated or departed completely, many demons have been forced to flee and water blessed by his hands becomes a preventive medicine"[25]. His public sphere of activity was thus the diocese rather than the church and the enemies he helped Theodoret to combat were not imperial Arianism or the universal Christological heresies, but the by now provincial sect of Marcionism, superannuated even in Gnostic circles by Manichaeism. Though he did not refuse Theodoret's calls for help, James was a more private person than either Macedonius or Simeon. "I did not come to the mountain for another's sake but for my own" he told Theodoret[26].

Vööbus, Festugière and Brown have all in different ways stressed the unity of North Syrian sanctity in the fourth and fifth centuries: its rigorism, orientation to prayer, its combination of somatization and social service[27]. Yet there was diversity as well as unity, and to relate it to the parts of the North Syrian corridor serves to set this in relief. Nonetheless that corridor was also a coherent *collection* of parts. The influence of the corridor *as a whole* may be seen in the special persona of Simeon Stylites.

22 Theodoret, p. 134.
23 Theodoret, p. 124.
24 Theodoret, p. 136.
25 Theodoret, p. 138.
26 Theodoret, p. 246.
27 A. Vööbus, *History of Asceticism in the Syrian Orient, A Contribution to the History of Culture in the Near East,* CSCO 184, 195 Subs. 14, 17 (Louvain, 1958, 1960); A.-J. Festugière, *Les Moines d'Orient* (Paris, 1960-1964); for Peter Brown, see the papers cited in N.I.

Simeon Stylites

Brown's Simeon was a mediator, the good patron between town and country: this relationship, "transvalued" as he put it, made Simeon (and of course the other holy men) mediators in other, further, relations between church and state, between earth and heaven. This interpretation was at once recognized as superior to that of martyr manqué, peasant spokesman, austere enthusiast. Yet there is perhaps more to be said about "the great wonder of the world", Theodoret's μέγα θαῦμα τῆς οἰκουμένης and perhaps the concept of a corridor system will elucidate what that is.

First, Theodoret stresses the vast diffusion of Simeon's fame (φήμη) — "known by all the subjects of the roman empire and has also been heard of by the Persians, the Medes, the Ethiopians, and the rapid spread of his fame as far as the nomadic Scythians has taught his love of labor and his philosophy"[28]. There is a similar passage in ch. 11, including Iberians, Armenians, Himyarites, Spaniards, Britons. It was surely the fact that the transit zone in which his pillar stood linked two populous, developed termini that ensured this wide diffusion, so that both Rome and Ctesiphon were aware of his extraordinary witness. The termini guaranteed his fame.

Second, Theodoret presents the population traversing the area as extremely diverse, ethnically, linguistically, culturally. A Saracen chief, an Ishmaelite queen, bands of Bedouin, locals, not-so-locals, Persian courtiers, Christian deacons "a sea of men standing together in that place, receiving rivers from every side"[29]. While Simeon does of course address the crowds, giving two exhortations (παραινέσεις) a day, Theodoret clearly recognizes that his true message is as a sign or spectacle (θέαμα καινὸν καὶ παράδοξον), something metalinguistic, an arresting *logo* along the journey that both Greek and Syrian, literate and illiterate could all comprehend: the man on the pillar himself. But to be a traffic logo there must be traffic, to be a street lamp there must be a street. So the floating world of the corridor is closely related to the message it is given. One could even go on to speculate on a true "feedback" effect whereby Qalat Seman drew pilgrims to its vast basilica in later centuries, thus itself ultimately altering the character of the system.

Universal and metalinguistic, Simeon was a mediator in a further sense than the other North Syrian ascetics. While he, like they, was a mediator between static groups of the population (this is an aspect emphasized particularly by the Syriac life), he was also a mediator between mobile people: police and robbers, nomads and sedentarists, different groups of

28 Theodoret, p. 160.
29 Theodoret, p. 165.

nomads. Though immobile himself, he was a man of the road, the unifying factor of the topographical system, and not really conceivable without it. He needed the corridor just as the corridor needed him: a mutual implication of topography and sanctity which can last light on the question of North Syrian spirituality to earlier Judaeo-Christian ascetic tradition.

North Syrian sanctity and the Judaeo-Christian ascetic tradition

Recent scholarship has tended to interpret North Syrian asceticism in terms of an ongoing Judaeo-Christian ascetic tradition. There are several reasons for this. First, there is the tendency, exemplified by the work of Helmut Koester, to see developed Christianity as the product of the confluence of distinctive primitive Christianities, among which the Judaeo-Christian stream, stressed by Jean Daniélou and others, was an important one too often underestimated by Western "Pauline" Christians. Second, there has been the delayed but profound impact of the work of Vööbus, which undertakes to provide a systematic account of that stream from its Jewish origins through Tatian and the Encratites to later Christian Syriac piety. Third, traces remain, even in Vööbus, of an orientalizing interpretation: a wish to associate the North Syrian ascetics with fakirs, gymnosophists, Persian dualists, Manichaean *perfecti*, Messalian extremists, etc., and a failure to see the different basis of Christian asceticism as somatization of the Spirit rather than pneumatization (or rejection) of the body. As a result of these reasons, North Syrian asceticism has seemed to require a genealogy and the Judaeo-Christian ascetic tradition has seemed to provide one.

An advantage of the approach through systemic human topography is that it makes any such appeal to long term history less necessary. While background can never fully explain foreground and history must always accept a principle of insufficient reason, it may be argued that North Syrian asceticism can be adequately explained in terms of its own time and place. It was the product of a post-persecution, post conciliar, triumphalist Christianity for which there were no limits to the somatization of the Spirit; a single orthodox culture in two languages along the corridor; and a compression, as a result of the rendition of Nisibis, of that orthodoxy to a new degree of organization and articulation. As noted above, the notion of systemic topography includes not only the spatial, but also the temporal and cultural. For the human geographer, who is thinking in terms of systems rather than possibilities, there can be no pure "milieux naturels". As Jean-Robert Pitte says, once this is appreciated, "personne ne songera plus à couper la géographie dite

30 J.-R. Pitte "Le Retour de la Géographie" *Vingtième Siècle* 23 (1989) p. 88.

'physique' de la géographie dite 'humaine'"[30]. It is not merely that the geography conditions the history, but the history actualizes the geography. Between the two there is a relation of mutual implication, and it is this relationship which constitutes them as parts of a system. Within this perspective, it may be suggested that North Syrian asceticism will be more fruitfully explored through its spatiotemporal conjuncture than through distant antecedents and crosscultural comparisons. North Syria was a movement in space as well as in time.

FREDERIK WISSE

The Naples Fragments of Shenoute's 'De certamine contra diabolum'

THE CODEX

In *Oriens Christianus* 59 (1975), 60-77, I published with Klaus Koschorke and Stefan Timm an edition of the last part of a sermon by the most important Coptic author, the archimandrite Shenoute (died A.D. 451), which we called *De certamine contra diabolum*. The text is preserved in a manuscript owned by the Institut français d'archéologie orientale in Cairo (IFAO 1)[1]. The first part of this sermon did not survive in IFAO 1 and, as far as we knew, also not among the many other fragments of Shenoute's writings which were taken from the White Monastery in Sohar and are now scattered in library collections in Western Europe, Egypt, and the United States.

In the introduction to our edition we pointed out that the incipit to the sermon appeared in a table of contents consisting of the incipits of the various sermons and speeches in IFAO 1, and written by a later hand on the verso of the last page of the codex[2]. On the basis of this incipit — which translates "A loved one asked me years ago" — I was able to identify seven pages from the beginning of the sermon which come from a different codex with the same content as IFAO 1. Most of the surviving pages of this codex are now part of the Borgia collection of the Bibliotheca Nazionale in Naples. These folios of the "Naples Codex" were described and in part excerpted by Georg Zoega[3]; the text was edited and translated into French by E. Amélineau[4].

1 The text of the surviving pages of the codex (pp. 175-375) was published by Émil Chassinat, *Le quatrième livre des entretiens et épître de Shenouti* (Mémoires de l'Institut français d'archéologie orientale, Tome 23), Le Caire 1911.

2 Neither Chassinat nor P. du Bourguet, who edited and translated two and a part of a third of the tractates in IFAO 1 (see notes 14, 16 and 20), recognized the list of incipits. Afterwards I discovered that Hans Quecke had properly identified the list in his article, "Ein Pachomiuszitat bei Schenute", in: *Probleme der koptischen Literatur*, ed. P. Nagel (Wissenschaftliche Beiträge der Martin-Luther-Universität Halle-Wittenberg 1968/1), Halle 1968, p. 157. He already intimated some of the conclusions which are presented here more fully.

3 *Catalogus codicum copticorum manuscriptorum qui in Museo Borgiano Velitris adservantur*, Rome 1810 (reprint Hildesheim/New York 1973), pp. 455-470 (= Num. 194).

4 *Œuvres de Schenoudi* I, Paris 1907, pp. 365-441. Johannes Leipoldt used one folio (Naples Codex, pp. 277-8) in *Sinuthii archimandritae vita et opera omnia* III (CSCO 42, script. copt. 2), Louvain 1960 (reprint of 1908), pp. 74-76.

The pages of the Naples Codex measure 25 by 31.5 cm. with two columns of 28 to 31 lines per page. Zoega assigned the writing to his class VIII.

Thanks to the fact that the content of the Naples Codex runs parallel to IFAO 1, it proved possible to arrive at a precise reconstruction of the content of these two fragmentary codices, and to find further attestation for the tractates contained in them. The pagination ratio between the Naples Codex and IFAO 1 proved to be a constant of 1 to 1.21, which made it possible to estimate the pagination of the incipits in the lost parts of the codices. I have been able to find the following information on each of the tractates:

1. *De idolis vici Pneueit I*

This is the famous sermon on Psalm 18:13-17 (17:14-18 LXX) which Shenoute preached at the so-called Water Church in Antinoe after his Christian supporters had prevented his trial on charges of temple plunder[5]. The incipit is found in the table of contents of IFAO 1, but the text, which must have occupied pages 1-108, is lost. This sermon would have covered the first ninety pages of the Naples Codex; of these pp. 15-18, 35-50, 55-56 and 83-84 survive[6]. One other fragmentary codex is known which included this sermon as its first tractate. A folio in the Bibliothèque Nationale in Paris (P 130^5 fol. 68) preserves the superscript and first part of the sermon[7]. The pagination of this folio is missing but it must involve pages 1-2. Two further fragments of this sermon, probably from the same codex, are preserved in the Bibliotheca Nazionale in Naples (pp. 19-28 and 37-44)[8].

2. *Adversus diabolum*

The incipit of the second tractate is found in the table of contents of IFAO 1 as well as in the fragmentary incipit list of Shenoute's writings preserved in Vienna, where it occupies number 84[9]. The incipit translated: "Since it is necessary to pursue the devil". The theme of the struggle against the devil links this sermon with the preceding and following ones. The text must have occupied pages 109-20 in IFAO 1. In the Naples Codex the incipit would have been on page 90, while the ending is preserved on page 100. The

5 Leipoldt, *Schenute von Atripe und die Entstehung des national-ägyptische Christentums*, TU n.F. 10, Leipzig 1904, pp. 179-80.

6 Edited by Amélineau, *Œuvres* I, pp. 365-387.

7 Leipoldt, *Sinuthii* III, pp. 84-86.

8 Zoega, *Catalogus*, pp. 517-8 (= Num. 208) and Amélineau, *Œuvres* II, pp. 134-43 and I, pp. 371-380.

9 Published by Carl Wessely in *Griechische und koptische Texte theologischen Inhalts* I (Studien zur Palaeographie und Papyruskunde IX), Leipzig 1909, pp. 167-8.

surviving fragment begins with page 97[10]. The ending of the sermon is also preserved on a folio from another codex in the Biblioteca Nazionale in Naples (p. 239)[11]. It is followed by a different tractate than in IFAO 1 and the Naples Codex[12].

3. *De certamine contra diabolum*

Only the last eleven pages (175-85) of this lengthy sermon survive in IFAO 1. The incipit can be estimated to have been on page 120. The Naples Codex preserves the beginning pages and two later folios (100-2 and 111-4) which are edited here[13]. The ending of the sermon can be estimated to have been on page 154.

4. *Adversus daemonem*

The text is fully preserved in IFAO 1 on pages 185-204. A fragment of the Naples Codex in the Egyptian Museum in Cairo preserves the last three pages (165-7) of this sermon[14]. The incipit would have been on page 154.

5. *Epistula ad servum quemdam daemonis*

The text is fully preserved in IFAO 1 on pages 204-16. The text of the letter in the Naples Codex survives on the Cairo fragment 8006 (pp. 167-76) and on a poorly preserved folio (pp. 177-8) in the Bibliothèque Nationale in Paris (P 131^{5} fol. 8)[15].

6. *De disciplina ecclesiastica*

The full text is preserved in IFAO 1 on pp. 216-28. Also the copy in the Naples Codex is complete. The first page (178) is supplied by the Bibliothèque

10 Zoega, *Catalogus*, p. 459 and Amélineau, *Œuvres* I, pp. 387-390.

11 Zoega, *Catalogus*, pp. 415-29 (= Num. 188), published by Amélineau, *Œuvres* I, pp. 211-12. He was unaware that he had edited and translated the ending of the same sermon twice.

12 The sermon must have begun approximately on page 230 of this codex. The order of tractates agrees with the Vienna list of incipits, for the tractate which follows it is number 85.

13 Zoega, *Catalogus*, pp. 460-3 and Amélineau, *Œuvres* I, pp. 391-397.

14 This sermon was edited by P. du Bourguet, "Diatribe de Chenouté contre le démon", *BSAC* 16 (1962), 17-71. The text of the sermon on the Cairo fragment was published by W. E. Crum in *Coptic Monuments*, Le Caire 1902, p. 3. The fragment is Nr. 8006 in the "Catalogue général des antiquités égyptiennes du Musée du Caire". It was also included by Leipoldt in *Sinuthii* III, pp. 77-8; he gave it the less fortunate title *Adversus Saturnum I.*

15 The part on the Cairo fragment was published by Leipoldt under the title *Adversus Saturnum II* (*Sinuthii* III, pp. 79-84); the Paris folio was published by Amélineau, *Œuvres* I, pp. 443-4. The letter was translated by John Barns, "Shenoute as Historical Source", in *Actes du Xe congrès international de papyrologues*, ed. J. Wolski, Warsaw 1964, pp. 151-9.

Nationale (P 131⁵ fol. 8), and the rest (pp. 179-88) are preserved among the folios in Naples[16]. There is a further folio of this tractate from another codex in the Bibliothèque Nationale (P 130⁵ fol. 23). It involves pages 177-8 and is equivalent to IFAO 1, pp. 121,32-123,17[17].

7. *Ad Jobinum comitem*

The full text is extant in IFAO 1 on pages 228-50. Only the first part (pp. 188-194) of the address is preserved in the Naples Codex[18]. The ending would have been on page 208.

8. *Ad Flavianum ducem*

The full text is extant in IFAO 1 on pages 250-91. The table of contents on the verso of the last page of IFAO 1 and the Vienna incipit list treat this long address as three distinct items[19]. The reason for this is that Shenoute quoted his letter to Bakanos (pp. 260-263) in the body of the text which created the impression of three distinct parts[20]. Of the Naples Codex two folios survive near the beginning of the tractate (pp. 211-4) and most of the third part including the ending (pp. 223-42)[21]. There are two folios in the Bibliothèque Nationale (P 130⁵ fol. 47 and 53) from two other codices (pp. 133-4 and 27-8) which correspond to IFAO 1, pp. 259,25-262,37 and 273,43-276,3.

9. *Ad Heraclammum ducem: de modestia clericorum et magistratuum*

The full text is extant in IFAO 1 on pages 292-319. Only the superscript and the first few lines survive in the Naples Codex (p. 242)[22]. Four folios of the same address from a different codex are in the British Museum (pp. 197-204).

16 The address was edited by P. du Bourguet, "Entretiens de Chenouté sur des problèmes de discipline ecclésiastique et de cosmologie", *BIFAO* 57 (1958), 99-141. He used Chassinat's edition of IFAO 1 as well as Zoega, *Catalogus*, pp. 463-5 and Amélineau, *Œuvres* I, pp. 397-406 which represent the Naples Codex. He was unaware of the Paris folio, since Amélineau had failed to make the connection with the Naples codex (*Œuvres* I, p. 444).

17 Amélineau, *Œuvres* I, pp. 401-2.

18 Zoega, *Catalogus*, p. 466 and Amélineau, *Œuvres* I, pp. 406-410 and 414-416. Amélineau mistook p. 213 for 193 and 214 for 194. This mistake was compounded when he numbered page 194 as 213 and page 193 as 214.

19 It must have involved numbers 34-36 of the Vienna incipit list. Nr. 34 was on the preceding page which is lost. For Nr. 35 only part of the incipit survives.

20 The first part, IFAO 1, pp. 250,35-260,16, was edited by P. du Bourguet, "Entretien de Chenouté sur les devoirs des juges, *BIFAO* 55 (1956), 85-109.

21 Zoega, *Catalogus*, pp. 466-9 and Amélineau, *Œuvres* I, pp. 410-14 and 416-34. His p. 193 is 213 and his p. 194 is 214.

22 Zoega, *Catalogus*, p. 469 and Amélineau, *Œuvres* I, p. 435.

They correspond to IFAO 1, pp. 292,50-300,17[23]. This tractate is Nr. 37 in the Vienna incipit list.

10. *De bonis operibus* and *Pseudo-Liberius: Oratio consolatoria de morte Athanasii*

The full text is preserved in IFAO 1, pages 319-75. The table of contents on the verso of IFAO 1, page 375 and the Vienna incipit list treat this sermon as two distinct tractates, Nr. 38 and 39 in the Vienna list. Of the Naples Codex only three folios of *De bonis operibus* have been identified (pp. 277-8, 287-8 and 293-4) and none of the *Oratio*[24]. A section of *De bonis operibus* equivalent to IFAO 1, pages 333,35-337,55 was excerpted for a florilegium[25]. The *Oratio* (IFAO 1, pp. 366,34-375,26) is a full citation by Shenoute, introduced at the end of *De bonis operibus*, of what he believed to be an oration by pope Liberius on the occasion of the death of Athanasius. Of course, since Liberius died in 366, seven years before Athanasius, it could not have been written by him[26]. The *Oratio* is also partially preserved on three folios from another codex in which it is treated as an independent tractate[27].

THE TEXT

Unfortunately, Amélineau's edition of the Naples fragments of *De certamine contra diabolum* is very untrustworthy. The many mistakes in his transcription of the text are due to his usual carelessness[28], but the serious shortcomings in

23 Coptic Ms. Nr. 208 transcribed by W. E. Crum, *Catalogue of the Coptic manuscripts in the British Museum*, London 1905, pp. 90ff. The text was edited by Leipoldt, *Sinuthii* III, pp. 33-37.

24 Zoega, *Catalogus*, p. 470 and Amélineau, *Œuvres* I, pp. 435-441.

25 Leipoldt called it *De Aethiopum invasionibus III* in *Sinuthii* III, pp. 5-6, 69-77, 244-246. Of the nine fragments which he assigned to this florilegium G and J and possibly also H are actually not part of it but belong to *De bonis operibus*. G is British Museum Coptic Ms. Nr. 207 (Crum, *Catalogue*, pp. 89-90) and begins before the section excerpted in the florilegium; its text is parallel to IFAO 1, pp. 333,20-336,13. J is a folio from the Naples Codex (pp. 277-8).

26 I have published an edition of *Pseudo-Liberius: Oratio consolatoria de morte Athanasii* in *Le Muséon* 103 (1990), pp. 43-65.

27 Bibliothèque Nationale P 130[5] fol. 128 (pp. 329-30; the *Oratio* begins on p. 330) and Biblioteca Nazionale in Naples Casetta I.B. 14, fasc. 465 (pp. 335-338). The Naples fragment was described and partially transcribed by Zoega, *Catalogus*, p. 634. It is preceded in this codex by *Adversus Graecos de mortibus hominum* (see Leipoldt, *Sinuthii*, III, pp. 3-4, 41-44) which is Nr. 69 in the Vienna incipit list.

28 Where he differs with Zoega's transcription the latter is always correct. Zoega transcribed of the Naples fragments of *De certamine* pp. 100,30-101,19; 102,13-24; 111,1-114,57. Where Zoega departs from the manuscript (see my note for 101,6f.) Amélineau follows him. The serious shortcomings of Amélineau's edition of Shenoute's writings are well known. This necessitated a complete reediting begun by J. Leipoldt, with the help of E. W. Crum, in

his translation may find some excuse in Leipoldt's comment: "Im übrigen gibt dieses Schenutestück dem Übersetzer mehr als ein zur Zeit unlösbares Rätsel auf"[29]. A reediting of this interesting and challenging piece is clearly warranted.

The text follows classical Sahidic orthography. The scribe used few supralinear strokes. They are found consistently on *nomina sacra* and sporadically as a syllable marker, limited largely to MNT and the final syllable of a word. If an initial mu or nu has syllabic value it never has a supralinear stroke but occasionally a supralinear dot.

Decorations separate the author's name from the descriptive title, and the superscript from the beginning of the sermon. The edited text follows the paragraphing of the manuscript. In the manuscript paragraphs are marked by an enlarged letter, usually the first one in the paragraph, written in the left margin of the column. Spacing within the line is used to separate some sentences or parts of sentences. This spacing has been indicated in the edited text.

A rosette was placed in the margin next to the incipit (100,37) no doubt to mark the liturgical annotation at the bottom of the page which is also preceded by a rosette and which reads "Apa Zenobios". The reference is most likely to the monastery founder Zanufius whose feast was celebrated on the sixth day of ʿAmsir. It appears that the number marks the ninth liturgical annotation in the Naples Codex[30]. Portions of Shenoute's writings are among the liturgical lessons included in the Coptic lectionaries[31]. They were listed in liturgical directories of which fragments survive[32].

Sinuthii archimandritae vita et opera omnia III and IV, CSCO 42 and 73, script. copt. 2 and 5, Louvain 1960 and 1954 (reprint of 1908 and 1913).

29 *Schenute*, p. 71, note 4.

30 Other liturgical annotations preserved in the fragments of the Naples codex are:
p. 45, # 5 "concerning catechumens" (the marginal annotation in the parallel text, Zoega, Num. 208, p. 43 reads: "5 concerning catechumens being about to be baptized").
p. 167, # 15 "concerning the ninth day of Toubi, the day on which our father Shenoute caught the devil".
p. 182, without the expected number 16, "the second day of Pauni" (the marginal annotation in the parallel text, IFAO 1, p. 221 reads: "concerning John the Baptist and concerning the sun of Gibeon").
p. 188, # 17 "concerning the archangel Gabriel".
p. 225, # 21 "concerning the fast of 40 days" (i.e. lent).
p. 231, without a number, "concerning our father Pachomius" (for this see Quecke, "Pachomiuszitat", pp. 155-71).
p. 242, # 22 "concerning our father Apa Shenoute" (the marginal annotation in the parallel text in IFAO 1, p. 294 reads: "concerning our holy father Shenoute").
p. 287, # 27 "the feast of Apa Macarius" (the marginal annotation in the parallel text in IFAO 1 reads: "concerning Apa Macarius".

31 Nine of these are included in "The Homilies or Exhortations of the Holy Week Lectionary" edited by O. H. E. Burmester in *Le Muséon* 45 (1932), pp. 1-70.

32 See Quecke, "Pachomiuszitat", pp. 161-64. He prefers the Greek term "typikon" for these

There is also a rosette in the middle of 111,4 marking the quotation from Job 40:18a (23a LXX) "If the inundation comes he does not notice". Today there is no longer a marginal annotation visible in the manuscript, but Zoega reports the gloss "concerning the ascent of the water"[33]. No doubt the reference is to the yearly inundation of the Nile at which time Shenoute's comments on Job 40:18a in *De certamine contra diabolum* 111,4-112,7 were to be read in the liturgy[34].

There are only two scribal errors in the fragments[35]. The text was established on the basis a microfilm copy of the manuscript[36]. Zoega's extensive excerpts from the fragments proved to be very accurate except for 101,6f. where he introduces a curious variant reading without specifying manuscript support[37]; Amélineau follows Zoega in this reading.

THE SUPERSCRIPT

The Greek form of Shenoute's name in the genitive case (100,30) is found in the superscripts of many of the surviving tractates. Leipoldt's conclusion that this indicates that the writings so introduced were originally written in Greek is unwarranted[38]. The Greek form in the genitive introduces all the Shenoute entries in the liturgical directories (typika). Even though some of Shenoute's letters and speeches must originally have been written in Greek, this is only clear from the occasion for which they were written.

Both the name and the descriptive title in the superscript are likely secondary editorial additions. The surviving folios of the sermon in the Naples Codex and in IFAO 1 do not reflect the content of the descriptive title. Since the beginning of the sermon is based on the Leviathan account in Job 40 and 41[39], it is possible that the title refers to something in the missing

liturgical directories. They include the incipit of the Shenoute reading followed by the incipit of the tractate. Marginal annotation in some of the codices containing Shenoute's writings facilitated finding the appropriate lessons. The advantage of numbering the annotations is not clear; the numbers are lacking in IFAO 1.

33 *Catalogus*, p. 468, note 102.

34 The obelus in the margin of 112,7 marks most likely the end of the reading.

35 See my notes for 101,52 and 112, 56.

36 I am grateful to Tito Orlandi for supplying me with microfilm prints and for his invaluable advice.

37 See my note for 101,6f.

38 *Schenute*, p. 71, note 5.

39 Job 40:15-23a in Hebrew = 40:15-23 in Greek = 40:10-18 in Coptic; 40:23b-24 is missing in Greek and Coptic; 41:1a and 2a in Hebrew = 40:25 in Greek = 40:20 in Coptic; 41:2b in Hebrew = 40:26 in Greek = 40:21 in Coptic; 41:3-11 in Hebrew = 40:27-32 and 41:1-3 in Greek = 40:22-28 and 41:1-2 in Coptic; 41:12 is missing in Greek and Coptic; 41:13-16b in Hebrew = 41:5-8 in Greek = 41:4-7 in Coptic; 41:16a and 17 are missing in Greek and Coptic; 41:18-34 in Hebrew = 41:10-26 in Greek = 41:9-25 in Coptic (41:23b, 29a and 22a

folios, perhaps extended comments on Job 41:7 (Coptic) "and a spirit (or wind) shall not pass through" combined with John 3:8. Shenoute's point would have been that Satan cannot hinder the Spirit.

CONTENT

De certamine is part of a series of four sermons and a letter in the Naples Codex and IFAO 1 which focus on the need for Christians to struggle against the devil. Evidently they were grouped on the basis of the shared topic. Demonology was a frequent topic in early Christian literature and especially in monastic writings[40]. Shenoute's comments on the subject conform to a large extent to those found elsewhere in Patristic literature, but he makes a notable contribution in his own right. It is clear that he was familiar with Athanasius' *Vita Antonii*, which speaks often about Antonius' successful struggle against demons (chapters 6, 10, 13, 14, 16, 19, 21, 23, 51 and 70). Shenoute also follows the lead of *Vita Antonii* chapters 5 and 24 in interpreting the Leviathan figure in Job 40 and 41 as a description of the devil. He may have known some of the other writings of Athanasius, and perhaps the *Catecheses illuminandorum* by Cyril of Jerusalem, which often counsel the reader to fight against demons.

The *Vita Sinuthii* includes a legendary account of Shenoute's own struggle with the devil. It was commemorated in the liturgy on the ninth day of Toubi. Apparently at that occasion the first part of the "Epistula ad servum quemdam daemonis", the fifth treatise in the Naples Codex and IFAO 1, was read[41]. The passage in the *Vita Sinuthii* translates:

> Furthermore it happened one day, when my father lived in the monastery, that, behold, the devil entered together with a multitude of demons. And he spoke to my father threateningly and wickedly. And my father, when he saw the devil, recognized (him) immediately. Forthwith he leaped up, he grabbed for him and seized him throwing him on the ground. And he put his knee upon him and cried out to the brethren who were with him, "Catch these others who follow him". And immediately they (i.e. the demons) dissolved like smoke[42].

It is likely that the sermon followed a public reading of the section on Leviathan in Job 40 and 41, and it is assumed that the dragon is the

are missing in Greek and Coptic). The Coptic version was translated from the Greek which often varies in meaning from the Hebrew.

40 For a summary see A. Kallis, "Geister (Dämonen) II. Griechische Väter", *RAC*, IX, pp. 700-15.

41 See the liturgical annotation # 15 listed above in note 30. The rosette indicate that the reading starts at the beginning of the letter.

42 Translated from the text published by J. Leipoldt, *Sinuthii vita bohairice* (CSCO 41, script. coptici, 1), Louvain 1951 (reprint of 1906), ch. 73.

Demon[43]. Shenoute begins with the Greek etymology of the word δαιμόνιον. He is aware of the etymology δαήμων "knowing", suggested by Plato in *Crato* 398b, as well as the more common δαίομαι "to distribute"[44], though he gives them decidedly negative connotations (100,37-101,28).

The transition to the commentary on verses from Job 40 and 41 is rather abrupt. The link is supplied by "shamelessness" which, according to Shenoute, is closely associated with the name "demon" and a basic characteristic of the devil. He sees this implied in Job 40:13[45] which describes the Dragon (δράκων) as having ribs of iron. This makes it possible for the devil not to be ashamed when being trampled by the faithful, and to return time and again for another fight and another defeat. In this way the righteous have multiple chances of winning imperishable crowns. Indeed, one could say that "if there were no devil... there would not be a difference betweens the pious and the impious" (101,28-102,43). This claim becomes the occasion for Shenoute to refute the view that "if Satan had not come into being every person would have been good" (102,44ff.).

Pages 103-110 are missing and it is uncertain which verses from Job 40 and 41 were commented on in this section, since Shenoute may not have commented on all the verses and did not treat them in order. On page 111,4 a commentary begins on the inundation mentioned in Job 40,18. Shenoute rejects the opinion that the inundation refers to the coming of Christ, or to the prayers of the faithful, or to the cross. Rather, he claims, it refers to the heresy of those who "do not confess the trinity". If their deeds increase, Satan takes no notice of them and heedlessly tramples upon them (111,4-112,47).

In the next section Job 41:17. 15b. 21a. 13b. 6b; 40:11. 16; 41:15a and 12 are all interpreted with reference to the enemies of God, i.e. heretics and idolaters. They are not able to oppose the devil and end up being his servants. The "terror which is around his teeth" (Job 41:5b) refers to idols which "instill fear in the foolish". Shenoute is familiar with idols for he has personally been involved in taking them from pagan houses (112,8-114,32)[46]. In 114,33 a new section begins with a commentary on Job 40:26. It is impossible to say how far the commentary on the Dragon in Job continued in the lost section of 31 pages in the Naples Codex and IFAO 1. The final part

43 Shenoute often uses the name "demon" for the devil (cf. Leipoldt, *Schenoute*, p. 83). He is even identified with the pagan god Cronos whose temple was near Shenoute's White Monastery (du Bourguet, "Diatribe", p. 53).

44 Cf. *RAC*, IX, 600.

45 All references will be to the Coptic verse numeration. For the equivalent verse numbers in Hebrew and Greek see note 38.

46 See Leipoldt, *Schenute*, pp. 178-82.

of the sermon preserved in IFAO 1 continues on the theme of the struggle against the devil, but no longer with references to the book of Job[47].

The nineteen biblical quotations in the Naples fragments of *De certamine contra diabolum* conform closely to the published editions of the Sahidic Old and New Testament[48]. They have been marked and identified in the translation; textual variants are discussed in the notes to the text and translation[49].

ⲥⲓⲛⲟⲩⲑⲓⲟⲩ

> ⲛⲑⲉ ⲉⲧⲉ ⲙⲛ ⲣⲱⲙⲉ ⲉϥⲟ ⲛⲧⲉⲝⲟⲩⲥⲓⲁ· ⲙ̇ⲡⲉⲡⲛ̅ⲁ̅ ⲉⲧⲣⲉϥⲕⲱⲗⲩ ⲙ̇ⲡⲉⲡⲛ̅ⲁ̅ ⲙ̅ⲛ ⲡⲉⲧⲉⲓⲙⲉ ⲟⲛ ⲉⲧⲉϩⲓ̈ⲏ ⲙⲡⲉⲡⲛ̅ⲁ̣̅

ⲁⲟⲩⲙⲉⲣⲓⲧ ϫⲛⲟⲩⲓ̈ ϩⲁⲑⲏ ⲛ̇ⲛⲉⲓⲣⲟⲙⲡⲉ ⲉϥϣⲓⲛⲉ ⲉⲧⲃⲉ ⲡⲇⲓⲁⲃⲟⲗⲟⲥ· ϫⲉ ⲟⲩ ⲡⲉ ⲡⲉⲓⲣⲁⲛ· ϫⲉ ⲇⲁⲓ̈ⲙⲱⲛⲓⲟⲛ ⲛⲧⲁϥϭⲱⲗⲡ ⲛⲁⲓ ⲉⲃⲟⲗ ϩⲙ ⲡⲥⲏⲩ ⲙ̇ⲡⲉⲓⲡⲓⲣⲁⲥⲙⲟⲥ ⲧⲉⲛⲟⲩ·

ⲇⲁⲓⲙⲱⲛⲓⲟⲛ ⲡⲉ ⲡⲣⲁⲛ ⲉⲧⲉ ⲙⲛ ⲕⲉⲣⲁⲛ ⲥⲏϣ ⲉⲣⲟϥ

ⲛϩⲉⲗⲗⲏⲛ ⲙⲉⲛ· ⲛⲣⲉϥϫⲉ ϣⲃⲱ· ⲉⲩⲥⲡⲟⲩⲇⲁⲍⲉ ⲉⲕⲟⲥⲙⲉⲓ ⲛ̇ⲛ̇ϣⲁϫⲉ ⲉⲧϩⲟⲟⲩ ϣⲁⲩⲃⲱⲗ ⲙⲙⲟϥ ⲛⲧⲉⲓϩⲉ ||**101** ϫⲉ ⲇⲁⲓⲙⲱⲛⲓⲟⲛ ⲡⲉ ⲡⲉⲧⲥⲟⲟⲩⲛ ⲏ̣ ⲡⲉⲧⲡⲱϣ ⲛϩⲉⲛⲙⲉⲣⲓⲥ ⲉϫⲙ ⲡⲟⲩⲁ ⲡⲟⲩⲁ·

ⲁⲛⲟⲕ ϩⲱⲱⲧ ϯⲛⲁⲟⲩⲱϣⲃ ⲟⲩⲃⲉ ⲛⲉⲩϣⲁϫⲉ ⲛⲧⲁϫⲟⲟⲥ ϫⲉ ⲇⲁⲓⲙⲱⲛⲓⲟⲛ ⲡⲉ ⲡⲉⲧⲥⲟⲟⲩⲛ· ⲙⲡⲱϣ ⲛϩⲉⲛⲧⲟⲉ ⲉϫⲛ ⲛⲁⲧⲛⲟⲩⲧⲉ· ⲉⲧⲉ ⲛⲁⲓ ⲛⲉ ⲙⲙⲛⲧⲁⲡⲓⲥⲧⲟⲥ· ⲛ̇ϫⲱϩⲙ· ⲙ̇ⲙⲛⲧⲁⲧⲁⲙⲁϩⲧⲉ· ⲛϫⲓ̈ ⲛϭⲟⲛⲥ ⲙⲛ ϩⲱⲃ ⲛⲓⲙ ⲉⲧⲥⲧⲏⲩ ⲉ̇ⲃⲟⲗ·

ⲛⲛⲁϩⲣ̅ⲛ ⲛⲉⲧⲟⲩⲁ͡ⲁⲃ ⲇⲉ ⲛⲧⲟⲟⲩ· ⲇⲁⲓⲙⲱⲛⲓⲟⲛ ⲡⲉ ⲡⲣⲁⲛ ⲉⲧⲥⲧⲏⲩ ⲉⲃⲟⲗ· ⲁⲩⲱ ⲉⲧϩⲟⲟⲩ· ⲉⲣⲉⲛⲉⲓⲕⲉⲣⲁⲛ ⲧⲏϭ ⲉϩⲟⲩⲛ ⲉⲡⲉⲓⲣⲁⲛ ϫⲉ ⲥⲟϭ· ⲁⲑⲏⲧ ⲁⲧϣⲓ̈ⲡⲉ· ⲧⲁⲓ ⲧⲉ ⲑⲉ ⲛ̇ⲧⲁⲩϫⲟⲟⲥ ⲉⲛⲉϥⲥⲡⲓ̈ⲣⲟⲟⲩⲉ ϫⲉ ϩⲉⲛⲡⲉⲛⲓⲡⲉ ⲛⲉ· ϫ̣ⲉ̣ ⲛ̅ϥϣⲓⲡⲉ ⲁⲛ̣ ⲉⲩϩⲱⲙ ⲉϩⲣⲁⲓ̈ ⲉ̇ϫⲱϥ ⲙⲛ ⲛⲉϥⲕⲁⲕⲓⲁ· ϩⲓⲧⲛ ⲛⲉⲧϫⲣⲟ ⲉⲣⲟϥ ⲛⲟⲩⲟⲉⲓϣ ⲛⲓⲙ ⲉⲩⲣ ⲡⲟⲗⲩⲙⲟⲥ ⲛⲙⲙⲁϥ ⲉⲩⲕⲱⲛ̅ⲥ̅ ⲙⲙⲟϥ ϩⲛ̅ ⲧⲉⲩⲡⲓⲥⲧⲓⲥ· ⲁⲗⲗⲁ ⲙⲛⲛⲥⲁ ⲧⲣⲉϥⲡⲱⲧ ⲉⲃⲟⲗ ⲙ̇ⲙⲟⲟⲩ ⲉϥϭⲟⲧⲡ· ⲉⲩⲡⲏⲧ ⲛⲥⲱϥ ϩⲛ ⲛⲉⲩⲡⲣⲁⲝⲓⲥ ⲛⲁⲅⲁⲑⲟⲛ· ⲉⲙⲟⲟⲩⲧϥ ⲛⲑⲉ

47 See K. Koschorke, S. Timm and F. Wisse, "Schenute: De certamine contra diabolum", *OrChr* 59 (1975) 60-77.

48 E. Amélineau, "The Sahidic Translation of the Book of Job", *Transactions of the Society of Biblical Archaeology* IX, London 1893, pp. 470-72; J. Schleifer, "Sahidische Bibel-Fragmente aus dem British Museum zu London II", *Sitzungsberichte der Kais. Akademie der Wissenschaften in Wien.* Philosophisch-Historische Klasse. 164.6, Wien 1911, pp. 21-23; William H. Worrell, *The Proverbs of Solomon in Sahidic Coptic according to the Chicago Manuscript*, Chicago 1931; L.-Th. Lefort, M. Wilmet et R. Draguet, *Concordance du Nouveau Testament sahidique*, CSCO 124, 173, 183, 185, 196, Louvain 1950-1960 (based on Pierpont Morgan manuscripts of the Gospels); H. Thompson, *The Coptic Version of the Acts of the Apostles and Pauline Epistles in the Sahidic Dialects*, Cambridge 1932.

49 Since Shenoute's writings include numerous, precise biblical quotations they are of great text-critical value for the Sahidic Old and New Testament (cf. Leipoldt, *Schenute*, pp. 83f.).

ⲛⲛⲉⲧⲉⲣⲉϩⲉⲛⲥⲏϥⲉ ⲛ̇ⲧⲟⲟⲧⲟⲩ ⲙⲛ ϩⲉⲛϩⲛⲁⲁⲩ ⲙ̇ⲙⲓϣⲉ ⲉⲩⲡⲏⲧ ⲛⲥⲁ ⲛⲉⲩϫⲁϫⲉ ⲉϥⲟⲧⲟⲩ ⲉⲃⲟⲗ

ⲡⲁⲗⲓⲛ ⲟⲛ ϥ<ⲕⲧⲟ> ⲙⲙⲟϥ ϩⲛ ⲟⲩⲙⲛ̄ⲧⲁⲧⲃⲁⲗ ϥⲧⲟⲗⲙⲁ ⲉϯ ⲟⲩⲃⲏⲩ

ⲡϫⲟⲉⲓⲥ ⲡⲛⲟⲩⲧⲉ ⲡⲡⲁⲛⲧⲟⲕⲣⲁⲧⲱⲣ ⲡⲉⲧϯ ⲙⲙⲟϥ· ⲉ̇ϩⲣⲁⲓ ⲉⲛⲉⲓⲇⲓⲙⲱⲣⲓⲁ· ⲛⲧⲉⲓϩⲉ· ⲭⲱⲣⲓⲥ ⲡⲕⲱϩ̄ⲧ ⲛ̇||**102**ⲧ̣ⲅⲉϩⲉⲛⲛⲁ ⲉ̣[ⲧⲥⲃ]ⲧⲱⲧ ⲛⲁϥ ⲉⲧⲣⲉⲛⲉϥⲇⲓⲕⲁⲓⲟⲥ ⲡⲱⲧ ⲛⲥⲱϥ ⲛⲟⲩⲟⲉⲓϣ ⲛ̇ⲓ̈ⲙ ⲛⲑⲉ ⲛϩⲉⲛϣⲁϩ ⲛⲕⲱϩⲧ ϩⲛ ⲧⲉⲩⲙⲛ̄ⲧϩⲁⲣϣ ϩⲏⲧ ϩⲛ ⲧⲉⲩϩⲩⲡⲟⲙⲓ̈ⲛⲏ

ⲉⲣϣⲁⲛⲡⲉⲧϣⲱϫⲉ ϫⲣⲟ· ⲛⲟⲩⲥⲟⲡ ⲛⲟⲩⲱⲧ ⲟⲩⲕⲗⲟⲙ ⲛⲟⲩⲱⲧ ⲡⲉ ϣⲁϥϫⲓⲧϥ ⲁⲩⲱ ⲉⲃⲟⲗ ϫⲉ ⲟⲩⲉⲧ ⲛⲁⲑⲗⲟⲛ ⲛⲛⲉⲧϩ̄ⲛ ⲛⲁⲅⲱⲛ ⲟⲩⲉⲧ ⲛⲁⲑⲗⲟⲛ ⲛ̇ⲛⲉⲧⲡⲏⲧ ϩⲛ ⲛⲉⲓ̈ⲙⲁ ⲙⲡⲱⲧ ⲛⲁⲓ ϫⲉ ⲡⲱⲧ ⲛ̇ⲧⲉⲓϩⲉ ϫⲉ ⲉⲧⲉⲧⲛⲁⲧⲁϩⲟ ⲟⲩⲉⲧ ⲛⲉⲕⲗⲟⲙ ⲛⲁⲧⲧⲁⲕⲟ· ⲟⲩⲉⲧ ⲛⲉⲕⲗⲟⲙ ⲉⲧⲛⲁⲧⲁⲕⲟ·

ⲧⲁⲓ ⲧⲉ ⲑⲉ ⲉⲧⲉⲣⲉⲡⲛⲟⲩⲧⲉ· ⲁⲛⲉⲭⲉ ⲙⲡⲇⲓⲁⲃⲟⲗⲟⲥ· ϫⲉⲕⲁⲥ ⲉⲣⲉⲛⲉϥⲇⲓⲕⲁⲓⲟⲥ ⲛⲁϫⲓ ⲉⲟⲟⲩ· ⲉⲃⲟⲗ ϫⲉ ⲙ̇ⲙⲛ ⲇⲓⲁⲃⲟⲗⲟⲥ ⲉϥϯ ⲟⲩⲃⲏⲕ· ⲙⲙⲛ ⲕⲗⲟⲙ ⲟⲛ ⲉⲕⲛⲁϫ[ⲓⲧϥ] ⲟ̣ⲩⲇⲉ ⲙⲙⲛ ⲡⲱⲣ̣ϫ ⲉⲃⲟⲗ ⲙⲙⲁⲩ ⲙ̇ⲡⲉⲛⲧⲁϥϫⲣⲟ· ⲉⲡⲛⲟ̣ⲃⲉ ⲙⲛ ⲡⲉⲧⲁⲩϫⲣⲟ ⲉⲣⲟϥ ϩⲓⲧⲙ ⲡⲛⲟⲃⲉ

ⲟⲩⲇⲉ ⲙⲙⲛ ϣⲓⲃⲉ ⲛⲁϣⲱⲡⲉ ⲙⲡⲣⲙⲛⲛⲟⲩⲧⲉ ⲙⲛ ⲡⲁⲧⲛⲟⲩⲧⲉ ⲁⲩⲱ ⲡⲉⲧⲟⲩⲁⲁⲃ ⲙⲛ ⲡⲁⲕⲁⲑⲁⲣⲧⲟⲥ

ⲉⲣϣⲁⲛⲛⲉⲧϫⲱ ⲛ̇ϩⲉⲛϭⲱⲱⲙⲉ ⲛ̇ⲑⲉ ⲉⲧⲥⲏϩ ϫⲉ ⲉⲛⲉ ⲙⲡⲉⲡⲥⲁⲧⲁⲛⲁⲥ ϣⲱⲡⲉ ⲣⲱ· ⲛⲉⲣⲉⲣⲱⲙⲉ ⲛⲓⲙ ⲛⲁϣⲱⲡⲉ ⲉⲛⲁⲛⲟⲩϥ ⲡⲉ·

ⲛⲉⲧⲟⲩⲱⲛϩ ⲇⲉ ϩⲱⲟⲩ· ⲛⲛⲉⲧⲥⲟⲩⲧⲱⲛ ⲉⲃⲟⲗ· ϩⲓ ⲛⲉⲩⲥⲡⲟⲧⲟⲩ· ⲥⲉⲛⲁϫⲟⲟⲥ ϫⲉ ⲱ̇ ⲛ̇ⲣⲱⲙⲉ ⲛⲧⲉⲧⲛ ⲛⲓⲙ ⲉⲟⲩⲱϣⲃ ⲟⲩⲃⲉ ⲡⲛⲟⲩⲧⲉ ⲡⲇⲩⲙⲓ̈ⲟⲩⲣⲅⲟⲥ ⲙⲡⲧⲏⲣϥ ⲉⲃⲟⲗ ϫⲉ ⲛ̇ⲑⲉ ⲉⲧⲉⲛⲁⲛⲟⲩ ⲛⲉϥϩⲃⲏⲩⲉ ⲧⲏⲣⲟⲩ ⲛⲉⲧⲛⲛⲁⲩ

[Pages **103-110** are missing]

||**111** ϫⲱⲟⲩ· ⲙⲛ ϩⲉⲑⲛⲟⲥ ⲛⲓⲙ ⲛⲁⲧⲛⲟⲩⲧⲉ ⲉⲧⲥⲧⲱⲧ ⲉⲡⲧⲁⲕⲟ

ⲉⲣϣⲁⲛⲧⲉⲙⲏⲣⲉ ϣⲱⲡⲉ ⲙⲉϥⲁⲓⲥⲑⲁⲛⲉ· ⲙⲡⲣϫⲟⲟⲥ ϫⲉ ⲉⲣϣⲁⲛⲡⲥⲟⲟⲩⲛ ⲁϣⲁⲓ· ⲉⲕⲃⲱⲗ ⲙ̇ⲡϣⲁϫⲉ ⲉ̣ϫⲛ ⲧϭⲓⲛⲉⲓ ⲙⲡⲉⲭ̄ⲥ̄ ⲉⲡⲕⲟⲥⲙⲟⲥ ϫⲉ ⲧⲉⲙⲏⲣⲉ ⲧⲉ· ⲛⲑⲉ ⲛⲧⲁⲓⲥⲱⲧⲙ ⲉϩⲟⲓⲛⲉ ⲛⲁⲑⲏⲧ· ⲁⲗⲗⲁ ⲕⲱ ⲛ̇ⲥⲱⲕ ⲛⲧⲙⲛⲧⲁⲑⲏⲧ ⲛ̇ⲛⲉⲧⲙⲙⲁⲩ· ⲛⲅⲉⲓⲙⲉ ⲉⲧⲙⲉ

ⲉϥⲧⲱⲛ ⲡⲉⲓⲕⲁⲕⲉ ⲧⲏⲣϥ ⲉⲧϣⲟⲟⲡ ϩⲛ ⲧⲉⲩϣⲏ· ϩⲙ ⲡⲧⲣⲉⲡⲣⲏ ⲡⲉⲓ̈ⲣⲉ ϫⲉⲕⲁⲥ ⲉⲕⲉⲉⲓⲙⲉ ϫⲉ ⲙⲡⲁⲓ ⲁⲛ ⲡⲉ·

ⲉϣϫⲉ ⲁⲡⲕⲁⲕⲉ ϭⲉ ϥⲓ ⲙⲙⲁⲩ ϩ͡ⲙ ⲡⲧⲣⲉⲡⲣⲏ ⲡⲓⲣⲉ· ⲛⲁϣ ⲛⲧⲟϥ ⲛ̇ϩⲉ ⲙ̇ⲡⲉⲑⲏⲣⲓⲟⲛ· ⲏ ⲡⲉⲇⲣⲁⲕⲱⲛ ⲉⲧ̄ⲙⲙⲁⲩ ⲛⲁⲣ ϭⲱⲃ ⲁⲛ· ⲛ̇ϥ̄ⲧⲙⲁϩⲉⲣⲁⲧϥ ϩⲙ ⲙⲧⲣⲉⲧϭⲟⲙ ⲁⲩⲱ ⲡⲟⲩⲟⲉⲓⲛ ⲉⲓ ⲉⲡⲕⲟⲥⲙⲟⲥ·

ⲏ ⲛⲧⲉⲧⲛϫⲱ ⲙⲙⲟⲥ ⲁⲛ ϫⲉ ⲟⲩⲛ ⲟⲩⲃⲟ· ⲛⲁⲟⲙⲥϥ ⲉⲧⲉ ⲡⲁⲓ ⲡⲉ ⲡⲉϣⲗⲏⲗ ⲛⲟⲩϩⲗⲗⲟ· ⲙⲛ ⲟⲩϩⲗⲗⲱ· ⲉⲣⲉ ⲡⲉⲩϩⲏⲧ ⲥⲟⲩⲧⲱⲛ ⲉϩⲟⲩⲛ ⲉⲓ̄ⲥ̄ ⲛⲁⲟⲙⲥϥ·

ϫⲉ ⲛⲛⲁϫⲟⲟⲥ ϫⲉ ⲟⲩⲉⲓⲟⲟⲣ· ⲉϥⲥⲱⲕ ϩⲛ̇ ⲟⲩϭⲟⲙ ⲉⲧⲉ ⲡⲁⲓ ⲡⲉ ⲟⲩϩⲣϣⲓⲣⲉ ⲉϥϣⲗⲏⲗ ⲕⲁⲗⲱⲥ· ϥⲛⲁⲧⲣⲉϥⲣ ⲑⲉ ⲛⲛⲉⲧⲉ ⲛⲥⲉϣⲟⲟⲡ ⲁⲛ·

ⲙⲁⲗⲓⲥⲧⲁ· ⲛⲉⲓⲉⲣⲱⲟⲩ ⲉⲧⲥⲱⲕ ⲉⲧⲉ ⲛⲉϩⲃⲏⲩⲉ ⲛⲉ ⲛⲁⲅⲁⲑⲟⲛ ⲛⲛⲉⲧⲟⲩⲁⲁⲃ ⲧⲏⲣⲟⲩ· ⲛⲧⲁ̣ⲩⲙⲉϩ ⲡⲕⲁϩ ⲧⲏⲣϥ ⲛⲑⲉ ⲛⲟⲩⲙⲟⲟⲩ ⲉϥⲟϣ

ⲡϩⲱⲃ· ⲟⲛ ⲛⲟⲩϣⲏⲣⲉ ϣⲏⲙ ⲡⲉ ⲗⲉⲥ· ⲟⲩϥⲛⲧ ϩⲛ̄ ⲧⲉϥⲟ̣ⲩⲉ̣ⲣⲏ||112ⲧⲉ· ⲁⲩⲱ ⲉ̀ϫⲟⲧϥ ⲁⲛ ϩⲛ ⲟⲩⲙⲉⲣⲉϩ·

ⲉⲧⲉ ⲡⲁⲓ ⲡⲉ ⲡⲡⲱⲣϣ ⲉⲃⲟⲗ ⲛⲛⲉϥϭⲓϫ ⲉⲧⲟⲩⲁⲁⲃ· ⲛⲁⲃⲟⲧⲡϥ· ⲛ̄ϥⲧ̄ⲙⲁϩⲉⲣⲁⲧϥ ⲟⲩⲃⲏϥ·

ⲏ ⲉⲣⲉⲛⲉⲧϣⲗⲏⲗ ⲉϫⲛⲱϫⲛ ϣⲡϩⲓⲥⲉ ⲉⲡϫⲓⲛϫⲏ· ⲏ̑ ⲛⲧⲉⲧⲛϫⲱ ⲙⲙⲟⲥ ⲁⲛ ϫⲉ ⲁϥⲱϫⲛ̄ ⲉⲡⲧⲏⲣ̄ϥ ϩⲓⲧⲙ ⲡⲉⲥ⳨ⲟⲥ·

ⲉⲛⲉ ⲙⲛ̄ ⲟⲩⲕⲉⲣⲁⲩⲛⲟⲥ ⲅⲁⲣ ⲡⲏⲧ ⲛ̀ⲥⲱϥ ⲉϥⲟⲧϥ ⲉⲃⲟⲗ· ϩⲓⲧⲛ ⲧⲙⲛⲧϩⲁⲣϣϩⲏⲧ ⲙⲡϫⲟⲉⲓⲥ ϩⲓ ⲡϣⲉ· ⲛⲉⲩⲛⲁϫⲟⲟⲥ ⲁⲛ ⲡⲉ ϫⲉ ⲁϥϥⲓ ⲙ̀ⲡⲛⲟⲃⲉ ⲙⲡⲕⲟⲥⲙⲟⲥ· ⲉⲧⲃⲉ ⲡⲁⲓ ⲙⲡⲣⲧⲣⲉⲛⲣ ⲁⲧⲥⲟⲟⲩⲛ ⲉⲧⲉⲭⲁⲣⲓⲥ ⲙ̀ⲡⲛⲟⲩⲧⲉ·

ⲙⲁⲣⲛⲕⲧⲟⲛ ⲇⲉ ⲉϫⲙ ⲡⲉⲛⲧⲁⲛϫⲟⲟϥ· ϫⲉ ⲉⲣϣⲁⲛⲧⲉⲙⲏⲣⲉ ϣⲱⲡⲉ ⲙⲉϥⲁ[ⲓ]ⲥⲑⲁⲛⲉ· ⲉⲧⲉ ⲡⲁⲓ ⲡ̣[ⲉ] ⲉⲣϣⲁⲛⲛⲉϩⲃⲏⲩ[ⲉ] ⲛⲛⲉⲧⲧⲁⲉⲓⲟ̣ ⲙⲡⲉⲓ̈ⲱⲧ ⲉⲩϫⲓ ⲟⲩⲁ ⲉⲡϣⲏⲣⲉ· ⲁ̣ⲩⲱ ⲛⲉⲧⲧⲁⲉⲓⲟ ⲙⲡϣⲏⲣⲉ· ⲉⲩϫⲓ ⲟⲩⲁ ⲙ̣ⲡ̣ⲉⲓⲱⲧ ⲉⲩϣⲁ̣ⲛⲁϣⲁⲓ ⲛϩⲟⲩⲟ ⲉⲡⲙⲟⲟⲩ ⲛ̀ⲧⲉⲙⲏⲣⲉ ⲙⲉϥⲁⲓ̈ⲥⲑⲁⲛⲉ ⲁⲩⲱ ⲙⲉϥⲣ ⲣⲟⲟⲩϣ ⲛⲁϥ ⲉⲧⲙϩⲱⲙ ⲉϩⲣⲁⲓ ⲉϫⲛ ⲑⲁⲓⲣⲉⲥⲓⲥ· ⲑⲁⲓⲣⲉⲥⲓ̈ⲥ ⲉⲧⲉ ⲛⲥⲉϩⲟⲙⲟⲗⲟⲅⲉⲓ ⲁⲛ· ⲛⲧⲉⲧⲣⲓ̈ⲁⲥ

ϩⲓⲧⲛ ⲟⲩ ⲇⲉ ⲟⲛ· ⲁⲩϫⲟⲟⲥ ϫⲉ ⲉⲣϣⲁⲛϩⲉⲛⲗⲟⲅⲭⲏ ⲧⲱⲙⲛⲧ ⲉⲣⲟϥ· ⲛ̄ⲛⲉⲩⲣ ⲗⲁⲁⲩ ⲛⲁϥ· ⲛⲁϣ ⲛϩⲉ ⲉϥⲛⲁⲟⲩⲱⲱⲙⲉ ⲛϥⲧⲣⲣⲉ ϩⲏⲧⲥ ⲛⲧⲉⲡⲣⲁⲝⲓⲥ ⲛⲛⲉⲧⲉⲛⲧⲟ{ⲟ}ⲩ ⲛⲧⲟⲟⲩ ⲟⲛ ⲡⲉⲧϥⲁϩⲉⲣⲁⲧϥ ⲛⲛⲁϩ̣ⲣ̣ⲁ̣ⲩ ||113 [ⲛⲑ]ⲉ ⲛⲟⲩ`ⲉ´ⲙⲏϣ [ⲉ]ⲙⲉϥⲕⲓ̈ⲙ ϫⲉ ⲙ̣ⲛ ⲡⲉⲧϯϭⲟⲙ ⲛⲛⲉⲃⲓⲏⲛ ⲉⲧⲙⲙⲁⲩ ⲉϯ ⲟⲩⲃⲏϥ ⲉⲧⲃⲉ ϫⲉ ⲙⲙⲛ ⲡⲓⲥⲧⲓⲥ ⲛ̀ϩⲏⲧⲟⲩ

ⲏ̣ ⲉⲩⲛⲁ̣ⲙⲓ̈ϣⲉ ⲙⲛ ⲡⲉⲧⲟ̣ⲩ̣ⲣ ϩⲱⲃ· ⲏ [ⲉ]ⲩⲥⲱϩⲉ ⲉⲡⲉⲓ[ⲡⲣ]ⲏϣ ⲛⲁϥ ⲉⲧϫⲏⲣ· ⲉⲓ̈ϫⲱ ⲙⲙⲟⲥ ⲉⲧⲉⲩⲙⲛⲧⲁⲧⲛⲁϩⲧⲉ ϫⲉ ⲛ̀ⲧⲟⲥ ⲡⲉ ⲡⲉⲡⲣⲏϣ ⲛⲧⲁⲩϫⲟⲟⲥ ⲉⲣⲟϥ ϫⲉ ϩⲉⲛϩⲟⲃⲉⲗⲓⲥⲕⲟⲥ ⲉⲩϫⲏⲣ ⲡⲉ ⲡⲉϥⲡⲣⲏϣ

ⲡⲉⲓ̈ⲧⲁⲕⲟ· ⲣⲱϣⲉ ⲉⲧⲙⲟⲟϣⲉ ϩⲁⲑⲏ ⲙⲙⲟϥ ⲉⲁⲁⲩ ⲛϫⲁϫⲉ ⲉ͡ⲡⲛⲟⲩⲧⲉ ϩⲛ ⲧⲉⲩⲙⲛⲧⲁⲡⲓⲥⲧⲟⲥ ⲛⲑⲉ ⲛⲧⲁⲩϫⲟⲟⲥ ϫⲉ ⲉⲣⲉⲡⲧⲁⲕⲟ ⲡⲏⲧ ⲙ̀ⲡⲉϥⲙⲧⲟ ⲉⲃⲟⲗ·

ⲛⲧⲟⲟⲩ [ⲟ]ⲛ ⲛⲉ ⲧⲉϥⲙⲣⲣⲉ [ⲉ]ⲧⲟ ⲛⲑⲉ ⲛⲟⲩⲱ̑ⲛⲉ ⲛⲥⲙⲓⲣⲓⲧⲏⲥ ⲁⲩⲱ ⲧⲉϥϩⲁⲡⲉ ⲁⲩⲱ ⲧⲉϥϯⲡⲉ ⲉⲧⲉⲣⲉⲧⲉϥϭⲟⲙ ⲙ̣ⲛ̣ ⲧⲉϥⲛⲟⲙⲧⲉ [ⲛϩⲏ]ⲧⲟⲩ· ϫⲉ ⲁⲩ[ⲁⲣ]ⲛ̣ⲁ̣ ⲉⲃⲟⲗ ⲙⲡⲛⲟⲩⲧⲉ

ⲛⲧⲟⲟⲩ ⲟⲛ· ⲛⲉ ⲡϫⲟⲟⲩϥ ⲙⲛ ⲡⲕⲁϣ ⲙⲛ ⲡⲧⲣⲃⲏⲉⲓⲛ ⲉⲧϥⲛ̀ⲕⲟⲧⲕ ϩⲁⲣⲟⲟⲩ ⲁⲩⲱ ⲉϥⲙⲧⲟⲛ ⲙⲙⲟϥ ⲛϩⲏⲧⲟⲩ· ⲉⲁϥⲣ ⲡⲉⲩϩⲏⲧ ⲛⲱⲛⲉ· ⲛⲑⲉ ⲙ̀ⲡⲱϥ ⲡⲉϫⲁϥ ⲅⲁⲣ ϫⲉ ⲁⲡⲉϥϩⲏⲧ ϫⲣⲟ· ⲛ̀ⲑⲉ ⲛⲟⲩⲱⲛⲉ·

ⲁⲩⲱ ⲁϥⲣ ⲧⲉⲩⲯⲩⲭⲏ ⲛϫⲃⲃⲉⲥ· ⲉⲥϫⲉⲣⲟ ϩⲛ ⲁⲕⲁⲑⲁⲣⲥⲓⲁ ⲛⲓ̈ⲙ ⲛⲑⲉ ⲛⲧⲱϥ· ⲛⲑⲉ ⲛⲧⲁⲩϫⲟⲟⲥ ϫⲉ ϩⲉⲛϫⲃⲃⲉⲥ ⲛⲉ ⲧⲉϥⲯⲩⲭⲏ ⲟⲩϣⲁϩ ⲛ̀ⲕⲁⲧⲁⲗⲁⲗⲓⲁ ϩⲓ ϭⲟⲗ ϩⲓ ⲗⲁ· ⲉⲛⲉ ⲙ̀ⲛ̄ⲧⲟⲩ ϣⲁϫⲉ ⲉϫⲱ ⲉⲣⲟⲟⲩ ⲡⲉⲧⲛⲏⲩ ⲉⲃⲟⲗ ϩⲛ̄ ||114 ⲣⲱⲟⲩ· ⲛⲑⲉ ⲛ̀ⲧⲁⲩϫⲟⲟⲥ ⲉⲧⲃⲏⲏ̀ⲧϥ· ϫⲉ ⲟⲩϣⲁϩ ⲡⲉⲧⲛ̣ⲏ̣ⲩ ⲉⲃ̣ⲟⲗ ϩⲛ ⲣⲱϥ [ⲁⲩ]ⲱ̣ ϫⲉ ⲟⲩϩⲟⲧⲉ ⲡ̣ⲉ̣ [ⲡⲕ]ⲱⲧⲉ ⲛⲛⲉϥⲟⲃϩⲉ ⲛⲛⲁϩⲣⲛ̀ ⲛⲉⲧⲟⲩⲱϣⲧ ⲁⲛ ⲛⲓ̅ⲥ̅ ⲙⲏ ⲅⲉⲛⲟⲓⲧⲟ· ϥⲣ ϩⲟⲧⲉ ⲅⲁⲣ ϩⲏⲧϥ ⲙ̀ⲡϥⲓ ⲉϩⲣⲁⲓ

ⲛ̀ⲛⲉⲩϭⲓϫ ⲁⲗⲗⲁ ⲟⲩϩⲟⲧⲉ ⲡⲉ· ⲛⲛⲁϩⲣⲛ ⲛⲉⲧⲟⲩⲱϣⲧ ⲙⲡⲉϥⲉⲓ̈ⲛⲉ·
ⲛ̀ⲧⲁⲩⲥⲁϩϥ ⲉϩⲉⲛϩⲓⲕⲱⲛ ⲙⲛ ⲛϫⲟ ⲛⲛⲉⲩⲧⲁⲙⲓⲟⲛ ⲁⲩⲱ ϩⲛ ⲛⲉⲩϩⲛⲁ ⲁⲩ·
ⲛⲟⲩⲱⲙ· ⲙⲛ ⲛⲉⲩϩⲛⲁⲁⲩ ⲛ̀ⲥⲱ ⲁⲩⲱ ϩⲛ ϩⲁϩ ⲛ̀ϩⲛⲁⲁⲩ ⲙⲛ ϩⲁϩ ⲛⲧⲟⲡⲟⲥ
ⲏ ⲉⲓⲥ ⲛⲉϥⲉⲓⲛⲉ ⲧⲏⲣⲟⲩ ⲁⲛ ⲙⲛ ⲡⲉⲓⲛⲉ ⲛ̀ⲛⲉϥⲛⲁⲁϫⲉ ⲉⲧϯ ϩⲟⲧⲉ
ⲛ̀ⲛⲁϩⲣⲛ ⲛⲁⲑⲏⲧ· ϥϩⲛ ⲛⲉⲓ̈ⲇⲱⲗⲟⲛ ⲛ̣[ⲧⲁⲛ]ϥⲓⲧⲟⲩ ⲉⲃⲟⲗ ϩⲛ̣ ⲛⲉⲩⲏⲓ·
ⲉⲣϣⲁⲛ ϫⲟⲓ ⲛⲓⲙ ⲉⲓ ⲉⲩⲙⲁ ⲛ̀ⲟⲩⲱⲧ ⲛⲛⲉⲩϥⲓ ϩⲁ ⲟⲩϣⲛ̣ϥⲉ ⲛⲟⲩⲱⲧ
ⲙⲡⲉ[ϥ]ⲥⲁⲧ· ⲕϥⲓ ⲛⲧⲟⲕ̣ ϩⲁ ⲛⲉϥϣⲟϫⲛⲉ ⲙⲛ̣ ⲛⲉϥⲙⲟⲕⲙⲉⲕ [ⲙⲛ] ⲛⲉϥ-
ⲕⲁⲕⲓⲁ ⲧ[ⲏ]ⲣ̣[ⲟⲩ] ⲁⲩⲱ ⲕϣⲱⲡ ⲉⲣⲟⲕ̣ ⲛⲛⲉⲥⲃⲟⲟⲩⲉ· ⲛⲛⲣⲉϥⲧⲁⲕⲉ ϩⲏⲧ·
ⲛ̀ⲣⲱⲙⲉ ⲛⲁⲧⲛⲟⲩⲧⲉ̣ ⲛⲧⲁⲛϫⲟⲟⲥ ϫⲉ ⲛ̀ⲧⲟⲟⲩ ⲡⲉ ⲡⲉϥⲥⲁⲧ
ⲛⲉϥϣⲛⲃⲉ· ⲇⲉ ⲟⲛ ⲛⲉ ⲛϣⲁϫⲉ ⲛⲧⲉⲩⲧⲁⲡⲣⲟ ⲉⲧⲟⲩϫⲱ ⲉⲣⲟϥ ⲛϩⲏⲧⲟⲩ·
ⲛ̀ⲑⲉ ⲛⲟⲩⲕⲓⲑⲁⲣⲁ ⲉⲁⲩⲥϩⲟⲩⲣ ⲡⲉϩⲣⲟⲟⲩ· ⲛ̀ⲛⲉⲥⲟⲩⲉⲗⲗⲉ ϩⲓⲧⲙ ⲡⲛⲟⲩⲧⲉ
ⲉⲃⲟⲗ ϫⲉ ⲟⲩⲉⲧ· ⲡⲉⲛ̣ⲧⲁϥϯ ⲧⲁⲡⲣⲟ ⲉⲣ̣[ⲟ]ⲟⲩ· ⲉⲥⲙⲟⲩ ⲉⲣⲟϥ

[Pages **115**ff. are missing]

By Shenoute

How there is no one who exercises authority (ἐξουσία) over the Spirit (πνεῦμα) so as to hinder (κωλύειν) the Spirit (πνεῦμα); furthermore, there is no one who knows the way of the Spirit (πνεῦμα).

A loved one asked me years ago, while inquiring about the devil (διάβολος), "What is (the meaning of) this name 'demon' (δαιμόνιον) which was revealed to me during this present trial (πειρασμός)"?

'Demon' (δαιμόνιον) is the name which is more contemptible than any other one. The Greeks (Ἕλλην + μέν), the spinners of tales, being eager (σπουδάζειν) to camouflage (κοσμεῖν) evil words, explain it thus: **101** 'Demon' (δαιμόνιον) is he who knows, or (ἤ) he who distributes portions (μερίς) to each one. I, however, shall contradict their words and say, 'demon' (δαιμόνιον) is he who knows how to distribute portions to the ungodly, i.e. unfaithfulness (ἄπιστος), impurities, incontinence, iniquities, and everything that is to be rejected. Rather (+ δέ) to the saints 'demon' (δαιμόνιον) is a rejected and evil name with these other names joined to it: foolish, senseless, shameless.

This is why *his ribs* were referred to as "*they are of iron*" (Job 40:13), [for] he is not ashamed to be trampled, together with his vices (κακία), by those who conquer him everytime they wage war (πόλεμος) against him, (and) pierce him with their faith (πίστις). But (ἀλλά) after he flees from them he is overtaken, since they pursue him with their good (ἀγαθόν) deeds (πρᾶξις) to kill him, like those who with their swords and weapons pursue their enemies to destroy them. Yet again (πάλιν) he <returns> shamelessly and dares (τολμᾶν) to fight against them. It is the Lord God Almighty (παντοκράτωρ) who delivers him up to these punishments (τιμωρία), thus — apart from (χωρίς) the fire of **102** Gehenna which is ready for him — to cause his righteous ones (δίκαιος) to pursue him all the time, like flames of fire, with their long suffering (and) their endurance (ὑπομονή).

If the one who contends is victorious once for all, there is a single crown that he would receive. And since there are contests (ἆθλον) of those who engage in sport events (ἀγών) and other contests (ἆθλον) of those who run in these race courses, — these namely: to *run thus that you* (pl.) *may obtain* (it) (1 Cor 9:24b) — (so) there are imperishable crowns (and) there are other crowns which will perish. Thus God put up with (ἀνέχειν) the devil (διάβολος), in order that his righteous ones (δίκαιος) may receive glory. Because if there were no devil (διάβολος) fighting against you (sg.) there would also be no crown for you to receive, nor (οὐδέ) would there be a separation between he who has conquered sin and he who has been conquered by sin, nor (οὐδέ) would there be a difference between the pious and the impious person, and between the pure and impure (ἀκάθαρτος).

If those who *speak perversions* (Prov 23:33), as it is written, (say): "If Satan had not come into being, indeed every person would have been good", then (+ δέ) those who, in contrast, reveal with their lips what is right will say: "*O* (ὦ) *men, who are you to answer back to God* (Rom 9:20), the maker (δημιουργός) of everything. Because just as all his works which we see are good ...

[pages **103-110** are missing]

111 them, and every godless nation (ἔθνος) that is doomed to destruction.

If the inundation comes he does not notice (αἰσθάνεσθαι) (Job 40:18). Do not say, "If the knowledge increases", thus explaining the verse with reference to the coming of Christ to the world (κόσμος), namely that it is the inundation, as I heard some fools (say). Rather (ἀλλά) repudiate the foolishness of those, and know the truth!

Where is all this darkness that is present at night, when the sun shines? (I say this) that you may know that it is not this. If, therefore, the darkness disappears when the sun shines, how then would the beast (θηρίον), or (ἤ) that dragon (δράκων), not weaken and loose footing when the Power and *the Light come into the world* (κόσμος) (John 3:19a)?

Nor (ἤ), surely, would you say, "A canal shall submerge him", — that is the prayer of an old man and an old woman, who have an upright heart towards Jesus, will submerge him — lest I shall say that a canal which flows forcefully is a youth who prays rightly (καλῶς). It would make him like things which do not exist.

Most certainly (μάλιστα) flowing rivers, which are the good (ἀγαθόν) works of all the saints, have filled the whole earth like much water. Also the task of a child is to crush a worm with its foot, **112** and not to pierce it with a spear. That is to say, the spreading out of its holy hands shall defeat him that he may not stand up against it. Or (ἤ) do those who pray without ceasing labour in vain?

Nor (ἤ), surely, would you say, "He perished completely due to the cross (σταυρός)", for (γάρ) if a thunderbolt (κεραυνός) were not pursuing him in order to obliterate him, through the suffering of the Lord on the tree, it would not be said: "*He took away the sins of the world* (κόσμος) (John 1:29b). Therefore, let us not be ignorant of the grace (χάρις) of God.

But (δέ) let us return to what we said: *If the inundation comes he does not notice* (αἰσθάνεσθαι) (Job 40:18). This means if the deeds of those who honour the Father while blaspheming the Son, and those who honour the Son while blaspheming the Father, if they increase more than the water of the inundation, *he does not notice* (αἰσθάνεσθαι). And he takes no heed not to trample upon the heresy (αἵρεσις), the heresy (αἵρεσις) that they do not confess (ὁμολογεῖν) the trinity (τριάς).

And (δέ) further as to what is said: *If spears* (λόγχη) *meet him they will do nothing to him* (Job 41:17), how will he be restrained by, and be afraid of the action (πρᾶξις) of their owners? Before them (i.e. spears) also he *stands* **113** *like an immovable anvil* (Job 41:15b), for there is nothing that enables those wretched ones to fight against him, because there is no faith (πίστις) in them. Would (+ ἤ) they fight against the one for whom they work, or (ἤ) are they weaving this spiked mattress for him? I say this concerning their unbelief, for it is the mattress of which it is said: *sharp spikes* (ὀβελίσκος) *are his mattress* (Job 41:21a).

This destruction which goes before him is responsible for making them enemies of God in their unbelief (ἄπιστος), as it is said: *destruction runs before him* (Job 41:13b). They are also *his ligaments* which *are like a smyrite* (σμιρίτης) *stone* (Job 41:6b), and *his navel, and his loins in* which are *his power and his strength* (Job 40:11), for they have [denied (ἀρνεῖσθαι)] God. They also are the *papyrus and the reed and the sedge* under which *he sleeps* (Job 40:16), and in them he rests himself having turned their heart to stone like his own, for (γάρ) it said: *His heart has become hard as stone* (Job 41:15a).

And he made their soul (ψυχή) into coal which burns with every impurity (ἀκαθαρσία) like his own, as it is said: *Coals are his soul* (ψυχή) (Job 41:12a). A flame of slander (καταλαλιά), lying and envy, which are indescribable, is what comes from **114** their mouth, (just) as it said of him: *A flame is what comes from his mouth* (Job 41:12b), and *terror is around his teeth* (Job 41:5b). (Terror) in face of those who do not worship Jesus? Of course not (μὴ γένοιτο)! For (γάρ) he is (only) afraid of the raising of their hands. Rather (ἀλλά) there is terror for those who worship his likeness which has been painted on images (εἰκών), and on the walls of their inner rooms (ταμεῖον), and on their eating and drinking utensils, and on many things and in many places (τόπος). Or (ἤ) are they not all his images and the image of his teeth which instill fear in the foolish? It (i.e. his image) is on the idols (εἴδωλον) which we took from their houses!

If all ships came together, they would not bear up under a single scale of his tail (Job 40:26). (And) you (sg.) would bear up under his scheming and his deliberations [and] all his vices (κακία), and accept the teachings of deceivers, the godless men of which we said that they are his tail? And (δέ) furthermore, his scales are the words of their mouth with which they sing to him like a harp (κιθάρα) of which the sound of its melodies has been cursed by God. For there is the One who has given a mouth to them to bless Him ...

[pages **115**ff. are missing]

NOTES TO THE TEXT AND TRANSLATION

100,35f. Cf. John 3:8.

100,49 In Shenoute's writings Ἕλλην means normally pagan. Here the reference is to the ancient Greeks.

100,50 The "tales" are fables and myths which, according to Patristic authors, are devoid of truth.

101,6f. Zoega and Amélineau read ⲁⲛⲟⲕ ϩⲱ ϯⲛⲁⲟⲩⲱϣⲃ ⲉ- "I, on the other hand, shall respond to". It is unclear on what basis Zoega adopted this reading.

101,13f. The Coptic has the plural "unfaithfulnesses" and "incontinences".

101,52 Ms. reads ϥⲙⲉ ⲙⲙⲟϥ; Zoega wants to emend to ϥⲕⲧⲉ (*Catalogus*, p. 460, note 47), but the *status absolutus* is needed.

102,11-13 Cf. 1 Cor 9:24.

102,18-20 The quotation from 1 Cor 9:24b is awkwardly integrated into the sentence to indicate what kind of race is meant. Shenoute reads the Future II in 1 Cor 24b instead of the Future III read by H. Thompson (see Introduction, note 48).

102,21-24 Cf. 1 Cor 9:25.

102,55-58 Shenoute has changed the vocative in Rom 9:20 to the plural and omitted ϩⲱⲱϥ.

102,60ff. The complete sentence likely stated that since all God's works are good, so God's creation of Satan must also have had a good purpose.

111,1 For the *spiritus asper* with ἔθνος, ὀβελίσκος (113,16f.), and εἰκών (114,16f.) see A. Böhlig, *Griechische Lehnwörter im sahidischen und bohairischen Neuen Testament*, München 1953, pp. 111f.

111,1-4 This is very likely the ending of Shenoute's commentary on Job 40:25 "Do the nations (ἔθνος) feed upon him; do the peoples (ἔθνος) of the Phoenicians divide him"?

111,4-6 (= 112,28-31) Shenoute reads ϣωπε μεϥ⁻ in agreement with the fragment from the British Museum edited by Schleifer against ϣωπε εμεϥ⁻ in the text edited by Amélineau (see Introduction, note 48).

111,7-14 It is unclear who the "fools" are who interpreted the inundation as the effects of the coming of Christ. The polemic fits Shenoute's general rejection of allegory (see Leipoldt, *Schenute*, pp. 73f.), though his own interpretation of the verse is not free from allegorization.

111,19-35 The point of the refutation is that just as darkness disappears before the light, so Satan was defeated at the coming of Christ. Since the quotation from Job 40.18 states that the Dragon, Satan, is not effected by the inundation, it cannot refer to the coming of Christ, or have another positive meaning, such as the prayers of the pious (111,38-43) or the cross (112,10-22).

111,29f. θηρίον and δράκων are used respectively in the Coptic and Greek text of Job 40:10 (LXX 15) and 40:20 (LXX 25).

111,35f. It appears that η (ἤ) introduces a rhetorical question (which continues the negative imperative in 111,7) expecting a positive answer: "Or you would not say that... would you"? See also 112,11f., 113,8-10 and 114,25f.

111,43-50 This is an argument *ad absurdum* which fits Shenoute's fondness of ridicule (Cf. Leipoldt, *Schenute*, p. 177). His point is that if a canal is the prayer of an old person then a fast flowing canal is the prayer of a youth. However, fast flowing (irrigation) canals belong to "things which do not exist" (cf. 1 Cor 1:28) in Egypt.

111,51-112,10 Shenoute wants to make clear that he did not mean to disparage prayer in the previous paragraph, for prayers and good deeds are indeed like flowing rivers which fill the earth. These however, Satan cannot ignore, for even the prayer of a child is effective against him.

111,58-112,5 The same point is developed more fully in the last part of the sermon ("Schenute: De certamine", 15,36-16,26).

112,3f. Spreading of holy hands in prayer.

112,8-10 Cf. 1 Thess 5:17 and Phil 2:16.

112,11f. See the note for 111,35f.

112,12-22 The point is that Satan could not ignore the effect of the cross which pursues him like a thunderbolt (cf. 102,3-6 "pursue him ... like flames of fire").

112,14 Ms. uses the common abbreviation of σταυρός with the tau-rho combined in the form of a cross.

112,21f. John 1:29b is understood to include the defeat of Satan. It is quoted with the same meaning in the last part of the sermon ("Schenute: De certamine", 17,39-46) which also makes clear that the Demon's continuing activities are allowed by God in order to give Christians a chance to share in Christ's victory (18,9-19,14).

112,24-26 By ignoring the defeat of Satan due to the cross one would be ignorant of the grace of God.

112,31-38 Cf. 1 John 2:23; the allusion is to the Arian heresy (Cf. "Schenute: De certamine", 16,27-32).

112,56 Ms reads ⲛⲛⲉⲧⲉⲛⲧⲟⲟⲩ probably due to dittography; lit. "those who belong to them (i.e. the spears)".

113,16-18 Shenoute read ϫⲏⲣ in Job 41,21a instead of ⲧⲏⲙ read by Amélineau (see Introduction, note 48).

113,28 The Greek and Coptic read sing. "ligament" (σύνδεσμος).

114,5ff. Shenoute interprets the "terror around his teeth" in two ways, i.e. as due to being frightened and as causing fright.

114,15-32 The reference is to images of pagan gods, such as Cronos, which Shenoute claimed to be likenesses of the devil.

114,33-37 Shenoute read ⲛⲛⲉⲩϥⲓ and ⲙⲡⲉϥⲥⲁⲧ with Schleifer instead of ⲛⲛⲉⲩⲉϣϥⲓ and ϩⲁ ⲡⲉϥⲥⲁⲧ read by Amélineau (see Introduction, note 48).

114,37ff. This is most likely not a statement of fact but a rhetorical question similar in form to Gal 3:3.

114,45f. Shenoute does not make this identification in the surviving fragments. Perhaps in the missing pages 103-110 there were comments on Job 40:12 which interpreted the Dragon's tail as godless deceivers.

115ff. The final 17% of the sermon survives in IFAO 1; it was edited by K. Koschorke, S. Timm, and F. Wisse, ("Schenute: De certamine", pp. 60-77).

LESLIE S. B. MACCOULL

The Coptic *Triadon* and the Ethiopic *Physiologus*

The fourteenth-century Coptic religious didactic poem *Triadon* is the cenotaph of a dead civilisation. It was composed in a period when Coptic had long been a dead language in Egypt, no longer understood even by the scribes who attempted to copy Coptic manuscripts, with only a few phrases being fossilised in the liturgy of the Orthodox (Monophysite) church. Four hundred and twenty-three of an original numbered 732 four-line stanzas of the poem are preserved in a unique bilingual manuscript, of the Coptic poem with an Arabic translation, in parallel columns, kept in the National Library at Naples (Zoega 312). The text was originally published by Oskar von Lemm in St. Petersburg in 1903[1]; the poem is now available in German translation with explanatory introduction and copious notes by Peter Nagel (Halle 1983)[2]. This latter modern work has begun to make scholars and readers aware of the striking literary qualities of the poem, of its religious thought, and of the many elements of Late Antique *Gedankengut* it still preserves. Study of this long poem will tell us much about the sensibility and the thought-world of a devout Egyptian Christian of the fourteenth century, one who was painfully aware that the language he had, it seems, taught himself to write in, the language of his old tradition, had been killed by the language of his alien political masters.

The *Triadon* is a Biblical didactic poem. In its overall structure, which Nagel has discerned follows a journey by the first-person narrator down the Nile from Upper to Lower Egypt, many Bible stories are considered in turn, with lessons being drawn from them for the pious conduct of the poem's listeners or readers. The poet treats the Prodigal Son, Noah's Ark, Balaam's ass, Abraham and the angels at Mamre, Jonah, Daniel, and of course many scenes, parables and miracles from the life of Christ. In the process of making a complete English translation of the *Triadon* (forthcoming; up to now there has been none), the present writer was struck by the frequency of nature, animal, and bird images in the poet's language and their echoes of earlier images that we associate with the "Bestiary" type of literature. "Consider the

1 O. von Lemm, *Das Triadon* (St. Petersbourg 1903).
2 P. Nagel, *Das Triadon: ein sahidisches Lehrgedicht des 14. Jhdts.* (Halle 1983).

falcon", says the poet, "the eagle ... the lion ... the antelope ... the dove ... the heron ... the sycamore ... the phoenix". This would immediately lead one to that perennial repertoire of Alexandrian Late Antique Christianised animal lore, the so-called *Physiologus*. This work is thought to go back to a pagan Hellenistic compilation of the third to second centuries B.C., and to have been reworked by an Alexandrian Christian in perhaps the late fourth or fifth century A.D. Its translations into Christian Oriental languages, Armenian, the fragmentary Coptic, and especially the classical Ethiopic or Ge'ez[3], clearly go back to a Greek *Vorlage* earlier than the Greek recensions as we now have them. It is with the Ethiopic version of the *Physiologus*, possibly made by an Abyssinian monk in Scetis, that the *Triadon*'s animal and bird parallels are particularly close.

The fifth of the *Triadon*'s preserved stanzas in the text that we have, no. 142, runs: "Come with me in haste / and I will let you into the garden / so you can spread out your net / and catch this great eagle". It is a commonplace of criticism that this eagle, which is a metamorphosis of the solar falcon of Horus (see below)[4], is Christ. And indeed the poet returns later to the Eucharistic image of Christ's body, in stanza 714: "If, my beloved brothers, we very much wish / for great strength and boldness, / let us catch the eagles in their nests, / for they gather in the place of the λειψανον" (the remains, i.e. the body of Christ nourishing and sustaining the universe). This is of course the traditional patristic interpretation of Mt 24:28, "Where the body is, there the eagles are gathered together". The Ethiopic *Physiologus* likens the solar eagle to the believing Christian, who renews his youth as on the Psalmist's eagle wings as he flies upward ever nearer to Christ, the Sun of Justice[5]. It may be further remarked that a double pun may underlie the Coptic image: "eagle" in Coptic is ⲁϩⲱⲙ, and the name ⲡⲁϩⲱⲙ, Pachomius, means "the eagle". The fourteenth-century poet, who often emphasises the virtues of the monastic saints and the desert way of ascetic life, may also be recalling for his listeners or readers the legacy of Pachomius the monastic founder, which lived on in its country-wide network of self-sufficient houses ("gardens") that perpetuated the Christian presence and sacraments in Moslem-ruled Egypt.

Another solar bird image occurs in stanza 638: "Beloved, come to gather beautiful precious / stones and delicate perfumes, / and take from the eighty eggs / to catch the falcon and the crane". Critics attuned to the echoes of Ancient Egyptian mythology as they are thought to survive in Egyptian

3 F. Hommel, ed., *Die äthiopische Übersetzung des Physiologos* (Leipzig 1877); C. Sumner, *The Fisalgʷos* (Addis Ababa 1982).
4 P. Houlihan, *The birds of ancient Egypt* (Warminster 1986) 46-49, 140, 149.
5 Sumner, *Fisalgʷos*, 16-17.

Christianity see in the falcon here of course again the solar Horus bird, symbolic of Osirian resurrection and so transferred to being a type of Christ. About the crane, matters are less clear. In the papyrus poem *Vision of Dorotheos* (ed. A. Hurst et al., Geneva 1984), preserved in one of the Bodmer papyrus codices, and surely by an Egyptian Late Antique poet, Christ speaks "with the voice of cranes" (line 295). But this is of course a Homeric simile, compare *Iliad* 3.3, the sound of the Trojan army being likened to the cry of a flock of cranes. The *Physiologus* text here affords us no Ancient Egyptian or Christian parallel stated as such. About the symbolism of the eighty eggs, I leave that to wiser heads.

In the very next stanza (no. 639) we find: "Then let us catch the great antelope / and smell the fragrance spread out / over us now, and level out / our threshing-floors and put wheat into our granaries". The Ethiopic *Physiologus* gives us the key to the Christological antelope, citing Song of Songs 2:8, "My beloved is like a hart upon the mountains of spices". The *derqodas*, gazelle or perhaps hartebeeste of § 41, is said to know the intent of whoever approaches it, a figure of Christ foreknowing Judas' kiss[6]. The wheat and sweet scent in the Coptic poet's discourse are probably Eucharistic. Also comparable is the Ethiopic *endrap*^{w}*os* of § 36, probably the oryx, whose two horns are likened to the Old and New Testaments, the twin weapons with which the Christian combats evil[7]. According to Damascius' Life of Isidore, the oryx responds to the rising of Sirius, the Sothic star (Photius *Bibl.* cod. 242, sec. 102), also an image later Christianised by Egyptian poets and exegetes.

In a context expressing his desire to be purified and find the solution to "mysteries" that are perplexing him, the *Triadon* narrator says, in stanza 707, "I will raise myself up to the house of the heron, / high exalted, and will not weaken / with those whose heart is weak / and do not endure in temptation". What can be signified by this striking image? The Ethiopic *Physiologus* says of the heron, the *erodios/-on* (§ 47): "It is the wisest of all the birds. It does not fly to many places; it has but one lodging. Do not look around for the multiple dwelling places of the impious, but let your cove be one and this is the holy church"[8]. The heron is the Ancient Egyptian mythological *benu* bird[9], later assimilated to the phoenix (see below). Now the context of the whole *Triadon* passage is the narrator's visit to the monks of Scetis, as in stanzas 701-702: "Blessed is the one who went to the place near the desert / and saw the ascetics in the wilderness. / Some of them uttered a saying from

6 *Ibid.*, 56-57.
7 *Ibid.*, 51-52.
8 *Ibid.*, 63. On the heron cf. D'Arcy Thompson, *A glossary of Greek birds* (Oxford 1936) 102-103, and J. Pollard, *Birds in Greek life and myth* (London 1977) 68-69.
9 Houlihan, *Birds of ancient Egypt*, 13-16.

Jeremiah, / while others read from Chronicles. / Still others enquired about the great oven, / and some asked questions about the great winepress. / But I said to them, 'Why, O great men, / do you think about these great mysteries?' " The poet is testifying to a still living tradition and practice of Biblical exegesis by the monks of the desert. In the context of the fourteenth century in Egypt, he is surely exhorting his hearers and readers to remain true to their traditional Christianity and not waver when they are exposed to Moslem counter-interpretations of scripture and accusations that the Christians have tampered with the Biblical texts.

One plant image is worth mentioning. When the *Triadon* poet mentions the sycamore in stanza 719, he of course refers to Lk 19:4, the sycamore tree climbed by Zacchaeus in his eagerness to see Christ: "From then on, my fathers, I must shake off / the old garment, and seek to climb the sycamore / and act like Zacchaeus, of the seed of Shem, son of Noah, / whose craft is that of ⲧⲉⲗⲱⲛⲓⲟⲛ (tax-collector)". Compare also stanza 474: "I am eager to climb up into the sycamore / and see the one who saved our father Noah[10]. / Again he said to his disciples: / 'Shake the dust of your feet upon the city of the lawless'". Throughout Coptic folklore the sycamore symbolises the Coptic people[11]: this folk symbolism is usually thought to derive from the Ancient Egyptian sycamore as the tree of the goddess Nut, whose body overarches the night sky. Here too the Ethiopic *Physiologus* in Christianising the image gives us a clue to its perennial force (§ 48): "The sycamore, once it has ripened, on the third day, becomes the food for all: likewise our Lord Jesus Christ, risen from the dead on the third day, gave His life and forgiveness, and became the food for all"[12].

In a short study one cannot give a resume of the totality of current scholarship on the phoenix as a Christian symbol[13]. Suffice it to say that a consensus posits an origin in Ancient Egyptian mythology for this miraculous bird. Here I shall simply juxtapose the *Triadon*'s image of the Phoenix with the legend given in the Ethiopic *Physiologus*[14]. The Coptic poet, after a section describing Lenten penitence, speaks of preparing his soul for Easter (stanzas 613-614): "... I shall rejoice in my good works / and be glad, when I see my abundant harvest, / and I shall be happy in this field of mine, which

10 This is Cyrillian exegesis. Christ is the truer Noah; the ark is the Church, surely constructed; the flood prefigures Christian baptism (*Glaph. in Gen.* 5 = *PG* 69.65B).

11 A recent book about the accomplishments of 1930s Coptic cultural figures was entitled *Les sycomores* (Cairo 1978).

12 Sumner, *Fisalgʷos*, 64-65.

13 Cf. R. van den Broek, *The myth of the Phoenix according to classical and early Christian traditions* (Leiden 1972); E. Brunner-Traut, "Altägyptische Mythen im Physiologus", *Antaios* 10 (1969) 184-198.

14 Noticed by Nagel, *Das Triadon*, p. 101 n. (citing the Greek).

will be left / after it was cultivated and bore spiritual fruit. / But when I shall see that my field is prepared, / I shall spread my net and hunt / the Phoenix, the great bird who remains ever existing, / who hides in himself the mystery of the true Resurrection". So too the *Physiologus* writer, associating the bird with the "priest of the city of the Sun (Heliopolis)" and the spring months of Phamenoth and Pharmouthi (roughly March and April), says: "the Phoenix is an image of our Redeemer"[15]. In a local touch, the Ethiopic translator has misrendered the Greek διὰ ἀγαθῶν πολιτειῶν, in speaking of how we are to pray and receive spiritual graces, as "in our beautiful homeland" rather than "by good conduct".

It is noticeable that a continuing thread tying these images together is the metaphor of catching them in a net ("Let us spread out our nets and catch the (X)" is the poet's formula), clearly a further image of intellectual and especially spiritual comprehension. The poet continually reminds his hearers and readers to hunt for and grasp the edifying Christian meaning of these types in nature. This image from hunting may reflect the difficulty of comprehension involved for those trying to grasp the import of a text in Coptic at a time when Coptic was no longer understood.

How can a Christian religious writer in fourteenth-century Arabophone Moslem-ruled Egypt, who had to go to the trouble (by a process we cannot really reconstruct), not only to learn the dead Coptic language in its classical Sahidic dialect, but to learn it complete with embeddings of rare classical Greek and even Latin words — how, one asks, could such an *érudit*, steeped in the Bible and in the local Christian traditions that ranged up and down the Nile Valley, have had access to a Christian "Bestiary" to weave its stories into his text? What line of descent can be postulated from Ancient Egyptian bird and animal symbolism, through a Christian Greek compilation from Late Antique Alexandria, to a fourteenth-century Coptic writer, the last of his kind? All that has been established is that the Greek text of the *Physiologus* from which the Ethiopic translator worked, probably in the fifth century, was older than and contained matter not found in the Greek recensions of the *Physiologus* as we now know it. It was fuller and contained more things relevant to how the *Triadon* poet treated the creatures he uses in his imagery. The line of descent one might posit goes back to the well-documented presence of Ethiopian monks in Scetis, the later Wadi Natrun, from the fifth century right down to the Ottoman period. The early Greek text the Ethiopian translator worked from is essentially the same as that translated into Coptic, which latter version has come down to us only in fragments but must have been extant in its full length and scope throughout the Egyptian

15 Sumner, *Fisalgʷos*, 19.

middle ages, later with an Arabic version attached, most particularly in a monastic library or libraries. From the Ethiopic as it was later copied and transmitted we can form an idea of the Coptic *Physiologus* as it would have been read by Egyptian Christians as long as they could read Coptic. This in turn would have been what was rendered into Arabic, to give an Arabic version again fuller than the one we have now. Thus Christianised Ancient Egyptian nature stories would have remained part of people's mental furniture even in a period when people were more and more losing touch with their Christian past.

This has been a short survey of one aspect of source research in a long and interesting text that has only begun to be read and to be excavated, as it were, for what it might contain. A fitting closing would be to review the poet's own plea for his own intention, a purpose devoted to a dead cause: "Brothers, come, hear these sweet words / and understand these comforting thoughts, / as I have begun and have taught you / the usefulness of this language, Coptic. ... Do you not know the number of ideas I have gathered together in this *Triadon*? ... Brother, do not tell me that these words need explanation, / but look rightly, for I have not taken them from outside, / and know, man of good sense, that without God's / providence I would not have been able to set aright this *Triadon*." (stanzas 413, 683, 441)[16]. It is to be hoped that people other than just specialists in Coptic philology — Byzantinists, Biblical scholars and historians of religion, students of other areas of the Christian Orient, social historians — will read this long and rich text, and find in it much food for thought[17].

16 Also for the most part noticed by Nagel, *Das Triadon*, pp. 26-27.

17 A first version of this paper was given at the Fifteenth Annual Byzantine Studies Conference, Amherst, Massachusetts, October 1989. I should like to thank Levon Avdoyan, Monica Blanchard, Theodore Natsoulas, and Lucas Siorvanes for their help.

ERICA C. D. HUNTER

An inscribed reliquary from the Middle Euphrates

During the 1987 excavation season conducted by Prof. Graeme Clarke at Djebel Khaled, a reliquary inscribed in Syriac was discovered at the nearby village of Khirbet Khaled[1]. It was, apparently, found along with another basin that is uninscribed, but is shaped like a deep bath and also with two lengths of monolithic columns[2]. In the 1988 excavation season, a limestone block bearing a uniquely incised cross also came to light, functioning as a prop for a villager's sleeping platform[3]. However, such is the precariousness of this material that, by the 1989 excavation season, the limestone block had already disappeared, probably having been broken up.

PHYSICAL DESCRIPTION OF THE RELIQUARY

The limestone reliquary is rectangular in shape with dimensions 65 cm × 38.5 cm × 38.5 cm. It has a rectangular rim 7.5 cm thick. Whilst the internal dimensions of the reliquary are 50 cm × 23.5 cm, the short sides only measure 11 cm in depth[4]. The reliquary's floor slopes down to the deepest internal point of 22 cm, forming a 'V' junction with an included angle of 132°[5]. Thus, the base of the reliquary is 16.5 cm thick at its midpoint and 27.5 cm thick at its edges. Indeed, the reliquary is a fairly solid item, with its weight being

1 The author wishes to thank Prof. Clarke for sending her the photographs of the inscribed reliquary and the other finds, Dr. S. P. Brock for his helpful suggestions and Dr. S. A. Durrani for the mathematical calculations.

2 See Plate I: *Uninscribed bath from Khirbet Khaled.*

3 See Plate II: *Stone incised with a unique cross.* The block is shown *in situ* as a prop for a sleeping platform. The tripartite head is probably representative of the Trinity, but this style is not included in the vast array of crosses reproduced in A. Desreumaux and J. B. Humbert, "Ḫirbet es-Samra. Contribution à l'épigraphie syro-palestinienne augmentée de quatre inscriptions en grec", *Annual of the Department of Antiquities* (Hashemite Kingdom of Jordan), XXV, (1981), plates XII-XX. Nor does it occur in A. N. Palmer, *Monk and mason on the Tigris frontier*, (Cambridge, 1990), fig. 48 "Crosses on stone from Ṭur ʿAbdin and its environs".

4 Measurements supplied in private correspondence between Clarke and Hunter (26 October 1987). Recorded 18 May 1987.

5 See Plate III: *Internal view of the inscribed reliquary.* The position of the inscription on the short side is also visible.

estimated at approximately 207 kg, and with a capacity of holding 19.4 litres of liquid[6].

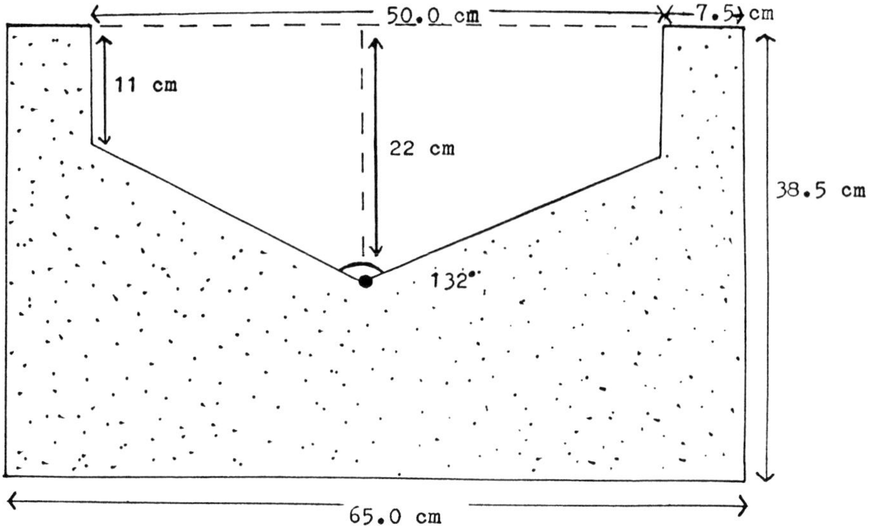

Fig. 1. *Cross-section (long side) of the reliquary*

At the point where the 'V' junction occurs within the reliquary an outlet hole has been drilled, emerging equidistant between a pair of discs that have been carved in bas-relief on one of the long sides[7]. The discs, which are 15 cm in diameter, feature identical motifs of four-petalled rosettes. To the upper right of the aperture is a lozenge-shaped depression which has been incised, rather than having been the result of an overflow of liquid. Apart from this decoration, the reliquary is unadorned and without joins since it was carved from one block of limestone. The dressing marks of the mason are still visible, for the reliquary has suffered little physical deterioration.

On one of the short sides, a Syriac inscription of four lines has been incised, covering an area of 31 cm × 14 cm[8]. In its drafting, the inscription conveys an impression of clarity and regularity with the well-cut characters

6 The volume of the reliquary, if solid = 65 × 38.5 × 38.5 cm = 96,346.25 cm^3

The volume of the hollow portion of the reliquary is given as:

(i) volume of the rectangular slab = 50 × 11 × 23.5 cm = 12,925 cm^3

(ii) volume of the prismatic section = ½ × (50 × 11) × 23.5 cm = 6,462.5 cm^3

= 19,387.5 cm^3

Hence, the volume of the actual solid material of the reliquary = 76,958.75 cm^3

The reliquary's weight is calculated on the assumption of the density of the limestone being 2.7 gm per cm^3.

7 See Plate IV: *View of the reliquary, showing the long, decorated side.* The awkward juxtaposition of the aperture and the lozenge-shaped depression is evident, as is the vertical alignment of the inscription on the short side.

8 See Plate V: *View of the reliquary, showing the short side with the Syriac inscription.*

being evenly spaced. The downward inclination of both ll. 2 and 4 suggest that the lines have not been plotted, as does the re-adjustment of the text which occurs midway through l. 3. The right-hand margin of ll. 2, 3 and 4 has been aligned with the cross that occurs above 1.1, but the left hand margin is irregular. Ll. 3 and 4 both measure 24 cm, in comparison to ll. 1 and 2 that are 26 cm and 31 cm respectively, but their length may have been determined by the natural irregularities which occur in the rock[9].

The inscription is legible, with only minor difficulties occurring at the commencement of l. 4 where there has been some slight weathering. The rubrication of the characters is still visible, providing a noticeable contrast against the buff-coloured limestone. However, the inscription is distinguished by its vertical alignment when the reliquary is set on its base; in what presumably was its functional position[10]. Of course, the convention of vertically aligned inscriptions was common, *viz* the specimen from Babiska, dated A.D. 547 and the corpus from Heshterek, spanning 8C A.D. - 12C A.D., amongst others[11].

TRANSCRIPTION & TRANSLATION OF THE INSCRIPTION[12]

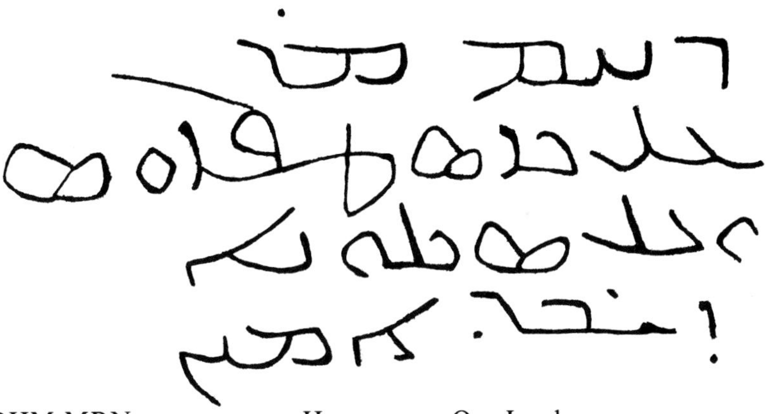

l. 1	RḤM MRN	Have mercy, Our Lord
l. 2	ʿL KRSṬPRWS	upon Christopher
l. 3	WʿL SKLWNʾ	and upon SKLWNʾ
l. 4	DʿBD ʾMYN	who made (this). Amen.

9 Measurements supplied in private correspondence between Clarke and Hunter (26 October 1987). Recorded 18 May 1987.

10 Palmer, *op. cit.*, p. 224 attributes the phenomenon of vertical inscriptions to scribal convention, reproducing the manner in which manuscripts were written.

11 E. Littmann, *Semitic inscriptions*, (New York, 1904), pp. 33-34, *re* the A.D. 6C stoa at Babiska where the two panels in the parapet of the colonnade have dovetailed plates with Syriac inscriptions written vertically. See H. Pognon, *Inscriptions sémitiques de la Syrie, de la Mésopotamie et de la région de Mossoul*, (Paris, 1907), p. 191 *sqq.* and A. Palmer, "A corpus of inscriptions from the Ṭur ʿAbdin and environs", *OrChr*, 71 (1987), p. 64.

12 See Plate VI: *Syriac inscription.*

Palaeographic summary

The eight-word inscription, consisting of 33 letters, has been written in a clear Estrangela. There are no examples of Gamal, He, Ṣadhe, Qoph, Shin and Tau; but the remaining letters exhibit the majuscule features of this script. In their duplication, the characters Alaph, Kaph and Ayin show little variation beyond the chirographical. Similarly, the three examples of Lamadh exhibit a conservative form. The three specimens of Semkath each have a pronounced 'V' at the junction of the left and right hand loops and characteristically remain unattached to the following letter — in two of the cases[13]. The single final Mim shows the expected closed, square form, whilst the rubrification of the base-line of the two medial examples of Mim, indicates that this letter is open.

However, some promiscuity of form may occur in the case of Waw. In l. 3, the example that is ligatured to the preceding Lamadh exhibits the straight, vertical stroke leading to the rounded head and is typical of Estrangela. By contrast, the penultimate letter of l. 2, an unattached Waw, is closed. Exceptions do, of course, occur as is shown by the inscription from Qartmin Abbey, Ṭur ʿAbdin (dated A.D. 534), where the single, closed Waw is differentiated from the usage of this letter otherwise[14]. However, the angular, diamond form of the specimen on l. 2 is reflected by the letter at the beginning of l. 3, even though it is open. Of course, the sharp opening stroke may have been executed by the mason, as a convention.

That square forms were used for initial letters in a line may be seen in the examples of Resh and Dalath at the beginning of ll. 1 and 4 respectively. Although some deterioration has taken place in the case of the latter letter, the vertical and horizontal strokes intersect to form a right-angle, as is also found in l. 1. Yet, in both ll. 1 and 4, the Resh and Dalath that are reproduced later in the lines exhibit an obtuse angle. In addition to the two types of Resh that are found in l. 1, a third form appears; twice in the proper name KRSṬPRWS. Here the letter consists of a vertical stroke that ends in a 'foot', but culminates in a wedge instead of the expected horizontal stroke. In neither instance, is any diacritical point discernable.

The mason may have attempted to reproduce the rounded or comma form of Resh which was used interchangeably with the angulaı form of this letter in manuscripts that were written in the Estrangela script from as early as

13 E. Littmann, *Syria: Publications of the Princeton University Archaeological Expeditions to Syria in 1904-5 and 1909. Division IV. Semitic inscriptions*, (Leiden, 1934), p. 19 notes that in majuscule script Semkath was left unconnected even as late as A.D. 13C, in contrast to the minuscule and semiminuscule scripts.

14 Palmer, *op. cit.*, p. 59.

A.D. 5C[15]. Yet as might be expected, in inscriptions the angular type seems to have gained precedence, probably because its execution would have been easier to render. Hence, the rounded form occurs only rarely; in two undated inscriptions from Dêr Simʿân[16]. Whilst it is possible that the mason may have been copying a blueprint of the inscription in which the proper name KRSṬPRWS was written with the rounded form of Resh, if he was incising his own name, he may have just reproduced his 'signature' in the current letter forms.

Due to the classic tendencies of the Estrangela script, where certain conventions that were established in A.D. 5C continue even in A.D. 13C, the dating of the inscription on purely palaeographic grounds is problematic. However, an earlier rather than a later date can be proposed, in the light of the context for which the reliquary was manufactured.

Commentary

Line 1 RḤM MRN "Our Lord have mercy". Although the diacritical point of the initial Resh is not visible, this letter may be read with certainty. Indeed, from the position of the diacritical point belonging to the Resh in MRN, it might be inferred that the diacritical point of RḤM was included in the cross that was incised to the upper left of l. 1. The appeal for divine mercy is expressed by the 1 singular Imperative Pa'el $\sqrt{\text{RḤM}}$, but as the epithet MRN indicates, it is directed to Christ[17]. The tenor and tense of the petition is reminiscent of the inscription: MŠBḤT' TLYTYWT' RḤM ʿLY "Praised Trinity, have mercy upon me", which is found on two jamb-stones of the east portal on the north side of the Trinity Church at Dar Kita and is dated to the second half of A.D. 6C[18].

Line 2 ʿL KRSṬPRWS "upon Christopher". The preposition ʿL can be read, even though the base-line of the Lamadh appears to be connected to the head of the Kaph. That this ligature has only been produced in the course

15 W. H. P. Hatch, *An album of dated Syriac manuscripts*, (Boston, 1946), p. 36 notes that in A.D. 5C, the rounded form of Resh was more common than the angular form, which gained ascendancy in A.D. 6C. See Plate V, Vatican city, Bibliotheca Apostolica Vaticana, Cod. Vat. Sir. 160, fol. 68, dated A.D. 473.

16 Littmann, *op. cit.*, (1934), pp. 29, 37. The Dalath in Inscription 29 has a diacritical point, whilst the Resh in Inscription 46 is without. However, the shape of both of these characters would conform to Littmann's comment on p. 27; "their form is not ˥, but ⟩ or ⟩", which was made in reference to an undated inscription, also from Dêr Sim'ân.

17 *Ibid.*, p. 36 mentions that, on occasion, MRN was used "with the names of Biblical prophets, and also as the titles of political rulers" and cites the examples of MRN Tiberias Caesar and MRN Abgar, the king.

18 *Ibid.*, pp. 4-6. For the earlier discussion of this inscription, when the second part had not yet been discovered, see Littmann, *op. cit.*, (1904), pp. 32-33.

carving the inscription and is unintentional, is suggested by the rubrification which does not extend for the entire length of the stroke. The proper name, KRSṬPRWS "Christopher" or "Christophorus" is one of the two persons on whose behalf mercy was sought. Whilst the combination Waw-Semkath expresses the Greek suffix ιος, otherwise the orthography of KRSṬPRWS suggests an internal reduction of vowels[19]. According to Littmann, this trend indicates the adaptation of Greek names, which presumably may have been cumbersome for Semitic speakers to pronounce[20].

Line 3 WʿL SKLWNʾ "and upon SKLWNʾ". The repetition of the preposition "upon" extends the plea for mercy to a second person. The final Alaph is characteristic of Aramaic nomenclature, but in the light of the trend towards the internal reduction of vowels, SKLWNʾ may be a Greek name which has been Semiticised[21]. Alternatively, this proper name may have derived from √SKL Paʾel, thus conveying the connotation of intelligence or knowledge[22].

Line 4 DʿBD ʾMYN "who made (this). Amen". Due to the physical deterioration at the beginning of this line, only the perpendicular stroke and the diacritical point of the Dalath, together with the tip of the oblique stroke and the base line of the Alaph can be discerned. However, the reading of DʿBD can be confidently proposed, even though the use of 3 masculine singular Peʾal √ʿBD is enigmatic given the two named subjects. Similarly, an inscription dated A.D. 784/5 from Qartmin Abbey, Ṭur ʿAbdin uses the singular verbal form of ʿBD together with none less than six men, whose names and occupations are specified[23]. As Littmann points out, the silent Waw at the end of verbs was often omitted by scribes, possibly because they may have worked from oral instructions, instead of from a written text[24]. The final word, ʾMYN, can be clearly read and is a fitting conclusion to the inscription.

19 R. Payne Smith, *Thesaurus Syriacus*, (London, 1879-1901), vol. II, col. 1821 records under the entry KRYSṬWPWRWS "Christophorus", the variant spellings: KRYSṬʾPWRWS, KRYSṬWPRʾ, KRYSṬPWRʾ, KRYSṬWPRWS.

20 Littmann, *op. cit.*, (1934), p. 12.

21 *Ibid.*, p. 21 comments that the "rendering of the Greek termination by the Syriac ܐ is very unusual", when discussing the proper name GYWRGʾ. That the paradigm was applied to the proper name Christopher can be seen in n. 19.

22 Payne Smith, *op. cit.*, Vol. II, col. 2627.

23 Palmer, *op. cit.*, pp. 69-71, specifically p. 71 where he proposes that there was "one main subject and several subsidiary subjects".

24 Littmann, *op. cit.*, (1934), p. 28.

THE MANUFACTURE OF THE RELIQUARY

The short dedicatory inscription immediately raises questions about the manufacture of the reliquary. The semantics of √ʿBD Pe'al "do, make, prepare" are wide-ranging, but from its often synonymous usage with √BN' Ethpe'al "it was built, erected, founded" and √ḤDT Ethpa'el "it was renewed restored, repaired", the most obvious application seems to be physical. That DʿBD may connote the hewing of the reliquary from the solid limestone block and possibly its transportation from the quarry, is suggested by an inscription from the monastery of St. Gabriel, Qartmin in the Ṭur ʿAbdin[25]. Given the estimated weight of the reliquary this task may have been worth recording, even if the limestone was from a nearby source.

Additionally, DʿBD may refer to the carving of the inscription and possibly even the decoration on the front of the reliquary by KRSṬPRWS and SKLWN'. In the aforementioned inscription from Qartmin, and also in a collection of epitaphs, that are dated A.D. 8C - A.D. 12C, from Hachtarak in the Ṭur ʿAbdin, this action is distinguished by √QRṬ Pa'el "he incised" (literally "he gnawed")[26]. On rarer occasions, the specifically physical effort of inscribing the inscription is expressed by √SRṬ, either as a Pa'el "he cut/engraved/scratched" or as a Pa'el "he set down in writing"[27]. √GLP Pe'al

25 Pognon, *op. cit.*, p. 42 records, ʿBD ZKRY' ... WMN D'SB 'PYS L'ŠʿY' PPYY' ŠWŠBYNH DNYTYH WʿBD 'ŠʿY' "Zacharie ... a fait ce travail ... et lorsqu'il eut détaché ce bloc de pierre, il supplia Isaie, du village de Fafa, son parrain de l'apporter. Isaie se donna beaucoup de peine ...". Some controversy surrounds Pognon's interpretation of D'SB "lorsqu'il eut détaché", claiming its derivation as Aphel √SB, citing as collateral evidence the Arabic √NZʿ "pull out, extract, remove" and √MZʿ II "pick, pluck, tear to pieces". See H. Wehr, *A Dictionary of Modern Written Arabic*, 3rd ed., (New York, 1976), pp. 954 and 906 respectively. Whilst Pognon did consider the possibility of 'SB being an orthographic error for S'B'; Aphel √SʿB "he became old/aged", Palmer, *op. cit.*, p. 66 adopts this interpretation, citing biographical information to support his reading. If Zechariah was an old man, then WMN D'SB "from the moment when he aged" may be a fitting reading, especially since Palmer claims that the clause is an "error for the phonetically indistinguishable WMN D'S'B". However, the emphasis on the physical actions associated with the manufacture of the inscription, *viz*: W'YTYWH WMRQWH WSMWH BDWKT' "on l'apporta, on le polit, on le mit à sa place" would lend weight to Pognon's suggestion, particularly in view of the time lapse of eight years. Payne Smith, *op. cit.*, Vol. II, col. 2498 lists √SB, Aphel, "abstulit, abstruxit, divulsit, evulsit", but apart from this inscription its usage elsewhere is unattested; a *hapax legomenon*?

26 Pognon, *op. cit.*, pp. 191-202. Specifically Inscriptions 95, 99, 100, 101, 102, 103, 104, 106, 107, 110, 113 and 116*. Excepting Inscriptions 101 and 116*, in each case the verb is accompanied by the name of the stone mason, being qualified either by his ecclesiastical rank or by ḤṬY' "sinner", possibly denoting a novice. However, Inscription 110, dated to A.D. 11C, uses the singular of QRṬ together with two names; ŠMW'YL and BNYMN "Samuel and Benjamin", both of which are unaccompanied by any qualifying epithets. The entry in Payne Smith, *op. cit.*, vol. II, col. 3741 indicates that this root is not frequently used, and then only in Pa'el and Ethpa'el.

27 *Idem*. Specifically Inscriptions 105, 108, 111 and 115, all emanating from A.D. 12C. See the entry for this root in Payne Smith, *op. cit.*, vol. II, col. 2738.

"he carved/engraved" appears to have been used as a synonym of $\sqrt{\text{SRṬ}}$, possibly for emphasis[28]. That the comprehensive term DʿBD was used, may be due to the genre of the inscription, for several physical actions might be combined in dedications.

Alternatively, DʿBD may have implied the sponsorship or patronage by which means the reliquary was created[29]. Hence, an A.D. 8C inscription again from Qartmin in the Ṭur ʿAbdin names Patricia, daughter of Elusṭriya as the subject of ʿBDT[30]. Undoubtedly, the finances of this woman "whose name and patronymic betray an attachment to Byzantine aristocratic culture", allowed the stoa to be 'made'[31]. Were KRSṬPRWS and SKLWN' the patrons of the reliquary, presumably they would have at least identified their patronyms, and possibly the villages from which they came. Further, had the two men been of any ecclesiastical or civil standing, their titles would have been mentioned, and even the frequent epithet ḤṬY' "sinner" is notably absent.

If DʿBD does imply the physical manufacture of the reliquary, then KRSṬPRWS and SKLWN' may have been the craftsmen; possibly one as the hewer of the limestone block and the other as the monumental mason. Such a division of labour is suggested in the previously discussed inscription from the monastery of St. Gabriel in Qartmin. Thus the pair of names might be a 'firm' signature[32], and possibly that of local artisans since had the men travelled from afar, then they may have advertised their origins. The qualifying phrase "from this village" is only occasionally included in inscriptions, presumably because this fact would have been implicit if no location was cited[33]. Hence, KRSṬPRWS and SKLWN' may have been attached to the monastery complex at Djebel Khaled.

28 *Ibid.*, p. 201. Inscription 115, ll. 5-6 reads: SRṬ MWŠ' ḤṬY' BR' DYLH DHW GLP LWḤ' HN' "Son fils Moïse, le pecheur, a écrit, et c'est lui qui a sculpté cette inscription avec son encadrement". Pognon notably justifies his translation to include "son encadrement", on the basis of his interpretation of LWḤ'. The inscription might be also rendered, "His son, Moses, the sinner, set it (i.e. the inscription) down in writing. *He* carved this tablet". Here GLP may be used to stress the physical action which was undertaken. See Payne Smith, *op. cit.*, vol. I, col. 732.

29 H. C. Butler, *Early Churches in Syria. Fourth to Seventh Centuries*, (Princeton, 1929), p. 256 points out the discrepancy in modern English surrounding clauses such as "he built and founded this church", in that they have a causative rather than literal meaning. Littmann, *op. cit.*, (1934), p. 20 queries the expression "made and built" (ʿBD WTQN), suggesting from Greek parallels a dual role of sponsorship and supervision. Palmer, *op. cit.*, (1990), p. 204 summarizes the diverse semantics of ʿBD, including that of sponsorship.

30 Palmer, *op. cit.*, (1987), p. 121.

31 *Idem.*

32 Butler, *op. cit.*, p. 257.

33 Pognon, *op. cit.*, p. 199, Inscription 111, dated A.D. 12C.

FUNCTION AND CONTEXT OF THE RELIQUARY

The massive, rectangular shape of the reliquary together with its decoration is reminiscent of Jewish ossuaries[34]. Thus, the arrangement of two rosettes, filling the two metapes of the front panel, with the intermediate space being occupied by a central motif; in this case a lozenge, is commonly attested[35]. The direct legacy of reliquaries from Jewish ossuaries is postulated by Grabar, being a result of the common *milieu* in the first centuries A.D.[36]. Yet, the reliquary from Khirbet Khaled shows some adaptation; for the 6-pointed star which often forms the central motif of the disc in Jewish ossuaries, is replaced by the much rarer 4-petalled rosette[37]. This may have been a stylised cross[38].

If the external appearance of the reliquary is similar to that of an ossuary, several internal features differ quite dramatically. Rather than being merely a receptacle, the design of the reliquary which has been hollowed out to form a 'V' shape, culminating in an outlet hole which at 22 cm forms the deepest internal point, suggests that fluid was drained. Had the accompanying cover survived, presumably it would have had a hole drilled through which fluid might have been poured; to emerge from the lower part of the reliquary. Although the cover of the specimen from Khirbet Khaled has been lost, it may well have been gabled with an acrotère at each of the four corners.

Indeed, the form of the reliquary, with the outlet hole being placed on one of the long sides is one of two types. In the second category, the outlet hole is situated on one of the short sides, often in the form of a chalice from which the oil would be scooped[39]. Thus the 'Cosmos and Damian' reliquary found

34 E. R. Goodenough, *Jewish Symbols in the Graeco-Roman Period*, v. III, (New York, 1953) fig. 105-223 provides a comprehensive collection of Palestinian ossuaries. See also H. Leclerq, "Ossuaires", *DACL*, v. 30, (Paris, 1937), col. 22-7, figs. 9277-70.

35 P. Figueras, *Decorated Jewish Ossuaries*, (Leiden, 1983), pp. 36-41 discusses rosettes as a decorative element on ossuaries, positing on p. 39 that this common design symbolised the handle-rings which were attached to wooden coffins. P. 69 discusses the lozenge motif, and in particular refers to ossuaries 365 (Plate 29) and 577 (Plate 28), where it forms the central motif, flanked by rosettes.

36 A. Grabar, "Recherches sur les sources juives de l'art paléochrétien", *Cahiers archeologiques*, XIV (1964), p. 53.

37 Figueras, *op. cit.*, p. 37 comments that "the six petals appear almost automatically, and this is the commonest form on the ossuaries". Figueras lists two specimens with four-petalled rosettes; ossuaries 341, 511. See plate 9.

38 *Ibid.*, p. 41 notes the transformation of rosettes into crosses, citing ossuaries 232 and 341. See Plate 10. In these two examples, however, the cruciform shape is well-defined, in comparison to the example from Khirbet Khaled.

39 W. Gessel, "Das Öl der Märtyrer: Zur Funktion und Interpretation der Ölsarkophage von Apamea in Syrien", *OrChr*, 72 (1989), p. 186.

by Mayance at Apamea, featured this device[40], as did two specimens which Lassus included in his *Inventaire Archaeologique de la region du nord-est de Hama*, from the villages of Qerrāté and ʿAṭšan[41]. And, another reliquary of the same form, from Restan-Arethusa is shown by Lassus in *Sanctuaires Chrètiens de Syrie*, along with a reliquary from Kafer Nabo, where the design and also the decoration — two disks with crosses rather than four-petalled rosettes — is similar to that from Khirbet Khaled[42].

The reliquary could be easily mistaken at first glance for a holy water basin, or an aqueduct-type of installation, as did Prentice when a basalt specimen was found at Mo'allaq in Syria at the turn of the century[43]. What function reliquaries fulfilled was surmised by Mayance, *viz*:

> Ils consistent en un bloc de marbre, de forme rectangulaire dans lequel, à la partie supérieure, á été creusée une petite cavité destinée à contenir des reliques, et reliée par un étroit conduit à une sorte de petit godet ámenagé sur la face latérale droite. Le couvercle de reliquaire affect la form d'un couvercle de sarcophage; il est percé, au sommet, d'un trou en forme d'entonnoir par où l'on pouvait verser, dans la cavité contenant les reliques, un liquide qui était ensuite recueilli dans le petit godet latéral et qui était sans doute considéré comme sanctifié par le contact avec les reliques[44].

That the specimen from Khirbet Khaled operated similarly, seems without question.

As Mayance mentioned, the contact of the liquid; always oil, with the relics sanctified it. Indeed, the bones of martyrs were reputed to have miraculous properties, so much so that an A.D. 13C inscription from Karakoche narrates the metamorphosis of pillaging Tatars (Mongols), who upon finding the bones of saints in a monastery which they were ransacking "became sheep instead of wolves"[45]. Eight centuries earlier, Philoxenus of Mabbug highlighted the curative powers of the martyrs bones for he wrote; "and demonic spirits cry out bitterly at his power within them, for sicknesses are driven off and illnesses chased away"[46]. Yet Philoxenus stressed that these miracles

40 A detailed description of the reliquary inscribed to the martyrs Cosmas and Damian occurs in J. Napoleone-Lemaire and J.C. Balty, *L'Église à Atrium de la Grande Colonnade*, (Brussels, 1969), p. 60. See p. 58, fig. 13 for a cross-section and an overhead view of the reliquary.

41 J. Lassus, *Inventaire Archaeologique de la region au nord-est de Hama*, 2 vols., (Damascus, 1935), vol. I, pp. 17 and 105 respectively. See also, figs. 17 and 112.

42 J. Lassus, *Sanctuaires Chrétiens de Syrie*, (Paris, 1944), p. 160.

43 *Ibid.*, p. 166, n. 6.

44 F. Mayance, "La quatrième campagne de fouilles à Apamée", *Bulletin des Musées Royaux d'art et d'histoire*, VII:1 (Jan-Fev. 1935), p. 4.

45 Pognon, *op. cit.*, pp. 129-30, Inscription 74, ll. 6-9.

46 S.P. Brock, *The Syriac Fathers on Prayer and the Spiritual Life*, (Kalamazoo, 1987), pp. 122-3. A French translation together with the Syriac text is provided by A. Tanghe, "Memra de Philoxène de Mabboug sur l'inhabitation du Saint-Esprit", *Le Muséon*, LXXIII (1960), pp. 53 (Syriac), 78.

were not effected by the bones *per se*, but by the indwelling of the Holy Spirit.

Philoxenus of Mabbug was, of course, writing contemporaneously with the rise of the cult of martyrs which flourished in Syria in A.D. 5C. His comments presumably were a reaction to this phenomenon, or more particularly to the superstitious elements therein. The growth of cult-centres appears to have been two-pronged; either developing around the burial-place or site associated with a martyr or saint, as happened in regard to St. Sergius at Resapha or St. Simon Stylites at Qal'at Sêm'ān respectively[47]. Or, involving the transportation of a martyr's relics to a location with which he was unconnected during his lifetime. Hence, one of the reliquaries found at Apamea, was dedicated to St. Theodore, from Asia Minor[48].

Indeed, so prevalent appears to have been the cult of martyrs in Syria, that Lassus notes an innovation in church architecture to accommodate this phenomenon. Based on a survey which he conducted in the regions of Jebel Sêm'an and Jebel Baricha, Lassus claims that edifices which were built after A.D. 420 incorporated a "chapel of the martyrs" which was characteristically located in the south sacristy of the sanctuary or presbyterion[49]. Butler had not recognised this development, prefering the *diaconium-prothésis* arrangement for the triple-room structures found in many of the churches[50]. Yet the discovery of reliquaries *in situ*; at the Atrium church in Apamea and village churches attests that the "chapel of the martyrs" was a common feature[51].

Given the proportions reached in Syria in A.D. 5C, when thousands of pilgrims visited cult-sites, Lassus proposed that reliquaries were used to manufacture the "oil of the martyrs", which was drained into terra-cotta

47 For the development of Resapha as a shrine and pilgrimage-centre see, J. Spencer Trimingham, *Christianity amongst the Arabs in Pre-Islamic times*, (London, 1979), pp. 235-8, P. Peeters, *Le tréfonds oriental de l'hagiographie byzantine*, (Brussels, 1950), pp. 68-70. The church at Qal'at Sem'ân is discussed in detail by Butler, *op. cit.*, pp. 96-105; Lassus, *op. cit.*, (1944), pp. 129-132; A. Grabar, *Martyrium: recherches sur le culte des reliques et l'art chrétien antique*, 2 vols., (Paris, 1946), vol. 1, pp. 364-5.

48 H. Delehaye, "Saints et reliquaires d'Apamée", *AnBoll*, 53 (1935), p. 238 comments that St. Theodore was one of the reknowed martyrs from Asia Minor, whose grave at Euchaïta in the Pontus, was visited by many pilgrims. A detailed description of the Theodore reliquary is provided by Napoleone-Lemaire and Balty, *loc. cit.*

49 Lassus, *op. cit.*, (1944), p. 177, based on an architectural analysis on pp. 173*sqq*. Grabar, *op. cit.*, vol. I, p. 340 notes "un usage... dans un grand nombre d'autres églises syriennes (Ve et VIe siècle), a fait fixer les mêmes *martyria* dans l'une des deux petites salles à côté de l'abside, de préférence dans celle du Sud", with further discussion on pp. 341-2.

50 Butler, *op. cit.*, p. 175.

51 Lassus, *op. cit.*, (1944), pp. 175-6, quoting an (unpublished) report of Tchalenko which was sent in October, 1940 to Seyrig, the Director of Antiquities, lists sixteen churches. See also, Napoleone-Lemaire and Balty, *op. cit.*, pp. 57-9 for a detailed description of the *situ* of the reliquaries at the Atrium church in Apamea. Pp. 63-4 attempts a reconstruction of the placement of the reliquaries in the "chapel of the martyrs".

phials (εὐλογία)[52]. Of course, the prophylactic value of this product was highly prized, even being considered a cure for inebriation, and apart from fulfilling the requirements of the pilgrim-trade, the "oil of the martyrs" may have also been used by local communities for quasi-medical purposes[53]. That reliquaries served the needs of villagers and pilgrims may be suggested from the large number of specimens which have been found in the restricted areas of Jebel Sem'ân and also Jebel Baricha, indicating that each church may have had a "chapel of the martyrs".

A further role is assigned to the reliquaries by Gessel in his recent article, "Das Öl der Märtyrer". From a reconstruction of the baptismal ceremony, based on the groundplan of the "cathedral de l'est" at Apamea, he claims that the reliquary, presumably the pink marble specimen which Mayance found, supplied the chrism[54]. Problems surround Gessel's suggestion that the tre-foil room (CD) was the place of pre-baptismal unction, since the recent excavator of the site, Balty designates instead the baptistery at (BL), distinguished by its semi-circular apse set into the eastern wall[55]. Whilst the location of the baptistery remains disputed, Balty does acknowledge the anointing process and may therefore uphold Gessel's association of the reliquary with the production of chrism[56].

The relationship between the "chapel of the martyrs" and the baptistery had already been noted by Lassus during his discussion of the churches at Taklé and Kseijbé, where the rooms were adjacent being connected by a door

52 Lassus, *op. cit.*, (1944), pp. 163-5.

53 Gessel, *op. cit.*, pp. 189-90, including the recommendation of St. John Chrysostrom, *Homilia in Martyribus*, (PG 50,664f.) of the usage of the "oil of the martyrs" to combat drunkenness, by means of a total corporeal unction. Grabar, *op. cit.*, vol. II, p. 343 summarises the comprehensive powers of relics.

54 Gessel, *op. cit.*, pp. 199-20, although the reliquary which is placed within the tre-foil room is not identified. However, Mayance, *op. cit.*, p. 7 reports the discovery of a rose marble reliquary during the excavation of the "cathedral de l'est", but does not specify its *locus*.

55 See the report by J. C. Balty, "Le group épiscopal d'Apamée dit 'cathédral de l'est'. Premières recherches", *Apamée de Syrie: bilan des recherches archéologiques 1969-1971*, (Brussels, 1972), pp. 198-200. He postulates that the candidates disrobed in (BR) and (BU) which were cloakrooms and then proceeded to their baptism which included unction in (BL). Gessel, *op. cit.*, pp. 199-200 postulates that after unction in the tre-foil room (CD), the naked candidates would have walked through the *piscina* in the eastern niche, which connected rooms (CB) and (CC). He makes no reference to the possible function of the apse set into the eastern wall of room (BL), but on the other hand, Balty does not proffer any interpretation of the role of the tre-foil room (CD) in their plan. Furthermore, both sets of scholars cite paradigms for their arguments; Balty specifies the baptistery attached to the church of Sts. Paul and Moses at Dār Qītā and also make a footnote reference to the martyrion of Antioche-Kaoussie. Gessel bases his proposal on the baptismal font that, like the postulated *piscina*, was both walk-through and oriented on a south-north axis at Qal'at Sem'ân.

56 Balty, *op. cit.*, p. 200 which mentions "l'onction sur tout le corps", whilst suggesting that the three semi-circular niches between the columns of the apse were places to set flasks of oil used in the anointing process. However, no specific mention is made of a reliquary.

in the southern wall[57]. On the basis of this physical proximity, Lassus stated, "[n]ous aurions aussi une preuve intéressante d'une relation qui semble exister entre les lieux de pèlerinage — ou, plus simplement, le culte des saints — et les cérémonies baptismales"[58]. Undoubtedly, the reliquaries that were found at Taklé and Kseijbé would have fulfilled both functions; i.e. producing holy oil for pilgrims and villagers and also supplying chrism since the two activities probably were mutual.

By contrast, at Apamea, Gessel implies that the manufacturing process was specialised, being divided between the "cathedral de l'est" and the Atrium church. If the former location appears to have been the source of the chrism used in the baptism ceremony, in the latter the three specimens which Mayance found in 1932 were, in Gessel's opinion, "vollauf das Begehren auch zahlreicher Pilger nach Märtyreröl dank ihrer gut durchdachten technischen Anlage befriedigen konnten"[59]. No reason is given for the differing roles of the reliquaries at Apamea, but these may have been due to its standing both as the capital of *Syria Secunda* in A.D. 5C and also as a metropolitanate with seven bishoprics.

APPLICATION TO KHIRBET KHALED

The discovery of the reliquary at Khirbet Khaled indicates that this site was associated with the cult of martyrs which reached its apogee in Syria during A.D. 5C. Hence one of the Byzantine buildings whose ruins are still visible at Khirbet Khaled may originally have been the church in which the reliquary was housed[60]. The two lengths of monolithic columns that were found nearby may have supported a ciborium which had been erected over the reliquary, as occurred at Kafer Nabo[61]. To this "chapel of the martyrs" pilgrims may have come to obtain *ampullae* of holy oil, consecrated by its contact with the relics held within the reliquary and possibly also to receive baptism in an adjacent baptistery.

The nearby limestone outcrop of Djebel Khaled was an area of anchoritic activity and the assemblage of previously discussed evidence from the site has all the hallmarks of a cult of a holy man[62]. The crosses and Christian graffiti

57 Lassus, *op. cit.*, (1944), pp. 173-4, 222.

58 *Ibid.*, p. 227.

59 Gessel, *op. cit.*, p. 191.

60 Communication between Clarke and Hunter (17.VII.89) notes two ruinous older buildings (?Byzantine date) within the village.

61 Lassus, *op. cit.*, (1944), p. 174.

62 See G. W. Clarke, "Syriac inscriptions from the Middle Euphrates", *Abr Nahrain*, XXIII (1984-85), pp. 73-82 and specifically p. 78 for discussion and description of the graffiti and the crosses. Clarke only fleetingly mentions the Syriac inscriptions on p. 79, but these are

which were carved at the entrance to the sepulchre attest that numerous pilgrims paid their respects. The three-forked cross incised on the outside of the tomb-chamber and the Maltese-type cross which was painted within, assures that the erstwhile occupant's status was saintly. Finally, the two Syriac inscriptions which were written on the walls of the 'cella' and which have been allocated, on palaeographic grounds, to the medieval period, support a continuing veneration of a saint or a martyr.

If a centre of pilgrimage had developed at the site of Khirbet Khaled, it is possible that the remains of the holy man may have been taken from his abode, the sepulchre at Djebel Khaled, to be enshrined in a church that was built for his commemoration. Such a phenomenon was not unknown in Syria, as the *Historia Philotheos* attests concerning the celebrated example of Mar Maron[63]. Yet, the identity of the saint is enigmatic, for the reliquary's inscription does not divulge any information about the contents contained therein. Nor, can it even be presumed that the bones of one person were held, for multiple deposits seem to have been made, as is illustrated by the Greek inscription dedicated to "Jude and D... and saint Callinicus and saint John the soldier and the forty martyrs", from the "cathedral de l'est" at Apamea[64].

However, would it not be fitting for a saint of the stature of Marcianus to be associated with the reliquary, especially since Clarke makes the suggestion attractive by noting that the followers of this holy man "gathered up his mortal remains in a stone chest they had made"[65]. Of course, the problem remains as to where Marcianus actually established his cell. Its distance from Beroea was noted as four *stathmoi* in the *Historia Philotheos*, but Theodoret does not specify in which direction the cell could be found[66]. Vööbus would place the monastery "in the direction of Apamea"[67], but by specifying that

discussed at length by T. Muraoka, "Two Syriac inscriptions from the Middle Euphrates", *Abr Nahrain*, XXIII (1984-85), pp. 83-9 and by Erica C. D. Hunter, "Syriac inscriptions from a Melkite monastery on the Middle Euphrates", *Bulletin of the School of Oriental and African Studies*, LII:1 (1989), pp. 1-17. For the anchoritic activity at Djebel Khaled see G. W. Clarke and P. J. Connor, "Inscriptions, Symbols and Graffiti near Joussef Pasha", *Abr Nahrain*, XXV, (1987), pp. 33-6.

63 Theodoretus, *Historia Philotheos*, XVI, col. 1420. (PG 83). An English translation is supplied by Theodoret of Cyrrhus, *A History of the Monks of Syria*, trans. R. M. Price, (Kalamazoo, 1985).

64 Lassus, *op. cit.*, (1944), p. 164 wrongly ascribes the reliquary to the Atrium church at Apamea, but provides a transcription and translation of the Greek text, as does Delehaye, *op. cit.*, pp. 238-40, together with a discussion of the named saints. Regarding multiple reliquaries, see Lassus, *op. cit.*, (1944), p. 171 and also *Historia Philotheos*, XXI, col. 1449.

65 Clarke, *op. cit.*, p. 80 referring to *Historia Philotheos*, III, col. 1337.

66 *Historia Philotheos*, III, col. 1329.

67 A. Vööbus, *History of Asceticism in the Syrian Orient*, 2 vols., (Louvain, 1956-60), v. II, p. 249. P. Canivet, *Le monachisme Syrien selon Théodoret de Cyr*, (Paris, 1977), p. 185 does not propose any location for the monastery.

the Djebel Khaled complex was precisely four *stathmoi* from Beroea, Clarke presents an alternative proposal[68].

Indeed, had the relics contained within the reliquary included those of a 'megalomartyr', would it not be plausible that the masons may have hoped, via their inscription, to secure a blessing? Certainly the Syriac inscription is unique, in that it is not a commemoration of the saints held within, but rather a dedication of the reliquary. Although dedications are found on a wide range of liturgical items, including episcopal thrones and wine-presses, no other reliquary is extant with this genre of inscription[69]. Could it be that the dedication distinguished the reliquary which was otherwise left unmarked, ostensibly, in respect of Marcianus' wishes for anonymity after his death[70]? At this stage, the identity of the martyr for whom the reliquary was manufactured can only remain conjecture.

It is paradoxical that the names of the two presumed masons have remained for posterity. Despite the inscription being written in Syriac, the combination KRSṬPRWS and SKLWN' may indicate that the monastery complex at Khirbet Khaled was bilingual. As it is attested in the *Historia Philotheos*, Greek and Syriac appear to have been spoken concomitantly at the monastery which was established further north on the Euphrates at Zeugma[71]. Greek may, however, only have been the preserve of a minority of monks, in comparison with the autochtonous language, Syriac[72]. Whilst the masons probably emanated from the indigenous population, the morphology of KRSṬPRWS suggests the infiltration of Hellenistic influences in the Aramaic culture[73].

68 Clarke, *loc. cit.*

69 See Littmann, *op. cit.*, (1934), pp. 65-6 for the inscription on a parapet at Zebed: — 'R' RWBL' 'BDYT TRWNWS' "AR(D)A Rabula made this throne". Palmer, *op. cit.*, pp. 69-71 discusses the inscription dedicating the wine-press (M'ṢRT' HD') from Qartmin Abbey in the Tur 'Abdin. Particular note may also be made of the dedication, BDYT BSHD(') HN' "I made this *martyrion*", which Littmann, *op. cit.*, (1934), p. 43 records from Kafer Nabo.

70 *Historia Philotheos*, III, col. 1337.

71 *Ibid.*, V, col. 1354.

72 Canivet, *op. cit.*, p. 250 claims that Syrian monasticism derived from men who were educated in Greek culture, pointing out on p. 248 that the monks whom Theodoret immortalised in his *Historia Philotheos* bore, with one exception (Aphraates), Greek names, thus indicating their social origins and *milieu*. In commenting on the petition of the monks from Apamea after the expulsion of Severus in A.D. 512, Peeters, *op. cit.*, p. 90 notes that the majority of signatures were in Syriac, with only a minority in Greek, but including those of the archimandrites, thus lending support to Canivet's social divisions.

73 C. Cannuyer, "Langues usuelles et liturgiques des Melkites au XIIIe s.", *OrChr*, 70 (1986), p. 111 in discussing the languages of the Melkites prior to A.D. 636 makes a tripartite division with (a) a Greek-speaking elite, (b) an indigenous Hellenised population which was bilingual, (c) rural/peasant communities speaking Syriac. Whilst the masons may have belonged to (c), by virtue of their trade skills they may have been incorporated into an artisan class that might be accommodated by (b).

Furthermore, the proper names may lend cautious support to the previous identification of the monastery site at Djebel Khaled as Melkite, on the basis of the palaeography of the two Syriac inscriptions from the 'cella' of the holy man[74]. Whilst these have been dated as late as A.D. 12C, the reliquary may be placed within the *milieu* of A.D. 5C. Hence, it would seem probable that the cult-centre at Khirbet Khaled was established prior to the emergence of the Melkite church in the wake of the Chalcedonian controversies *circa* A.D. 450. If the site became associated afterwards, the chronology of the monastery complex would be compatible with the pattern of Melkite dominance in northern Syria, which continued until the medieval period.

Per se, the reliquary is material evidence of a phenomenon which flourished in A.D. 5C, perhaps being the expression of an 'heroic' age prior to the irreversible division of the Syrian Church. Most of the other reliquaries have been concentrated in areas which became Chalcedonian; in the Jebel Sem'ân and Jebel Baricha regions of *Syria Prima* or at Apamea and the vicinity of Hama in *Syria Secunda*[75]. Moreover, specimens, or fragments thereof, have been located at Gerasa and also at Ras Siaga, their presence indicating that the cult of martyrs spread south to the cities of the Decapolis[76]. That this practice also extended eastwards is attested by the discovery at Khirbet Khaled; on the borders of Euphratesie and Oshroene.

74 See Hunter, *op. cit.*, pp. 7, 13.

75 It should be pointed out that, had other regions of Syria also been subjected to the scrutiny of Littmann and Lassus, other reliquaries may have come to light. Further, the problem of mis-identification of these objects is serious and probably has attributed to numerous reliquaries not having been recorded as such.

76 C. H. Kraeling, *Gerasa: city of the Decapolis*, (New Haven, 1938), p. 182 lists reliquaries from the churches af St. Peter's and St. George's as well as from the Cathedral. However, their siting behind or beneath the altar differs from the placement of reliquaries in Syria. Pp. 245-6 discusses the specimen that was set before the bishop's throne in St. George's church. Plate LI (a) and Plate L (b) show items from the church of SS. Peter and Paul, listed on p. 253. The reliquary from Ras Siaga is described by B. Bagatti, "Edifici Cristiani nella regione del Nebo", *Rivista di Archaeologia Christiana*, XIII, (1936), pp. 125-6. See also Fig. 16.

Plate I: *Uninscribed basin from Khirbet Khaled*

Plate II: *Stone incised with a unique cross*

Plate III: *Internal view of the inscribed reliquary*

Plate IV: *View of the reliquary showing the long, decorated side*

Plate V: *View of the reliquary, showing the short side with the Syriac inscription*

Plate VI: *Syriac inscription*

WAHEED HASSAB ALLA

Discours pour la fête de la croix attribué à saint Cyrille d'Alexandrie

Texte commenté, édité et traduit

INTRODUCTION

Aujourd'hui, nous réalisons en partie le désir du P. M. Chaîne qui a édité la version copte[1] de ce discours, par l'édition du texte arabe de celui-ci d'après le *Ms. Par. ar. 132, fol. 116V-123V*, qui date du XVIIe siècle[2], en prenant en considération le *Ms. München ar. 242, fol. 1r-9V*, qui date du XIXe siècle[3].

Il y a une phrase dans le texte arabe définissant à quel moment de l'année liturgique il faudra lire ce discours, et pour quel but? Celle-ci est d'ailleurs en accord avec le titre du manuscrit copte. Il est donc souhaitable que cette erreur soit corrigée dans les catalogues des manuscrits arabes chrétiens de la Bibl. Nat. de Paris et celle du München.

Toutefois, nous suggérons de prendre note de la correction de certaines erreurs dans la traduction française de la version copte:

A. *Omissions*

p. 499 «ⲓⲏⲥ ⲡⲭⲥ»; le terme «ⲡⲓⲣⲱⲙⲓ» est très souvent omis, ou remplacé par l'«*ouvrier*».

B. *Erreurs du traduction*

p. 505: ⲡⲓϫⲱⲙ ⲛ̀ϩⲟⲩⲓⲧ la première lecture au lieu: le premier livre;
p. 506: ϩⲁⲛⲙⲁⲧⲟⲓ des instructions au lieu: des soldats;
p. 510: ⲉⲑⲃⲏⲧⲟⲩ des Juifs au lieu: à leur sujet;
p. 512-3: ϣⲫⲏⲣ frère au lieu: compagnon (deux fois);

1 P. M. Chaîne, «Sermon sur la pénitence, attribué à saint Cyrille d'Alexandrie», in MUSJ, T. VI (1913), pp. 493-528.

2 G. Troupeau, Catalogue des manuscrits arabes de la Bibliothèque Nationale de Paris (Paris 1972-74), p. 96; Slane, Catalogue des Manuscrits arabes de la Bibl. Nat. de Paris (Paris 1883-1895), p. 29; G. Graf, GCAL, I, p. 363; M. Geerard, Clavis Patrum Graecorum, t. III, No 5278, p. 29.

3 J. Aumer, Catalogus codicum manuscriptorum Bibliothecae Regiae Monacensis: Die Arabischen Handschriften der K. Hof- und Staatsbibliothek in Muenchen, t. I, pars II: Codices arabicos continens, p. 81.

p. 514: ⲉⲁⲩⲥⲁϫⲓ les Juifs lui dirent au lieu: ils dirent;
p. 516: ϩⲁⲛⲉϥϭⲁⲗⲁⲩϫ devant lui au lieu: sous ses pieds;
p. 517: ⲛ̀ⲇⲓⲁⲕⲱⲛ du prêtre au lieu: du diacre.

PARTICULARITÉS DU P: *Par. ar. 132*

Hauteur 20½ c., largeur 15 c., 18 lignes par page.

Nous faisons les remarques suivantes:

1° l'absence de la ponctuation;
2° l'absence du hamza «ء» en position initiale: الأب – الاب; le hamza finale de la racine par tā' marbūṭa: فقراء – فقرة et la substitution du hamza par yā' ou ī: خطيئة – خطية;
3° L'absence du point diacritique pour distinguer les différentes lettres comme dans les cas suivants où nous avons procédé à quelques corrections:
dāl au lieu de ḏāl: ذ – د
ʿayn au lieu de ġayn: غ – ع
yā' au lieu de yā'hamza: ئ / ي
ḥ au lieu de ḫ: خ – ح
alif au lieu de yā': ى – ا
hā'marbūṭa au lieu d'alif-yā': اء – ه
alif au lieu de hā'marbūṭa: ه – ا
lām-mīme au lieu de lam-alif: لا – لم
tā' au lieu de ṯa': ث – ت
tā' au lieu de yā': ي / ت
tā' au lieu de tā'marbūṭa: ة / ت
ḥ au lieu de ǧim: ج – ح
4° la confusion totale entre la forme singulière et plurielle:
الذى au lieu de الذين
لأنا au lieu de لأننا
أوره au lieu de أورده
5° l'absence partielle du tašdid, waṣla, maddh et du sukūn, ainsi que l'omission du hamza dans le cas du alif mamduda: لايشا/لايشاء
6° nous signalons que dans certains endroits, le copiste a cité les mots suivants en marge de la page:
p. 117R, ligne 1, au-dessus: يترك
p. 120R, ligne 8, marge à gauche: مكتوب
p. 122R, ligne 6, marge à gauche: مذهبه
p. 122V, ligne 11, marge à droite: على

Nous pouvons conclure par cette remarque que notre texte a été traduit dans un language dialectal, voir populaire.

LA COMPILATION DEFINITIVE DU TEXTE ET LA DATATION DE CELUI DE L'ARABE

Si le P. Chaîne a placé la date de la compilation du texte copte vers le IXe siècle, nous constatons que les différentes parties du texte étaient rédigées avant cette date. Car, certains éléments de ce discours nous laissent croire que ces deux récits ont été écrits avant la conquête arabe, mais pas nécessairement à l'époque de saint Cyrille, puisqu'il ne fait aucun doute que ce discours s'inscrit dans le cadre de la littérature hagiographique apocryphe. Il ressort de l'analyse philologique de nos sources deux hypothèses: la première, c'est que le traducteur arabe a eu recours à un autre manuscrit copte que celui qui a été édité; et la deuxième, qu'il y avait un seul texte à l'origine, que le copiste copte a omis de transcrire certaines parties, ou que le traducteur arabe a ajouté lui-même les textes qui ne se trouvent pas en copte pour adapter son discours aux nouveaux environnements ecclésiastiques. Il n'est pas facile d'opter, en ce moment, pour l'une ou l'autre hypothèse, mais nous proposons de retenir la première hypothèse. Parce que nous avons constater que les deux manuscrits arabes P et M ont été recopiés, eux aussi, d'après deux autres manuscrits différents plus anciens, et que ces derniers ont été traduits d'après un ou deux manuscrit(s) copte(s) indépendamment l'un de l'autre.

Notre hypothèse s'appuie sur les variantes et le style. Le στέμμα ci-dessous montrera l'évolution et l'origine du texte. Cela ne veut pas dire que nous arriverons à donner une date précise, faute manuscrites plus anciennes que celles que nous possédons actuellement. Nous avons tenu compte, pour le récit du crucifix, du texte du synaxaire qui contient certains éléments qui ne se retrouvent pas dans P, M et V. Les variantes du synaxaire nous ont posé une question: est-ce que le compilateur du synaxaire a eu entre ses mains une autre source manuscrite où ne figure pas le récit de la manichéenne? Ou s'est-il contenté de retenir le récit du crucifix qui répond à son but? Dans ces conditions nous ne saurions prendre en considération que l'hypothèse suivante: c'est qu'il y avait à l'origine deux manuscrits, l'un contient le titre et le but avec le préambule homélitique et le récit du crucifix, l'autre est celui de la manichéenne. Cette hypothèse réside dans le fait que le nom de «Cyrille» ne figure que dans le titre et le récit du crucifix. Nous supposons que la compilation définitive du discours a eu lieu vers le milieu du IXe siècle, comme l'a proposé le P. Chaîne. Quoi qu'il en soit, les deux récits viennent du milieu alexandrin:

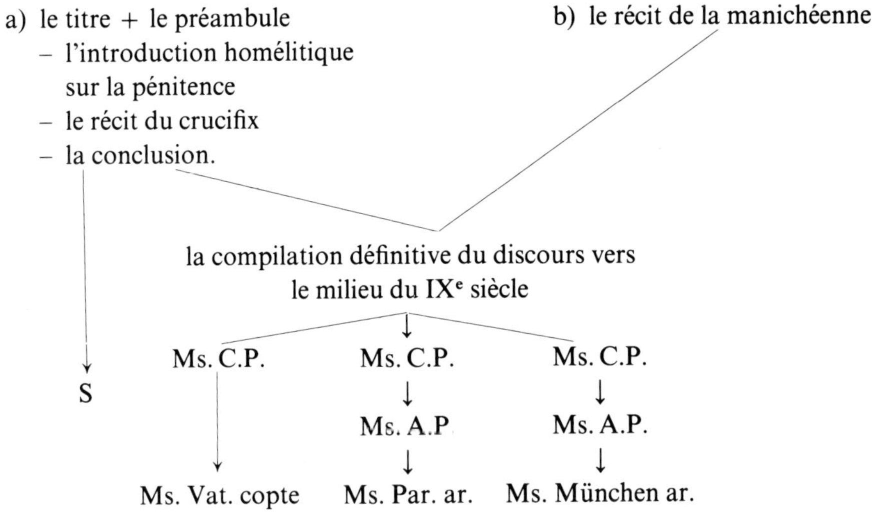

Quant à la datation de la première version arabe, nous sommes assez perplexes. Car, nous avons examiné la partie homélitique du texte arabe (et qui ne figure pas dans le copte) avec un article écrit par l'évêque Sévère ibn al-Muqaffa d'Aschmounain, intitulé: «Traité pour consoler les fidèles et pour les encourager à supporter avec patience les chagrins qu'ils éprouvent»; ce traité fait partie de son ouvrage: «Le livre de la Perle Précieuse dans l'éclaircissement de la religion»[4], où nous avons constaté certaines concordances du point de vue du style et des idées. Il ressort de cette comparaison qu'il s'agit très vraisemblablement des deux hypothèses: soit que la traduction arabe a eu lieu avant l'époque d'ibn al-Muqaffaʿ; soit que celui-ci a traduit lui-même ce discours en ajoutant certains commentaires, ainsi que certaines paraphrases. Nous ne saurions y répondre dans l'état actuel de cette question.

BUT DU DISCOURS

Le P. Chaîne a évoqué dans son commentaire sur ce sermon, deux points que nous ne saurions admettre en aucune manière, faute des preuves historiques: le premier point concerne le phénomène d'«antipathie» entre Grecs et Égyptiens manifesté dans le récit du crucifix[5]. Cela laisse entendre que le narrateur est d'une origine grecque. Mais, cette hypothèse est dificile à prouver. Parce que, premièrement, les mots grecs dans la langue copte sont abondants; deuxième-

4 Sévère Ibn al-Muqaffaʿ, «Le livre de la Perle Précieuse dans l'éclaircissement de la religion» (Le Caire 1925), 1re édition, pp. 336, 337, 164-5 [en arabe].

5 Art. cit., p. 495.

ment, il était, et il est toujours, habituel dans les récits, ainsi que dans le langage courant, que les narrateurs fassent allusion aux villes natales de leur personnages sans qu'il y ait un rapport d'«antipathie» d'ordre racial ou confessionnel.

Quant au deuxième point, le P. Chaîne a formulé toute une théorie concernant le but de la compilation du récit du crucifix prétendant que celle-ci est réalisée dans le but de rivalité [6]. Cette opinion, qui ne concerne que le récit du crucifix, est une interprétation autant fantaisiste que la première. Parce que, d'abord, le récit du crucifix a été inséré dans le synaxaire copte dans le sens commémoratif d'un miracle sans aucun caractère national. Nous savons, par ailleurs, que le synaxaire a été composé vers la fin de la première moitié du XIIIe siècle.

Ensuite, historiquement parlant, la fête de la croix est, selon le calendrier copte, le 17 Tout (14 septembre). Cette date est conforme aux deux manuscrits P et M; aux «Ménologes Évangéliaires coptes-arabe» [7]; dans le calendrier d'Abu'l-Barakât [8]; dans «les fêtes des chrétiens coptes dans les provinces Égyptiennes» de Taqî ed-Din Ahmad ibn Ali al-Maqrîzî (1364-1442 AD) [9]. Nous ne trouvons nulle part dans toutes ces sources historiques une trace de ce miracle du crucifix, ni de la manichéenne. D'ailleurs, l'Histoire des patriarches d'Alexandrie d'ibn al-Muqaffa ne contient aucune allusion à ces miracles dans la vie, ni de Théophile [10], ni de celle de Cyrille d'Alexandrie [11].

Enfin, le synaxaire copte retient quatre fêtes ou commémorations de la croix:

1° la fête officielle de la croix le 17 Tout;
2° la commémoration de la découverte de la croix par l'impératrice Hélène le 10 Barmahat (6 mars); aussi à l'honneur de la découverte de la croix par Héraclios;
3° l'apparition d'une croix au milieu du ciel dans la ville de Jérusalem à l'époque de saint Cyrille de Jérusalem le 12 de Bachons (6 mai);
4° la commémoration de ce prodige (notre sujet) le 14 Mésori (7 août).

Nous venons de constater que le but du narrateur n'était en aucun cas de fournir des raisons justifiant l'institution de la fête de la croix en Égypte. Mais, pensons-nous, le narrateur avait d'autres raisons d'ordre théologiques, liturgiques et pastorales. Pour aborder cette hypothèse, nous rappelons que le discours a été compilé postérieurement à l'époque mentionnée, et par conséquence, nous le supposons, après la crise chalcédonienne, avec tous les effets qui ont découlé de celle-ci: la persécution de l'Église d'Alexandrie accusée d'hérésie monophysite.

6 Art. cit., p. 496.
7 F. Nau, PO, t. X, p. 188.
8 E. Tisserant, PO, t. X, p. 254.
9 R. Giveau, PO, t. X, p. 328-333.
10 PO, t. I, pp. 425-430.
11 PO, t. I, pp. 430-443.

La raison théologique: le narrateur a voulu mettre en valeur la foi christologique en rejettant, indirectement, l'accusation selon laquelle l'Église d'Alexandrie est une Église monophysite au sens strict du terme. Le texte du récit de la femme manichéenne est riche en vocabulaire christologique concernant la transsubstantialité eucharistique. En outre, ce texte n'est pas le seul dans la littérature hagiographique copte, puisque Evelyn White a publié un fragment copte trouvé dans le couvent d'Abû Maqâr, sans préciser la date de celui-ci[12], où l'on constate une forme du terminologie christologique très frappante: le récit de ce fragment du «Miracle eucharistique» contient certains éléments semblables à celui de la manichéenne: un païen, un coffret d'or et un parfum odorant, ce qui nous laisse supposer qu'il a été écrit à l'époque où on donna encore «le saint corps» dans la main. Voici ces formules: «il nota qu'il (le saint corps) avait pris la forme d'un fils de l'homme ⲛ̇ⲟⲩϣⲏⲣⲓ ⲛ̇ⲣⲱⲙⲓ dans sa main»[13]; la formule suivante a été répétée trois fois dans ce fragment: «le corps et le sang de Notre-Seigneur Jésus-Christ: «ⲡⲥⲱⲙⲁ ⲛⲉⲙ ⲡⲓⲥⲛⲟϥ ⲙ̇ⲡⲉⲛⲟ̅ⲥ̅ ⲓ̅ⲏ̅ⲥ̅ ⲡⲭ̅ⲥ̅». Une troisième formule de ce même récit: «le païen le regarda en notant qu'il était devenu (un) corps dans sa main ⲛ̇ⲥⲱⲙⲁ ϧⲉⲛ ⲛⲉϥϫⲓϫ», les deux récits ont un point commun, c'est la christologie alexandrine qui n'a rien de commun avec le monophysisme déjà condamné avant Chalcédoine.

Les raisons liturgiques et pastorales: celles-ci sont liées indéniablement à la vie socio-religieuse mise en désordre suite à des persécutions ménées contre les chrétiens d'Alexandrie et le reste du pays après le concile de Chalcédoine. Celles-ci ont engendré certains laisser-aller, voire des négligences, à assister à la liturgie dès le début selon la tradition. Le narrateur a profité de l'occasion pour attirer l'attention de son auditeur sur l'importance de la liturgie de la Parole. Certes, ce point aurait pu être formulé autrement de façon à ce qu'il ne soit pas en contrediction avec la théologie eucharistique qui consiste dans la transsubstantiation par l'Esprit-Saint. Hélas! le narrateur a lui manqué de discernement théologique. Toutefois, un aspect positif, que nous pouvons relever, c'est le lien entre la liturgie de la Parole et de la liturgie eucharistique, dans le sens où la Parole s'est fait chair. C'est une valeur christologique qu'il faut retenir.

Le récit du crucifix, à part la raison fondamentale concernant la réalité toujours présente de la mort de Jésus-Christ, a une justification qui s'inscrit dans le contexte de la pastorale et de la vie socio-religieuse: les persécutions et les désordres qui frappèrent la communauté par la pauvreté ont déclenché des doutes chez un grand nombre de membres de celle-ci. Donc le but était de mettre en évidence la supériorité de la foi et de la vie éternelle par rapport à la richesse de ce bas-monde, une idée ancienne et très fréquemment évoquée dans la Bible.

12 H.-G. Evelyn White, The monasteries of the Wadi'n-Natrun: New coptic texts from the monastery of saint Macarius (New York 1973), t. II, pp. 176-7.

13 Ibid., p. 177.

Notons aussi, qu'il était possible d'avoir un autre but qui vise à changer l'image de l'Église d'Alexandrie, surtout ses chefs religieux, accusés de mener des persécutions contres les Juifs d'Alexandrie, en démontrant que c'est par des prodiges que ces derniers ont embrassé la foi chrétienne.

Nous concluont en réaffirmant que les hypothèses avancées par le P. Chaîne, ainsi que par P. Peeters[14] dans son compte rendu manquent des fondements solides.

TABLES DES ABRÉVIATIONS

M	= Ms. München ar. 242.	S	= synaxaire copte.
P	= Ms. Par. ar. 132.	[ ]	= leçons retenues du M.
V	= Ms. Vat. copte 59.	{ }	= leçons retenues du V.
Ms. C.P.	= Ms. copte perdu.	< >	= ajouter.
Ms. A.P.	= Ms. arabe perdu.		

14 Paul Peeters, in Analecta Bollandiana, t. 33 (1914), pp. 343-4.

p.116V بسم الله العظيم الربوبية المنفرد بالوحدانية [1]

ميمر وضعه الأب المكرم [2] كيرلص [3] بطريرك مدينة [4] الاسكندرية. يقرأ [5] فى [6] عيد الصليب [المجيد] [7] فى [8] سابع عشر توت لأجل التوبة النقية [9] بركة مابه تكون معنا أمين [10]. وأظهر فيه كيف [11] يحتمل الله الخاطئ بكل نوع حتى يرده إلى التوبة، بالأمراض والأعراض [12]. لأن [13] الله [14]، سبحانه وتعالى [15]، لا يشاء أحدا يهلك أبدا، {لأنه عمل يديه} [16]، ألا ييقظه إلى التوبة بالأمراض والأعراض [17]، والأحزان والفقر وموت الأولاد، حتى يتفكر فى خطاياه وما صنع من الشرور. فيتوب إلى الله [تعالى] [18] بسرعة، فيقبل الله [19] توبته، ويعوضه فى الدنيا] [20] ماضاع [21] منه أضعاف، وفى الآخرة بالحياة المؤبدة. وكل من يهمله الله فى خطاياه، ولا يفتقده بمرض، ولا بألم، ولا بمصيبة ولا بفقر، فيعلم أن ماله عند الله فى الآخرة نصيب. لأنه تركه يعيش فى الدنيا، يعيش جسدانى بذخ.

وأيضا [22] تكلم [23] فى هذا الميمر من أجل [24] امرأة {مانوية} [25] كانت فى مدينة الاسكندرية {فى أيام طفولته} [26]، وكيف أرشدها الله حتى دخلت فى دين النصرانية.

وأيضا ذكر فيه [27] فلكسيانوس رئيس [28] اليهود، وكيف [29] تعمد وصار نصرانى هو وأهل بيته من أجل الأعجوبة التى كانت من الصليب المجيد [30]، وكيف نظرت أبنته [31] العمياء عندما لطخ عينيها بالدم الذى خرج من [صليب] [32] المسيح [33] {فى وسط المجمع} [34]، وأمنوا جماعة كبيرة [35] من اليهود بسيدنا [36] يسوع [37] المسيح [له المجد دائما إلى الأبد] [38]، بسلام من الرب أمين [39].

1 M "بسم الآب والأبن والروح القدس الاله الواحد" 2 M om., V "القديس" 3 M "كيرلس" 4 M om.
5 M "يقـــرى" 6 M om. 7 P om. 8 M om. 9 V om.
10 M "بركته علينا أميـــن" 11 V om. 12 V om. 13 M "لأنــه", V "هــو" 14 MV om.
15 AjP. 16 PM om. 17 M om. 18 AjM. 19 M om. 20 P om. 21 M "بما ضاع"
22 AjP. 23 M "وتكلـم". 24 V om. 25 P "صا بيـــه", M "صبيـــه" 26 PM om.
27 M "وذكـر فيـه أيضـا", V "تكلم أيضـا". 28 PM "ريس". 29 M "كيـف", V "بعد أن حصـل"
30 M om, V "المسيح". 31 M "أبنـة". 32P "الصليـب". 33 M "عندما لطخ بالدم الذى خرج من صليب المسيح عينيهـا"
34 PM om. 35 M "كثيرة", V om. 36 V om. 37 V om.
38 AjM. 39 M cm.

قال صالح [1] ومكرم [2] هو أسم سيدنا يسوع المسيح الذى قربنا من بيعته ، وعلمنا P.117R كلام [3] الأنجيل المقدس ، كما قال فى بشارة [4] متى عن: "أنسان [5] كان له [6] ماية خروف [7] ، فأذا ضل واحد منه [8] ، إليس يترك التسعة [والتسعين] [9] على الجبل، ويطلب الضال الذى هلك. فأذا [هو] [10] وجده ، حمله على عاتقه [ويفرح] [11] به. ويدعى أصدقاؤه وجيرانه ويقول [لهم] [12] أفرحوا معى اليوم لأنى وجدت خروفى الذى هلك." [13] هكذا [14] يكون فرح عظيم فى السماء قدام اللّه [تعالى] [15] وملائكته بخاطئ واحد يتوب. وقال أيضا يدعونا [اللّه] [16] إلى التوبة: "هلموا إلى ياكل التعبنين [17] الثقيلى الحمل وأنا أريحكم. أحملوا نيرى عليكم وتعلموا منى ، فأنى متواضع فى قلبى ، فتجدوا نياح [لنفوسكم] [18]، لأن نيرى حلوا وحملى خفيف." [19] "أيها الحاملون أوساخ [20] خطاياهم التى تفوحت [21] فيهم وكثرت [22] جدا ، هلموا إلى لأغفر لكم ، لأنى لا أشاء موت الخاطئ ، قال الرب ، حتى يعود من طريقه السوء ، ويتوب ويعيش فى الحياة الأبدية." [23] وقال أيضا: "يكون فرح عظيم قدام ملائكة اللّه بخاطئ واحد إذا تاب. فإذا كان الفرح العظيم بخاطئ واحد {إذا تاب عند اللّه وملائكته} [24] ، فكم بالحرى يكون الفرح العظيم للسمائيين والأرضيين {والملائكة ورؤساء الملائكة والطوباويين السمائيين} [25] بجماعة خطاة أذا تابوا. فالآن أيها الأخوة الأحباء لا نتوانا عن أنفسنا ولا نقول أن خطايانا [26] كثيرة ، رحمة اللّه أكثر من خطايانا "وليس أحدا بلا خطية إلا اللّه وحده." [27]

1 M om. 2 M om. 3 M "بكلام". 4 M "فصل". 5 M "الأنسان". 6 M "الذى كان له".
7 M "خاروف". 8 M "منها". 9 P "وتسعين". 10 P om. 11 P "وفرح به".
12 P om. 13 Lc.15,4-8. 14 M "هكذى". 15 AjM. 16 P om.
17 M "المتعوبين". 18 P "نفوسكم". 19 Mt.11,28-30. 20 M "أوساق".
21 M "وتقرحت". 22 MP "وكثرة". 23 Ez.33,11. 24 PM om. 25 PM om.
26 V "الآن أيضا يا أحبائى لا نحتقر أنفسنا بسبب خطايانا"
27 Mc.10,18; Lc.18,19.

أعلموا [1] أن [2] أبليس يوقعنا فى الخطايا بمناميه [3] الشريرة ، ويحسن لنا الشهوة واللذات [4] . فلنبادر نحن [5] إلى التوبة [6] ونسأل الله محب البشر بتواضع عظيم ليغفر لنا خطايانا ، { وتوجد عنده العناية لنا } [7] . وعلامة [8] الأتضاع إبن الأنسان لا يكافئ عدوه بما صنعه [9] ، ولا يجازيه بالشر ، ويرى أن جميع الخطاة ، حتى سافكين الدماء والزناه ، أنهم أخير منه . ولا يدين أحدا أبدا ، [ولا يعيبه] [10] P.117V ولا يعيره ، ولا يوبخه ، إلا [11] يعاتبه بينه وبينه . ولا يؤذى أحدا ، ولا يكذب على أحدا ، ولا يطرد أحدا ، ولا يمنعه من خيره [ولا مرقده] [12] . ومن سأله يعطيه [13] ومن طلب منه يقرضه [15] ، ولو كان عدوه . [ولايضحك على أحدا] [14] ، ولا يحقد على أحدا ، ولايستهزئ بأحدا . فهاذاك [هو النصرانى] [16] بالحقيقة ، الذى يهتم بخطاياه ويتوب ، ولا يؤذى أحدا بكلمة ردية . لأن كلمن يتحدث [17] فى الناس ، يجيب الله خطاياهم عليه . لأنه كذب ونم [18] . وأما النصرانى المتواضع الذى هو [19] مهتم [20] بخلاص نفسه ، لا يخلى أحدا [متوجع] [21] من جهته ، ولا يتناول السراير الطاهرة [22] حتى يصطلح مع عدوه [23] ، كما أمر السيد [المسيح] [24] فى إنجيله المقدس [25] . أو لعل يتوانى [26] ويقول: خطايانا كثيرة جدا ، وكيف يغفر لنا الله [27] ؟ أنظر ياحبيب لا تقول [28] شيئا هكذا ، [فأنه ليس] [29] شيئا من الخطايا تقبل قدام الله [30] ، لأنه ، سبحانه وتعالى [31] ، غفور رحوم [32] ، يغفر لنا . فأن كنت خاطئ جدا ، أذكر أهل نينوى ، وكيف غفرت [33] لهم مسباتهم [34] بالتوبة . وأن كنت [35] زانى ، أذكر الامرأة [36] الزانية [37] التى جعلت عينيها مثل قصرية ماء [سائبة] [38] ، [39] وغسلت رجلى سيدنا [40] [يسوع] [41] المسيح [42] بدموعها [43] ومسحتهم بشعر رأسها . وأن كنت لصا ، فأذكر اللص الذى أعترف بالسيد المسيح [44] على الصليب ، فنال غفران خطاياه <فى نفس الوقت> [45] . وأن كنت ظالما [46] أو عشارا [47] ، فأذكر العشار الذى جعله سيدنا تلميذا له مبشرا . وأن كنت ساحرا مجوسيا [48] ، [فتب] [49] وأذكر المجوس

1 MV om. 2 V "وإذا". 3 M "بمصايبه". 4 V "وإذا أظلم قلوبنا فى الشهوات"
5 M om. 6 V "فلنجأ بجوار صلاح الله". 7 PM om. 8 M "وعلامت"
9 M "بما صنع". 10 P om. 11 M "ولا". 12 P "ولا رفده"
13 M "ومن سألك تعطيه". 14 P om. 15 M om. 16 P "نصرانى". 17 M "يحدثا".
18 M "ونم". 19 M om. 20 M "يهتم". 21 P "متجع". 22 M "الالهية"
23 M "هو وعدوه". 24 P om. 25 M "الإنجيل المقدس". 26 M "ولا يتوانا أحدا".
27 M "الله لنا". 28 M "ولا تقول". 29 P om. 30 V "لا تأتى قائلا: أرتكبت خطايا عديدة وعظيمة ، من الصعب أن يغفر الرب لى ، أحذر ، أحذر أن تتكلم هكذا ، ليست خطية عظيمة تقبل قدام الله ، ولا يستطيع أن يغفرها لنا".
31 AjP. 32 M "رحيم".
33 M "غفر". 34 M "سياتهم". 35 V "خاطئ" 36 M "لامرأة".
37 M "الذى". 38 PV om. 39 M "وغسلة". 40 M "ربنا". 41 P om.
42 AjPM. 43 AjP. 44 AjP. 45 PM "فى ساعة واحدة". 46 M "ظالم".
47 M "عشار". 48 AjPM, V "لكن أخيرا ستقول لى: أنا ساحرا". 49 AjPM.

الذين جاؤا للسيد [1] المسيح وقدموا له قرابينهم ، ونالوا منه غفران خطاياهم {فى نفس الوقت} [2] . وأن كنت عملت كل الخطايا [3] ، لا<تتوانى> [4] عن التوبة ، {الآن أذن ياأحبائى} [5] ، ولا تقطع رجائك [6] من مراحم اللّه ، سبحانه [7] ، {بعلة P.118R
الخطية} [8] . لأن اللّه ، سبحانه وتعالى ذكره [9] ، {مملوء عطف فى الواقع} [10] <وهو> رؤوف رحيم لا يشاء هلاك أحدا من خليقته [11] ، {ولكن ليعود من طريقه السيئ وليحيا} [12] ، ولا يضيع لأحدا أجرا أبدا ، ويشاء أن تخلص [13] الناس جميعهم بالتوبة . لأن التوبة تقيم الساقطين ، وتثبت [14] <القائمين> [15] . التوبة تغسل الأنسان من الخطايا مثل ما [يغسل] [16] الثوب ولا يعلم أحدا أين مضى الوسخ. قال اللّه، سبحانه [17] ، على لسان الأنبياء: تعالوا إلى أيها الأبناء ، ولو كانت خطاياكم مثل [البشر] [18] ، أنا أبيضها مثل الثلج ، ولو كانت السيخ [19] [الأسود] [20] ، أنا أنقيها جدا ، وأسامحكم بها ، أذا لم تغيبوا [21] على غيركم ، وإن نممتوا [22] وكذبتوا على أنسان ، فأنى [23] أغفر [له] [24] خطاياه ، وأجددها على الذى أفتخر وكذب على [رفيقه أو] [25] قريبه وضحك عليه.

أسمعوا [26] الآن بيان تحقيق الكلام [27] ، إن اللّه ، سبحانه وتعالى [28] ، لايشاء موت الخاطئ ، بل ييقظه [29] للتوبة والخلاص [30] .

كان بمدينة [31] الاسكندرية [فى أيام] [32] البطريرك ثاوفيلس ، وكنت أنا [شـاب] [33] أتعلم فى المكتب. وكانت امرأة {مانوية} [34] ساكنة فى شارع معلمى ، [وكـان] [35] لها أبنة صغيرة عمرها نحو تسعة [36] سنين أو عشرة. وكانت أم هذه [37] الصبية تزينها وترسلها إلى الكنيسة المقدسة [38] من وقت أن يقرأ [39] البولس [40] الكتاب الأول {حسب التقليد} [41] . وتقول لها أمها [42] [هكذا] [43] : أنظرى ياأبنتى ، لا [44] تخرجى من الكنيسة [45] حتى يعطوا السلام ويصرفوا [الجميع] [46] ، والذى يعطيه

1 AjPM. 2 PM "فى لحظة واحدة". 3 M "الخطية".
4 P "لا تتوانا", M "ولا تتوانا". 5 PM om. 6 M "رجاك", V "لا تيئسوا من مراحم اللّه".
7 AjP. 8 PM om. 9 AjP. 10 PM om. 11 M "لهلاك أحدا من الخليقه". 12 PM om.
13 M "يخلص". 14 M "وتبت". 15 PM "القايمين". 16 M "تغسل". 17 AjP.
18 P "اليسر". 19 M "المسح". 20 P "السودانا". 21 M "تعيبوا". 22 M "تممتوا".
23 M "فأنا". 24 P om. 25 P om. 26 M "أسمع". 27 V "أسمع حقيقة الكلام".
28 AjP. 29 M "ييقضه". 30 V "ساقص لك خبرا عظيم حدث فى مدينة الاسكندرية ستتعجب من القصة".
31 M " ". 32 P om. 33 P om.
34 PM om; P "صابيه", M "صبيه". 35 P "وأن". 36 M "تسعت". 37 M om.
38 MV "النصارى". 39 M "يقرى". 40 AjPM. 41 PM om. 42 AjP. 43 M "هكذى"; P om.
44 AjPM. 45 AjPM. 46 AjPM; P "الجمع".

لك الكاهن لا تأكليه حتى تجئ إلى ها هنا[1] . [وكانوا][2] أولا يعطوا القربان المقدس للناس فى أيديهم إلى زمان أبى البطريرك[3] ثاوفيلس. ولما[4] جرى هذا الأمر ، أبطلوا عطية القربان فى اليد[5] ، وصاروا الكهنة[6] يقربون[7] الناس[8] فى أفواههم[9] . وتثبتت[10] هذه[11] العادة[12] فى الكنيسة[13] حتى[14] يومنا هذا.

118V حينئذا تلك الصبية .أبنت[15] الامرأة[16] كانت تمضى تختلط مع جماعة نساء[17] النصارى من أول القداس[18] إلى عند تناول القربان[19] [وتدخل][20] مع < النساء >[21] ، وتمد يدها للبطريرك[22] وتأخذ منه [الجسد المقدس][23] الذى [لربنا يسوع المسيح][24] سرقة من غير إن يعرفها أحدا أنها غير نصرانية[25] ، [وتقف][26] حتى يعطوا السلام، فتخرج خفية[27] . لأن الاساقفة والبطاركة كانوا يقربون[28] النساء بأيديهم <فى > ذلك الزمان. [وكانوا][29] لابسين[30] الكتان. وما ترهبوا الاساقفة وتركوا نسائهم إلا من زمان الأب البطريرك[31] ديمتريوس. وكانت أم الصبية إذ جابت لها أبنتها[32] [الجسد][33] المقدس ، كل دفعة تجربه لتعلم[34] إن كانت الصبية[35] < قـد > سمعت الكتب أم لا. فتغرس فيه شوكة أو أبرة ، فإذا خرج منه[36] الدم ، تلفه فى منديل حرير وتجعله فى درج ذهب وتحفظه عندها. فقامت الامرأة دفعة وأرسلت أبنتها[37] إلى الكنيسة كالعادة لتأخذ القربان المقدس ، الذى هو الحياة الدائمة وبه غفران الخطايا والذنوب[38] ، ولذلك[39] سمى الجسد المقدس. فعندما خرجت الصبية لتمضى إلى الكنيسة[40] ، وجدت بنات من أهل شارعها، فألتهت [معهن][41] ، ولم تمضى إلى الكنيسة إلا وقت رفع { الذبيحة }[42] . فلما دخلت الكنيسة[43] ، أخذت من القربان المقدس مع الشعب ، ومضت كالعادة إلى أمها خفية. حينئذا أمها أرادت < أن > تعلم إن كانت أبنتها[44] < قد > سمعت الكتب[45] أم لا. فأخذت الشوكة <وغرستها >[46] كالعادة[47] ، فلم يخرج منه

V "لتحمليه إلى هنا". 2 P "وكان". 3 M om. 4 M "لما".
M om. 6 M om. 7 M "أن يقربوا". 8 M om. 9 M "فمهم". 10 M "وتبت".
M "هذا". 12 M om. 13 M "البيعة". 14 M "إلى". 15,16 AjPM. 17 AjPM.
AjPM, V "القراءة". 19 V "حتى يعطوا السلام". 20 P "تدخل"
P "النسوان", M "النسوة". 22 M "إلى البطريرك".
P "من القربان من القدس", V "المحيى". 24 P "لسيدنا", V om. 25 V om.
P "تقف". 27 M "خفيا". 28 M "يقربوا". 29 P om. 30 M "لابسى".
M om. 32 M "بنتها". 33 P "القربان". 34 M "لعلم". 35 M "إن الصبية كانت
M om. 37 M "بنتها". 38 M "والحياة". 39 M "وكذلك". 40 AjP.
P "معهم". 42 P "الابرسفارين", M "الابروسفارين". 43 M "البيعة". 44 M om.
M "الكتاب". 46 P "وتغرسها", M "ونغسته". 47 M om.

دم ، لأنها لم تسمع الفصول. لأن كلمن لا يسمع الفصول ويتأملها جيدا ، ما يحل له أن يتقرب. لأنها أنهار[1] ماء الحياة. فعند ذلك[2] مسكتها[3] أمها[4] وضربتها [ضربا][5] وجيعا حتى بلغت الموت من أجل غضبها[6] عليها. فلما سمع معلمى[7] P.119R [ضرب][8] الصبية ، تعجب من ذلك[9] ، لأن بيته كان فى مقابل[10] بيت الامرأة، كما بدئنا وقلنا. حينئذا [وجدها][11] معلمى[12] عشية النهار[13] ، لم تكن أمها حاضرة. فقال لها معلمى : أيش [الذى][17] صنعتيه[16] حتى[15] ضربتك أمك هذا الضرب العظيم؟[14] فأما هى فأظهرت الأمر لمعلمى وقالت: أمى كانت تسيرنى إلى كنيسة النصارى لأخذ القربان[19] وأجيبه لها. فقال لها: وأيش تعمل به؟ قالت[18] له: تجعله فى درج ذهب ، وتحفظه حتى تبيعه للنصارى فى بلادنا بثمن كثير[20] . فلم <يتوانى>[21] معلمى فى هذا الأمر ، بل قام ومضى إلى البيعة ، إلى عند الأب البطريرك ثاوفيلس[22] وأعلمه بهذا الأمر. وللوقت أرسل كهنة وجند خلف الامرأة وإبنتها حيث لا يعلموا [بالأمر][24] ، وجابوهم[23] إلى الكنيسة. فقال لها البطريرك: أقسم عليك أيتها الامرأة بالاله[28] الضابط[27] [الكل][26] الذى [تترجيه][25] إن تعلمينى كيف هذا الأمر؟ إما تخافى الله حيث تسرقى أعضاء المسيح سيدنا[29] وتبيعه بالمال؟ فأعترفت الامرأة قبل أن يعذبوها بشئ من العذاب[30] وقالت: لست أبيعه ، بل [أنا][32] أحفظه فى بيتى. وللوقت أرسل البطريرك[31] قسوس وشمامسة وأقوام مؤمنين[34] إلى بيت تلك[33] الامرأة. فلما قربوا من الموضع الذى فيه الدرج ، نظروا عليه لميع عظيم. فصلوا هناك صلاة عظيمة ، وتعجبوا من ذلك وأخذوا الدرج الذهب ، وأتوا به إلى الأب[35] البطريرك. فعندما فتحه ، وجد الجسد المقدس[38] [فيه][37] ، وفاح[36] منه عطرا. حينئذا وقع خوف الرب على تلك الامرأة ، وسجدت[42] له[41] قائلة: ياسيدى الأب[40] البطريرك[39] إن كان يستطاع

1 M om. 2 M om. 3 M "فمسكتها", V "عند ذلك مسكت الطفلة" 4 M om. 5 P om.
6 M "عيضها". 7 M "المعلم". 8 P om. 9 AjPM. 10 V "بجوار", le terme copte: ⲚⲞⲨⲈϨⲞⲞⲨ "ϨⲀⲐⲞⲨⲰⲤ"
11 P "أوجدها". 12 M om. 13 AjPM, V "يوما ما بعد ذلك ، ملاحظا أن أم الطفلة الصغيرة ليست هناك".
14 V "تكلم مع الطفلة بملاطفة". 15 P om. 16 M "ضيعتيه".
17 V "حتى أستحقيت هذا الغضب العظيم والعقاب الكبير". 18 V "ⲚⲚⲒⲀⲨϢⲀⲚⲞⲚ".
19 M "فقالت". 20 V om. 21 PM "يتوانا". 22 M "ثاوفيلس البطريرك".
23 P "مالأمر". 24 V "فأتوا بالمرأة وأبنتها الصغيرة". 25 V "بالله". 26 AjPM.
27 P om. 28 P "ترتجيه". 29 AjPM. 30 V "ⲬⲰⲢⲒⲤ ⲂⲀⲤⲀⲚⲞⲤ : بدون تعذيب".
31 P om. 32 M om. 33 V "مؤمنين أرثوذكس". 34 AjP. 35 M "عند الأب".
36 P om. 37 M "ففاح". 38 AjP. 39 M "فسجدت". 40 V "أمام البطريرك".
41 M "الان". 42 AjP.

لقدسك أن تترحم على أنا الخا طية ، [فأغفر][1] لى ولأبنتى[2] ، لأننا تائبين على يديك. فعرض عليهما الأب البطريرك قانون صوم أربعين يوما ، ووعظهما .119V [وثبتهما][3] ، وعمدهما بأسم الآب والأبن والروح القدس ، الاله الواحد[4] ، ونالوا من السرائر المقدسة [جسد ربنا يسوع المسيح ودمه الكريم][5] . [ودفعت][6] الامرأة[7] للبطريرك[8] كل مالها ليصرفه[9] على المساكين ، وبنت دارها كنيسة. وبعد ذلك حلقوا رووسهم ، وترهبوا فى دير الزجاج[10] ، خارج مدينة الاسكندرية، وأقاما[11] فيه إلى يوم وفاتهما. وكملوا سيرتهما بأستقامة ، بسلام من الرب. أمين.

وأيضا[12] ظهرت <أ>عجوبة[13] عظيمة لا ينبغى السكوت عنها[14] . وذلك بمدينة الاسكندرية[15] فى أيام صباى كما عرفت محبتكم[16] أولا أنا الحقير كيرلس[17] . قال أن اللّه الصالح لايشاء موت الخاطئ ، بل يسعى فى طلب الخروف الضال ليعيده إلى القطيع الناطق. والآن يا حبيب[18] لا تتوانى[19] عن خلاصك[20] {بسبب الخطية[21] } ، وتقول [أن][22] خطاياى عظيمة جدا[23] وليس يصفح اللّه عنى. لا تؤمن[24] بهذا أبدا ، ولا تعطى الخطية قوة. فإن كان أبليس قد أضلك وأرماك فى خطية عظيمة[25] ، أسرع[26] أنت [وعد][27] إلى اللّه محب البشر ، وأطلب منه بدموع <وقل>[28] اللهم أغفر لى أنا[29] الخاطئ سريعا[30] ، فتدركك رأفته ورحمته بسرعة[31] . لأنه، سبحانه وتعالى جل ذكره[32] ، قال: عندما تنطق وتطلبنى ، فأقول [هوذا أنا هاهنا][33] حى أنا يقول الصباؤوت ، أنى أغفر له فى ساعة توبته ، ولا أطالبه بذنب قديم أبدا إذا لم[34] يعود إلى الخطية ثانية[35] ، ويموت بلا توبة ، ولا صدقة تفديه من جهنم[36] . أسمعوا[37] [الآن][38] لأخبركم[39] <بهذه الأعجوبة>[40] التى أبتدئنا بسببها[41] ، {لكى تعلم<وا> صلاح اللّه الذى لا يريد هلاك أحدا من

1 P " وأغفر لى ". 2 AjP. 3 P om. 4 AjP. 5 P om. 6 P " ودفعة ".
7 M " له الامرأة ". 8 M om. 9 M " وفرقه ". 10 V " دير العذارى ".
1 M " وبقيا فيه ". 12 MV " هذه الاعجوبه ". 13 S " صنع الله عجوبة عظيمة ". 14 AjP.
5 MV " فى مدينة ". 16 V " كما قلت سابقا. لقد رويتها بمحبة لكم لأعلمكم... ". 17 V om.
8 V " يا أحبائى ". 19 PM " لا تتوانا ", V " لا تيئسوا ". 20 V " خلاصكم ". 21 PM om. 22 P om.
3 V " مهما عظمت ", 24 M " لا تظن ", V " لقد أرتكبت خطايا عديدة وعظيمة أحذروا أن تتكلموا هكذا ، الخطية ....".
5 M " فى الخطية ". 26 M " فأسرع ". 27 P om. 28 PM " وقول ".
9 M " فأنى ". 30 AjP. 31 M " سرعة ". 32 AjP. 33 P " فأقول هأنذا ". 34 M " ولم ".
5 M " ثانيا ". 36 V " لا يريد موت الخاطئ ، ولكن ليعود من طريقه السيئ ويحيا ".
7 M " اسمع الآن ", V " أسمع أيضا ". 38 P om. 39 M om.
0 M " معجزة آخرى ", V " سأحكى لك قصة آخرى ". 41 AjP.

عمل يديه } [1] :

كان فى مدينة [2] الاسكندرية فى أيام أبى [3] الأب البطريرك [4] ثاوفيلس ، وكنت أنا شماس عنده فى القلاية [5] [أتعلم] [6] عظم محبة الله للبشر ، أنه لايشاء إن يمضى أحدا من خليقته للهلاك مثل ما يعود ويحيا. كان أنسان يهودى فى مدينة P.120R الاسكندرية أسمه فلكسيانوس [7] ، عظيم فى المجمع ، وكان غنيا جدا بالذهب والفضة والمواشى والعبيد. وهذا كان { أنسان } [8] خائف من الله ، سبحانه [9] ، عاملا بشريعة موسى ، يصنع عبادة عظيمة فى مجمع اليهود ، وصدقات كثيرة كما هو مكتوب فى ناموس موسى [10] . وكان له [صيت] [11] فى جميع المجامع [12] فى أخذه وعطاه ، ومشكور السيرة لأجل تحننه على المساكين ، وكان كل أحد يعطيه الطوبى [13] . ولكن الله ، سبحانه وتعالى ذكره [14] ،[الصالح] [15] ، < حسب محبته > [16] للبشر ، [لم يشاء < أن > [17] يترك هذا الأنسان] [18] اليهودى هكذا فى الظلمة ، بل أراد أن يطهره من خطاياه ، كما هو مكتوب فى الابركسيس [19] :"أن جميع الخائفين من الله ، الذين يصنعون هواه وأرادته هم مقبولين عنده " . وكانوا أيضا رجلين نصارى فعلة [20] ، سكان فى مدينة الاسكندرية ، وهؤلاء كانوا [21] من أهل مصر. وكانوا سكان فى شوارع [22] اليهود. فنظروا أولئك [23] النصارى الفعلة [24] إلى اليهود وهم أغنياء بالذهب والفضة. فتحدثوا يوما مع بعضهما قائلين: نحن متعجبين من هؤلاء اليهود وهم أناس خطاة ، وهم صالبى [25] المسيح { أبن الله الحى } [26] سيدنا [27] ، أذ نراهم أغنياء أكثر من جميع النصارى. وأن أحدهما كان خائفا من الله ، فأجاب وقال لرفيقه [28] : حقا [29] بالحقيقة ياأخى ليس أمانة على الأرض أعظم من أمانة النصارى الذى أعطاهم السيد الطوبى فى الانجيل قائلا: طوبى للمساكين بالروح ، فأن لهم خاصة ملكوت الله. وأعطى

1 PM om. 2 M " مدينت ". 3 AjP. 4 AjP. 5 V " sous sa juridication". 6 P " لتعلموا ".
7 MV om. 8 PM om. 9 AjP. 10 M om. 11 P " صيط ". 12 AjPM. 13 PM " الطوبا ".
14 AjP. 15 M " صالح ". 16 M " محبته ". 17 PM om.
18 Il semblerait que cette phrase a été adaptée au cas de l'homme juif par le traducteur arabe, puisqu'elle ne figure pas ainsi dans le texte copte. 19 AjPM. 20 M " فعلة نصارى ".
21 M om. 22 M " شارع ". 23 M om. 24 M om. 25 M " صالبين ". 26 PM om.
27 AjPM. 28 S " فأجابه ذاك قايلا ياأخى مال الدنيا ماله عند الله قدرا ، ولو كان له قدر ما اعطاه لعباد الاوثان والزناة واللصوص والقتلة ، والانبياء لم يزالوا فقرا مضطهدين وهكذا الرسل والرب يقول اخوتى الفقرا ".
29 AjP.

P.120V الويل لليهود الأغنياء [1] قائلا: "الويل للشباعة الآن فأنهم سيجوعون ، الويل لهم فأنهم أخذوا نياحهم على الأرض." وكذلك [2] قساة القلوب ، والذين يقلقون ولا يصبرون من النصارى أيضا ، بل يجحدون المسيح لأجل مال الدنيا ، ولأجل < شهواتهم > [3] الردية. ومدح الصابرين من النصارى قائلا: "طوباهم [4] الجياع [5] فأنهم شبعون ، طوبى [6] للعطاش من أجل البر ، فأنهم يفرحون. طوبى [7] للحزانى، فأنهم يعزون. طوبى [8] للمطرودين من أجل البر ، فأنهم يرثون [9] أرض الحياة."
[وأكد] [10] حزن اليهود والكفرة بقوله: الويل للضاحكين البذخين [11] ، فأنهم يبكون [12] وينوحون. " أجابه رفيقه ، ذلك الشقى [13] ، وقال له: ما أسمع منك شئ ، إلا أن أقوم [وأمضى] [14] وأعمل [15] يهودى وأبقى [16] غلام لفلكسيانوس [17] اليهودى ، وأدخل فى دينه [18] . فقال له: لا يا أخى ، أمن وأمن [19] بصلاح سيدنا يسوع المسيح أبن الله الحى ، فأنه يبارك فى القليل الذى لنا ، وهو أفضل من أموال ذلك الرجل اليهودى. لأن الله ، سبحانه وتعالى [20] ، قال على لسان داوود النبى: "اليسير من الصديق أخير وأفضل من كنزة [غنى] [21] الخاطئ. " وأيضا " أن مجد الخاطئ لم [22] يصل معه إلا إلى القبر فقط ، وأن غناه لا ينفعه فى يوم شدته ، بل يدينه الله عليه ، الذى أكتنزه وبخل به على المساكين [23] ، ولم يعطى [منه] [24] صدقة ، بل دفنه فى الأرض وأؤتمنها عليه أكثر من خالقه [ما أوعد له] [25] .
P.121R وبولس ، لسان العطر ، [26] يقول ، فى رسالته إلى طيماتاوس [27] ، قال: "وأما الذين يطلبون [28] الكنز [29] والغناء سيقعون فى البلايا وفى أمور صعبة ، وينبغى [30] لنا أن نقنع بالقوت [31] والكسوة [32] . وقال أيضا بعد وصف هذه الأشياء كلها، قال [33] : "وأنت ياولى الله ، أهرب من هذا كله ، وأوصى أغنياء هذه الدنيا، القساة القلوب [34] ، أن لا [35] يتكبروا فى همهم ولا يتكلوا [36] على [الغنى] [37] الذى

1 AjMPV. 2 M " كل قسات ". 3 P " شهوتهم ", M " سهواتهم ". 4 M " طوبا ".
5 M " للجياع ". 6,7,8 M " طوبا ". 9 M " يرثوا ". 10 P " وكد ". 11 M om.
12 M " يبكوا ". 13 AjP. 14 P " امضى ". 15 M " وابقا ". 16 M " وابقا ".
17 V " ولكن الآخر أجاب وقال له سأقوم وسأعمل سنة عمل عند فلكسيانوس ". 18 V om. 19 AjP.
20 AjP. 21 P om. 22 M " ما ". 23 M " وبخل على المساكين به ". 24 P om.
25 P " ما اودعه ". 26 AjP. 27 M om. 28 M " يطلبوا ". 29 M " الترف ".
30 M " ينبغى ". 31 M " بالقوة ". 32 M " الكسوه ". 33 AjP. 34 Mom.
35 M " الكفره لا يكفروا فى همهم ". 36 M " ولا يتوكلوا ". 37 P " الغنا ".

الذى لا [أتكالا][1] عليه ، بل على الله الحى. " وقال القتاليقون: " الويل لكم أيها الأغنياء الكفرة ، فقد أخذتم عزاكم على الأرض ، وذهبكم[2] يتغير ، وفضتكم تصدأ ، وثيابكم [الفاخرة تسوس وتبلى][3] . وقال سيدنا [يسوع المسيح][4] : "لا [يقدر][5] المتوكلون على [الأموال][6] <دخول>[7] ملكوت السموات. وأقول لكم أن دخول الجمل من ثقب الأبرة أهون من غنى يدخل ملكوت الله. " وقال أيضا: "لا تستطيعوا أن تعبدوا الله والمال" وسائر الكتب[8] تعطى[9] الطوبى للفقرا<ء>[10] المؤمنين ، وتعزيهم ، وتيقظ[11] عقول الأغنياء الكفرة أن يرجعوا إلى الله ولا [يتوكلوا][12] على أموالهم ، فأن أرواحهم تمضى وتنقطع[13] منهم إلى الجحيم وما [يفديهم][14] لذات هذه الدنيا كلها بعذابهم فى جهنم ساعة واحدة. ياأخى الحبيب طوبى[19] لنا[18] [أن][17] صبرنا على[16] الفقر والمسكنة لأجل أسم سيدنا[15] يسوع المسيح ، فقد ننال ما ناله العازر المسكين الذى ذكره الأنجيل. وأما هذا الغنى مثل [ذلك][20] الغنى الذى كان يتلذذ[21] ويتنعم ويلبس البرفير والارجوان [فآخر]<ة>[22] ذلك ورث العذاب الدائم فى جهنم. [وأما][23] ذلك النصرانى الشقى لم يسمع كلام[27] رفيقه ، ذلك الخائف من الله[26] ، وتعب[25] وهو[24] يكرر عليه القول P.121V ولم يوافقه[28] . بل قام ماضيا[29] إلى فلكسيانوس {رئيس مجمع اليهود}[30] ، وتحدث معه[32] قائلا: أسألك ياسيدى أن تقبلنى عندك غلاما وفاعلا[31] . فقال له ذلك اليهودى[34] :[33] أنت من أى صقع ، وماهو جنسك ، وماهى أمانتك؟ أجابه ذلك الرجل وقال: [أنا][35] نصرانى. فقال له فلكسيانوس[36] : لا يمكنا أن نخالط النصارى إلا أخوتنا الأسرائيليين. فأن كنت ياولدى محتاج لشئ من الصدقة[37] ، أنا أعطيك ماتحتاجه[41] ، ولا تغير[40] مذهبك ولا أمانتك[39] . فقال[38] ذلك النصرانى الشقى لفلكسيانوس[45] : أنا أقسم عليك بالله الضابط[44] [الكل][43] [وبشريعة][42] موسى

1 P "لا تكـــلان". 2 M "ذهبكـم". 3 P "وثيابكم الفخرة تستاس وتبـــــلا". 4 P om.
5 P "تقدر". 6 P "المـال". 7 PM "يدخلـــون". 8 M om. 9 M "الطوبا".
10 P "للفقـــره", M "للفقـــرا". 11 M "تيقـظ". 12 P "ولا يتكلـــوا". 13 M "وتقلـع".
14 P "وما يفيدهـــم". 15 M "طوبـــا". 16 P om. 17 M "على". 18,19 M om. 20 P om.
21 M "يلـــذ". 22 P "واخـــر". 23 M "فامـا". 24,25 AjP. 26 M om.
27 V "بعد أن تعب فى تعقيلـــــــه". 28 S "فلم يتركه عدو الخير أن يقبل شيئا من هذا القول ، بل حركه إلى أن ....".
29 M "ومضـــى", S "واتـــى". 30 PM om.
31 V "ارجوك ارحمنى واجعلنى عاملا لك هذه الســـــنة". 32,33 AjP, V "فلكسيانوس ساله".
34 AjP. 35 P om. 36 M "فلكسيانوس اليهودى قايلا". 37 M "تطلب منى".
38 V "واعطى مجد لله فى ايمانك". 39 AjP. 40 V "هذا الرجل". 41 AjP. 42 M "لفلكسينوس اليهودى".
43 V om. 44 P om. 45 P "وشـــريعـــة".

لا تردنى عنك بل أقبلنى اليك. أجابه فلكسيانوس قائلا: ياولدى [1] [مانقدر < أن >نخالط أحدا من الناس أذا لم يجحد أمانته وعبادته ويقبل] [2] شريعتنا وعبادتنا. أجابه ذلك [الرجل] [3] وقال له: إن أنت قبلتنى { عندك } [4] فأنا أصنع عبادتك فى كل شئ ، ولا أتجاوزك [5] أبدا إلى يوم مماتى. [فقال] [6] له فلكسيانوس: أمضى حتى أتحدث .مع أصحابى اليهود من أجلك. فمضى [7] ذلك [8] النصرانى [9] الشقى [11] إلى بيته. حينئذا تحدث فلكسيانوس مع اليهود لأجله ، فقالوا[له] [10] إن جحد أمانته وصنع ناموسنا ويدخل مجمعنا ، قبلناه [12] .[حينئذا فلكسيانوس اليهودى دعى [15] الرجل الفاعل] [14] وقال له: هوذا قد تحدثت [13] مع أصحابى { اليهود } لأجلك ، فقالوا [19] : إن قبل [18] ناموسنا وصنع [17] عبادتنا ، نحن نقبله [16] . فقال ذلك النصرانى الشقى [21] : أنا أقبل كل ماتأمرونى به. فأجابه [20] فلكسيانوس وقال : أمضى إلى P.122R بيتك ، وأذ كان [25] يوم السبت تعالى [24] إلى [المجمع] ،{نحن سنستقبلك} [23] [22] ، لنعلمك ناموسنا [31] وشرائع أبائنا [30] . فمضى [29] ذلك [28] النصرانى [27] الشقى [26] إلى بيته . ولما كان [37] يوم السبت ، بكر [36] ذلك [35] النصرانى [34] الشقى [33] ، وسبق سائر اليهود [32] ، وجاء إلى مجمعهم [40] . [فعندما نظره] [39] فلكسيانوس ، أجازه إلى جو [38] المجمع ، { [41] وبعد أن سألوه اليهود ، أجاب: سأكمل عبادتكم فى كل ماتقولونه لى } ، ثم أنه [43] أعترف قدام سائر اليهود أنه يبقى [42] يهودى . فقالوا له: نحن لنا عادة [47] ، من أراد< أن> يصير [46] يهودى يجحد [45] عبادته وينكر مذهبه ، وبعد ذلك [44] نحم<ي>ه [50] بالماء [49] لتنسلخ معموديته [48] . وبعد ذلك نعمل له صليب من خشب الزيتون مرتفع [54] نحو أربعة أذرع [53] ويشتد [52] ذلك الرجل الذى [يريد] [51] < أن > يصير يهودى ويأخذ سفنجة مملوة خلا ويجعلها [55] على قصبة ويمدها فوق رأس الصليب كما فعل بيسوع. وبعد هذا يأخذ حربة ويطعن بها الصليب فى جنبه. وفى

1 AjPM. 2 P "لم تقدر تخالط احدا من اليهود اذ لم تجحد امانتك وعبادتك وتقبل".
3 P "الشقى". 4 PM om. 5 V "ولا اتركها". 6 P "وقال". 7 M "فمضا".
8 AjP. 9 V "الرجل". 10 AjP. 11 P om. 12 V "الذى يجحد عبادته ليحيا حسب ناموسنا ، هذا نحن نقبله فى مجمعنا." S "ان كان يريد ان يجحد دينه ويكفر بمسيحه ، فنحن نقبله ونختنه".
13 P "فعند ذلك ارسل فلكسيانوس اليهودى واحضر ذلك النصرانى الشقى" 14 M "تحدت".
15 PM om. 16 M "وقالوا". 17 M "يصنع". 18 S "نحن من يقبل ناموسنا ويتابع عادتنا ، نحن نقبله بيننا".
19 M "فاجاب". 20 AjP. 21 M "فقالوا له". 22,23 M "الى".
24 P "مجمعنا". 25 PM om. 26,27 V "سنعطيك الناموس كذلك عادتنا". 28 AjP.
29 V "l'homme". 30 AjP. 31 M om. 32 M "الى". 33 M "ابكر". 34 AjP. 35 M "الرجل".
36 AjP. 37 AjPM. 38 MV "المجمع". 39 P "فعند ذلك لما نظره". 40 "داخل". 41 PM om.
42 S "فجحد المخدوع المسيح إلاهه امام اليهود واضاف الى فقره من المال فقره من الايمان". 43 AjP.
44 V "كانت عادة بين اليهود". 45 M "يبقا", "أرد". 46 M "فيجحد". 47 M "هذا".
48 M "فغسلوه بالماء لتنسلخ معموديته". 49 M "تعمل". 50 M om. 51 M "جدا". 52 V om, PM om.: V "ونضعه فى المجمع"
53 AjPM. 54 P om. 55 M "يجعلها".

تلك الساعة ، نجعل على رأسه تاج من خشب الصفصاف ونقرأ عليه الناموس

[ويصير] يهودى. تعمل هكذا ؟ فقال : نعم . وللوقت حموه بالماء ، وعملوا

له صليب من خشب الزيتون ، وأشتد ذلك المسكين الجاحد ، وأخذ بيده [سفنجه]

مملوّة خلا وربطها على قصبة ومدها إلى الصليب ، وبعد هذا أخذ حربة قوية

5   وطعن بها الصليب. وللوقت خرج منه دما كثير < ۱ > جارى [على] الأرض،

وأمتلأ [منه] الموضع حتى أن كثيرين من اليهود تعجبوا [مما] كان ، وصرخوا

جميعا قائلين: واحد هو إله النصارى {سيدنا} يسوع المسيح الذى صلب ،

P.122V   وبالحقيقة أستحقوا أبائنا نار جهنم . لأنهم صنعوا خطية عظيمة لا تغفر أبدا .

فأما فلكسيانوس فكان له أبنة عمرها أثنى عشرة سنة ، وولدها عمياء ، فعندما

10   نظر الدم نازلا من الصليب ، قال بأمانة عظيمة: وحق قوة الصليب [الذى

ليسوع المسيح لأغسلان وجه أبنتى بهذا الدم لتبصر] ، وإن أبصرت ، جحدت

أمانة اليهود وعبادتهم ومجمعهم ، وأصير نصرانى إلى يوم مماتى. ولما قال هذا

لطخ عينى أبنته بدم الصليب ، وقال بأسم يسوع المسيح أبن اللّه [الحى]

تبصر أبنتى. وللوقت أبصرت الصبية . ففرح كل من فى المجمع الذى لليهود،

15   وقالوا: [واحدا] هو إله النصارى يسوع المسيح أبن اللّه الحى . حينئذا

فلكسيانوس <رئيس > المجمع كتب رسالة إلى أبينا ثاوفيلس بطريرك الاسكندرية

هكذا: أنا الحقير فلكسيانوس اليهودى الغير مستحق أن يكتب إلى الطبيب

الحقيقى الذى ليسوع المسيح مخلصنا وينمى إلى قدسه ماجرى اليوم فى

مجمعنا من العجائب العظيمة من قبل صليب يسوع المسيح وعلامته المقدسة

20   الذى عليه صلب رب المجد . صليب خشب خرج منه دم [وجعلته] على

عينى أبنتى العمياء ، فللوقت نظرت. والآن قد علمنا بتحقيق أنه ليس

---

1 M "يجعل". 2 M "ويقرى". 3 P "وتصير". 4 V Les démarches se sont déroulées autrement, cela dit que les juifs ont posé leur condition après avoir dressé d'abord la croix au milieu de la synagog 5 P "قال", V "l'ouvrier s'y soumit". 6 M: cette phrase a été placée avant l'interrogatoire. 7 M "الوا له ابصق على هذه الصليب وقدم له هذا الخل واطعنه". 8 P السفنجة. 9 S "عملوا ذه الحربة وقل طعنتك ايها المسيح". 10 S "ماء ودم". 11 P "إلى". 12 P om. 13 P "الما كان". 14 PM om. 15 S "ثم آخذوا من ذلك الدم فعملوا على وجوههم وعيونهم". 16 M "ولدهما", V "ودة". 17 M "قوت". 18 P om. 19 P "واعتنق ايمان المسيحيين". 20 M "فلما". 21 P om. 22 P "واحد". 23 M "الاه". 24 V om. 25 P "ريس", M "راس". 26 AjPM. 27,28 ,29 V om. 30 V "الصليب المقدس". 31 ,32,33 V om. 34 V "ربنا يسوع". 35 P "جعلته". 36 M om.

إله[1] فى السماء وعلى الأرض إلا يسوع المسيح إله[2] النصارى. وبالحقيقة أستحقوا أبائنا[3] نار جهنم. وكنا متمسكين بسنة أبائنا[4] ونقول أنها حق حتى رأينا العجائب.[5] وأنا أسألك ياسيدى الأب أن تفرح مع هؤلاء [الخراف][6] الذين عادوا إلى قطيع المسيح، لأننا[7] رجونا رحمته[8]، أنا وأهل بيتى وكل[9] يهودى حاضر فى مجمعنا فى هذا اليوم[10]. فلما قرأ الرسالة، أعنى أبينا{ القديس }[11] ثاوفيلس البطريرك[12]، فرح جدا، ونهض مسرعا[13]، وجاء إلى المجمع[14] هو وجماعة[15] من الكهنة وأكابر الشعب[16]، وهو يمشى على رجليه.

123R *ولما رأى فلكسيانوس أبى البطريرك، خر على الأرض[17] ساجدا تحت رجليه[18] وقال: ياعبد[19] يسوع المسيح أرحمنى وأعطنى مغفرة خطاياى[21]. [ودخلوا قدامه المجمع[20] وأوروه الصليب][22] <ونظر> البطريرك إلى الصليب وهو مطعون والدم[23] يجرى منه، وخر ساجدا للصليب المعظم الذى لسيدنا يسوع المسيح*[24]. وأوروه[25] أيضا الصبية[26] أبنة[27] فلكسيانوس[28] التى أبصرت[29]. فأما ذلك [الرجل][30] النصرانى[31] الجاحد[32] الذى طعن الصليب، وقع عليه خوف [عظيم][33]، ويبس مثل الحجر، فوقع ميتا[34] وأسلم الروح للوقت ومات ميتة[35] ردية[36] شريرة[37]، وأخذ نصيبه مع يهوذا[38] الذى باع[39] سيده بالمال. حينئذا أمر أبى القديس البطريرك[40] أن يحمل[41] الصليب[42] إلى الكنيسة وجميع الكهنة يرتلوا قدامه متعجبين من الأمور التى كانت، ممجدين لله الصالح[43] من قبل علامة[44] الخلاص[45] التى رأوها من صليب سيدنا يسوع المسيح له المجد إلى الأبد.

1,2 M "الاه". 3 M "ابهاتنا". 4 M "ابانا". 5 V "وأذ استمرينا بحفظ تقاليد أبائنا، قلنا أنها ستكون خطية".
6 P om. 7 M "لانا". 8 V om. 9 M "وكان". 10 V om.
11 PM om. 12 V "أبى القديس البطريرك", M om. 13 S "فقام واخذ معه الاب كيرلس".
14 V "هذا المكان", S "مجمع اليهود". 15 M "هو وجماعته". 16 V "وأنا اصاحبهم".
* * Nous avons dû changer radicalement la structure de la phrase ici, afin qu'elle suit un ordre logique. 17,18 M "رجليه". 19 M "خر على رجليه ساجدا",
V La traduction française ne concorde pas avec le texte copte, qui est en accord les textes arabes.
19 M "ياعبد سيدى". 20 V "أغفر لى". 21 P om. 23,24 M "واوروه الصليب مطعون والدم يجرى منه". S "وابصر الصليب والدم والماء الخارجين منه فأخذ منه القديس وتبارك منه. ورشم على جبهته وجبهة الشعب من ذلك الدم وكشطه من على الارض وجعله فى اناء برسم البركة والمنفعة"
22 P "ولما", M om. 25 AjP. 26 M "والصبية". 27,28 AjP. 29 M "الذى ابصرة". 30 P om.
31,32 AjP. 33 P om. 34 AjP. 35,36,37 AjPM. 38 M "بوداس". 39 M "اباع".
40 V "ثاوفيلس". 41 M "بحمل". 42 M "المقدس". 43 AjPM. 44 M "علامت",
45 M "الصليب"

N.B. la note "22" devrait précéder celles de "23,24".

وأما فلكسيانوس وأبنه[1] وأبنته[2] وزوجته ، وبقية اليهود < الذين >[3] فى المدينة ، نحو ثلاثة آلاف نفس[4] . < و > دخلوا بهم إلى الكنيسة ، ووعظهم[5] البطريرك { ثاوفيلس }[6] من الكتب المقدسة[7] [التى][8] هى أنفاس الله . وبعد هذا هيؤا المعمودية[9] ، فعمدهم بأسم[10] الآب والأبن والروح القدس ، الإله الواحد[11] ، وناولهم من السرائر المقدسة[12] { جسد ودم ربنا يسوع المسيح } ، وأعطاهم السلام ، {وأرسلهم}[13] .

وأما فلكسيانوس فأعطى نصف ماله للبطريرك [ليصدقه][14] على المساكين. وفى الوقت الذى تعمد فيه ، أضاء وجهه مثل الشمس. وبعد سنة كرزه شماسا ثم قسا[15] ، وجعل أبنه { ألكسندر }[16] شماس.[17] [وزادوا][18] فى العبادة بالأكثر[19] .

P. 123V وكانت زوجته مؤمنة جدا ، فأعطت مالها جميعه للمساكين حتى أغنتهم[20] . وهكذا[21] كانت سيرتهم الحسنة[22] . وبعد ذلك تنيحوا ونالوا ملكوت السموات[23] ، فى الحياة الد< ا > ئمة[24] .

فقد[25] أخبرنا[26] محبتكم بهذا لكى تعلموا[27] أن الله رحوم محب للبشر ، لايشاء هلاك أحد ا ، إلا يمهله للتوبة ، والله ، سبحانه وتعالى جل ذكره[28] ، يغفر لنا وأياكم ويعطينا حظا[29] ونصيبا[30] فى ملكوته[31] الأبد < ى >[32] . بنعمة ورأفة[33] ومحبة البشر التى[34] لسيدنا[35] يسوع المسيح ، هذا الذى له[36] المجد والأكرام والتسبيح[37] والسجود[38] للآب معه والروح القدس ، الإله الواحد[39] ، الآن وكل آوان وإلى دهر الداهرين أمين. أمين[40] .

1 V om. 2 V confusion dans la traduction française du terme: ⲦⲈϤϢⲎⲢⲒ qui aurait dû être traduire par "fils". 3 P "الذى" , M "التى". 4 AjPM. 5 M "واوعظهم". 6 PM om. 7 V om. 8 P "الذى". 9 M "المعمودية المقدسة". 10 M "بسم" 11 AjP. 12 PM om. 13 PM om. 14 P "ليصدقوا". 15 M "ثم قسمه اسقفا" 16 PM om. 17 V "prêtre". 18 P "وزاده". 19 AjPM. 20 M "اعانتهم". 21 M "وهكذى". 22 M "الصالحه". 23 M "السماواة". 24 M om., V "هكذا كملوا حياتهم فى الارثوذكسية وذهبوا نحو المسيح". 25 M om. 26 M "فاخبرنا". 27 M "لتعلموا". 28 M "فالله تعالى". 29 M "حضا". 30 M "ونصيب". 31 M "ملكوت". 32 M "الابديه". 33 M "ورافت". 34 M "الذى". 35 M "لربنا". 36 M "من قبله". 37,38 AjP. 39 AjP.

40 La conclusion de ce discours est différent dans V. Il semblerait que chaque copiste a fini sa copie par une conclusion personnelle.

Traduction

AU NOM DE DIEU MAJESTUEUX <DANS> LA SOUVERAINETÉ p. 116v
L'UNIQUE DANS SON UNICITÉ
UN DISCOURS QUE L'HONORABLE PÈRE CYRILLE
PATRIARCHE DE LA VILLE D'ALEXANDRIE A COMPOSÉ
POUR QU'IL SOIT LU À LA FÊTE DE LA CROIX [GLORIFIÉE]
LE 17 DE MOIS DU TOUT, POUR CONDUIRE À LA PURE PÉNITENCE.
QUE LA BÉNÉDICTION QUI EST EN LUI, SOIT AVEC NOUS AMEN.

Il a démontré comment Dieu supporte le pécheur et prend tous les moyens, jusqu'à ce que celui-ci revienne à la pénitence[1], par les maladies et les accidents. Car, Dieu, soit loué, ne veut la perte de personne, car il est l'œuvre de ses mains. Mais aussi, Il l'éveille à la pénitence par les maladies, les accidents, les tristesses, la pauvreté et la mort des enfants, afin qu'il pense à ses péchés et tout ce qu'il a fait comme méchancetés; il se retourne rapidement vers Dieu, [qu'il soit loué][2], qui accepte sa pénitence, et Il lui compense, [dans ce bas monde], maintes fois ce qu'il a perdu, et dans l'au-delà de la vie éternelle. Quant à celui que Dieu abandonne dans ses péchés, Il ne le cherche ni par une maladie, ni par la souffrance, ni par une catastrophe, ni par la pauvreté; celui-là, il doit savoir qu'il n'a pas de part auprès de Dieu, puisqu'il l'a abandonné vivant somptueusement dans le monde selon la chair.

Il a aussi parlé dans ce discours d'une femme manichéenne qui se trouvait dans la ville d'Alexandrie {aux jours de mon enfance}, et comment, Dieu l'ayant guidée, jusqu'à ce qu'elle ait embrassé la religion chrétienne. Il a également parlé de Philoxène, chef des Juifs, qui après avoir reçu le baptême, devint chrétien avec toute sa maison, à cause du prodige qui arriva par la croix glorieuse; et comment la fille de ce dernier recouvrit la vue, après que ses yeux eussent été frottés du sang qui coula de la croix du Christ {au milieu de la synagogue}; et comment une foule de Juifs crurent à Notre-Seigneur Jésus-Christ [à qui la gloire pour les siècles des siècles], dans la paix de Dieu. Amen.

Il dit: bon et honorable est le nom de Notre-Seigneur Jésus-Christ qui nous a rapproché de son Église, et qui nous a appris les paroles du saint Évangile, comme Il a dit dans l'évangile de Mathieu concernant *«un homme possédant* p. 117r *cent brebis qui, si une d'elles s'égare, ne laisse pas les quatre-vingt-dix-neuf autres sur la montagne, pour chercher celle qui s'est perdue? Et s'il la trouve, il la prend sur ses épaules, il se réjouit avec elle. Il invite ses amis et ses voisins en [leur] disant: réjouissez-vous avec moi aujourd'hui; car j'ai trouvé ma brebis,*

1 Ez. 33,11.
2 Ces exclamations, qui ne figurent pas dans le texte copte sont un emprunt aux habitants musulmans.

qui était perdue. De même, est une grande joie dans le ciel, devant Dieu, [qu'il est Grand], et ses anges, pour un seul pécheur qui fait pénitence»[3]. Il a aussi dit [Dieu] en nous appelant à la pénitence: *«Venez à moi, vous tous qui êtes fatigués et qui êtes accablés de fardeaux et je vous soulagerai. Prenez mon joug sur vous et apprenez de moi que je suis doux et humble de cœur; vous trouverez le lieu du repos [pour] vos âmes, car doux est mon joug, et léger est mon fardeau»*[4]; *«Vous qui êtes accablés des souillures de vos péchés qui se sont répandus et multipliés en eux en abondance, venez à moi et je vous pardonnerai; car je ne veux pas la mort du pécheur, dit le Seigneur, mais qu'il se détourne de sa voie mauvaise, qu'il fasse pénitence et qu'il vive dans la vie éternelle»*[5]. Il dit encore: *«Il y aura de la joie chez les anges de Dieu pour un seul pécheur qui fait pénitence»*[6]. Si la joie est grande pour un pécheur {s'il fait pénitence devant Dieu et ses anges}, quelle ne sera pas la joie immense des habitants du ciel et de la terre {des anges, des archanges et des vertus célestes}, si une multitude de pécheurs fait pénitence.

Maintenant donc, ô frères bien-aimés, ne nous négligeons pas nous-mêmes en disant que nos péchés sont nombreux; la miséricorde de Dieu est plus abondante que nos péchés *«personne n'est sans péché, à l'exception de Dieu seul»*[7]. Sachez que le démon nous fait tomber dans les péchés par ses ruses, il nous rend agréables la passion et les plaisirs. Précipitons-nous vers la pénitence et sollicitons Dieu, l'ami des hommes, avec une grande humilité, afin qu'Il nous remette nos péchés, {il y a la sollicitude en Lui pour nous}. Le signe de l'humilité, c'est que l'homme ne répond pas à ce que son ennemi lui a fait, ni le punit par le mal; mais il voit que tous les pécheurs, même ceux qui sont des sanguinaires et des adultères, sont mieux que lui, mais il ne juge
p. 117v jamais personne; [ni ne blâme personne], ni ne les flétrit point et ne lui fait aucun reproche; mais il lui parle à part. Il ne doit mentir à personne, ni chasser quelqu'un, ni l'empêcher de puiser dans ses biens, [ni de sa maison]. Il donne à celui qui en fait la demande, il prête à celui qui lui sollicite quelque chose, même si celui-ci est son ennemi; [ni de tromper personne], ni détester quelqu'un, ni se moquer de quelqu'un. Celui-ci [est un vrai chrétien], qui est soucieux de ses péchés et fait pénitence; il ne fait aucun mal à personne par une mauvaise parole. Parce que, à celui qui dit du mal des autres, Dieu lui fait supporter les péchés de ceux-là; car, il leur a menti et calomnié. Mais le chrétien humble, c'est celui qui est préoccupé par le salut de son âme, et qui ne laisse personne [souffrant] à cause de lui; il ne communie pas des mystères

3 Mt. 18,12-14; Lc. 15,3-7; Ez. 34,4-16.
4 Mt. 11,28-30.
5 Ez. 33,11.
6 Lc. 15,7.
7 Mc. 10,18; Lc. 18,19.

jusqu'à ce qu'il se reconcile avec son ennemi, comme le Seigneur [Christ] l'a commandé dans son saint Évangile. Il se peut que quelqu'un se désintéresse en disant que nos péchés sont très abondants et comment Dieu nous les pardonne[8]? Regarde, bien-aimé, ne dis une pareille chose. Car il n'y a de péchés que Dieu accepte de remettre; Il est, soit loué, rédempteur et miséricordieux, Il nous pardonne. Si tu es un grand pécheur, souviens-toi du peuple de Ninive, comment leur blasphème a été pardonné par la pénitence[9]. Si tu es un adultère, souviens-toi de la femme adultère qui a transformé ses yeux en une fontaine d'eau [abondante] et qui lava les pieds de Notre-Seigneur [Jésus]-Christ par ses larmes, puis les essuya avec sa chevelure[10]. Si tu es un voleur, souviens-toi du larron qui fit son aveu au Seigneur Christ sur la croix et reçut {en même temps} le pardon de tous ses péchés[11]. Si tu es un oppresseur ou publicain, souviens-toi du publicain dont le Seigneur a fait son disciple évangéliste[12]. Si tu es un sorcier magicien, [fais pénitence et] souviens-toi des mages qui vinrent au Seigneur Christ lui offrir des présents; et ils reçurent de lui le pardon de leur péché {en même temps}[13]. Si tu as fait tous les péchés, ne néglige pas la pénitence {maintenant donc mes bien-aimés} et ne désespère pas de la miséricorde de Dieu {à cause du péché}. Car, Dieu, son invocation soit p. 118r
louée, {Il est plein de compassion en effet}, Il est miséricordieux, ne veut pas qu'une seule de ses créatures périsse; {mais qu'elle revienne de sa voie mauvaise et qu'elle vive}; Il ne fera perdre à personne sa récompense, et Il veut que les hommes soient sauvés par la pénitence. Car la pénitence relève les perdus, et consolide ceux qui sont debouts; elle lave l'homme des péchés comme tu laves un habit et personne ne sait où est partie la saleté. Dieu, qu'Il soit loué, a dit par la bouche des prophètes: *«Venez à moi, ô fils, si vos péchés sont comme le cramoisi, ils deviendront blancs comme la neige; s'ils sont rouges comme l'écarlate, ils seront comme la laine, et je vous les remettrai»*[14], si vous ne dites pas du mal des autres en leur absence; si vous ne calomniez point, ni ne mentez à quiconque, je lui pardonnerai ses péchés et je les remettrai à celui qui s'est enorgueilli et a menti sur [son compagnon ou] son proche et le trompant.

Écoutez maintenant les faits qui prouvent la vérité de ces paroles selon lesquelles Dieu, soit loué, ne veut pas la mort du pécheur; bien plus, Il l'éveille à la pénitence et au salut:

8 Jn. 4,13.
9 Jon. 3,5-9; Mt. 12,41; Mc. 11,32.
10 Lc. 23,39-43.
11 Lc. 23,39-43.
12 Mt. 9,9; Mc. 2,14; Lc. 5,27.
13 Mt. 2,1; Lc. 2,7.
14 Is. 1,18.

Le patriarche Théophile <régnait> sur la ville d'Alexandrie, [aux jours de mon enfance], étant [jeune] je m'instruissais à l'école. Il y avait une femme {manichéenne} habitant dans la rue de mon maître, et elle avait une fillette âgée de neuf ou dix ans environ. La mère de cette fillette la revêtit et l'envoya à l'église sainte dès le moment de la lecture de la première lettre de Saint Paul {selon la coutume}, en lui disant [ceci]: prends garde ma fille de ne pas sortir de l'église jusqu'à ce qu'on ait donné la paix et qu'on ait renvoyé l'assemblée: et ce que le prêtre te donnera, ne le mange pas jusqu'à ce que tu reviennes ici. On avait tout d'abord donné aux gens le saint sacrement dans leur mains jusqu'à l'époque de mon père le patriarche Théophile; mais depuis cet événement, on a cessé de donner le saint sacrement dans la main; et dès lors, les prêtres donnent le saint sacrement aux gens dans la bouche, et on a établi
p. 118v cette coutume dans l'église jusqu'à ce jour-ci.

Alors, la fillette de cette femme s'en alla en se mêlant avec les femmes des chrétiens dès le début de la liturgie jusqu'à la communion du saint sacrement. À ce moment, elle entra avec les femmes, tendant sa main au patriarche et elle lui prit frauduleusement [le saint corps], celui de Notre-Seigneur [Jésus-Christ], sans que personne ne s'aperçoive qu'elle n'était pas chrétienne. Après avoir attendu qu'on eût donné la paix, elle sortit secrètement. Car, les évêques et les patriarches en ce temps-là, communiaient les femmes par leur mains, ils étaient vêtus d'étoffe de lin. D'ailleurs, les évêques n'ont embrassé la vie monastique et quitté leur épouse que depuis l'époque du père patriarche Démétrius. La mère de cette fillette avait coutume que chaque fois que sa fille lui apportait le saint [corps], elle vérifiait au moyen <de celui-ci> si la fillette avait entendu ou non les Livres; aussitôt elle enfonça un stylet ou une épine dans le saint sacrement. S'il rendait du sang, elle l'enveloppait dans un linge de fin lin et l'emportait pour le mettre dans une casette d'or, le conservant chez elle. Une fois, cette femme envoya sa fille à l'église, comme d'ordinaire, pour recevoir le saint sacrement, qui est la vie éternelle, et c'est par lui que sont pardonnés les péchés et les fautes; et c'est pourquoi il est appelé le saint corps. Quant la fillette sortit pour aller à l'église, elle rencontra des fillettes qui étaient de sa rue. Elle s'amusa avec elles, de sorte qu'elle arriva juste à l'église au moment où on offre {le sacrifice}. Quant elle rentra dans l'église, elle prit part au saint sacrement avec l'assemblée; elle partit secrètement comme d'habitude chez sa mère. Alors, sa mère voulut savoir si elle avait entendu ou non les Livres: elle prit donc une épine, l'enfonça dans <le saint sacrement>, selon son habitude, mais celui-ci ne rendit point de sang. Car la fillette n'avait pas entendu les Livres. Parce que celui qui ne les entends pas, et qui ne les contemple pas bien, il ne lui est pas permis de communier; car il est de fleuves d'eau vivante. À ce moment, la mère la saisit et la frappa de coups, au point qu'elle arriva aux bords de la mort à cause de sa colère.

Quant mon maître entendit la raclée de la fillette, il s'étonna de cela. Car, sa p. 119r
maison était en face de la maison de la femme, comme nous l'avons dit au début.

Alors, mon maître alla [la trouver] au coucher du soleil, et sa mère n'était pas présente. Mon maître lui dit: «Qu'est-ce que tu as fait, pour que ta mère t'ait frappé ainsi à si grands coups»? Quant à elle, elle révéla la chose à mon maître en disant: «Ma mère m'envoie à l'église des chrétiens pour recevoir le saint sacrement en je le lui apporte chez elle». Et il lui dit: «Qu'en fait-elle»? «Elle le renferme dans une casette d'or», répondit-elle, «et elle le garde chez elle, pour le vendre très cher aux chrétiens dans notre pays».

Aussitôt, mon maître ne <négligea> pas cette affaire, mais il se leva et alla à l'église chez le père patriarche Théophile, lui rapportant cette affaire. Sur-le-champ, il envoya des prêtres et des soldats chez la femme, puisqu'elles ne savaient pas pourquoi, on les conduisit à l'église. Le patriarche <s'adressa> à la femme, lui dit: «Je t'adjure par Dieu tout-puissant, ô femme, en qui [tu espères], fais-moi savoir comment est arrivée cette chose? N'as-tu pas la crainte de Dieu puisque tu dérobes les membres du Christ Notre-Seigneur et en les vendant pour de l'argent»? La femme avoua aussitôt, avant qu'elle soit tourmentée, et dit: «Je ne les ai pas vendus, mais [je] les conserve dans ma maison». Immédiatement, le patriarche envoya des prêtres, des diacres et une foule de fidèles à la maison de la femme. Arrivés à l'endroit où se trouvait la cassette, ils virent une grande lueur de feu et, après avoir dit une grande prière, ils s'émerveillèrent de cela. Ils prirent la petite cassette d'or et ils la portèrent chez le père patriarche. Lorsqu'il l'ouvrit, il y trouva le saint corps qui exhalait un suave parfum. Alors, la crainte du Seigneur s'empara de la femme. Elle se prosterna devant lui (le patriarche) en disant: «Monseigneur le père patriarche, est-il possible que votre sainteté ait pitié de moi, la pécheresse, accorde-moi ton pardon, ainsi qu'à ma fille, parce que nous ferons pénitence entre vos mains». Le patriarche les proposa une
règle de jeûne de quarante jours; et il les avait instruit, [il les a oint avec le p. 119v
huile des catéchumènes], ensuite il les baptisa au nom du Père, du Fils et du Saint-Esprit, un seul Dieu; et il les communia des saints mystères [corps de Notre-Seigneur Jésus-Christ et son sang honoré].

La femme donna au patriarche tout ce qu'elle possédait, pour qu'il distribue aux pauvres; elle transforma sa maison en église. Après cela, elles rasèrent leur tête; elles embrassèrent la vie monastique dans le couvent du verrier, (zaǧǧāǧ) à la périphérie de la ville d'Alexandrie, elles demeurèrent en lui jusqu'au jour de leur mort, et elles achevèrent leur vie droitement dans la paix du seigneur. Amen*.

* «Amen» indique que le texte, dans une première forme, se terminait là et donc que le récit suivant a été ajouté dans un deuxième temps.

Aussi, un grand prodige s'est manifesté qu'il ne faut pas ignorer. Cela sa passait dans la ville d'Alexandrie, aux jours de mon enfance, comme je vous ai fait part précédemment, bien-aimés, moi l'humble Cyrille. Il est dit que Dieu le Bon ne veut pas la mort du pécheur, mais qu'Il va toujours chercher la brebis égarée, pour la ramener à son troupeau doué de parole. Maintenant donc, ô bien-aimé, tu ne négliges pas ton salut {à cause du péché} en disant que j'ai commis de très grands péchés que Dieu ne me pardonnerait pas; ne crois absolument pas en cela, et ne donne pas de force au péché, si le démon t'a trompé et t'a fait tomber dans un grand péché, hâte-toi [et retourne] vers Dieu l'ami des humains; demande-Le avec des larmes en disant: ô Dieu, pardonne-moi rapidement, moi le pécheur, et sa miséricorde te sera vite accordée. Car, que Son Nom soit loué, Il a dit: *«Quand tu parleras encore et me demanderas, Je dirai: me voici Vivant, dit le Sabaoth, Je le pardonnerai au moment de sa pénitence, et Je ne lui réclame plus son ancien péché, s'il ne retourne encore une fois au péché et meurt sans qu'il fasse pénitence; et l'aumône ne le rachettera de l'enfer»*[15].

Écoutez [maintenant] pour que je vous informe de ce prodige par lequel nous avons commencé, pour que vous apprenniez la bonté de Dieu que ne veut pas que nulle {œuvre de ses mains} périsse.

Il y avait dans la ville d'Alexandrie, aux jours de mon père le père patriarche Théophile, alors que j'étais diacre auprès de lui dans la cellule**, afin d'apprendre le grand amour de Dieu pour les humains, et qu'Il ne veut
p. 120r qu'aucune de ses créature n'aille à la perdition, mais qu'elle retourne et qu'elle vive.

Il y avait un homme Juif dans la ville d'Alexandrie, nommé Philoxène, qui était un grand de la synagogue. Il était fort riche en or, en argent, en serviteurs et en troupeaux. C'était [un homme] qui avait la crainte de Dieu, pratiquant la Loi de Moïse; il remplissait de nombreux ministères dans la synagogue des Juifs, et offrant beaucoup d'aumônes, selon ce qui est écrit dans la Loi de Moïse, il était célèbre dans toutes les synagogues pour ses revenus comme pour ses aumônes. Il était remercié de sa conduite pour ses affections pour les pauvres; et chacun lui a rendu louange. Mais, son invocation soit louée, le Bon, à cause de son amour pour les humains, n'a pas voulu laisser cet [homme] Juif ainsi dans les ténèbres, mais Il a voulu le purifier de ses péchés comme il est écrit dans les Actes: *«Ceux qui craignent Dieu et qui font sa volonté, Lui sont agréables»*[16].

15 Ps. 49,7-8; Ez. 33,11-19.

** «Cellule»: le sens du mot arabe «qallaya» = episkopeion, pris d'abord au sens locatif, puis désignant les personnes qui habitent avec l'évêque ou le patriarche, du fait que ce dernier était choisi parmi les moines qui habitent une *cellule*.

16 Ac. 10,35.

Il y avait aussi deux ouvriers chrétiens habitants dans la ville d'Alexandrie, faisant partie des habitants d'Égypte «Miṣr»*, qui logèrent dans les rues des Juifs. Or, ces ouvriers chrétiens qui voyaient les Juifs riches en or et en argent, se sont parlés un jour disant: nous nous étonnons de ces Juifs, qui sont des hommes pécheurs qui ont crucifié le Christ {Fils de Dieu Vivant} Notre-Seigneur, que nous les voyons plus riches que tous les chrétiens. Or, l'un des deux, qui avait la crainte de Dieu, répondit à son compagnon en disant: En vérité, il est vrai, mon frère, qu'il n'y a pas, sur terre, une foi glorieuse comme celle des chrétiens, pour qui le Seigneur a donné la béatitude dans l'Évangile disant: *«Bienheureux les pauvres de l'esprit, parce que le royaume des cieux est particulièrement à eux»*[17]; et Il a promis aux Juifs riches le malheur en disant: *«Malheur à ceux qui sont rassasiés maintenant, parce qu'ils auront faim;* p. 120v
malheur à eux parce qu'ils ont eu leur repos sur terre»[18]. Ainsi pour ceux dont le cœur est dur, et ceux qui sont angoissés et impatients des chrétiens, mais ils nient le Christ à cause de l'argent du monde et de leur mauvaise passion. Il a fait l'éloge des chrétiens patients en disant: *«Bienheureux ceux qui ont faim, car ils seront rassasiés; bienheureux ceux qui ont soif de la justice, car ils auront la joie; bienheureux ceux qui sont tristes, car ils seront consolés; bienheureux ceux qui ont été chassés à cause de la justice, car ils hériteront la terre de la vie»*[19]. Il a également attristé les Juifs et les infidèles en disant: *«Malheur à ceux qui rient et vivent dans le luxe, parce qu'ils pleureront et ils se lamenteront»*[20]. Mais, son compagnon, ce malheureux, lui dit: je n'écoute rien de ta part, mais je me lèverai et j'irai me faire juif, et je demeurerai ouvrier chez Philoxène le Juif et j'embrasserai sa religion. Il répondit: non, mon frère, crois et fais confiance dans la bonté de Notre-Seigneur Jésus-Christ, Fils de Dieu Vivant qui bénit le peu que nous avons bien davantage, car il est mieux que les richesses de cet homme Juif. Car Dieu, soit loué, dit par la bouche du prophète David: *«Le peu du juste est bon et meilleur que le trésor du pécheur»*[21]; et *«la gloire du pécheur ne l'accompagnera pas au tombeau; et ainsi sa richesse ne lui servira à rien le jour de sa peine»*, mais Dieu le condamnera pour ce qu'il a accumulé en privant les pauvres de sa propre richesse, et il n'a pas donné [d'elle] d'aumône, mais il l'a caché dans la terre, lui faisant confiance plus que la promesse de son Créateur. Et Paul, la langue odoriférante, dit dans sa lettre à Timothée: *«Mais ceux qui veulent s'enrichir* p. 121r
tomberont dans les misères et dans des affaires difficiles et il nous fait nous

* Paul Casanova, Les noms coptes du Caire et localités voisines, in B.I.F.A.O., t.I (1901), pp. 139-180.

17 Lc. 6,20.

18 Lc. 6,24.

19 My. 5,6,15.

20 Lc. 6,25.

21 Ps. 37,16; 49,17.

contenter de la nourriture et des habits»[22]; il dit aussi, après avoir exposé toutes ses choses: *«Toi, homme de Dieu, fuis tout cela et recommandes aux riches de ce monde, les cœurs durs, de ne pas s'enorgueillir dans leur soucis, et de ne pas s'appuyer sur leurs richesses si incertaines, mais de la mettre en Dieu Vivant»*[23]. Il est dit aussi dans les lettres catholiques: *«Malheur à vous les riches incrédules, parce que vous avez eu vos consolations sur terre, et votre or changera et votre argent rouillera, vos vêtements luxueux seront rongés par les vers»*[24]. Et Notre-Seigneur a dit: *«Ceux qui s'appuyeront sur la richesse ne pourriont pas entrer dans le royaume des cieux»*[25]; *«Et je vous le dis: il est plus facile qu'un chameau passe par le trou d'une aiguille qu'un riche entre dans le royaume de Dieu»*[26]; et Il dit aussi: *«Vous ne pouvez pas adorer Dieu et l'argent»*[27]. Tous les Livres donnent la béatitude aux croyants pauvres en les consolant et ils réveillent les consciences des riches incrédules, afin qu'ils reviennent à Dieu et qu'ils ne s'appuient plus sur leurs richesses. Car, leur esprits les quittent allant à l'enfer ; et toutes les passions de ce monde ne les sauveront après qu'ils se retrouvent en enfer une seule heure. O frère bien-aimé, que nous serons heureux si nous patienterions à l'encontre de la pauvreté et de l'humilité, pour le nom de Notre-Seigneur Jésus-Christ, c'est alors que nous obtenions ce que Lazare l'humble a obtenu, ce que l'Évangile a évoqué; et que ce riche héritera du même sort que ce riche qui était dans les passions, vivant dans le luxe, se vêtant de pourpre et de fin lin. La fin de celui-là était d'hériter de la souffrance éternelle dans l'enfer[28].

p. 121v Mais, ce malheureux chrétien ne voulut pas écouter les paroles de son compagnon, celui qui a la crainte de Dieu, qui se fatigua en lui répétant ces mêmes paroles; non seulement il n'était pas d'accord avec lui, mais encore il se leva en le laissant, et il s'en alla chez Philoxène [le chef de la synagogue juive], et il s'entretint avec lui, disant: monseigneur, je vous demande de m'accepter chez vous en tant que ouvrier. Il le dit, ce Juif; De quelle région es-tu? De quelle race? De quelle religion? Cet homme lui répondit disant: Je suis chrétien. Philoxène lui dit: Il nous est impossible d'avoir de contact avec des chrétiens, mais seulement avec nos frères israélites. Si tu as, mon fils, besoin de quelque aumône, je te donnerai ce dont tu as besoin; mais tu ne changes pas, ni ta religion, ni ta foi. Mais, ce malheureux chrétien dit à Philoxène: Je t'adjure, par Dieu tout-puissant, et la Loi de Moïse, ne me repousses pas de toi, mais accepte-moi. Philoxène lui répondit, disant: [Nous

22 I Tm. 6,8-9.
23 I Tm. 6,11-17.
24 Jc. 5,1-3.
25 Lc. 18,24.
26 Lc. 18,25.
27 Lc. 6,16.
28 Lc. 6,19-31.

ne pouvons pas, mon fils, contacter quelconque s'il ne renie pas sa foi et son culte, et il accepte] nos lois et nos cultes. Cet [homme] lui répondit, disant: Si tu m'acceptes [chez toi] j'accomplirai ton culte en toute chose et je ne te quitterai jusqu'au jour de ma mort. Philoxène lui [dit]: Va-t-en jusqu'à ce que j'aie parlé de toi avec mes compagnons les Juifs. Et le malheureux chrétien s'en alla à sa maison.

Philoxène parla alors de lui aux Juifs et ceux-ci lui dirent: S'il renie sa foi et pratique nos lois et entre dans notre synagogue, nous l'accepterons. [Alors, p. 122r
Philoxène le Juif appela l'homme ouvrier], il lui dit: Voici, j'ai parlé de toi avec mes compagnons [les Juifs], ils m'ont dit: S'il accepte nos lois et pratique nos cultes, nous l'accepterons. Alors, le malheureux chrétien répondit: J'accepte tout ce que vous me demanderez. Philoxène lui répondit disant: Va à ta maison et viens le jour du samedi à la synagogue, {nous t'accueillerons}, afin que nous t'apprenions nos lois et les coutumes de nos pères. Le malheureux chrétien alla à sa maison. Et quand arriva le jour du samedi, ce malheureux chrétien, se leva de bonne heure, devançant tous les Juifs en venant à leur synagogue. Quand Philoxène le vit, il l'introduisit à l'intérieur de la synagogue; {et après que les Juifs l'eurent interrogé, il répondit: «J'accomplirai votre culte en tout ce que vous me direz»}; puis il confessa devant tous les Juifs qu'il restera Juif. Ils lui dirent: Nous avons pour coutume que celui qui veut devenir Juif doit renier son culte et abjurer sa confession, et ensuite nous le laverons avec l'eau pour le dépouiller de son baptême; et après cela, nous lui ferons une croix de bois d'olivier d'une hauteur de quatre bras environ; et l'homme, qui [veut] devenir Juif, s'affermit et prend une éponge remplie de vinaigre, pour l'élever avec un roseau et la diriger en haut vers la tête de la croix, comme cela a été fait à Jésus. Et après cela, il prend une lance aiguisée pour frapper la croix dans son côté. À cette heure là, nous lui mettrons une couronne en bois de saule sur la tête, nous lui lirons la loi, et ainsi il deviendra Juif. Veux-tu faire cela? Il dit: Oui. Ils le lavèrent immédiatement avec de l'eau, et ils lui firent une croix de bois d'olivier; et il se raffermit, ce pauvre incrédule, et il prit dans sa main une éponge remplie de vinaigre et l'ayant attaché au roseau, il la dirigea contre la croix; ensuite il prit une lance aiguisée puissante par laquelle il frappa la croix. Et immédiatement, un sang abondant sortit d'elle remplissant la terre et l'endroit tout entier, à tel point qu'une foule de Juifs, émerveillés du fait, s'écrièrent ensemble en disant: Un est le Dieu des chrétiens, [Notre-Seigneur] Jésus-Christ, qui a été crucifié! En vérité, nos pères ont mérité le feu de
l'enfer, parce qu'ils ont commis un grand péché irrémissible! Quant au p. 122v
Philoxène, qui avait une fille âgée d'une douzaine d'années, et qui était née aveugle, lorsqu'il vit le sang couler de la croix, il se dit avec une grande foi: Par la dignité de la force de la croix, [celui de Jésus-Christ que je laverai le

visage de ma fille par ce sang, afin qu'elle recouvre la vue], et si elle recouvre la vue, je renoncerai à la foi des Juifs, à leur culte et à leur synagogue, et je deviendrai chrétien jusqu'au jour de ma mort. Quand il dit cela, il frotta les yeux de sa fille avec le sang de la croix en disant: Au nom de Jésus-Christ le Fils de Dieu [Vivant], que ma fille recouvre la vue; et à l'instant la fillette recouvra la vue. Tous ceux qui étaient dans la synagogue des Juifs, se réjouirent et ils s'écrièrent: Un est le Dieu des chrétiens[29], Jésus-Christ, Fils de Dieu Vivant.

Alors, Philoxène, chef de la synagogue, écrivit ainsi une lettre à notre père Théophile, patriarche d'Alexandrie:

> *Je suis l'humble Philoxène le Juif indigne d'écrire au médecin véritable de Jésus-Christ Notre Sauveur, annonçant à sa sainteté ce qui est arrivé aujourd'hui dans notre synagogue des grands prodiges survenus par l'emblème de la croix de Jésus-Christ et son signe saint, sur laquelle fut suspendu le seigneur de la gloire. Du sang ayant coulé d'une croix en bois, <sang> que je mis sur les yeux de ma fille aveugle et aussitôt elle a recouvert la vue. Maintenant, nous connaissons véridiquement qu'il n'est pas d'autre Dieu dans le ciel et sur la terre que Jésus-Christ, le Dieu des chrétiens et, en vérité, nos pères ont mérité le feu de l'enfer. Nous avons observé les traditions de nos pères en disant qu'elles sont la vérité jusqu'à ce que nous ayons vu les prodiges. Et je te demande, Monseigneur, le père, de te réjouir avec ces brebis qui reviennent au bercail du Christ. Parce que nous avons espéré sa miséricorde, moi et toute ma maison, ainsi que chaque Juif présent aujourd'hui dans notre synagogue.*

Lorsqu'il lut la lettre, je veux dire notre père [le saint] Théophile le patriarche, il eut une grande joie. Il se leva rapidement, il alla à la synagogue avec une foule de prêtres et d'autres hommes de mérite. Il marche à pied.
p. 123r Quand Philoxène vit mon père le patriarche, il se prosterna sous ses pieds en disant: Serviteur de Jésus-Christ, aie pitié de moi, donne-moi le pardon de mes péchés. [Ils entrèrent devant lui à la synagogue, et ils lui montrèrent la croix]. Le patriarche vit la croix frappée et le sang qui a coulé d'elle, et il se prosterna devant la croix majestueuse de Notre-Seigneur Jésus-Christ; on lui montra la fillette de Philoxène qui avait recouvert la vue. Quant à cet [homme] incrédule, qui avait donné le coup de lance à la croix, il fut saisi de [grande] terreur et, devenu rigide comme une pierre, il tomba mort, et il rendit l'esprit; il eut une mauvaise mort, et il reçut sa part avec Judas, qui a vendu son Seigneur pour de l'argent.

Alors mon père le patriarche demanda à porter la croix à l'église, et tous les prêtres chantèrent devant elle, s'émerveillèrent de ces choses qui étaient arrivées; ils rendirent gloire à Dieu le Bon pour le signe du salut qu'ils venaient de voir à cause de la croix de Notre-Seigneur Jésus-Christ, gloire à Lui pour les siècles des siècles.

29 Cette formule est très ancienne (on la voit souvent sur les stèles coptes et on la lit dans des martyria coptes); voir Erik Peterson, «εἷς θεός», Göttingen 1926, VIII.

Quant à Philoxène, son fils, sa fille, sa femme et tous les Juifs qui sont dans la ville, trois milles âmes environ, on les admit dans l'église. Le patriarche {Théophile} les instruisit des Livres Saints qui sont les souffles de Dieu, et après cela, on prépara le baptistère et il les baptisa au nom du Père, du Fils et du Saint-Esprit, Un seul Dieu, il les communia aux saints mystères {le corps et le sang de Notre-Seigneur Jésus-Christ}, et leur donna la paix et les {renvoya}.

Philoxène, de son côté, donna au patriarche la moitié de tout ce qui lui appartenait pour qu'on l'employât comme aumône pour les pauvres. Au temps où il fut baptisé, son visage devint resplendissant comme le soleil et, l'année écoulée, le patriarche le consacra diacre, puis prêtre, et son fils {Alexandre} diacre, et ils progressèrent dans la pitié encore plus. Sa femme, qui était très croyante, donna toutes ses ressources aux pauvres, au point qu'elle les enrichit. Et c'est ainsi que leur conduite fut bonne. Et après cela, ils p. 123v
s'endormirent, obtenant le royaume des cieux dans la vie éternelle.

Ainsi, nous avons porté à la connaissance de votre charité ceci pour vous faire connaître la miséricorde de Dieu, l'ami des humains, qui ne veut la perdition de personne, mais qui lui accorde le temps de faire pénitence; et Dieu, son invocation soit louée, nous pardonne et vous aussi, et Il nous offre une chance et une part dans son royaume éternelle par sa grâce, sa bonté et l'amour des humains qui est de Notre-Seigneur Jésus-Christ, celui par qui est toute gloire, tout honneur, toute louange et toute adoration est au Père, avec Lui et avec L'Esprit-Saint, Un seul Dieu, maintenant et toujours, pour les siècles des siècles. Amen. Amen. Amen.

DORA PIGUET-PANAYOTOVA

L'église d'Iškhan: patrimoine culturel et création architecturale

L'église se dresse sur un haut plateau à l'extrémité ouest d'Iškhan, ville située sur la rive droite de la rivière Olty affluant de la Čorokh, dans l'ancienne province géorgienne de Tao, actuellement en Turquie orientale. La cathédrale d'Iškhan fit l'objet d'études de Takajšvili [1] qui a déterminé les deux périodes de son existance, répondant à deux constructions de type différent. Ayant déchiffré les inscriptions conservées sur les parois, il a établi que sa reconstruction s'était poursuivie en 954-955, et que des renovations furent effectuées à deux reprises, vers 1023 et en 1032. En outre, Marr [2] eut le grand mérite de la découverte des sources écrites offrant des données indéniables quant à l'élévation de l'église. Or, ses recherches sur la «Vie de Grigor Khandzijski» lui ont permis d'identifier l'église érigée à Iškhan par Nerses, avant son élection de catholikos d'Arménie (640-661), laquelle fut détruite et abandonnée lors de la domination arabe. Selon le texte, l'église fut restaurée à l'initiative de Saban, évêque d'Iškhan qui par respect pour l'œuvre de Nerses a conservé la colonnade du sanctuaire. Vraisemblablement, les travaux de refection ont eu lieu pendant la troisième décennie du IXe siècle.

C'est une église cruciforme à coupole [3] dont la partie est se détache par sa disposition élaborée et par sa construction qui offre des éléments de deux époques différentes (fig. 1). Ainsi s'impose la colonnade dont l'abside est percée et qui impressionne par ses chapiteaux. En réalité, elle appartient à la

1 E. Takajšvili, Arkheologičeskaja ekspedicija 1917-go goda v južnye provincii Gruzii, Tbilisi 1952, p. 23-44, pl. 1-38. Les dessins-plans, coupes, façades sont de A. Kalgin, C. Kldiašvili, I. Zdanević; pl. 1, 2, 3, 4, 15, 16 figurent dans la présente étude.

2 N. Marr, Georgij Merčul. Žitie sveti Grigorija Khandzijskogo s dnevnikom poezdki v Šavšiju i Klardžiju. Teksti i Razijskvanija po Armjano-gruzinskoj filologii, VII, Saint-Petersbourg 1911, § 13 - p. XIV-XV.

3 La partie ouest de l'église fut transformée en mosquée actuellement abandonnée. L'espace central garde sa coupole, mais les voûtes des bras de la croix ont disparu. Jadis l'église était toute recouverte de peintures dont une partie fut détruite par les musulmans. Les fresques qui ont échappé au feu et aux piques des soldats, furent identifiées par Takajšvili qui a déchiffré aussi toutes leurs inscriptions ainsi que les grafitis, témoins de la longue existence de l'église. E. Takajšvili, op. cit., p. 35-41, dess. 12-18. Au sujet des peintures voir aussi: N. et M. Thierry, «Peintures du XIe siècle en Géorgie Méridionale et leurs rapports avec la peinture byzantine de l'Asie Mineure», Cahiers Archéologiques, XXIV (1975), p. 88-105.

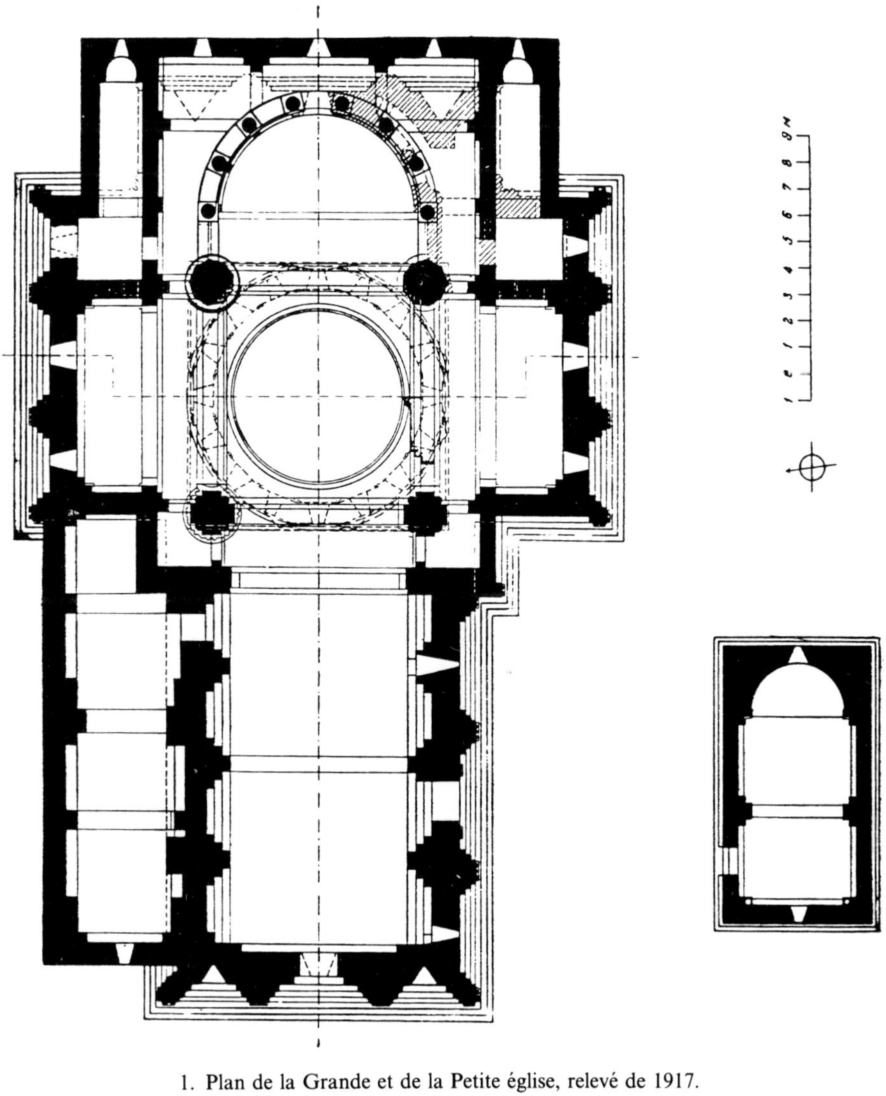

1. Plan de la Grande et de la Petite église, relevé de 1917.

conque orientale d'un quatre-feuilles avec déambulatoire, plus ancien qui fut construit par Nerses au VIIe siècle. Ses chapiteaux, toutefois, n'ont pas fait l'objet d'étude, ce dont je me propose.

J'envisage aussi de m'occuper des modes de reconstruction appropriés à l'architecture de Tao-Klardžeti[4] au IXe-XIe siècle, quant au renouvellement

4 E. Takajšvili, Materialy po Arkheologiju Kavkasa, XII, Moscou 1909, p. 114-116; V. Beridze, Architecture de Tao-Klardjetie, Tbilisi 1981, p. 52, 70, 96, 150, pl. 62-69, 83-84, 87-89.

fondamental d'un temple à plan quadrilobé avec déambulatoire, remontant au VIIe siècle: plus précisément, d'examiner la façon dont la première construction d'Iškhan a influencé l'aménagement des pièces dans la nouvelle partie est de l'édifice, ainsi que le choix des formes unifiant la colonnade et les surfaces avoisinant le sanctuaire.

D'autres problèmes essentiels se lient à la présente étude — celui de l'élévation de la coupole et de son système d'appui nouveau. Aussi, cette recherche a pour but de relever les innovations auxquelles procède la construction à plan cruciforme au IXe-Xe siècle; d'analyser les formes architecturales qui en découlent; enfin, de poursuivre leur décor sculptural: chapiteaux et bases des supports du corps central, à l'intérieur de l'église.

La dernière partie de cet ouvrage sera consacré à la sculpture architecturale des façades laquelle nécessite un examen approfondi des encadrements des ouvertures, leurs composantes sculptées, leurs motifs ornementaux, leurs origines, enfin leur valeur artistique déterminant de l'œuvre d'Ivan Morčaidze, de 1032[5].

1. *Colonnade de Nerses et ses chapiteaux du VIIe siècle*

Une arcade à huit colonnes perce l'abside[6] à l'est, sur son axe de symétrie, en suivant son tracé curviligne (fig. 1, 2). Les colonnes d'une hauteur de 2,48 m, leur base simple, se posent sur un stylobate. Leurs entrecolonnements d'une largeur de 1,88 m sont surmontés des arcs en forme de fer à cheval. La conque étant en à jour, reçoit ainsi, un allégement des maçonneries, cependant qu'elle est animée par le contraste vif entre la surface lisse lumineuse et les ouvertures assombries.

Les chapiteaux qui couronnent les colonnes surprennent par leur type et leur décor inhabituel. Tous d'une même taille, ils ont la forme d'un cube dont les faces sont, néanmoins, arrondies dans leur partie inférieure. Plus précisément, les angles du chapiteau sont graduellement rognés vers le bas, d'où leur retrait par rapport au champs ornementé qui, étant ortogonal évoque une surface en saillie. Dans la plupart des cas, les faces représentent des lobes (fig. 3, 4). Leur décor varié se caractérise par la simplification des ornements en accord avec leur traitement linéaire, répondant en effet, à l'abandon définitif des dérivés directs des ordres classiques. Les chapiteaux se détachent complètement des créations byzantines de l'époque. Ces œuvres d'art qui ne

5 E. Takajšvili, Arkheologičeskaja ekspedicija 1917-go goda v južnye provincii Gruzii, p. 28.

6 E. Takajšvili, Materialy po Arkheologiju Kavkaza, p. 114-116; Idem, Arkheologičeskaja ekspedicija, p. 28; S. Mnacakanjan, Zvartnotz, Moscou 1971, p. 48; R. Mepisašvili, V. Zinzadse, Die Kunst des alten Georgien, Leipzig 1977, p. 98, 148.

2. Vue vers l'abside, colonnade du VIIe siècle.

3. Sanctuaire, détail, côté sud.

manquent pas de charme demandent, néanmoins, un critère nouveau pour être appréciées.

Le chapiteau qui épaule l'arc central — côté nord — peut être qualifié par commodité «bilobé». Ses quatre faces offrent une même ornementation, sculptée en méplat: un motif de feuilles d'acanthe schématisées et qui, à dire vrai, est doublé (fig. 2, 5). Sur l'axe de symétrie de chaque côté, frontal ou latéral, se dresse une feuille qui sert de trait d'union entre les deux parties identiques du décor. Celles-ci représentent deux lobes retracés par deux tiges sortant à sa base, lesquelles encerclent aussi les feuilles déterminantes l'extrémité gauche et droite du chapiteau. Ces feuilles font pendant à l'axiale, voire à ses deux moitiés relatives aux deux lobes. En outre, chaque acanthe extrême pousse une grappe de raisin qui retombe au milieu du lobe dont la disposition

4. Sanctuaire, détail, côté nord, galerie et prothèse.

symétrique est évoquée d'ailleurs, par l'ourlet convexe d'une feuille très basse placée sur son point inférieur.

Les lobes coiffent d'habitude les minces pilastres élancés qui figurent à la rencontre des surfaces orthogonales ainsi qu'à la retombée des arcs et les voûtes, comme ils se voient à Ptigni et Aruć[7]. Comportant souvent des ornements végétaux les lobes apparaissent à l'extérieur: ainsi, sur les demi-colonnettes engagées à Zvartnotz et Artik[8]. Ailleurs, par exemple à Talin et Irind[9] les côtés larges des chapiteaux-pilastres offrent deux lobes agrémentés

7 Ptigni/Aruć, Documenti di Architettura Armena, 16, Milan 1986, fig. 1, 8, 9.

8 J. Strzygowsky, Baukunst der Armenier und Europa, Vienne 1918, fig. 93; Architettura Medievale Armena, Roma-Palazzo Venezia 1968, fig. 26.

9 J. Strzygowsky, op. cit., p. 138, fig. 141-142 (Irind), p. 172, fig. 201-202 (Talin).

5. Chapiteau central nord.

d'un même motif floral. Partout, ledit décor bilobé se développe suivant une frise, cependant qu'à Iškhan il s'associe au chapiteau d'un support libre.

On peut ainsi poursuivre le motif doublé sur les chapiteaux des demi-colonnes du pourtour extérieur de Zvartnotz[10]: la palmette sassanide révèle ici, grâce à son emplacement et à sa forme, une étape dans la formation du chapiteau «bilobé». Les demi-colonnes qui se joignent sur le rebord de chacune des 28 faces de l'édifice, font, en effet, apparaître leurs palmettes l'une à côté de l'autre, en constituant deux lobes unifiés.

La transposition des deux éléments identiques sur une même surface était donc, facile. De plus, elle fut pratiquée beaucoup avant le VIIe siècle, de

10 S. Mnacakanjan, Zvartnotz, Moscou 1971, p. 51, 121.

6. Chapiteau central sud.

même qu'au début du IVe, ce dont témoignent les chapiteaux des pilastres de la salle en forme de fer à cheval, dans la villa de Mascene (306-312) à la piazza Armérina[11].

On est surpris de voir ici le motif des feuilles d'acanthe doublé, traité de la même façon qu'à Iškhan. De plus, au-dessus de la feuille commune apparaît un calice adventice qui marque l'axe de symétrie du chapiteau. Il donne naissance à une tulipe qui rejoint l'abaque. À sa gauche et à sa droite, deux tiges recourbées épousent les extrémités de deux enroulements qui partent des feuilles externes en se dirigeant vers le centre. Comparables à un «S» allongé,

11 H. Kähler, Die Villa des Maxentius bei der Piazza Armerina. Monumenta Artis Romanae, XII, Berlin, 1973, p. 25, pl. 12c.

ceux-ci courent au-dessus des deux motifs d'acanthe «jumelés», dont chacun reçoit sur son axe de symétrie la spirale par laquelle ledit «S» se termine.

Cette ressemblance est très significative, quant au changement survenu dans les conceptions décoratives des sculpteurs. La déformation des ordres classiques est déjà en cours au tout début du IVe siècle, et elle se poursuit sur la voie des créations nouvelles au VIIe. En fait, l'évolution artistique se plie aux changements socio-politiques, religieux et culturels. Les formes antiques sont désavouées ainsi que les règles déterminantes l'ornementation architecturale. L'exemple d'Iškhan montre définitivement, l'abandon de l'ancien principe de lien entre le détail de construction et son décor approprié, ce qui amène à la transposition des motifs réservés aux frises, sur les chapiteaux. La suppression du haut relief et la technique du traitement linéaire qui s'en suit, va de paire avec le nouveau critère d'esthétique.

Le chapiteau de la colonne contiguë du centre — côté sud — offre aussi une ornementation rare (fig. 6). Sur son axe de symétrie se dresse une palmette à sept lobes, dont les deux derniers épousent la courbe des grandes feuilles qui, disposées par deux partent, à gauche et à droite, de sa base. Ayant arrondi les angles de la surface décorée, elles montent, leur galbe ample, le sommet recourbé, rappelant un «S». De plus, ces feuilles dégagent à leur départ le bourrelet situé en dessous qui ressort d'une hauteur variée, sur toutes les colonnes. Sur ce petit dégagement s'installe un élément qui descend de la palmette nouée plus haut, et qui rappelle les tiges réunies à la base d'un bouquet lacé.

Le chapiteau adjacent, le deuxième vers l'ouest — côté sud — est très caractéristique par ses lobes, si recherchés à Iškhan (fig. 7). Sur sa face frontale deux spirales d'une section plate s'enroulent et se relient par le bas, en retraçant le contour précis d'un lobe. Le champs libre dans sa partie inférieure est réservée à une «palmette» renversée à trois pétales qui s'étale sur son axe de symétrie respectée également par les spirales. Sur le côté latéral du chapiteau ce même décor orienté, cependant, verticalement — la palmette raccommodée à cinq pétales — se voit doublé afin de constituer une composition bilobée.

Les comparatifs de la face latérale bilobée se signalent sur les chapiteaux des pilastres évoqués plus haut, de même que ses ornements se retrouvent dans des combinaisons variées, en pleine expansion en Transcaucasie au VIe-VIIe siècle, comme par exemple à Agrak[12]. Par contre, les chapiteaux aux faces lobées dépourvues de décor couronnent les colonnes engagées dans l'abside de Zoravar[13].

12 J. Strzygowsky, op. cit., p. 315, fig. 93, 351.

13 V. Arutjunjan, S. Safarjan, Pamjatniki armjanskogo zodčestva, Moscou 1951, p. 21, fig. 44, 46; M. Asratjan, Egvard. Obščestvo Okhrany Pamjatnikov, Erevan 1984.

7. Chapiteau, côté sud, deuxième du centre vers l'ouest.

Le chapiteau avoisinant celui du centre — côté nord — figure également sur les deux colonnes placées aux extrémités de l'arcade. Il est le seul qui soit représenté trois fois ici. Sur sa face frontale apparaissent deux enroulements repartis, à gauche et à droite, qui encerclent deux médaillons, se dirigent vers le bas et se relient en esquissant un troisième médaillon, sur son axe de symétrie (fig. 8). Les deux médaillons supérieurs sont d'une taille plus grande et comprennent des rosettes de belle forme à huit pétales. Leurs encerclements (côté intérieur) sont doublés par deux galons qui descendent en côtoyant l'axe vertical du chapiteau et qui renferment le médaillon inférieur, contenant deux hélices reliées par le bas. Constitués ainsi, les trois médaillons trouvent leur équilibre, tandis que le ruban qui les relie assure leur unité inséparable par ses

8. Chapiteau, côté nord, deuxième du centre vers l'ouest.

mouvements sinueux. Il s'agit, en effet, d'un motif d'entrelacs bien adapté à la surface du chapiteau.

Malgré tous ces enroulements, le chapiteau est loin de l'ordre ionique, mais il n'exclut pas une inspiration des disques ornementés auxquels se sont réduit les volutes, ayant subi des transformations fondamentales, comme par exemple à Mirʿayeh et Ksedjbel en Syrie où figurent aussi les entrelacs (Ve siècle)[14].

14 H. Butler, Ancient architecture in Syria, Northern Syria, Leyden 1909, p. 69, fig. 73, 86; p. 159, fig. 170c; Idem, Early churches in Syria, Princeton 1929, p. 49-50, fig. 47c (Ksedjbel, église est de 414), fig. 51b. Les disques entrelacés se retrouvent sur la colonnade de la maison de Mirʿayeh et celles des deux églises, du Ve siècle où les entrelacs renfermant des rosettes et une croix sur l'axe du symétrie, courent tout autour du chapiteau. Des motifs qui rappellent celui d'Iškhan se signalent à Bakirha, Qalat-Seman, Qalb-Luzeh; J. Vogt-Göknil, Frühislamische Bogenwände, Graz 1982, p. 105, fig. 168.

9.Chapiteau des avant dernières colonnes.

Cependant à Iškhan, la composition est plus évoluée sur le plan décoratif. On s'efforce de préciser les formes telles qu'elles sont définies par la géométrie, et cette exactitude va de paire avec leur traitement linéaire. En fait, le décor ici discuté exploite des formes et des motifs connus depuis toujours, mais leur organisation et leur transposition sur une surface plane n'obéit plus aux règles respectées par les œuvres antiques et leurs dérivés directs. En revanche, ce même motif se retrouve sur les stucs sassanides[15]. Il est fort probable qu'il fut en vogue à l'époque, ayant été adopté en Syrie comme en Transcaucasie, et aussitôt transmis au répertoir artistique qui innove.

15 L. Golvin, Essai sur l'architecture religieuse musulman, 1. Généralités, Paris 1970, p. 31, fig. 15.

La face latérale du chapiteau reçoit les mêmes motifs que la face frontale, mais le nombre des encerclements s'accroit, tandis que leur disposition se modifie (fig. 8). Les deux grands médaillons gardent leur place établie par les galons d'entrelacs qui, cependant, forment en dessous, deux rondelles symétriques au lieu d'une seule — côté frontal. Puis, les galons montent afin de s'enrouler pour une troisième fois, auprès des médaillons desquels ils sont partis. En même temps, les galons enfermant les médaillons inférieurs convergent sur l'axe vertical du chapiteau et se rencontrent sous l'abaque, après avoir retracé un éléments lancéolé qui tente à unifier les deux parties du décor.

Évidemment, la distinction entre le côté latéral et frontal ne se traduit plus par la figuration de face et de profil d'un élément tridimensionnel, mais par un dessin modifié, en accord avec le style linéaire en vigueur.

En outre, les chapiteaux de ce même type qui couronnent les deux colonnes externes de l'arcade offrent, néanmoins, des nuances. Sur leur face frontale, en réalité, le médaillon du centre ne comporte plus d'hélices, mais, une grosse goute en accord avec le contour de ses encerclements légèrement élancés. Sur la face latérale, en revanche, des volutes d'une section plate figurent à la place des médaillons garnis de rosettes. Ces changements minutieux que l'on constate à Iškhan, montrent le soin d'éviter à tout prix la monotonie dans le décor architectural.

Le seul chapiteau qui puisse être appelé «ionisant» apparaît sur la troisième paire de colonnes, l'avant dernière, vers l'ouest. Il comprend un coussin muni de deux balustres qui se posent sur un bourrelet épais, mais, l'ensemble atteint la même hauteur que le reste (fig. 10, 11). Sur sa face frontale s'enroulent les volutes, sans pour autant se relier et de ce fait, semblent plus amoindries. De plus, la disparition des ornements sur le champs qui les sépare les rend plus éloignées.

Mais, ce manque de décor est en quelque sorte compensé par le profil même du chapiteau. Sa partie ortogonale descend jusqu'aux deux tiers de la hauteur des volutes, après quoi, elle subit un retrait sous 90° et donne naissance au bourrelet. Vu frontalement, ce retrait apparaît comme une platebande assombrie, entre les deux spirales.

La face latérale du chapiteau comprend la balustre, nouée à son milieu par un bandeau tripartite qui, dans sa partie inférieure est gradué horizontalement. Cette graduation est reprise sur le corps de la balustre dont les surfaces, de part et d'autre du bandeau, sont divisées en deux et il en résulte quatre travées presques égales. Habituellement, les balustres nouées à leur milieu s'évasent vers leurs extrémités. Cependant ici, cet évasement est saccadé et il se produit à deux reprises: d'abord, il touche aux travées avoisinantes du bandeau, puis, il recommence sur celles qui les suivent, à gauche et à droite.

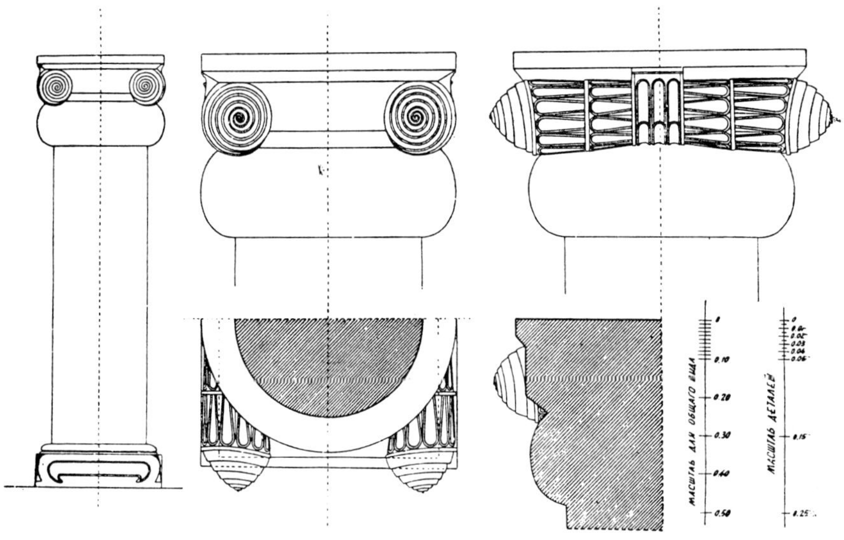

10. Chapiteau «ionisant», dessin.

Les travées ressemblent à des cônes tronqués, rayonnants du bandeau. Ce traitement de la balustre tente à dynamiser sa forme par la confrontation des surfaces retrécies et évasées.

Mais pour éviter les effets de morcellement on a recours à une ornementation unifiante. Des feuilles lancéolées déformées se rangent horizontalement l'une au-dessus de l'autre, leur sommet étant dissimulé derrière l'encadrement vertical qui délimite l'étendue de chaque travée. Des ornements semblables mais d'une orientation verticale regagnent la surface graduée du bandeau.

Le bourrelet demuni d'ornements comprend la demi-hauteur du chapiteau, l'autre partie étant réservée au coussin des volutes et à l'«abaque». Il faut noter que le bourrelet ici fait partie de la composition, à la différence des cas où lui-même est chargé de la fonction du chapiteau. Les comparatifs d'Iškhan se signalent surtout en Transcaucasie: c'est le cas du chapiteau de Dvin du Musée Historique d'Erévan[16], dont le bourrelet reçoit néanmoins un décor de vannerie qui agrémente aussi les fronts des volutes.

Le bourrelet se retrouve à Irind, mais l'exemple le plus spectaculaire fournit Bana[17] où il apparaît sur toute une colonnade, étant recouvert d'entrelacs de

16 Ereruk, Documenti di Architettura Armena, 9, Milan 1977, p. 29; D. Piguet-Panayotova, «Recherches sur les tetraconques à déambulatoire et leur décor en Transcaucasie au VIIe siècle», OrChr 73 (1989), p. 166-212, fig. 9.

17 D. Piguet-Panayotova, «Recherches sur les tétraconques à déambulatoire et leur décor», p. 170, 174, fig. 4-6.

treillis. Il obéit au même principe de répartition qu'à Iškhan, par son éloignement léger du coussin des volutes qui, cependant, se détachent par la richesse de leur décor. Plus précisément, la partie ionienne du chapiteau est très proche de l'ordre classique, de même qu'elle remonte au VIIe siècle. Bana et Iškhan traduisent, en fait, des règles décoratives diamétralement opposées, révélatrices des conceptions diverses, au sein de deux courants artistiques bien distincts.

L'usage des volutes sans respect de l'ordre ionique se signale en Transcaucasie déjà au VIe siècle, comme par exemple à Ereruk et Avan où figurent des spirales non reliées[18]. Le même phénomène s'observe à Ptigni datant du VIIe siècle[19]. Sur le pilon nord, le chapiteau comprend — côté frontal — deux volutes d'une section plate, reliées par le haut et entre elles, une rosette encerclée, tandis que la balustre — côté latéral — représente une simple bobine autour de laquelle une corde est enroulée. Les minces pilastres adjacents reçoivent des demi-chapiteaux du même type. L'ensemble fait allusion à une frise.

Le chapiteau de Cromi[20], en Géorgie, fournit un autre équivalent du VIIe siècle. Les volutes ne se relient pas, mais entre elles apparaissent deux rangées horizontales de petites feuilles de fougère, disposées en éventail et qui marquent le passage de la surface ortogonale vers l'echine. La balustre est divisée en travées ornementées et comme d'habitude, nouée par un bandeau. En outre, les fronts des volutes, transformés en rosettes rappellent les médaillons du chapiteau aux entrelacs d'Iškhan. Évidemment, Cromi et Iškhan révèlent les variantes d'un modèle, d'usage courant au VIIe siècle.

Les chapiteaux d'Iškhan à l'exception des deux du centre, offrent des éléments agréés par l'ordre ionique lesquels cependant, se retrouvent dans des combinaisons diverses avec des motifs locaux ou adoptés des cultures voisines. Leur décor est moins riche et il se plie aux impératifs du nouvel ordre qui domine la sculpture architecturale en Transcaucasie au VIIe siècle, mais qui se fait jour beaucoup avant. En effet, bon nombre d'exemples en Syrie, se prêtent à démontrer ce phénomène qui s'observe dès le IVe siècle[21]. En réalité, il s'est manifesté avant l'établissement du christianisme de religion

18 V. Arutjunjan, S. Safarjan, Pamjatniki armjanskogo zodčestva, fig. 21-2,6 (Ereruk), 21-5 (Avan), 21-11 (Ptigni). V. Arutjunjan, Kamennaja letopis armjanskogo naroda, Erevan 1985, p. 159.

19 B. Brentjes, S. Mnacakanjan, N. Stepanjan, Kunst des Mittelalters in Armenien, Vienne/Munich 1973, fig. 77.

20 G. Čubinašvili, Cromi, Moscou 1969, p. 25, pl. 80; Ereruk, Documenti di Architettura Armena, 9, p. 29, fig. 3, 4, 5.

21 H. Butler, Ancient Architecture in Syria, A. Part 3, Southern Syria, Leyden 1913, p. 161, fig. 141 (praetorium, daté de 371); Idem, Southern Syria, Leyden 1919, p. 330, fig. 375, 376 (Batuta); fig. 338 (Brad).

d'État et après, a trouvé un accueil favorable dans l'architecture tant civile que religieuse du pays.

À l'évidence, chaque spécimen apparenté à un motif «ionisant» d'Iškhan trouve ses prédécesseurs ornementaux en Syrie. Les volutes réduites à des rouleaux figurent à Kefr nabu, remontant au milieu du IVe siècle[22]. À Qasr Beyt 'Ali du Ve comme aussi à la maison de Fidren datée de 531, elles sont transformées en disques et s'avancent sur la surface orthogonale de demi-chapiteaux[23]. En revanche, sur les portiques de Keratin[24] de 474-478, les volutes sont enroulées en spirale et associées aux entrelacs des trois médaillons qui intercalent entre elles, tandis que les balustres gardent leur forme.

Quant au motif des spirales qui se relient par le bas en esquissant une rondelle, il se signale à Déir Seman[25] datant de 479, mais la palmette est absente. Aussi les combinaisons concernant les motifs végétaux sur les chapiteaux d'Iškhan, sont connues également des monuments syriens.

Cependant, en Transcaucasie tous ces motifs apparaissent sur des chapiteaux qui ne sont pas les mêmes. Les faces orthogonales se font jour en Syrie, mais ni leur forme, ni les ornements auxquels elles sont réservées ne correspondent à celles d'Iškhan. En fait, les motifs sont engagés ici dans des compositions plus compliquées qui sont inséparables des lobes enracinés dans la tradition transcaucasienne. Constitués ainsi, les chapiteaux d'Iškhan révèlent une phase plus évoluée dans la sculpture architecturale qui poursuit son développement sur la voie médiévale.

2. *Aménagement du sanctuaire. Caractères de la construction du IXe-Xe siècles. Décoration sculpturale de l'intérieur*

L'espace auquel donne accès la colonnade, embrasse l'abside mais, il est limité par des murs rectilignes: celui à l'est, muni de fenêtres, ceux au nord et au sud, adjacents la prothésis et le diaconicon, tandis qu'à l'ouest, il s'aligne à des pièces précédant ces deux annexes, en atteignant de même les piliers orientaux de la coupole (fig. 1). Cet espace, souvenir du déambulatoire, gaine à l'extérieur, le corps est de l'édifice, lequel se dresse en dissimulant la conque derrière ses parois planes (fig. 11). Celle-ci, en revanche, contribue par sa grande hauteur à l'élévation de la branche est au même niveau que le reste de la croix vue sur les toits. En s'inspirant de l'ancienne construction, les

22 H. Butler, Northern Syria, p. 295, fig. 323 (Kefrnabu), 326, 346.

23 H. Butler, Northern Syria, 1914, p. 251, fig. 260 (Fidreh, baptistère daté de 513), fig. 261 (Fidreh, maison de 531); fig. 255, 256 (Zarzita).

24 H. Butler, Northern Syria, 1909, p. 82, fig. 86, 89 (Keratin).

25 H. Butler, op. cit., p. 126, fig. 120 (Deir Seman).

11. Façade est.

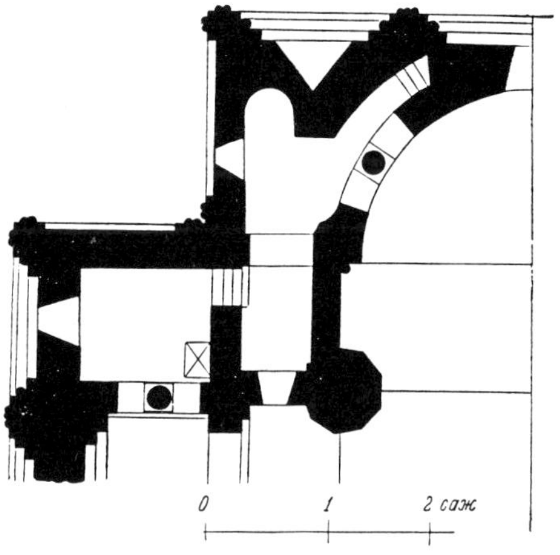

12. Plan de la galerie, côté nord.

galleries côtoyant l'abside ont été aménagées (fig. 12, 13). Accessibles par deux escaliers symétriques de départ à l'est, elles communiquaient à l'étage avec les deux pièces reparties à son extrémité nord et sud. Celles-ci, alignées à la paroi ouest du sanctuaire, s'associent néanmoins, au transept qui bénéficiait ainsi, vue de l'extérieur, de la même largeur que les autres branches de la croix (fig. 14, 15).

Le lien entre l'ancien et le nouveau si recherché dans l'organisation de l'espace, se reconnaît aussi dans les formes architecturales et leur décor. La colonnade, en effet, détermine l'aspect des ouvertures de l'étage, percées dans la conque auprès des galleries, ainsi que dans les murs plans des pièces contiguës. Ce sont des fenêtres bilobées, dotées d'une colonne couronnée d'un chapiteau varié et, qui reprennent le rythme de ses entrecolonnements arqués, en répondant à la splendeur de l'intérieur. Elles transmettent comme l'arcade un éclairage diffus, à la différence des fenêtres cintrées qui introduisent une lumière directe, et dont la forme convient au traitement des façades.

On observe aussi que les colonnettes et les chapiteaux des fenêtres bilobées sont récupérés de l'ancien tétraconque. Plus précisément, les chapiteaux s'apparentent aux œuvres connues en Syrie au VIe siècle et auparavant, lesquelles respectent le style linéaire conforme au courant artistique qui s'oppose à la continuité des ordres classiques. Ils sont tous différents. Celui de la fenêtre perçant la conque du nord, s'impose par la distinction nette entre ses deux parties symétriques (fig. 2, 4, 16). Or, de ses extrémités supérieures partent deux tiges horizontales qui, arrivées à son milieu se plient à 90 degrés et descendent en côtoyant, de part et d'autre, son axe de symétrie. À la base du chapiteau elles divergent et donnent naissance, chacune à trois feuilles dont les deux grandes montent en retraçant ses côtés extérieures, pour

13. Coupe transversale.

14. Vue du nord-est.

atteindre en haut, la limite fixée par les tiges. De cette manière, le motif est enfermé de tous côtés, cependant que la troisième feuille, la plus petite se replit vers l'intérieur, en lui offrant un accent unifiant. Le chapiteau constitué ainsi, de deux parties indépendantes, reçoit à sa base un tracé «bilobé», tandis qu'à son sommet il est couronné d'une plaque, voire d'une «abaque». Ce même décor réapparaît sur ses quatre faces.

Le chapiteau qui lui fait face sur la colonne de la fenêtre sud de l'abside, offre des éléments décoratifs appropriés aux frises et aux panneaux. Quatre pommes de pin d'une taille plus importante sont réparties sur chacune des quatre faces, les plus externes en constituant les angles (fig. 2, 3, 17). Toutes se relient par de petits arcs aveugles, en saillie légère sur la surface haute du chapiteau, laquelle cependant s'achève en dessous, par des découpures parallèles à leurs courbes. De plus, le fond sous cette petite arcade est très en retrait, les pommes de pin semblant ainsi suspendues aux arcs.

La fenêtre de la pièce à l'extrémité sud de l'étage, qui donne sur le transept fournit le chapiteau le mieux conservé. Son ornementation comprend un motif floral qui apparaît quatre fois sur les axes de symétrie de ses côtés et autant de fois sur ses rebords (fig. 18). C'est un fleuron à cinq pétales dont les trois principaux élancés, se rangent sur une même hauteur, en rappelant ainsi, un crocus, tandis que les deux externes s'enroulent en hélices. Les trois pétales

15. Façade sud, détail transept.

médians sont sanglés par un petit galon horizontal qui laisse sortir néanmoins leurs tiges latérales lesquelles descendent en divergeant, et rejoignent à la base du chapiteau leurs correspondantes voisines. En fait, elles enferment par le bas l'espace dans lequel s'intègrent les hélices, en épousant leurs courbes. Or, dans sa partie haute ce même espace est encadré par les pétales latéraux des crocus avoisinants. Ainsi constitué, le champs libre entre le fleuron axiale et angulaire offre, lui aussi, un motif décoratif.

La quatrième fenêtre qui éclairait jadis la pièce contiguëe à l'étage et qui fut orientée vers le transept — côté nord — a disparu tout comme le chapiteau. Cependant, la photographie prise en 1917 permet de s'en faire une idée: elle montre un chapiteau en forme de pyramide tronquée et renversée dont les

16. Galerie nord, fenêtre bilobée vers l'abside, détail, chapiteau.

faces sont sillonnées verticalement par des motifs de flûte[26] (fig. 42). Ce chapiteau est bien connu en Syrie au Ve-VIe siècle.

Enfin, ces quatre chapiteaux réutilisés pour les fenêtres bilobées comme ceux de la colonnade dans le sanctuaire, sont d'autant plus intéressants qu'ils offrent des spécimens appartenant au modèles repris lors de ladite renaissance géorgienne, mais on y reviendra après.

Une autre question fondamentale se pose ici, celle du mode d'appui utilisé pour la coupole qui se dresse sur le carré central (fig. 1, 25), constitué par quatre supports — poligonaux à l'est (fig. 21) et piliers munis de pilastres, à l'ouest (fig. 1, 19). Or, chacun de ces supports est inclus dans un système

26 E. Takajšvili, Arkheologičeskaja ekspedicia, pl. 26.

17. Galerie sud, fenêtre bilobée vers l'abside, détail, chapiteau.

d'appui et d'éléments de transmission, chargés de contrebuter les poussées venues des parties hautes de l'édifice. Un examen des piliers ouest permet, en effet, de découvrir le principe d'allégement de la charge des maconneries, mis en œuvre ici. À une hauteur précise, chacun de ces supports libres se relie avec les deux parois extérieures contiguës, par deux murs courts, surmontant des baies élancées. De cette manière, les murs intérieurs et extérieurs constituent ensemble un appui de section carrée, percé de deux baies étroites arquées, en réalité, un appui creusé, dont fait partie intégrante le pilier même (fig. 19, 20). Quant aux piliers à l'est, ils obéissent au même principe de résistance, étant allégés de plus, par l'appui des pièces voisines, aux extrémités nord et sud de l'étage (fig. 21).

Pour préciser, les maîtres géorgiens ayant renoncé à la pratique des appuis

18. Galerie sud, fenêtre bilobée donnant sur le transept.

massifs en vigueur au VIIe siècle, ont eu recours aux piliers creusés pour l'élévation de la coupole au IXe, laquelle a survécu jusqu'à nos jours. Ce mode nouveau de contrebuter les poussées, apparaît dans sa forme finale à Bana[27] où les quatre immenses supports abritent de petites chapelles, à chaque étage du tétraconque renouvellé au début du Xe siècle. Par contre à Ani[28], dans le même type d'édifice avec déambulatoire, remontant à l'an 1001, les piliers sont massifs et ils n'ont pas tardé à s'écrouler comme il est arrivé aux édifices du VIIe siècle.

27 E. Takajšvili, Materialy po Arkheologiju Kavkaza, fig. 64-68; pl. XVIII,34.
28 N. Marr, Ani. Knižnaja istorija goroda i razkopki na mesto gorodišča, Moscou/Leningrad 1934, pl. XXIII, XXIV.

19. Piliers ouest.

20. Support creusé nord-est, détail, vue d'en bas.

21. Pilier sud-est, détail, chapiteau.

Iškhan montre le type de construction à coupole adoptée au Xe siècle pour le renouvellement des édifices quadrilobés du VIIe siècle, pratiquée enfin, avec succès dans l'architecture du Tao-Klardžeti, lors de ladite renaissance géorgienne.

Les formes qui traduisent ce type de construction offrent leur concours à l'organisation de l'espace, étant enrichies par le décor approprié à leurs détails accentués. Voyons à Iškhan, les supports déterminants du carré central, leurs chapiteaux, leurs bases ornementées. Les grands piliers ouest qui se dressent à une hauteur de 11,80 m sont de section carrée, tandis que des pilastres s'avancent de leurs côtés. De cette manière, leur capacité de résistance est augmentée et leur éloignement des murs extérieurs, diminué. En fait, les pilastres sont nettement exprimés sur leurs côtés qui en haut, se

22. Pilier sud-ouest, détail, chapiteau.

prêtent à appuyer les retombées des grands arcs, sous la coupole. Par contre en bas, les pilastres ouest des deux piliers ainsi que le nord, du nord-ouest, et le sud, du sud-ouest, sont engagés dans les pieds-droits des ouvertures flanquées des murs extérieurs, ces derniers offrant leur pilastre à l'autre pied-droit. Intéressants ici sont les chapiteaux qui coiffent les montants de ces ouvertures, et notamment, leurs faces en forme de lobe, une replique de celles de la colonnade du sanctuaire du VIIe siècle.

Cependant, les baie orientées vers l'est sont très élancées (fig. 19). En effet, elles s'élèvent à la hauteur de leurs correspondantes orientales qui, associées à la paroi occidentale du sanctuaire, s'alignent sur les fenêtres bilobées des pièces nord et sud de l'étage. Toutefois, les pieds-droits des baies est sont demunis de ce chapiteau à lobes mais, ils gardent le double tailloir. Ainsi, leur

23. Pilier sud-ouest, base, détail.

décor s'associe-t-il aux montants des fenêtres bilobées, accentuées d'ailleurs, par leur beau chapiteau (fig. 13).

Les chapiteaux, des piliers ouest à dosserets et à boudins d'angle, s'imposent par leur bande large, garnie des ornements déterminants de leur aspect (fig. 22). Ce sont des feuilles d'acanthe dessechées et modifiées: d'abord, leur galbe a disparu et avec ceci, la distance entre elles-mêmes et leur fond, d'où le manque de tâches claires et sombres en contraste. Les feuilles ainsi ramenées à une surface plane ont perdu leur ourlet, tandis que les lobes rangés sur une même ligne verticale se sont géométrisés. À la place de la nervure médiane s'intercale une entaille déterminée par deux lignes qui se joignent au sommet de l'acanthe. Aussi, importantes sont les découpures créées par le frôlement des lobes des feuilles voisines, et qui se transforment en ornements négatifs.

En fait, ces découpures asombries, d'un contour raide, sont en concurrence avec les lignes éraflées et les encoches profondes, auquelles sont réduites les nervures des lobes. La forme a perdu son unité, l'acanthe son identité.

Ces feuilles d'acanthe disposées sur un seul rang sont limitées par deux boudins: l'un, inférieur est suivi par la rangée de petits lobes en retrait, qui achèvent le chapiteau; l'autre, supérieur en saillie, au-dessus duquel se détache l'abaque garni de petits arcs aveugles, reposant sur des colonnettes.

Ce type de décor trouve ses prédécesseurs sur les chapiteaux d'acanthe répandus en Transcaucasie au VIe-VIIe siècle. Les spécimens connus se présentent sous deux variantes: la première, à laquelle se rattache le chapiteau de Bana[29], ses feuilles arrondies, sa forme plastique, est fidèle à l'art antique; la deuxième, qui comprend ceux de Tékor, d'Aruć et surtout de Kassakh[30] montre, par contre, le dessèchement des feuilles déjà survenu, comme aussi les découpures du fond et les nervures, rappelant un dessin de losanges. De plus, sa structure est modifiée, son profil, applati. Ces deux variantes du chapiteau d'acanthe s'offraient comme modèle au maître d'Iškhan qui s'est inspiré de la deuxième variante, apparentée au même courant artistique que les chapiteaux de la colonnade du VIIe siècle. Or, il a créé son œuvre, de manière conforme à la sculpture architecturale du Xe siècle et au style avancé de son temps.

Quant aux piliers orientaux, ils se distinguent par leur trônc polygonal, tout en obéissant au même principe d'associé au support creusé, dont on a déjà parlé. Ils se relient à l'est, avec la conque en haut, par des parois courtes, surmontant des baies qui s'ouvrent vers le sanctuaire, au sud et au nord. En fait, leur proximité de la conque explique leur forme similaire aux colonnes si nombreuses ici (fig. 21, 25).

Le chapiteaux qui couronne ces supports polygonaux de l'est, a ses surfaces arondies. Il offre comme celui de l'ouest, une zone importante, réservée au motif principal, constitué ici de pommes de pin. Au-dessus d'elles s'avancent deux rangées de petites rondelles placées horizontalement et qui sont suivies en haut, par une scotie, en retrait. Après, vient une moulure convexe, dominée enfin, d'une plaque ronde agrémentée de petits disques dressés. En bas, la zone des pommes de pin est limitée par une grosse corde torsadée, sous laquelle une rangée de lobes ajustés au fût de la «colonne» achève le décor.

Ce chapiteau peut être comparé avec un bracelet ou un anneau, d'un profil bombé, et dont la partie médiane, la plus large qui reçoit les ornements essentiels, est bordée de part et d'autre, de minces bandes convexes — décorée ou dénudées.

29 E. Takajšvili, op. cit., fig. 38.
30 J. Strzygowsky, op. cit., fig. 434, 438, 439, 441.

Cependant à Iškhan, les pommes de pin s'associent à deux chapiteaux différents conformément à leur allure (fig. 3, 17, 25). D'abord, nouées par le haut, à l'aide de petites archivoltes, elles se succèdent sur le chapiteau de section carré qui domine la fenêtre bilobée sud de la conque et qui est très proche des spécimens syriens du Ve-VIIe siècle. Puis, ce même motif décoratif réapparaît sur le chapiteau des grands piliers est, au milieu cependant, d'une composition qui est adaptée à une forme architecturale nouvelle, en vigueur au Xe-XIe siècle. Il s'agit dans ce cas, d'une création de chapiteau et de son décor, inspiré d'éléments relevés du patrimoine artistique.

De plus, ces ornements appropriés aux chapiteaux, se retrouvent sur la base des piliers ouest (fig. 23). Ici les pommes de pin sont liées par le haut, à l'aide de minces tiges dont les courbes évoquent les petits arcs du chapiteau du VIIe siècle de la fenêtre bilobée sud du sanctuaireé discuté plus haut[31].

En fait, cette ornementation s'accorde au fût du support, tandis que la vraie base en forme poligonale commence en dessous, étant séparée de plus, par deux moulures plates. Elle offre un tore divisé horizontalement par des cavets, et à partir d'ici s'installe une bande importante où des champs sillonnés verticalement se sucèdent avec des champs libres, tandis qu'une dernière moulure plate passe au ras du sol. En outre, ce décor de la base encadre, de part et d'autre, les niches accollées aux piliers ouest dont l'un abrite le trône d'archevêque[32] (fig. 19, 23).

Ce même phénomène de déplacement des motifs, du chapiteau vers la base, se reconnaît aussi sur les piliers orientaux d'Iškhan. Ici sont repris, par contre, les minces moulures au lieu de la zone principale qu'ils délimitent. Ainsi, sont descendus les petits disques qui faisant le tour en couronnent la base. Ils sont suivis comme sur le chapiteau, par la grosse corde torsadée, sous laquelles vient la bande large des motifs principaux qui cependant, se démarquent complètement de tout ce décor unifié, de l'intérieur (fig. 24). En réalité, ces ornements inattendus sont pénétrés des façades où ils figurent obligatoirement dans toute sorte d'encadrement, mais on y reviendra après. Quant à la partie inférieure de la base, elle est identique avec celle des piliers ouest, examinée plus haut.

Enfin, l'usage des mêmes motifs ornementaux sur la base et sur le chapiteau des supports, tant est qu'ouest, démontre une négligence de l'emplacement du décor réservé jadis, à un détail fort précis. Dans le cas d'Iškhan, les ornements déterminent son étendue sans pour autant souligner sa nature. Évidemment, la sculpture architecturale obéit à des principes nouveaux qui se

31 A comparer avec les bases des piliers d'Oški. V. Beridze, L'architecture de Tao-Klardjetie, fig. 104, 105.

32 V. Beridze, op. cit., fig. 12 (Otkhta Eklesia), fig. 13 (Parkhal). Deux niches sont amenagées dans les deux supports à Manglisi. M. Dvali, Manglisi, Tbilisi 1974, fig. 34, 35.

24. Pilier sud-est, base, détail.

25. Construction de la coupole, vue du nord.

sont imposés dans ce type de constructions. En effet, ces bases et ces chapiteaux de colonnes ont connu un succès remarquable au Xᵉ-XIᵉ siècle. Entrés dans le répertoire artistique géorgien, ils seront exploités et développés largement à l'avenir.

À travers ces innovations émergent les traces de la tradition transcaucasienne voire géorgienne. Ainsi, les pendantifs qui se prêtent à constituer le pourtour circulaire du tambour (d = 9,67 m) offrent-ils, à leur milieu des maçonneries rangées comme dans le cas des trompes d'angles (fig. 25). Ces dernières ayant été utilisées, dès les plus anciens temps pour la construction à coupole, apparaissent ici en tant qu'éléments décoratifs. Par ailleurs, les quatre grands arcs entre lesquels s'avancent les pendantifs, ont leur forme brisée. L'arc brisé que l'on doit à l'Iran fur adopté par les constructeurs des pays voisins et aussitôt transmis à la tradition géorgienne.

L'idée de la coupole suspendue du ciel est réalisée grâce à une construction solide qui dans son agencement gradué reçoit son dernier accent, la calotte. De plus, le tambour à l'intérieur, est agrémenté par des colonnettes géminées qui ajoutent leur apport à cet élancement recherché (fig. 13, 25). Ce mode de construction approprié aux Abbassides fut largement exploité par l'architecture islamique et diffusé jusqu'à la Tunisie (IXᵉ) et à l'Espagne (Xᵉ siècle)[33]. À plus forte raison il pouvait être adopté par les pays adjacents la Mésopotamie, sans oublier la Syrie et la Palestine où des constructions semblables n'ont pas manqué auparavant. Son choix à Iškhan s'explique par l'affinité avec des éléments, tans hellénistiques que sassanides, apparentés à l'héritage culturel de la Transcaucasie.

3. *Vue de l'extérieur, décor des façades*

À l'atmosphère solennelle, créée par l'espace si bien organisé, à l'intérieur, répond la grandeur de l'édifice, à l'extérieur. La construction impressionne par l'agencement de ses volumes et par ses formes nettes qui traduisent les quatre branches de la croix, leur intersection dominée par la coupole (fig. 11, 14, 15). Celles-ci montrent leur façade à pignon qui se détache sur chaque côté de l'église par leur décor distinct: une arcade aveugle tripartie, dont l'arc médian s'élance beaucoup plus haut que les latéraux, conformément à la surface disponible[34]. Ce motif décoratif s'exprime par une archivolte à cinq profils: trois arrondis et deux plats, qui sont repris par les montants. Or, le

33 L. Golvin, Essai sur l'architecture religieuse musulmane, 1. Généralité, p. 129, 131, fig. 49, 50.

34 Ce décor est largement répandu en Géorgie. N. Aladašvili, Monumentalnaja sculptura Gruzii, Moscou 1977, fig. 145, 152 (Nikorcminda), fig. 186 (Sveti Tskhoveli); V. Beridze, op. cit., fig. 70-72 (Tbeti), fig. 82 (Savane).

26 Façade ouest, détail.

premier et le troisième des pieds-droits représentent de demi-pilastres, le reste offrant des boudins (fig. 14, 15, 26).

Tous les montants reçoivent des chapiteaux, mais on remarque qu'il en manque un sur le cinquième, le dernier boudin des archivoltes latérales. En fait, ce cinquième montant est commun pour l'archivolte centrale et l'archivolte latérale. Or, il dépasse la retombée de l'arc supérieur latéral, mais, en s'élançant au-delà, il reçoit son chapiteau à la retombée de l'arc supérieur central. Ainsi est évité l'encombrement d'éléments verticaux qui auraient provoqué des déformations d'apparence, indésirables pour l'œil. On reconnaît ici le soin du décorateur de présenter son œuvre achevée au spectateur et en agissant sur sa sensibilité esthétique de le faire comprendre le langage artistique (fig. 26).

Les chapiteaux qui couronnent les montants sont en général, de deux types.

27. Façade ouest, arcade aveugle tripartie, détail, chapiteaux

Le premier, moins fréquent, comprend une abaque sous laquelle vient une scotie; là-dessous, apparaît le motif le plus spectaculaire d'Iškhan — une feuille de fougère alterne de taille élevée, très découpée et enroulée en crosse au début de son développement, qui court, le sommet en bas (fig. 27). Ce chapiteau figure uniquement sur la façade occidentale. En revanche, le motif de fougère garnit la base des piliers est, à l'intérieur de l'église, où les champs libres entre ces feuilles renversées, recueillent une palmette dressée. En outre, ces fougères insolites de grande taille couronnent la corniche à la base de la coupole (fig. 28).

Le deuxième type chapiteau connaît néanmoins, des variantes qui relèvent de son décor et non pas de sa structure. Dans sa forme primaire il offre une abaque, suivie d'un boudin assez épais, sous lequel se pose en retrait une moulure convexe, bordée de deux listels. Le chapiteau s'achève par une rangée de petits lobes (fig. 26, 29).

Ce même chapiteau se voit paré de sculptures qui occupent des détails établis. Les rondelles en effet, agrémentent l'abaque, tandis que le décor principal remplit la moulure convexe par une frise d'entrelacs tressés du triple brin en forme de rondes, limitées par deux minces bordures plates (fig. 30, 33). Cette zone ornementée s'avance au-dessus des petits lobes qui sont, en fait, présents partout.

28. Coupole, vue de l'extérieur.

29. Façade sud, détail, fenêtre deuxième de l'ouest vers l'est, avec l'inscription d'Ivan Morčaïdze de 1032.

Ces deux variantes du deuxième type chapiteau se retrouvent sur toutes les façades de l'église. Cependant, il en existe une troisième, reconnaissable sur la partie seule qui ait subsisté de l'arcade aveugle nord, à son extrémité ouest; celle-ci ayant été dissimulée derrière le corps qui longe la branche ouest de l'église (fig. 31). Ses chapiteaux se distinguent par leur parure riche (fig. 32). Ainsi, la frise d'entrelacs: deux galons à triple brin partent sous 45 degrés et s'entrelacent, chacun en haut et en bas. Éloignés à une distance qui égale la hauteur du champs décoré, ils suivent leurs tracés en zigzag et s'entrecroisent à leur milieu, au-dessus d'une barre verticale laquelle cependant, ressort pour s'aligner aux deux bord de la frise. Sous la zone d'entrelacs se pose en retrait une petite bande qui introduit les lobes.

Par contre, l'abaque offre un décor végétal. On procède à l'apposition des demi-acanthes couplés, les lobes affrontés, qui, le sommet en bas, s'entrelacent à leur base de façon que leurs boucles nouées à distance égale, couronnent le chapiteau.

Par ailleurs, ces chapiteaux témoignent de l'aspect originel de la façade nord, et notamment, de sa partie ouest agrémentée jadis d'une belle arcade aveugle. En outre, leur parenté indéniable avec les sculptures datées de 1032 sur la façade sud et celles de la façade ouest, parle en faveur de la décoration simultanée du corps ouest de l'église, dont ils faisaient partie. En même temps ces chapiteaux ainsi que les restes de l'archivolte et du revêtement du mur à cet endroit, affirment que l'annexe nord accolé ici, fut erigé après la brillante renovation de l'église, effectuée par Ivan Morčaidze en 1032[35]. Suite de cet agencement, la façade nord s'est retrouvée à l'intérieur de l'annexe, en constituant sa paroi sud. Parallèlement, l'inscription de 955 qui figurait sur la façade septentrionale est tombée, elle aussi, à l'intérieur de la nouvelle construction[36]. Ainsi devient clair que les inscriptions annonçant les grands travaux et les donations princières toutes furent intégrées dans le décor des façades.

Quant aux supports de ces chapiteaux, ils ne se distinguent nullement des autres. En général, boudins et demi-pilastres s'achèvent par une base identique, composée d'un bulbe surmonté d'un tore. Cette petite base est séparée par un cavet de la grande base commune qui vient en dessous et qui, en descendant s'avance sur le socle. Cependant, les bases ne figurent pas sur la façade est où le corps moins élévé, fixé par le diaconicon et la prothésis gaine la branche orientale de la croix (fig. 11). En revanche, le relief qui annonce la

35 Ainsi, la grande rénovation de 1032 établit-elle, une date post quem pour l'érection de l'annexe nord, au plus tôt la deuxième moitié du XIe siècle.

36 L'inscription de 955 se reconnaît jusqu'à nos jours sur la même paroi sud de l'annexe, à droit de la porte par laquelle on y accède du corps ouest de l'église.

30. Façade est, arcade aveugle, chapiteaux, détail.

prothésis à l'extérieur, par le symbole de la croix fleurie reprend les motifs appropriés au décor des façades, en émerveillant le spectateur.

De plus, sur les façades à pignon est et ouest, les archivoltes latérales sont réservées aux niches triangulaires, élancées et agrémentées d'une coquille à leur sommet, si chère à l'architecture géorgienne (fig. 11, 26).

Ces mêmes archivoltes sont reprises par les arcs aveugles qui courent sur le côté sud de la branche ouest de la croix (fig. 29, 36, 38), son côté nord étant dissimulé derrière l'annexe rajoutée ici. Les pilastres régulièrement répartis sur la paroi méridionale comme à l'intérieur, recueillent les retombées des archivoltes d'une hauteur égale, en leur offrant des montants multiples, couronnés de chapiteaux similaires à ceux des façades à pignon (fig. 29, 30).

Les ouvertures percent les murs sur l'axe de symétrie des archivoltes, auxquelles elles associent leur forme cintrée. Portail et fenêtres, tous se détachent par leurs encadrements sculptés qui rythment leur accent sur la façade décorée. On s'efforce d'unifier ces détails par la nature de leurs ornements et par leur composition, cependant qu'un traitement distinct est accordé à chacun.

L'encadrement comprend, en effet, une archivolte ornementée qui retourne néanmoins, à ses retombées pour se dérouler horizontalement. De cette façon apparaissent deux prolongations à ses côtés, qui font allusion à des rubans

31. Façade ouest, détail, angle nord-ouest.

étalés. Aussi, l'étendue du décor est limité, à gauche et à droite, par des colonnettes accouplées, coiffées ou non d'un chapiteau commun, leurs bases étant soutenues par une console. Le champs libre entre l'ouverture et l'encadrement, ainsi constitué, est réservé aux chambranles qui s'achèvent souvent, par une bordure formée de consoles ou de plaques de pierre sculptées (fig. 36, 39). Quant à la fenêtre sur la façade ouest, elle reçoit une corniche importante, horizontale qui couronne le chambranle rectangulaire encadré sur ses quatre côtés (fig. 26).

Le décor réservé à l'arc surmontant les ouverture offre un motif principal, végétal ou géométrique, encadré d'une ou plusieures moulures prises dans une combinaison déterminée. Voyons d'abord le végétal et ses variantes. La première: l'archivolte est couronné d'une moulure plate, très en saillie qui, en

32. Arcade aveugle nord, détail, chapiteaux.

fait, court tout autour du champs ornementé, y compris les rallonges horizontales; une grosse corde torsadée vient d'habitude en dessous (fig. 40), sauf sur le portail sud où s'intercale un profil convexe comportant un texte en «asomtavruli» (fig. 34, 40). Plus bas se posent les grandes feuilles de fougère, motif principal ici, leurs sommets en bas, débordant l'encadrement. Ainsi se présente l'archivolte de la fenêtre centrale est, et de l'entrée principale sud. Cette dernière reçoit néanmoins, un décor complémentaire qui apparaît audessus de ses rallonges: quatre tronçons, leur face gravée en spirale, forment une rangée en saillie, suivis par quatre denticules modifiés dans des compartiments arqués, qui avancent sur les grandes feuilles de fougère. Or, les deux denticules du centre comme les deux tronçons du dessus, ressortent de la rangée même. Ce détail particulier, très en saillie, de part et d'autre de l'entrée fait appel aux stucs de Samara qui garnissaient jadis les portails, de même qu'ils laissaient flotter leurs rubans[37].

La deuxième variante procède à l'apposition des demi-palmettes dont les lobes se font face, le sommet en bas, cependant qu'à leur base celles-ci s'entrelacent avec un galon à triple brin, comme on l'a déjà vu sur les

37 J. Kröger, Sassanidischer Stuckdekor. Bagdader Forschungen 5, Mainz 1982, p. 78-79, fig. 37, 38.

33. Fenêtre centrale est.

chapiteaux de l'arcade aveugle nord. Ici leur boucles retracent néanmoins, l'extrados de l'archivolte, tandis qu'un boudin assez épais, en retrait par rapport au champs ornementé, court sur l'intrados, les rallonges étant décorées de la même façon. Ainsi sont coiffées les fenêtres de la façade sud (fig. 36).

Un autre motif végétal fournit une tige qui court tout le long de l'archivolte et de ses rallonges, en effectuant des mouvements sinusoïdaux. Dans les courbes ainsi décrites apparaissent des demi-palmettes «ailées», orientées de façon contrariée. Le champs du décor est bordé par des profils plats doublés. Cette ornementation végétale agrémente l'encadrement cintré de la fenêtre latérale sur la façade à pignon nord (fig. 37) ainsi que des oculi du tambour.

34. Entrée sud.

35. Inscription signée Ivan Morčaïdze.

En ce qui concerne les motifs géométriques des archivoltes, on doit mentionner celui qui fait ressortir un réseau de carrés entrelacés. Plus précisément, les galons à double brin qui se doublent, s'entrecroisent sous 90° et forment des carrés, alors qu'ils s'entrelacent au milieu de chacun de leurs côtés, où une boucle commune est nouée. Or, les deux rangées de carrés qui s'étalent sur l'archivolte sont encadrées sur tout leur pourtour, par des galons à double brin, lesquels se tressent de la même façon avec ceux qui viennent à leur rencontre. Les boucles ainsi obtenus sont repartis régulièrement sur les bords du champs ornementé en agrémentant chaque carré (fig. 38).

Les compositions offertes par les chambranles[38] sont les plus spectaculaires, elles aussi géométriques et florales. Les champs garnis du décor végétal procèdent, en effet, à des bouquets d'acanthe, leurs feuilles simplifiées, leurs lobes en forme d'hélice; des hélices encore sur les calices d'où s'échappent les bouquets (fig. 38). Ces derniers se développent en volute par des enroulement contrariées. Dans leur parcours ils embrassent la fenêtre de tous les côtés: ainsi sur la façade est (fig. 33). Mais parfois, ils s'arrêtent à la base des montants pour céder la place à un relief plus riche qui achève le chambranle sous la pierre d'appui, comme il se voit au sud (fig. 45). De même ils regagnent l'archivolte de la fenêtre latérale du transept sud (fig. 39). En outre, on aperçoit des nuances dans le traitement des bouquets: ainsi apparaissent-ils légèrement modifiés, leurs hélices intégrées dans les lobes, sur le chambranle central est et sur les corniches de la façade ouest. En définitive, l'acanthe est modifié mais loin d'être géométrisé: les bouquets qui libèrent les cornets s'enroulent d'un mouvement vivifiant.

Beaucoup plus compliquées sont les compositions purement géométriques que les diagrammes font ressortir sur les chambranles. Losangées ou en combinaison avec des cercles entrelacés, elles impressionnent par leur variété qui réside tantôt dans le nombre des galons tressés, tantôt dans les formes créées par les rubans qui entrepénètrent afin de s'entrelacer.

Précisément, les galons à triple brin qui se dirigent, de gauche et de droite sous 45°, s'entrecroisent et dessinent un réseau de losanges très régulier. Deux rubans distancés entrepénètrent parallèlement aux premiers galons et les croisent au milieu des tous les côtés des losanges. Mais en même temps, ces deux rubans se tressent au centre de chaque losange et créent ainsi des cercles lacés sur quatre points, en déterminant leur axe vertical et horizontal. Les

38 Les encadrements sculptés des ouvertures sont courants sur les façades des églises géorgiennes de l'époque. M. Dvali, Manglisi, fig. 20-23; N. Aladašvili, op. cit., fig. 157, 172 (Nikorcminda); N. Beridze, Quelques aspects de l'architecture géorgienne à coupole, Tbilisi 1976, fig. 32 (Katskhi), fig. 34, 35 (Mtskheta, église de Samtavro), fig. 36, 38-40 (Nikorcminda); Idem, L'architecture de Tao-Klatdjetie, fig. 89 (Ekhvevi).

36. Fenêtre sud, troisième de l'ouest vers l'est.

galons à triple brin encadrent aussi le champs ornementé et se nouent avec les rubans en complétant les cercles (fig. 36).

Cette composition géométrique connaît à Iškhan des variantes riches, en accord d'ailleurs, avec les dimensions des chambranles. Dans le cas où la surface disponible est moins large, le motif comprend une seule travée, au lieu de deux, mais il reçoit un encadrement complémentaire sur tout son parcours (fig. 26)[43], Le réseau qui procède aux entrelacs des galons met en valeur des cercles lesquels prédominent dans la composition. Or, ils donnent l'impression d'être concentriques, mais en fait, il s'agit d'une grande boucle d'enlacement, elle aussi circulaire qui occupe leur centre (fig. 29). Ainsi se présente le chambranle de la fenêtre, deuxième de l'ouest à l'est, sur la façade méridionale, comme aussi sur l'occidentale.

37. Fenêtre droite du transept nord.

Une autre variante fait ressortir une composition des losanges tout en évoquant des foyers rayonnants. Les doubles galons à triple brin sortent, de gauche et de droite, orientés sous 45° et s'entrecroisent en développant des losanges. Ici comme ailleurs, le champ du décor est encadré de galons, les mêmes à triple brin et doublés. Après avoir atteint ceux du pourtour ou la limite de leur travée, les galons constituant le réseau se plient sous 45° et se joignent sur l'horizontale, au centre de chaque losange, par un entrelac; de même, sur la verticale qui, côté extérieur, est offerte par les galons d'encadrement. Il en résulte des carrés noués au milieu de leur quatre côtés. Ainsi, figurent-ils, sur le chambranle de l'entrée sud (fig. 41).

Sur le tympan ici les carrés et les losanges se développent sur deux travées, mais leur forme se modifie, en obéissant aux impératifs d'une disposition

38. Fenêtre sud, première de l'ouest vers l'est.

rayonnante. De ce fait, les points de rencontre des motifs, au milieu de la composition et sur l'encadrements, s'effectuent sur des trajets semi-circulaires. En se réunissant sur des points communs, les galons nombreux à triple brin ressemblent à des rayons qui s'échappent d'un foyer. Enfin, ces faisceaux multiples s'imposent à l'ensemble, mais les effets de rigidité sont évités grâce aux entrelacs qui assoupissent les lignes droites (fig. 34, 40).

À ce décor aux tendances rayonnantes s'oppose le motif qui suit à l'intérieur du tympan. Il représente une écriture en lettres géorgiennes joliement réparties sur des demi-cercles concentriques. Remarquable, au point de vue artistique, est son intégration dans le champs ornementé où il achève une composition géométrique, en même temps qu'il a son sens littéraire, en révélant l'embélissement de ce portail même, vers 1023.

39. Fenêtre droite du transept sud.

Le motif d'écriture fait partie aussi du décor des archivoltes: ainsi, la deuxième sur la façade sud, qui surmonte la fenêtre, au-dessus du portail. Les belles caractères «asomtavruli» sont reparties sur une bande plate et forment un véritable ornement. Le texte qui annonce les rénovations effectuées à l'église, commence sur la partie horizontale gauche, suit le demi-cercle de l'arc, puis, rejoint la partie droite, enfin sort sur la paroi lisse (fig. 35). En réalité, l'écriture géorgienne soit le seul motif décoratif, réservé à l'archivolte, mais il reçoit un encadrement bien proportionné de moulures plates et convexes qui soulignent sa valeur (fig. 29).

Ces deux manières d'introduire les lettres en tant qu'ornement se voient réalisées ensemble sur le portail unique nord de la Petite église d'Iškhan, orienté vers la Grande église discutée ici. Le motif d'écriture figure d'abord,

40. Entrée sud, détail, inscription sur le tympan vers 1023.

41. Iškhan, Petite église de 1006, entrée nord, détail, tympan.

sur le tympan, à son emplacement central où il se déroule sur les demi-cercles concentriques, suivis d'une large bande ornementée et après, il réapparaît en caractères plus importants sur l'archivolte. En bas, de part et d'autre de ce décor central, on reconnaît sur l'horizontale la date d'érection de l'église, à savoir 1006, en lettres géorgiennes à gauche et, en arménienne, à droite. De cette façon s'établit un lien entre tous ces éléments scripturaux (fig. 41).

En ce qui concerne la bande décorée, elle a le fond légèrement creusé qui cependant, fait ressortir les ornements au même niveau que les surfaces garnies de lettres. Ce sont en effet, cinq volutes, chacune constituée de quatre segments d'une largeur égale qui s'échappent l'un de l'autre. Leur facture rélève quatre tiges sillonnées, parallèles qui courent ensemble et qui se développent en spirales par des enroulements contrariés (fig. 41). Leurs extrémités sont arrondies à la fin de chaque segment. Or, celles des tiges intérieures et extérieures prennent la forme d'hélices qui, par leurs accrochements répliquent aux entrelacs constitués par les volutes. De plus, ces mêmes hélices extérieures donnent naissance à des fleurons comparables à la moitié de la plante ailée qui sort de l'entrecroisement des volutes sur les champs symétriques du centre[39].

Tous les éléments porteurs d'écriture se réunissent autour de la zone des volutes, en constituant, pour ainsi dire, son encadrement, cependant qu'elle même encercle le tympan lettré. Cette entrepénétration des composantes démontre l'intégration parfaite de l'écriture en tant que motif décoratif dans l'ensemble.

Au delà de cette limite s'avance le motif animalier reparti sur l'archivolte du portail, encadrée de deux grosses cordelières. Plus précisément, les trapèzes qui sortent des entrelacs, renferment des différentes espèces tératologiques.

Ce tympan comme le précédent montrent une maîtrise extrême, quant à l'organisation du champs ornementé et à la combinaison des motifs variés — floral, géométrique, exceptionnellement animalier — souvent soumis aux impératifs des entrelacs. Aussi, les caractères géorgiens sont agréés dans une composition décorative où tout se tient dans un équilibre parfait.

Il faut évoquer enfin, la troisième variante du décor qui comprend à la fois, des éléments géométriques et végétaux. En effet, des tiges qui se terminent par deux crochets contrariés se voient confrontées, en s'inclinant l'une vers l'autre, tant sur le pourtour intérieur qu'extérieur du chambranle. Dans les champs libres entre elles s'installent, des deux côtés, des feuilles lobées d'un tracé lancéolé, leur orientation alternée. Or, ces ornements de remplissage et les tiges à deux crochets, constituant le motif principal, sont ainsi, à nombre

39 La bande ornementée comportant le motif des volutes à triple brin apparaît souvent dans des combinaisons avec des bandes offrant des motifs figuratifs. N. Aladašvili, op. cit., fig. 159 (Nikorcminda); V. Beridze, Quelques aspects de l'architecture à coupole, fig. 41 (Katskhi).

42. Galerie nord, fenêtre bilobée donnant sur le transept, d'après Takajšvili.

égal. Cette composition encadre la fenêtre centrale sur la façade à pignon, sud, en harmonie parfaite avec les grandes feuilles de fougère dominant sur son archivolte (fig. 43).

Au même groupe se rapporte le décor autour de la fenêtre centrale sur la façade à pignon nord (fig. 44). Un ornement lancéolé court sur toute l'étendue du chambranle. Le galon qui le constitue effectue un mouvement ininterrompu, comparable à celui d'un huit et, en se croisant il forme à sa base un petit cercle. De cette façon, toutes les lances qu'il esquisse, sont reliées par leurs cercles lesquels se rangent sur le rebord intérieur du champs ornementé. Près du rebord extérieur, cependant, au sommet de la lance un autre galon dessine deux petites crosses divergeantes, par lesquelles est introduit un élément de remplissage qui évoque le tracé simplifié d'une feuille

43. Fenêtre centrale du transept sud.

de fougère. En revanche, sur l'archivolte de la même fenêtre cet élément apparaît en tant que motif principal, tandis qu'un palmier remplit les champs libres.

Pour terminer avec ce décor, il faut évoquer, toujours à la Grande église, les colonnettes accolées et jumelées, leur tronc à torsades, qui se dressent, de part et d'autre des fenêtres ainsi que du portail sud, en offrant leur «appui» aux archivoltes (fig. 29, 36, 43, 52). Surmontées des arcs aveugles, elles font le tour du tambour polyèdre (h = 6,01 m), en délimitant ses champs où les «oculi» alternent avec les fenêtres cintrées (fig. 28). Chaque colonnette est couronnée d'un bulbe suivi d'une petite gorge qui la sépare d'un mince coussin serré par une gaine de feuilles lobées, orientées sur la verticale. La base est constituée du même bulbe et souvent comporte la gaine qui, à

44. Fenêtre centrale du transept nord.

l'envers, la précède, les lobes en haut. De plus, les colonnettes accouplées se posent sur une base commune, analogue à celle des minces pilastres et des boudins, déjà évoquée et qui, placée très haut ressemble à une console. Parfois, les deux bases communes fusionnent avec les reliefs riches qui occupent toute la surface en dessous de la pierre d'appui, comme sur la façade sud du corps occidental de l'église. Ainsi, la première fenêtre: les deux couples colonnettes, demunies complètement de bulbes reçoivent à l'emplacement de leur base commune, des oiseaux aquatiques, entre lesquels un dragon et un lion se livrent combat. Aussi les bases des godrons de la troisième fenêtre s'intègrent dans un haut relief non figuratif où, à la retombée des arcatures, des pommes de pin sont suspendues: les trois plus grandes occupent le centre, celles de petite taille, reparties par quatre, rejoignent les extrémités (fig. 36, 38, 45).

Original est le chapiteau-pilastre qui coiffe les colonnettes accouplées[40] et qui se présente sous formes légèrement variées. D'abord, sur son axe de symétrie se dresse une palmette nouée au-dessus de la base, qui laisse sortir à ses côtés deux feuilles d'acanthe triplées et nouées à ce même niveau. Celles-ci se libèrent vers le haut d'un mouvement ample en esquissant un «S», leurs sommets étant légèrement recourbés. Le chapiteau est d'autant plus intéressant que l'on reconnaît sur la colonnade même du VIIe siècle, le type de son inspirateur, offert par la colonne droite du centre. Bien entendu, les modifications survenues dans les feuilles d'acanthe répondent à des conceptions esthétique du Xe-XIe siècle, mais l'idée de cette combinaison d'éléments floraux se retrouve sur son prédécesseur (fig. 29, 36, 43).

Exemple de la «renaissance» géorgienne, le chapiteau suit l'ensemble décoratif d'Iškhan et se laisse influencé par les motifs d'entrelacs si appréciés à l'époque. Or, dans sa deuxième variante, la palmette est remplacée par une tige qui monte, s'entrelace au sommet et descend pour nouer, comme à son départ, une boucle, avec les feuilles qui sortent, à sa gauche et à sa droite.

Mais, ce n'est pas le seul exemple d'inspiration artistique de l'époque précédente. En effet, bon nombre des chapiteaux-pilastres du tambour reprennent les modèles adoptés pour la colonnade et les fenêtres bilobées remontant au VIIe siècle (fig. 28).

Tous ces motifs décoratifs dans leurs combinaisons variées offrent des créations artistiques de valeur exceptionnelle. Les reliefs non figuratifs dentelés des portails et des fenêtres vont de paire avec l'architecture la plus avancée de Tao-Klardžeti. Cependant, celle-ci n'est pas à l'écart de l'évolution architecturale du monde voisin, avec lequel des échanges culturels se poursuivent. En effet, elle exploite le fond artistique hérité des provinces orientales auquel ont puisé aussi d'autrres peuples.

Certains détails de constructions à Iškhan, réservés à ce décor opulent sont des exemples très significatifs, quant au renouveau dans l'architecture géorgienne du Xe-XIe siècle. En premier lieu, viennent les portails qui montrent une floraison exceptionnelle de la sculpture architecturale. Flanqués de

40 Le chapiteau a connu un grand succès en Géorgie, de même qu'il fut représenté sur les objets d'art sacré. On est surpris de le reconnaître sur une petite icône en schiste au Musée Cluny de Paris — N° 21002. La scène représente deux saints militaires en pied, bénis par le Christ du haut du ciel. Elle est surmontée d'un arc trilobé qui repose sur deux paires de colonnettes à torsade lesquelles sont couronnées des chapiteaux communs. Enfin, le décor architectural reprend les motifs des encadrements d'Iškhan et il suit jusqu'au moindre détail les godrons et leur chapiteau. Cette ressemblance frappante avec la sculpture transcaucasienne en pleine expansion à la fin du Xe-XIe siècle, permet de préciser les origines de l'icônes de schiste, à savoir de Tao-Klardžeti, ainsi que de lui attribuer la date de la première moitié du XIe siècle.

45. Fenêtre sud, première de l'ouest vers l'est, détail, relief figuratif.

colonnes qui sont surmontées d'architraves ou d'archivoltes multiples, ils sont connus en Syrie des premiers siècles du christianisme, par leurs formes majestueuses. De plus, leur présence sur le sol de la Transcaucasie même aux Ve-VIIe siècle, à Irind, Tékor, Ereruk, Džvari[41], pouvait influencer facilement leur reprise. Cependant, le portail se voit intégré dans un contexte nouveau, et son décor riche répond aux exigences esthétiques en vigueur au Xe-XIe siècle.

Les motifs inspirés du fond hellénistique sont modifiés et ils obéissent à des combinaisons nouvelles comme on l'a déjà constaté au sujet du chapiteau-pilastre des colonnettes accouplées, elles aussi témoins de la reprise des détails — tronc torssadé, chapiteaux et bases bulbeuses, si caractéristiques pour la tradition régionale. En revanche, les consoles décorés, de part et d'autre du portail sud trahissent des origines sassanides. Or, les stucs de Samara ont fourni ce motif approprié aux portails[42] dont les voûtes et les parois ornementées pourraient inspirer les panneaux des chambranles.

On constate des motifs qui appartiennent aux provinces orientales et à Byzance repris à Tao-Klardžeti, d'une part, et d'autre part, ceux de l'art

41 J. Strzygowsky, op. cit., fig. 442, 443, Ereruk; fig. 438, Tekor; G. Čubinasvili, N. Severov, Pamjatniki typa Džvari, Tbilisi 1948, p. 24-25, fig. 24; Quant aux rallonges horizontales des archivoltes de part et d'autre des encadrements des fenêtres, elles furent enracinées dans la tradition tant en Géorgie qu'en Arménie. N. Aladašvili, op. cit., fig. 17, 19, 24, 26; V. Arutjunjan, Kamennaja letopis, pl. XVIII, XIX.

42 J. Kröger, Sassanidischer Stuckdekor, pl. 15-3, fig. 39.

sassanide qui ayant pénétré à l'époque paléochrétienne avaient fusionné avec la tradition géorgienne, à la différence des éléments sassanides acquis à travers la culture des Abbassides.

Ainsi se présentent à la Petite église, les ornements des tiges quadruples d'origine syrienne[43], auxquelles s'ajoute la plante ailée sassanide qui a déjà envahi le fond artistique géorgien et syrien au Ve siècle. Par contre, le motif animalier dans un encadrement entrelacé semble avoir été adopté au Xe siècle, comme ce fut à Byzance et en Bulgarie à la fin du IXe - début du Xe siècle. Aussi les motifs sassanides sont passés à Bysance et aux provinces au Ve-VIe siècle, mais ils se grefent de nouveau sur le fond culturel de ces mêmes régions, lors de ladite renaissance du Xe-XIe siècle.

Il ne s'agit pas d'emprunt trait pour trait, mais des impulsions venues de ce qui est en vogue dans l'architecture de l'époque. À cet effet, il faut signaler la prédominance du décor non figuratif et surtout les compositions des entrelacs. En fait, leurs prototypes peuvent être indiqués dans les ensembles romains et hellénistiques[44]. Cependant les entrelacs ont connu une floraison spectaculaire dès le IXe siècle dans l'art du monde méditerranéen. D'abord, en Tunisie, à Kairouan[45] où ils ont été implantés par l'architecture islamique qui à son tour, avait déjà profité de l'héritage hellénistico-romain: ainsi, les Umayyades du répertoire syro-palestinien, puis les Abbasides, du mésopotamien, sans oublier l'apport artistique reçu en échange de Byzance. Introduits dans les panneaux des chambranles, les entrelacs démontrent néanmoins, l'interprétation appropriée aux Géorgiens, à leur égard.

Les ornements dentelés des fenêtres et des portails témoignent d'un répertoire riche en motifs géométriques, en même temps qu'en motifs végétaux, appuyés par la géométrie. Remarquables sont à ce propos, les demi-acanthes tressées sur les archivoltes. Le demi-acanthe fut largement utilisée dans l'art des Ummayades lequel cependant, a assimilé les emprunts à la fois syriens et sassanides[46]. Sa reprise ici s'explique par l'affinité des maîtres géorgiens avec les correspondants de leur patrimoine culturel.

43 J. Vogt-Göknil, Frühislamische Bogenwände, fig. 245.

44 Les entrelacs qui ont connu leur immense variété dans l'architecture islamique, se signalent cependant, au temps romain et hellénistique. K. Creswell, Early muslim architecture, I-1, Oxford 1969, 2e éd., fig. 110-1, Domus Augustiana de Palatin à Rome du temps de Domitien (81-96); fig. 51, 115, Qalb-Luzeh; fig. 116, temple de Bacchus à Baalbek; fig. 121-122, l'église de Procope de Jerach (536); fig. 119-120, église de Saint-Georges de Jerach; fig. 125, le Grand temple de Palmyre (80); fig. 118, pl. 59, la Grande Mosquée de Damas.

45 L. Colvin, Essai, 3. L'architecture religieuse des Grands Abbasides, p. 221, fig. 87, 90, 91, 92.

46 Le motif des demi-palmettes fréquent dans l'art des Ummayades pouvait être hérité de la culture hellénistique comme aussi des Sassanides. L. Colvin, Essai, 2. L'art religieux des Ummayades de Syrie, Paris 1971, p. 115, pl. 25-2, 5, 7; J. Kröger, op. cit., p. 124, fig. 3-a, b, pl. 37-a, b, pl. 50-4.

L'acanthe dans toutes ses formes variées sur les façades, s'écarte de sa nature, mais son allure n'enlaidit pas; sa stylisation poussée aboutit à des créations fructueuses. Quant aux bouquets d'acanthe, considérés d'origine sassanide, ils se voient enrichis de nombreuses hélices dues en fait, à Byzance, lesquelles cependant, ont pénétré en Transcaucasie au VIIe siècle, comme à Zvartnotz et été donc, assimilées par la tradition régionale. De plus, ces bouquets et leurs calices sont constituées en vue d'une composition qui a ses apports géométriques: en effet, ils courent, en se développant par les enroulements en volute.

De même, pour les tiges quadruples enroulées en spirale, qui donnent naissance à des fleurons et dont la précision est remarquable.

Un autre motif agréé par la géométrie représente la feuille de fougère qui offre la dernière phase d'une stylisation extrême à laquelle la flore obéit. Il est difficile de trancher sur ses origines. Dans ce but, il faut évoquer les variantes du motif où à la place des fougères figurent des palmettes qui se relient de la même manière, en renfermant de petits cercles par leurs lobes inférieurs[47]. Le motif constitué de palmettes est plus fréquent que celui des fougères[48] dans l'art géorgiens. Cependant, il est bien connu de l'héritage culturel sassanide. Aussi, sur le linteau du portail des bains omayyades de Kirbat-al-Mafjar[49] figurent ces mêmes palmettes, regroupées par quatre: reparties sur deux axes perpendiculaires croisés, mais orientés sous 45°, elles apparaissent, les bases réunies au centre, les sommets rayonnants.

Mais pour analyser l'apposition des fougères renversées d'Iškhan, il faut faire appel aussi, au fragment ornementé de stuc du Musée de Berlin-Est[50], remontant à la fin de l'ère sassanide. Son décor fournit, en effet, quatre feuilles dans la même disposition qu'à Kirbat-al-Mafjar, mais très découpées et d'un contour comparable aux fougères d'Iškhan; une boucle en forme de cercle, sur le croisement des deux axes, les réunit. En fait, ce motif dit de palme pouvait offrir le modèle au maître géorgien, par sa facture proche de fougère. Cependant, la feuille d'Iškhan se voit dans une autre combinaison: elle a adopté l'enroulement nécessaire pour son intégration dans une suite et de plus, sa stylisation fut poussée à la limite d'une forme géométriques.

47 Le motif des palmettes dont les lobes inférieurs forment des demi-cercles a connu un succès considérable en Géorgie. Il figure sur les arcs et les corniches des grandes églises, des premières décennies du XIe siècle: Tbeti, Džala, Savane, Nikorcminda, Sveti Tskhoveli. De même qu'à Manglisi, où il apparaît dans toutes ses variantes et de plus, sur les bases des colonnettes de la coupole, les palmettes sont dressées. M. Dvali, Manglisi, fig. 24-29.

48 Les fougères se retrouvent à Čangli. Rarement, le motif est introduit à l'intérieur des églises et notamment, sur les bases des colonnes comme à Iškhan et sur les socles: à Otkhta Eklesia, il agremente le contre pied de l'abside. V. Beridze, Architecture de Tao-Klardjetie, fig. 33, 12.

49 K. Kreswell, Early muslim architecture, I-2, linteau du portail des bains de Kirbat-al-Mafjar, datant de 743, pl. 105c.

50 J. Kröger, op. cit., fragment 202, pl. 55-1.

Étant réparties sur l'archivolte, les feuilles de fougère apparaissent, les bases sur l'extrados, les sommets sur l'intrados, de même qu'elles gardent cette disposition, le sommet en bas, sur les rallonges de l'arc. Enfin, il faut imaginer l'archivolte étalée pour aboutir aux fougères renversées qui courent sur les corniches horizontales. Cette orientation s'impose d'ailleurs, pour des raisons d'unification des motifs qui se déroulent sur une courbe ou sur une ligne droite.

Cependant il faut reconnaître ici, une distinction nette entre la feuille de fougère et la palmette: en effet, sur les bases des grands piliers ces mêmes feuilles, le sommet en bas, encadrent des palmettes dressées (fig. 24). Évidemment, dans le cas d'Iškhan il ne s'agit pas de modification de la palmette, mais d'une feuille à part qui a connu son évolution sur le sol de la Tao-Klardžeti. En définitive, le motif sassanide adopté, fut développé de façon qu'il aboutît à des créations nouvelles.

Enfin, l'unité indéniable du décor des façades est respectée aussi dans les compositions où s'engage le motif scriptural qui prend une forme originale tout en gardant son sens littéraire. Bien entendu, l'écriture coufique a imposée la mode de ses caractères qui furent imités sur les façades des églises byzantines[51], étant depourvus de sens textuel. Par contre en Géorgie, l'«asomtravruli» repartie sur les demi-cercles concentriques annonce une création authentique dans le but d'éterniser l'œuvre géorgienne.

Ich bedanke mich bei den Herren Kollegen G. Bruchhaus, F. Teichmann und B. Baumgartner für die Photographien von Iškhan.

51 G. Miles, «Byzantium and the Arabs: Relations in Crete and Aegean Area», Dumbarton Oaks Papers, 1964, 3-32, p. 22-25, fig. 24, 26, 31, 32, 35, 36.

BERICHTE

Georgischer Sommerkurs in Tbilisi

Vom 1. Juli bis 15. August 1990 veranstaltete die Philologische Fakultät der Universität Tbilisi den ersten internationalen Sommerkurs der georgischen Sprache und Kultur. Mit der Leitung und Organisation des Sprachstudiums waren der Prorektor der Universität, E. Khintibidze, und die Inhaberin des Lehrstuhls für die georgische Sprache, E. Babunašvili, betraut. Die georgische Akademie der Wissenschaften (E. Džavachišvili) und das Kulturministerium (N. Kakoyašvili) zeigten sich verantwortlich für die Durchführung des kulturellen Programms und die Exkursionen.

Die Medien nahmen an diesem Kurs regen Anteil. Das Fernsehen brachte Interviews, in zwei Zeitungen erschienen Fotoberichte.

Ungefähr 60 Teilnehmer aller Alterstufen, darunter viele Slavisten, aus West- und Osteuropa, Japan und den USA trafen zusammen. Die Spanne ihrer sprachlichen Voraussetzungen war breit. Manche beherrschten das Georgische genügend, um bereits eine Unterhaltung führen zu können; die Mehrzahl begann mit dem Erlernen des Alphabets.

Entsprechend ihrer Nationalität und den sprachlichen Voraussetzungen waren die Studenten in verschiedene Klassen eingestuft, die in der Regel fünf bis zehn Personen umfaßten und abwechselnd von zwei oder drei Lehrern betreut wurden. Auf dem Lehrplan standen morgens vier Stunden Grammatik und Sprachübungen, am Nachmittag die Konversationsstunde. Außerdem hielt der Nachmittagsunterricht Vorlesungen über literarische, philosophische, kunst- und kulturgeschichtliche Themen bereit. Großes Echo fand der Besuch georgischer Künstlerateliers, der Tbiliser Museen und des Handschrifteninstituts. Zweitägige Exkursionen führten die Gruppe nach Kachetien, ans Schwarze Meer (Batumi, Kobuleti), Vardzia, Qazbegi, Bordžomi, Kutaisi, Gelati und Mzchetha.

Leider ließ der gedrängte Veranstaltungskalender selten oder nur unter Ausfall von Programmpunkten Zeit zu eigenen Unternehmungen. Erschwerend kam hinzu, daß die Teilnehmer in einem Vorort von Tbilisi, fünfzehn Kilometer außerhalb der Stadt, geschlossen untergebracht waren. Daß privaten Unterkünften nichts im Wege stünde, bewiesen die vielen Einladungen. Zu dem beiderseits angestrebten privaten Kontakt und der höheren Effektivität im organisatorischen Ablauf wäre man auch der pädagogischen Zielsetzung des Kurses gerechter geworden, nämlich das aktive Sprechen der georgischen

Sprache zu fördern. Anzumerken ist noch, daß es dem Unterricht manchmal am methodischen und zielgerichteten Vorgehen mangelte. Die Lehrer waren in ihrem Lehrplan nicht aufeinander abgestimmt. Lehrmittel standen nicht genügend zur Verfügung. Ein Nachteil entstand zudem für diejenigen, die Russisch nicht beherrschten, weil vieles nebenbei auf Russisch erläutert wurde. Ein sprachlich aktiv umsetzbarer Lernerfolg ergab sich somit nicht in dem Maße, wie die starke Motivation von Lehrern und Studenten zu versprechen schien.

Jedoch müssen diese kritischen Punkte als künftig vermeidbare Anfangsschwierigkeiten gesehen werden. Unvergeßlich bleibt dagegen die den Teilnehmern entgegengebrachte Aufmerksamkeit und Freude, das große Engagement und der finanzielle Aufwand, um sie trotz einer politisch schwierigen Lage mit Georgien, seinen Menschen und seiner Kultur und nicht zuletzt mit der Sprache vertraut zu machen.

Andrea Schmidt

Internationales Symposium: Die Bibel in der armenischen Kultur

Am 16.-19. Juli 1990 fand im Internationalen Wissenschaftsforum der Universität Heidelberg (IWH) unter der Leitung von Prof. Dr. Michael E. Stone (Jerusalem) ein internationales Symposium zum Thema »Armenia and the Bible: Culture, Tradition, and Text — Die Bibel in der armenischen Kultur« statt. Es wurde veranstaltet von der Association Internationale des Études Arméniennes (AIEA) in Zusammenarbeit mit dem IWH und gefördert durch die Deutsche Forschungsgemeinschaft (Bonn), den Conseil international de la philosophie et des sciences humaines, eine Unterorganisation der UNESCO (Paris), und die Stiftung 600 Jahre Universität Heidelberg.

Das Ziel des Symposiums war, in einem internationalen Kreis von Fachleuten die Bibel als Faktor der armenischen Kultur längs durch die Jahrhunderte und quer durch die Fakultäten zu würdigen, nämlich einerseits auf schon bearbeiteten Feldern wie der Sprachgestalt der altarmenischen Bibelübersetzung, ihrer handschriftlichen Überlieferung, Edition und Wirkungsgeschichte bis an den Anfang der Neuzeit neue Akzente zu setzen, andererseits dort, wo wenig gearbeitet wurde, wie vor allem im Hinblick auf die jüngere Neuzeit und hier besonders auf die sich neben der Kirche herausbildende säkulare Kultur, möglichst viel Neuland zu betreten und schließlich Lage und neue Perspektiven der Forschung insgesamt zu bestimmen.

Deshalb war eine Reihe von Vorträgen zu den Themenkreisen Biblische Zitate und Motive in der bildenden Kunst und Epigraphik, neuarmenische Bibelübersetzungen, Nachwirkung der Bibel in der modernen armenischen Literatur, biblische Werte in Erziehung und Moral gezielt erbeten worden. Dazu wurden einige literarische Neu- oder Wiederentdeckungen präsentiert: Spuren der Nach-Septuaginta-Übersetzungen des Alten Testaments in armenischen Bibelhandschriften, Biblisches in armenischen Handschriftenkolophonen, die eine hervorragende Quelle für datierbare Alltagsgeschichte darstellen, Orakelverse in Bibelhandschriften, Identifizierung einer Psalmeneinleitung des als Philosoph bekannten David Anhaght.

Leider war die Liturgik nicht vertreten. Zwei zugesagte Vorträge über biblische Motive in der Literatur des 19. Jahrhunderts und Linguistische Aspekte neuarmenischer Bibelübersetzungen kamen dann doch nicht zustande. Dadurch war die Neuzeit weniger stark vertreten, als wünschenswert gewesen wäre.

Die Vorträge im einzelnen:

Rouben P. Adalian (Washington, D.C.): From Scripture to Text to Icon: The Armenian Bible in View of Modern Technology and Scholarship.

Joseph M. Alexanian (Deerfield, Ill.): Toward a Critical Edition of the New Testament in Classical Armenian.

Aida Boudjikanian (Beirut): Valeurs morales et religieuses dans la vie pratique des Arméniens du Liban. Résultats comparatifs d'une enquête menée parmi la population chrétienne libanaise en 1987.

Bernard Coulie (Louvain-la-Neuve): Répertoire des catalogues de manuscrits arméniens.

Claude Cox (Barrie, Ont.): The Translations of Aquila, Symmachus and Theodotion Found in the Margins of Armenian Manuscripts.

Patrick Donabédian (Paris): Les sujets bibliques dans la sculpture arménienne pré-arabe.

Armenuhi Drost-Abgarjan (Halle): Biblisches in moderner armenischer Literatur am Beispiel von Parouir Sewaks Gedicht »Nimmerverstummender Glockenturm«.

Michel van Esbroeck (München): Une exégèse rare d'Isaie 29,11-12 conservé en arménien.

Haçik Gazerian (Tübingen): Karapet Ter-Mkrttschians Versuch einer neuen armenischen Bibelausgabe.

Christian Hannick (Trier): Bibelexegese in armenischen Handschriftenkolophonen.

Friedrich Heyer (Heidelberg): Biblische Bezüge in den 95 Elegien des Gregor von Nareg.

Manuel Jinbachian (Straßburg): Modern Armenian Translations of the Bible.

Dickran Kouymjian (Fresno, Calif.-Paris): The Evolution of Armenian Gospel Illumination.

Louis Leloir (Clervaux, Luxemburg): Comment les premiers moines arméniens ont-ils lu la Bible?

Barbara J. Merguerian (Cambridge, Mass.): The Armenian Bible and the American Missionaries in the Ottoman Empire: The First Four Decades (1820-1860).

Parouir Mouradyan (Erevan): The Importance of the Biblical Quotations in the Literature and the Epigraphic Arts of Medieval Armenia.

Bernard Outtier (Saulieu-Paris): Réponses oraculaires dans des manuscrits bibliques arméniens.

Jean-Marc Rosenstiehl (Straßburg): Apocalypse 3,15 - Visio Pauli 31. Contribution à l'étude de l'Apocalypse apocryphe de Paul.

Avedis K. Sanjian (Los Angeles, Calif.): Esayi Nč'ec'i and Biblical Exegesis.

Gagik Sarkisyan (Erevan): The Early Stages of the Development of the Armenian Literature from the Point of View of an Historian.

Folker Siegert (Eschwege-Niederhone): Beobachtungen zur rhetorischen Qualität der armenischen Bibel.

Nira Stone (Jerusalem): 'And four rivers went forth from Eden': Some Images of Paradise in Armenian Art.

Abraham Terian (Berrien Springs, Mich.): The Bible in Verse by Gregor Magistros: On the Millennial of His Birth.

Joseph Weitenberg (Leiden): The Language of Mesrop: L'Arménien classique pour lui-même?

Andranik Zeytounyan (Erevan): Variant Readings in Greek and Armenian Manuscripts of Genesis.

Zwei weitere Vorträge lagen schriftlich vor, obwohl ihre Verfasser kurzfristig absagen mußten: Shahé Ajamian (Jerusalem), An Introduction to the Book of Psalms by David Anhaght, und S. Peter Cowe, Tendentious Translation and the Evangelical Imperative: Religious Polemic in the Early Armenian Church. Außerdem nahmen am Symposium teil Chr. Burchard (Heidelberg), V. Mistrih (Kairo), H. Palanjian (Regensburg) und gelegentlich interessierte Studierende.

Es ist geplant, die Vorträge zu veröffentlichen. Die von S. P. Cowe und P. Donabédian sind für die Revue des Études Arméniennes vorgesehen. Die übrigen sollen in einem Band der University of Pennsylvania Texts and Studies erscheinen.

Chr. Burchard

PERSONALIA

Mgr. Dr. Joseph Nasrallah, Exarch des melchitischen Patriarchen von Antiochien in Paris, begeht am 10. Oktober 1991 seinen 80. Geburtstag. Er hat sich große Verdienste um die Erforschung der Geschichte und Literatur der Melchiten erworben. Bis in unsere Tage herein arbeitet er noch an der Vollendung seines monumentalen Werkes »Histoire du mouvement littéraire dans l'église melchite du Ve au XXe siècle«, Louvain 1979f., von dem bis jetzt die Bände II/2 (1988), III/1 (1983), III/2 (1981), IV/1 (1979) und IV/2 (1989) erschienen sind. Seine früheren Arbeiten sind zusammengestellt in seiner Schrift »Cheminement d'un chercheur de la littérature arabe chrétienne«, Louvain 1983. Vergl. auch OrChr 68 (1984) 220.

P. Dr. rer. bibl. Heinz Kruse, SJ, em. o. Professor für Biblische Theologie an der Sophia-Universität, Tokio (ab 1953), emeritiert 1982, vollendet am 11. November 1991 das 80. Lebensjahr. Sein Hauptarbeitsgebiet ist die Theologie des Alten Testamentes. In unserer Zeitschrift veröffentlichte er mehrere Aufsätze über die Oden Salomos.

P. Dr. Hermenegild (Alfons) Biedermann, OSA, em. o. Professor an der Universität Würzburg, wird am 15. Dezember 1991 achtzig Jahre alt. Geboren in Hausen bei Würzburg, promovierte er 1939, habilitierte sich 1948 in Würzburg und lehrte dort bis zu seiner Emeritierung (1977) Geschichte und Theologie des Christlichen Ostens. Neben seinen eigenen Arbeiten erwarb er sich noch besondere Verdienste als Herausgeber der Reihe »Das östliche Christentum« (ab 1950) und vor allem als Begründer und Leiter der angesehenen Fachzeitschrift »Ostkirchliche Studien« (ab 1952).

P. Louis Leloir, OSB, Dr. rer. bibl. (2.10.56), Dr. theol. (25.3.62), Abbaye Saint-Maurice, L-9737 Clervaux, em. Professor der Katholischen Universität Löwen, begeht am 26. Dezember 1991 seinen 80. Geburtstag, In Namur (Belgien) geboren, lehrte er nach Studien in Lyon und Rom von 1959-1961 in San Anselmo, Rom, NT, AT und Armenisch; von 1973-1982 Armenisch, dann Äthiopisch an der Katholischen Universität Löwen. Seine zahlreichen Veröffentlichungen (bis 1989: 15 Bücher, 80 Artikel, viele Rezensionen) befassen sich u.a. mit dem Diatessaron Tatians, Ephräm dem Syrer, den Wüstenvätern und apokryphen Apostelakten.

Prof. Dr. Konstantin Tseretheli, Semitist am Orientinstitut der georgischen Akademie in Tbilisi, beging am 4. Februar 1991 seinen 70. Geburtstag. In Tbilisi geboren, promovierte er 1957 und befaßte sich innerhalb der semitischen Sprachen hauptsächlich mit der aramäischen Gruppe, auch mit den von den syrischen Christen noch in der Gegenwart gesprochenen Dialekten. Seine früheren Arbeiten sind verzeichnet in R. Macuch und E. Panoussi, Neusyrische Chrestomathie, Wiesbaden 1974, S. XXVI und XXIX. 1986 erschien seine syrische Grammatik in Leipzig.

Dr. William F. Macomber, St. Cloud, MN 56301, USA, wird am 21. Juli 1991 siebzig Jahre alt. Nach Studien am Harvard College (AB 1942), Boston College (MA 1951) und Weston College (SThLic 1957) promovierte er am Päpstlichen Orientalischen Institut in Rom (1964), wo er ab 1967 als Associate Professor und ab 1970 als Assistant Professor wirkte. Anschließend katalogisierte er die orientalischen Handschriften der Harold B. Lee Library der Brigham Young Universität bis zu seiner Pensionierung am 31.8.1989. Sein Hauptarbeitsgebiet sind die orientalischen Liturgien (griechisch und syrisch) und die Katalogisierung äthiopischer und christlich-arabischer Handschriften.

Prof. Dr. Avedis K. Sanjian, Los Angeles, wurde 70 Jahre alt. Geboren 1921 in Marasch (Türkei) kam er nach Studien in Beirut, Michigan und Harvard 1965 an die Universität von Kalifornien als Professor für armenische Studien. Seine Publikationen in englischer und armenischer Sprache befassen sich u.a. mit Themen der mittelalterlichen armenischen Geschichte und Literatur sowie mit armenischen Handschriften und Kolophonen.

Frau Dr. Mzek'ala Schanidze, Professorin für altgeorgische Sprache an der Universität Tbilissi, wurde am 16. Januar 1991 fünfundsechzig Jahre alt. Unter ihren zahlreichen Arbeiten, Untersuchungen und Textausgaben ragen insbesondere ihre mustergültige Edition der georgischen Psalmenübersetzung in drei Rezensionen (Tbilissi 1960) und die dazugehörigen Untersuchungen (Tbilissi 1979) hervor.

Frau Prof. Dr. Ruth Stiehl, Münster, beging am 13. März 1991 ihren 65. Geburtstag. Sie hat sich — meist in Zusammenarbeit mit Fr. Altheim — u.a. mit dem Christentum am Roten Meer und im übrigen Nahen Osten befaßt.

Prof. Lic., Dr. theol. Paul Van Moorsel, Leiden, vollendet am 14. Oktober 1991 das 60. Lebensjahr. Er lehrte von 1967-1990 altchristliche, vor allem koptische, Kunstgeschichte an der Universität Leiden und wurde am 1.1.1991 emeritiert. Seit 1981 leitet er das französische Projekt zur Erforschung der koptischen Wandmalerei. Er vertrat sein Fachgebiet auch als Gastprofessor in Löwen (1979), Jerusalem (1988) und Paris (1990). In seinen Arbeiten untersucht er hauptsächlich die koptische Kunst.

Prof. Dr. theol., Dr. phil. Siegbert Uhlig wurde am 1.10.1990 als o. Professor für Afrikanische Sprachen und Kulturen mit dem Schwerpunkt Äthiopistik (Nachfolge E. Hammerschmidt) an die Universtität Hamburg berufen. 1980 promovierte Uhlig mit einer Arbeit über Hiob Ludolf, den Begründer der wissenschaftlichen Äthiopistik, zum Dr. phil., 1985 habilitierte er sich mit einer grundlegenden Darstellung der äthiopischen Paläographie, wirkte an der Universität Osnabrück, wurde 1989 zum apl. Professor ernannt und lehrte 1989/90 noch zuštzlich in Addis Abeba und Tübingen. Zusammen mit Prof. Dr. Eckart Otto eröffnet Uhlig eine neue Reihe »Orientalia Biblica et Christiana« (bei Augustin, Glückstadt), die auch für den Christlichen Orient bedeutsame Arbeiten veröffentlichen wird.

Prof. Dr. phil. Manfred Kropp, Lund, wurde am 1.2.1991 an die Universität Mainz berufen. Der gebürtige Ludwigshafener (14.6.47) promovierte 1975, habilitierte sich 1984 in Heidelberg, wurde 1985 Professor, folgte 1990 einem Ruf an die Universität Lund und lehrt nun in Mainz Islamwissenschaft und Semitistik (Nachfolge H. Horst).

Frau Dr. phil. habil. Johanna Flemming, bis 1986 ao. Dozentin für Spätantike und Byzantinische Kunst an der Universität Jena, beging am 26. März 1991 ihren 65. Geburtstag. Sie promovierte 1953 in Jena mit der Dissertation »Die Ikonographie von Adam und Eva in der Kunst vom 3. bis 13. Jahrhundert« (maschinenschriftlich, 203 S.) und habilitierte sich 1963 in Jena mit der Arbeit »Der Lebensbaum in der altchristlichen, byzantinischen und byzantinisch beeinflußten Kunst« (maschinenschriftlich, 600 S.), wurde aber aus politischen Gründen erst 1983 zur ao. Dozentin ernannt. Sie veröffentlichte Artikel, auch in westlichen Zeitschriften und Lexika, besonders über georgische und armenische Kunst.

Julius Aßfalg

TOTENTAFEL

Dr. phil., Dr. h.c. mult. Bertold Spuler, em. o. Professor für Orientalistik und Islamkunde an der Universität Hamburg, verstarb am 9. März 1990. Am 5.12.1911 in Karlsruhe geboren, promovierte er 1935 in Breslau und habilitierte sich 1938 in Göttingen für Orientalistik und Islamkunde. 1948 wurde er an die Universität Hamburg berufen, wo er bis zu seiner Emeritierung (1980) lehrte. Neben seinen bedeutenden Arbeiten über die Geschichte des Nahen und Mittleren Ostens befaßte er sich auch sehr intensiv mit der Geschichte der orientalischen Kirchen. So schrieb er von 1939-1989 insgesamt 100 Beiträge »Die orthodoxen Kirchen« in der Internationalen Kirchlichen Zeitschrift, Bern, und veröffentlichte u.a. die Monographien »Die Gegenwartslage der Ostkirchen« (1948, 2. Aufl. 1968) und »Die morgenländischen Kirchen« (1964). Siehe H. Busse, in: Der Islam 67 (1990) 199-205.

Dr. Gérard Garitte, em. o. Professor der Katholischen Universität Löwen, starb am 30. August 1990. Mit ihm verlor die Wissenschaft vom Christlichen Orient einen ihrer hervorragendsten Vertreter, gleich bedeutend als vielseitiger und unermüdlicher Forscher wie als außerordentlich erfolgreicher akademischer Lehrer, dem viele junge Fachkollegen ihre Ausbildung verdanken. Von der lange Jahre von ihm geleiteten Zeitschrift Le Muséon wurde ihm Band 104 (1987) als Festschrift gewidmet. Darin finden sich am Anfang der wissenschaftliche Lebenslauf des Jubilars und eine Liste seiner sonstigen wissenschaftlichen Aktivitäten. Die reichhaltige Bibliographie seiner Werke findet sich in »Le Muséon. Tables générales des années 1932 à 1973«, par G. Lafontaine, Louvain-la-Neuve 1980, und in G. Garitte, »Scripta disiecta, 1941-1977«, Louvain-la-Neuve 1980, S. IX-XXIX (= Publications de l'Institut Orientaliste de Louvain, 21).

P. Dr. Edouard R. Hambye, SJ, Professor für Kirchengeschichte, Patrologie und Syrische Sprache, 1951-1987 in Indien, ab 1987 am Päpstlichen Orientalischen Institut in Rom, verstarb am 7. September 1990 in Namur (Belgien). Der am 3.7.1916 in Mons (Belgien) geborene Gelehrte befaßte sich vor allem mit der Geschichte des Christentums in Indien.

Professor David Marshall Lang, MA, PhD, DLit, LittD, 1964-1984 Professor für Kaukasische Studien an der Universität London, geboren am

6. Mai 1924, verstarb am 30. März 1991. Seinen unermüdlichen Studien verdanken wir wichtige Werke zur Geschichte und Literaturgeschichte Georgiens und Armeniens. Siehe OrChr 73 (1989) 224f.

Dr. P. Edmund Beck, OSB, Abtei Metten, geboren am 6. November 1902, starb an den Folgen eines zweiten Schlaganfalles am 12. Juni 1991. Neben einigen Studien über den Koran widmete er sich fast ausschließlich Ephräm dem Syrer, dessen Werke er im CSCO syrisch herausgab und ins Deutsche übersetzte und dessen Sprachgebrauch und Lehrmeinungen er in zahlreichen Arbeiten untersuchte. P. Beck war ein langjähriger treuer Mitarbeiter unserer Zeitschrift. Siehe OrChr 71 (1987) 225.

Julius Aßfalg

BESPRECHUNGEN

Silvia Ronchey, Indagini sul martirio di san Policarpo. Roma, Palazzo Borromino 1990, 241 S. (= Istituto storico italiano per il medio evo. Nuovi studi storici 6).

Bereits 1987 hat S.R. mehrere Übersetzungen und Einleitungen der Atti e Passioni dei Martiri geschrieben, die durch A. A. R. Bastiaensen und weitere im Originaltexte bei Mondadori in Vicenza herausgegeben wurden. Die vorliegenden Untersuchungen sind das Ergebnis einer langen Erfahrung, und erweitern die Probleme um das Martyrium des Polycarpus weit über die textuellen Einzelheiten hinaus. Überall werden die Parallelen zum Brief über die Märtyrer von Lyon oder zur Passio des Pionius und zu weiteren »Acta sincera« angeführt. Die Frage geht eigentlich um die Gültigkeit eines solchen Konzepts, und seine Wurzeln im 16. Jahrhundert. Was den Leser zuerst beeindruckt, ist die umfassende Bibliographie, welche sich in reichen Fußnoten als gründlich benützt erweist. S.R. setzt sich immer sorgfältig mit den vorliegenden Meinungen auseinander, auch wo die Lage der Forschung außerordentlich kompliziert ist. Um die Grundlinien ihrer Positionen kurz zu fassen, kann man einige Punkte erwähnen: der spätere Einfluß des Montanismus ist doch nicht so groß, daß man deswegen nicht Vieles in dem vorliegenden Text als Urtext betrachten könnte; die heutige Fassung sollte den Jahren 260-276 zugeschrieben werden, einer verfolgungslosen Periode; Polycarpus selbst ist jetzt sicher im Jahre 167, also unter Marcus Aurelius, gestorben wie 1980 P. Brind'Amour bewiesen hat. Die Autorin sucht, die philosophisch-politische *Matrix* (S. 153) des 3. oder des 2. Jahrhunderts gegenüber der des 4. Jahrhunderts zu entziffern. Die Hinrichtungen wären juristisch durch einen Kompetenzkonflikt zu erklären (S. 100); sie unterscheidet zwischen διωγμῖται als bürgerlicher Wache und ἱππεῖς als konsularischer Polizei, zwischen dem ὄχλος, der sich auf der Agora versammelt, und dem δῆμος im Theater; das ist im Falle Polycarpi, was an dem *Koinon* oder kaiserlichen Fest von Asia geschah. Die καινὰ δόγματα des Marcus Aurelius, die durch Melito von Sardes erwähnt wurden, müssen die *lectisternia* gewesen sein, die sowohl in der *Vita Abercii* wie in der *Vita Marci* vorkommen. S. 197 verwirft S.R. auf Grund eines Artikels von J. Rougé irgendeinen Zusammenhang zwischen dem *Aes Italicense* oder *Lex gladiatoria* mit der Hinrichtung der Märtyrer von Lyon. Sie erwähnt die Argumente von Palmer und Oliver nicht mehr. Diese hatten auch die religiöse Begründung unterzeichnet, wodurch die Märtyrer geopfert wurden: ἐτύθησαν; S.R. hat selbst βῆμα bei Eusebius' Bericht als »Tribunale« wiedergegeben (bei Bastiaensen, Zeile 172), während hier die Bedeutung θυμέλιον wahrscheinlich ist. Auch könnte τὸ κοινὸν τῶν ἐθνῶν (ebenda Z. 222) direkte Beziehungen mit den *Lectisternia*, haben. Am Ende S. 226-240 gibt S.R. eine Übersicht über den Einfluß von Cäsar Baronius in der Zeit der Entstehung des Martyrologium Romanum. Das Konzept »Acta sincera« hat hier seinen Ursprung. Viele interessante Gesichtspunkte sind überall in diesen Untersuchungen zu finden.

Michel van Esbroeck

Basile de Césarée: Sur le baptême. Texte grec de l'édition U. Neri. Introduction, traduction et annotation par Jeanne Ducatillon. Les Éditions du Cerf. Paris 1989 (= Sources Chrétiennes N° 357). Kart., 323 S.

Aphraate le sage persan: Les exposés. Tome II. Exposés XI-XXIII. Traduction du Syriaque. Notes et index par Marie-Joseph Pierre. Les Éditions du Cerf. Paris 1989 (= Sources Chrétiennes N° 359). Kart., S. 522-1042.

B. Altaner - A. Stuiber: Patrologie. Freiburg-Basel-Wien [9]1980 widmen »De baptismo« des Basilius keine Zeile, vermutlich, weil immer noch Zweifel an der Authentizität dieser Schrift bestanden, die jetzt endgültig (S. 7-12) aufgegeben werden können. Ducatillon übernimmt den von U. Neri: Basilio di Cesarea. Il battesimo, testo, trad., introd. e commento. Brescia 1976 eingerichteten Text, der mit 10 neuen Lesarten (S. 73) bereichert ist, die jedoch den Sinn der jeweiligen Passage nicht ändern. Gelegentlich ist die Punktation umgestellt. Das Jota subscriptum wird den Infinitiven zugefügt. Hilfreich ist die zusätzliche Angabe der Migne-Spalten am linken Rand des griechischen Textes. Die erstmalige Übersetzung in die französische Sprache bemüht sich um eine wortgetreue Wiedergabe des Originals. Das an asketische Kreise (Mönche?) gerichtete Werk datiert Ducatillon auf das Jahr 366-68, während W.-D. Hauschild für das Jahr 371 als Abfassungszeit eintritt (Bibliothek der Griechischen Literatur Band 32). Das erste Buch gibt Hinweise zur Vorbereitung auf den Empfang der Taufe und Eucharistie. Das zweite Buch, gestaltet als Frage- und Antwortspiel, erläutert die der Taufe entsprechende Lebensgestaltung. Die häufige Zitation von Röm 6,2-23 insgesamt und partiell ließe erwarten, daß über den Taufritus Aussagen vorgetragen würden. Bedauerlicherweise liegt die Taufliturgie und deren allenfallsige mystagogische Erörterung nicht im Interesse des Autors. Basilius gibt sich zu diesem Punkt noch wortkarger als Theodor von Mopsuestia und Cyrill von Jerusalem. D.h. »De baptismo« ist eine spirituelle Reflexion über die Taufe, keine Taufkatechese.

Die Sources Chrétiennes N° 359 setzen Band 349, der Einleitungsfragen und die Demonstrationes 1-10 behandelt hatte, fort und bringen das Werk Afrahats († nach 345) zum Abschluß. Der akrostischen Form der 23 Abhandlungen wurde von Pierre durch eine gebundene Sprache des Französischen und durch eine klare Markierung der einzelnen Zeilen Rechnung getragen. Die Leistung der Übertragung vom Syrischen in das Französische zeigt sich auch darin, daß die Texte wie Psalmen abgesungen werden könnten. Das Werk des »Persischen Weisen«, das seine Entstehung einer Anfrage verdankt, verdient besonderes Interesse, weil es von westlichen Einflüssen frei genuines syrisch-christliches Gedankengut vorlegt. Die Abhandlungen 11-23 sind folgenden Themen gewidmet: Beschneidung – Pascha – Sabbat – Argumente (= Synodalbrief) – Unterscheidung der Speisen – Das Volk Israel und die Völker – Der Messias als Sohn Gottes – Gegen die Juden über die Jungfräulichkeit und Heiligkeit – Endgültige Verwerfung der Juden – Die Stütze der Armen – Über die Verfolgung – Über den Tod und das Ende der Zeiten – Über die Weintraube. Afrahat setzt sich mit diesen Themen mit der im Sassanidenreich lebenden Judenschaft auseinander, die die Christenverfolgungen dort zu heftigen Angriffen gegen die Christen nutzten.

Beide Bände der Sources Chrétiennes sind mit übersichtlichen Indices ausgestattet.

Wilhelm Gessel

Studien zu Gregor von Nyssa und der christlichen Spätantike. Hrsg. von H. R. Drobner u. Ch. Klock (= Vigiliae Christianae supplement XII). E. J. Brill. Leiden-New York-København-Köln 1990. Ln., 418 S. 180,- holl. Gulden.

Dem etwas vollmundigen Vorwort und einer kleinen Tabula gratulatoria ist zu entnehmen, daß der Sammelband Prof. Dr. Andreas Spira zum 60. Geburtstag gewidmet ist. Die 21 Beiträge werden nach vier Stichworten aufgegliedert: Sprache – Philosophie – Theologie – Anhang. Umfängliche Register erschließen die Aufsatzsammlung. Besonders hilfreich ist die konsequent durchgeführte Absicht, jeden Beitrag mit einem Resümee abzuschließen. Der von Zeitnot bedrängte Leser wird dafür dankbar sein, zumal er in Kürze einen Überblick über Detailaspekte derzeitiger Gregor-von-Nyssa-Forschungen gewinnt. Besonderes Interesse findet die Oratio catechetica magna des Nysseners. Nach R. Kees (S. 211-231) weisen die Aussagen über den Tod im Oikonomia-Abschnitt der Großen katechetischen Rede in den drei Themenbereichen Schöpfungslehre, Soteriologie und Sakramentenlehre der jeweiligen Darlegungsabsicht entsprechend deutlich unterschiedliche Akzente auf. Im ersten Teil erscheint die Sterblichkeit als wohltätige Antwort Gottes auf den Fall des Menschen. Im zweiten Teil interpretiert Gregor den Tod als Eigentümlichkeit der zusammengesetzten menschlichen Natur. Erst im dritten Teil werden wichtige Grundentscheidungen über den Tod, über die Bestimmung des Menschen zur Unsterblichkeit und die Auferstehung Christi im Zusammenhang der Taufe aufgenommen.

J. Sancho Bielsa (S. 233-244) untersucht das eucharistische Vokabular in der Oratio catechetica magna und spricht diesem einen bedeutenden Einfluß auf die spätere Tradition zu. Mit den Verben γίνομαι, μεταποιέω, μετατίθημι, μεθίστημι und μεταστοιχέω sei die Vorstellung des Wechsels, des Übergangs einer Wirklichkeit in eine andere verbunden, vor allem in den mit μετά zusammengesetzten Begriffen. Damit rückt Sancho Bielsa die Eucharistieterminologie Gregors in sehr große Nähe zum Transsubstantiationsbegriff des 12. Jhs. Dies gleicht einem Anachronismus. Wenn überhaupt, dann läge ein Vergleich mit dem ambrosianischen Metabolismus nahe.

Überraschend ist die Hypothese von M. Starowieyski (S. 245-253), die ohne ersichtliche Begründung im Resümee S. 253 zur These stilisiert wird: »Die in der Vita Gregorii Thaumaturgi Gregors von Nyssa wiedergegebene Marienerscheinung an den Wundertäter nach seiner Bischofsweihe, um ihn im rechten Glauben zu unterrichten und zu bestärken, stellt den frühesten Bericht einer Mariophanie in der alten Kirche überhaupt dar und das erste Zeugnis für die Verehrung Mariens als Fürsprecherin im Kappadokien des 3./4. Jhs.«. Der einschlägige Text der Vita des Thaumaturgen (PG 46, 910-914) erzählt eine Erscheinung des Evangelisten Johannes und der »Mutter des Herrn«, die sich unterhalten. Von einer Fürsprecherin und einer Marienverehrung ist dort nicht die Rede. Solange die Zeitstellung der arg konfusen Vita und die Autorschaft Gregors von Nyssa noch völlig ungeklärt sind, sollte man solche Behauptungen unterlassen. Ihr Platz ist bestenfalls für die Populärliteratur reserviert. Vgl. dazu den profunden Artikel von H. Lais: Marienerscheinungen. In: LThK^2 7,64f.

Der Vergleich der Anmerkungsapparate aller Autoren des Sammelbandes verdeutlicht ein methodisches Problem. Der größere Teil der Autoren verzichtet auf die Inanspruchnahme der einschlägigen wissenschaftlichen Literatur, die in der Bibliographie (S. 382-391) unvollständig zusammengetragen ist. Der kleinere Teil der Autoren nennt diskussionslos das eine oder andere wissenschaftliche Werk. Der geringste Teil der Beiträge tritt ab und an in eine Auseinandersetzung mit schon Analysiertem, um den eigenen Standpunkt zu profilieren. Da die Literatur zu Gregor von Nyssa kaum mehr überschaubar ist, würde sich aus Gründen der Ökonomie der Mut zu äußerster Beschränkung in diesem Punkt empfehlen, zumal die Tendenz der Buchpreise nach oben immer hektischer wird, wie der vorliegende Band beweist. Und das trotz des unschönen Computersatzes, unter dem vor allem die Anmerkungen leiden.

Wilhelm Gessel

Jean Chrysostome: Trois catéchèses baptismales. Introduction, texte critique, traduction et notes par Auguste Piédagnel avec la collaboration du Louis Doutreleau (Sources Chrétiennes N° 366). Les Éditions du Cerf, Paris 1990, Kart., 288 S.

Mit diesem Band ist das Corpus Chrysostomianum auf insgesamt 18 Nummern der Sources Chrétiennes angewachsen. Dies entspricht dem literarisch sehr fruchtbaren Kirchenvater durchaus. Textedition, Übersetzung, einleitende Fragen sowie die Register sind im Rahmen dieser Reihe in etwa standardisiert worden. Die Qualität der Reihe ist inzwischen so bekannt, daß hier ein Detailhinweis genügen mag.

S. 54-56 wird im Zusammenhang einer liturgischen Einleitung der Taufakt behandelt und als Immersionstaufe geschildert. Während für Mailand und Rom eine Taufe durch Übergießen reklamiert wird, wird Antiochien und Johannes Chrysostomos als Zeuge für eine Taufe durch dreimaliges Untertauchen vorgestellt. Die Frage nach einer anderen Form des Taufritus wird nicht einmal gestellt. Dies verwundert im Blick auf den tatsächlichen Textbefund. Johannes behandelt eine Fülle von Themen, z.B. auch die dreigliedrige Taufformel, die seiner Auffassung nach den Taufliturgen ganz in den Hintergrund stellt und den dreifaltigen Gott als eigentlichen Taufspender ausweist. So beginnt die Taufformel nicht: »Ich taufe Dich«, sondern »Du wirst getauft auf den Namen des Vaters und des Sohnes und des Heiligen Geistes« (S. 224). Gewiß befaßt sich Johannes ähnlich wie Cyrill von Jerusalem allegorisch mit Röm 6,8 (S. 182-188), verbindet diese Stelle jedoch keineswegs mit einer Taufimmersion. Die Übersetzung von Katechese III 8 (S. 237) wird durch die Überschrift »l'immersion« hervorgehoben. Liest man diesen Abschnitt, stellt man fest, daß weder der Wasserritus erwähnt, noch ein Untertauchen geschildert wird. Lediglich das Hintreten zur Piscina »der heiligen Wasser« wird angesprochen, um dann breit zu erklären, warum der Täufling ohne jede Kleidung in den Taufbrunnen steigt. Der Grund hierfür findet sich in Gen. 2,25, also in der kultischen Nudität von Adam und Eva. Nachdem ein vollständiges Untertauchen aus dem Autor selbst nicht bewiesen werden kann, benennen Piédagnel und Doutreleau als unmittelbare Parallele Theodor von Mopsuestia und zwar Homélies catéchétiques, ed. R. Tonneau et R. Devresse. Vatican 1949. Diese französische Übersetzung aus MS Mingana Syr 561 bietet S.441 »t'immerges«, »t'immerger«, »étant immergé«, also untertauchen, versenken. Der syrische Codex dagegen hat f. III^r, Zeile 23 das Wort ʿmd, das in der deutschen Sprache nicht mit »untertauchen« wiedergegeben werden kann. Es heißt wie »baptizein« »waschen« und wird im Syrischen zum Terminus technicus für taufen (Belege bei Thesaurus Syriacus. Hrsg. v. R. Payne Smith Sp. 2906f. mit lateinischer Übersetzung: descendit in aquas, se abluit, lavit). Es entsprechen sich in der Tat Johannes Chrysostomos und Theodor von Mopsuestia, aber zum Ritus des Taufvorgangs ist damit nichts gesagt, erst recht nicht ist von einem Untertauchen die Rede. Da andere Zeremonien zum Vollzug der Taufe, z.B. die Ganzkörpersalbung vor der Wassertaufe, ausführlich vorgetragen und begründet werden, verbleiben wohl nur zwei Erklärungen. Entweder maß man der Wasserzeremonie keine allzugroße Bedeutung gegenüber anderen Taufriten bei oder die Arkandisziplin ließ den genauen Vorgang des Wasserritus verschweigen.

Wilhelm Gessel

Corpus Dionysiacum I. Pseudo-Dionysius Areopagita: De divinis nominibus. Hrsg. von Beate Regina Suchla (= Patristische Texte und Studien Band 33). Walter de Gruyter. Berlin-New York 1990. Ln., XXIXI, 238 S., DM 178,-.

Für die jetzt vorliegende Leistung der Nova editio critica maior ist sowohl für die Einrichtung des Textes, des kritischen Apparates und der drucktechnischen Anlage ohne Zweifel ein Superlativ am Platz: rückhaltlose Bewunderung. Gäbe es für jeden Autor der christlichen Antike eine vergleichbare Ausgabe, dann ließe sich die patristische Forschung in einem Maße bewegen, daß deren Früchte wie gut gereifte Äpfel vom Baume fielen. Sicherheit ist mit dieser Ausgabe angesagt. Dem Text des Areopagiten ist eine Einleitung vorangestellt, die den neuesten Forschungsstand berücksichtigend in das Gesamtcorpus einführt. Und, was in dieser Ausführlichkeit prinzipiell neu ist, es wurden graphisch hervorragende Falttafeln eingefügt, die die Qualität der Variantenträger und das Verhältnis der Zeugen zueinander nachprüfbar machen.

Das Werk 'Die Namen Gottes' aus der Feder des Areopagiten stellt eine geschickte Verbindung von Gotteslehre und Schöpfungslehre dar. Durch eine kompromißlos wirkende Verwendung der neuplatonischen Terminologie und durch eine konsequente Einbeziehung und Umdeutung von aristotelischer und neuplatonischer Metaphysik verchristlicht diese Schrift die heidnische

Philosophie, vor allem den Neuplatonismus. Ziel des Areopagiten ist dessen Überwindung. Das platonische Erbe des schlechthinnigen ἕν als des Urgrunds alles Seins kann durch die christliche Lehre des dreifaltigen ἕν als der Ursache der gesamten Schöpfung überwunden werden.

Auf der Basis des jetzt etablierten Textes hat Beate Regina Suchla schon 1988 eine kommentierte deutsche Übersetzung der Namen Gottes vorgelegt, die in der Bibliothek der griechischen Literatur (Stuttgart) als Band 26 erschienen ist. Beide Werke aus der einen Hand ergänzen sich bestens.

Wilhelm Gessel

Aleksander Kowalski. Perfezione e giustizia di Adamo nel Liber Graduum, Roma 1989, 256 S. (= Orientalia Christiana Analecta 232).

A.K. hat schon 1985 diese Untersuchung zum syrischen Liber Graduum als Dissertation an der Università Gregoriana vorgelegt. Nach einer Anregung von R. Murray hat er sich entschlossen, die Fragen um diesen alten syrischen Text gründlich zu erforschen. Als Zentralthema ergab sich dabei die Vollkommenheit und Gerechtigkeit Adams. Bessere Bestimmungen über die Entstehung dieses Liber Graduum hat er kaum erreicht. Wie die meisten Spezialisten schlägt er für die Abfassungszeit eine Periode um 400 vor, und schließt einen östlichen Ursprung nicht aus, denn die einzige geographische Anspielung weist auf den kleinen Zab hin. Den Beziehungen des Liber Graduum zu den Messalianern ist A.K. nicht nachgegangen. Der Schwerpunkt seiner Arbeit liegt auf dem syrischen Wörterverzeichnis und den Parallelen im Alten und Neuen Testament, bei den christlichen Adambüchern wie auch in den jüdischen Adamsvorstellungen. Manchmal hat A.K. hingewiesen auf die wichtige Bedeutung der Exegese von Gen. 2,15 in Anspruch, wo Adam im Paradies steht, um zu »arbeiten« und zu »bewachen«. Die jüdische entsprechende Exegese findet er in Bereshit Rabba 16,5 (S. 171, Fußn. 22); sehr gewundert hat sich A.K., daß dieser Vers nicht einmal im Liber Graduum ausdrücklich erwähnt worden ist, obwohl seine Wichtigkeit auf S. 45, Fußn. 23, S. 72, Fußn. 112, S. 121 für LG 21,20, und S. 167 für LG 24,8 immer wieder auftaucht. Die christlichen Parallelen bei Ephräm und in der Schatzhöhle gibt er S. 45, Fußn. 22. Offensichtlich hat er das 1982 erschienene Werk von Barsabaeus von Jerusalem nicht berücksichtigt (Patr. Orientalis 41, S. 208-252). Dort findet man nicht nur die ausdrückliche Exegese von Gen. 2,15 (S. 210), sondern auch mehrere Beziehungen zur Schatzhöhle (ibid., S. 199-201). Auch die langen Zusammenstellungen mit den Patriarchen des Alten Testamentes (S. 177) setzen gewisse Kontaktpunkte zwischen dem Liber Graduum und Barsabaeus voraus. Nur hat der Autor des Liber die Kategorien des Barsabaeus ganz asketisch umgearbeitet, am Rande der messalianischen Bewegungen um 400. In diesem Bereich wären weitere Untersuchungen nötig. S. 139 analysiert A.K., nach A. Lauf, die bemerkenswerte Interpretierung von Phil. 2,6-7 gegenüber Adams Sünde. S. 97, Fußn. 183 ist die Schatzhöhle nach C. Bezold zitiert, als eine Quelle des 4. Jahrhunderts, ohne Rücksicht auf A. Goetze's Arbeit über eine viel ältere Urschatzhöhle aus dem 3. oder 2. Jahrhundert. In derselben Fußnote wird Adam als Basileus als reine syrische Interpretation vorgelegt, obwohl sie bei den griechischen Kappadokiern ganz selbstverständlich vorkommt. Diese kleinen Punkte mindern keineswegs den Wert der zahlreichen Analysen im syrischen Bereich: rund 400 syrische Wörter liegen in dem Index S. 252-256 vor.

Michel van Esbroeck

Alexander Böhlig: Gnosis und Synkretismus. Gesammelte Aufsätze zur spätantiken Religionsgeschichte. 1. Teil (= Wissenschaftliche Untersuchungen zum Neuen Testament 47). J. C. B. Mohr (Paul Siebeck). Tübingen 1989, Ln., 370 S.

In diesem Sammelband sind dankenswerterweise bisher weithin verstreute Arbeitsergebnisse aus Zeitschriften, Kolloquiumsbänden und Festschriften zusammengetragen. »Allgemeine Probleme« und »Nag Hammadi« sind die Überschriften, unter denen Fragen aus der Erforschung der Gnosis versammelt wurden. In fast allen in diesem Buch vereinigten Beiträgen sind gegenüber der jeweiligen Erstfassung Änderungen vorgenommen und die Diskussion darüber aufgenommen worden. Damit überschreitet dieser Sammelband die Gestalt einer Reprise und verdeutlicht den inzwischen erreichten Fortschritt in der Auseinandersetzung mit der vielgestaltigen Gnosis der Spätantike.

Daß die Beschäftigung mit den Schriften aus der Nähe von Chenoboskion noch keineswegs abgeschlossen ist, beweisen auch die vorsichtigen Formulierungen Böhligs zu diesem Bereich. Was an Evangelien, Apokalypsen und Apokryphen aus der Bibliothek von Nag Hammadi vorliegt, ist samt und sonders gnostisch. So schließt hier Böhlig auf eine außerchristliche Gnosis und spricht von einem gnostischen Fluidum, das parasitär Religionen beeinflußte. In diesem Zusammenhang werden die bedeutenden christlichen Gnostiker Basilides und Valentin im Verein mit ihren Schülern als christliche Theologen einer besonderen Schule diagnostiziert. Im Gnostiker erkennt Böhlig den Disputant beim Entstehen der Großkirche, dessen Tätigkeit positive und negative Wirkungen auszeitigen kann. So wird dem Theologen vom Religionshistoriker ins Stammbuch geschrieben: Da Thesen häufig als Folge eines geistigen Kampfes formuliert wurden und werden, sollte der Theologe in extenso zur Kenntnis nehmen, womit sich die Großkirche in der Diskussion mit Gnostizismus und Manichäismus auseinanderzusetzen hatte. Das aus dem Sammelband sich ergebende Postulat lautet: die bekannten und schon grundsätzlich erschlossenen gnostischen Originaltexte sollten noch weiter literar- und formkritisch behandelt werden. Rezensent würde dieser Forderung die besondere Betonung der Redaktionsgeschichte anschließen, um zu einem abgerundeten Bild gnostischer Denkstrukturen zu kommen. Nicht zuletzt zeigt der verdienstvolle Sammelband die Notwendigkeit, die Gnosisforschung weiter intensiv voranzutreiben. Der Ist-Stand der Forschung aus religionshistorischer Sicht, wie er in diesem Band aufscheint, gibt eine gute Möglichkeit dazu und er sollte zugleich einen neuen Anstoß in diese Richtung bieten.

Wilhelm Gessel

Walter Selb, Orientalisches Kirchenrecht. Band II: Die Geschichte des Kirchenrechts der Westsyrer (von den Anfängen bis zur Mongolenzeit) (= Österreichische Akademie der Wissenschaften, philos.-hist. Kl., Sitzungsberichte, 543. Band = Veröffentlichungen der Kommission für Antike Rechtsgeschichte Nr. 6), Wien 1989. 309 S. und 1 Karte, 560,– öSchilling.

Das Buch setzt die Darstellung des orientalischen Kirchenrechts fort, die Selb mit seiner 1981 erschienenen Geschichte des Kirchenrechts der Nestorianer begonnen hat. Ebenso wie die ostsyrischen, so liegen auch die wichtigsten westsyrischen Rechtsquellen — teilweise schon seit längerer Zeit — in mehr oder weniger verläßlichen Ausgaben und Übersetzungen vor, doch hatte eine inhaltliche Beschäftigung damit bisher nur in Ansätzen stattgefunden. Selb beschreitet deshalb — wie beim Kirchenrecht der Nestorianer — auch jetzt weitgehend Neuland.

Das Werk besteht aus zwei Hauptteilen, von denen der erste die Quellen und der zweite die verschiedenen Rechtsinstitute behandelt. Vorangestellt ist eine knappe allgemeine Einleitung in das Kirchenrecht der orientalischen Kirchen. Außerdem findet der Leser ein Literaturverzeichnis und Register der zitierten Handschriften, der Personen und Sachen (S. 35-71) sowie eine Zeittafel und ein Sachregister (S. 305-309). Ferner ist eine Landkarte beigegeben.

Die Quellengeschichte geht weit über die bisher vorliegende Literatur hinaus, auch über die in den letzten dreißig Jahren erschienenen einschlägigen Arbeiten von Arthur Vööbus, die zweifellos wichtig, aber nicht recht zufriedenstellend sind. Selb bezieht sämtliche bekannten Texte, gedruckte, aber auch bisher nur handschriftlich überlieferte, ein und erfaßt ferner vollständig das zugängliche Handschriftenmaterial, das er zum Teil selbst auf mehreren Orientreisen an Ort und Stelle einsehen und photographieren konnte. Die einzelnen Texte sind zumeist in umfangreichen Sammelhandschriften (»Synodika«) enthalten, deren Entstehungsgeschichte bislang nur unzureichend untersucht worden war und die ebenfalls Gegenstand der Untersuchung sind (S. 139-154).

Die Institutionengeschichte umfaßt Synode (S. 198-211), die einzelnen hierarchischen Ränge (S. 211-251), kirchliches Vermögensrecht (S. 251-253), Eherecht (S. 253-263), Mönchtum (S. 264-284), Bußdisziplin (S. 284-294), »Recht und Häretiker« (S. 294-298), Verhältnis von Kirche und Staat (S. 298-302) sowie Rechtsquellenlehre (S. 302-304). Der Verfasser hat seine Darstellung ausnahmslos aus den Primärquellen erarbeitet, insbesondere den juristischen und historischen, zieht aber auch die Sekundärliteratur umfassend heran. Die behandelten Themen gehen über das in seinem Buch über das Kirchenrecht der Nestorianer Gebotene hinaus: er bezieht jetzt zu Recht auch das Eherecht und die Bußdisziplin mit ein. Das sonstige Sakramentenrecht fehlt allerdings auch hier. Da es aber im Hinblick auf die Art der einschlägigen Quellen wohl nur in enger Verzahnung mit der Liturgiewissenschaft behandelt werden kann und die Grenzen schwer zu ziehen sind, ist der Verzicht darauf verständlich. Entsprechendes gilt für die zeitliche Grenze: »bis zur Mongolenzeit«. An sich wäre natürlich auch die weitere Entwicklung bis in die Gegenwart von Interesse, doch versiegen nach dem 13. Jhdt. die Quellen für Jahrhunderte fast ganz, so daß für die Beschränkung gute Gründe sprechen.

Für das Recht des Mönchtums sei noch auf den 1989 in Löwen erschienenen dritten Band von A. Vööbus, History of Ascetism in the Syrian Orient (= CSCO 500), hingewiesen, in dem auch die Mönchskanones ausführlich behandelt werden; die Abschnitte Monasticism in the light of legislative sources (S. 68-71, 170-193, 279-295, 350-360, 411-427) weisen zwar deutliche Übereinstimmungen mit dem Kapitel »Die Kanones für das Mönchtum« in Vööbus' Buch »Syrische Kanonessammlungen« (dort S. 307-404) auf, doch gibt er zusätzlich Übersetzungen der Kanones.

Die vom Verfasser behandelten Themen waren bisher nur unzureichend oder gar nicht Gegenstand wissenschaftlicher Literatur. Selb faßt keineswegs nur bisherige Ergebnisse in Form eines Handbuches zusammen, sondern sein Werk stellt in weiten Bereichen einen wesentlichen eigenen Beitrag in der Erforschung des westsyrischen Kirchenrechts und einen bedeutenden Fortschritt dar.

Angemerkt sei noch, daß das Inhaltsverzeichnis nicht nur in deutscher, sondern auch in englischer und französischer Sprache vorangestellt ist. Der Verfasser will dadurch den Lesern, die des Deutschen nicht so kundig sind, den Zugang erleichtern. Angesichts der Erfahrung, daß deutschsprachige Literatur nicht von allen Autoren im erforderlichen Ausmaß berücksichtigt wird (häufig zum Schaden solcher Publikationen!), eine wohl nicht überflüssige Hilfestellung. Fest steht jedenfalls, daß die Benutzung des Buches von Selb für die weitere Beschäftigung mit dem westsyrischen Kirchenrecht unerläßlich ist.

Hubert Kaufhold

Walter Selb, Sententiae Syriacae. Eingeleitet, herausgegeben, deutsch übersetzt, mit einem syrischen und griechischen Glossar versehen und kommentiert (= Österreichische Akademie der Wissenschaften, philos.-hist. Kl., Sitzungsberichte, 567. Band = Veröffentlichungen der Kommission für Antike Rechtsgeschichte Nr. 7), Wien 1990. 219 Seiten, 630,– öSchilling.

Die Wissenschaft vom römischen Recht wurde 1880 durch die Ausgabe und Übersetzung des sogenannten Syrisch-römischen Rechtsbuches von Bruns und Sachau stark angeregt, eines Werkes, dessen griechische oder — wenn es sie je gab — lateinische Vorlage nicht erhalten ist und das nur in Übersetzungen in orientalische Sprachen, insbesondere ins Syrische, vorliegt. Völlig unerwartet ist nun vor etwa 25 Jahren ein weiteres syrisches Werk aufgetaucht, das ebenfalls römisches Recht aus verschiedenen Rechtsgebieten wiedergibt und dessen griechische oder gar lateinische Fassung gleichfalls fehlt. Es ist zwar nicht so umfangreich wie das Syrisch-römische Rechtsbuch (nur etwa ein Fünftel an Text), doch ohne Zweifel von ähnlich weitreichender Bedeutung für die rechtsgeschichtliche Forschung.

Selb veröffentlichte bereits 1968 (Zeitschrift der Savigny-Stiftung für Rechtsgeschichte, Romanistische Abteilung, Band 85) das erste Drittel nach fol. 27^{r-v} der fragmentarischen, aus dem 8./9. Jhdt. stammenden Hs. Vat. Syr. 560 (mit Photos des Blattes; eine Abbildung von fol. 27^{v} findet sich jetzt auf dem Buchumschlag). Er nannte den Text »Sententiae Syriacae«. Die Überschrift lautet eigentlich »Gesetze der christlichen und siegreichen Könige (in Kurzfassung)«. Seither wurden einige jüngere, aber vollständige Handschriften aufgefunden. Arthur Vööbus gab den Text, den er zu Unrecht für eine Version des Syrisch-römischen Rechtsbuches hielt, im zweiten Teil seines umfangreichen Werkes »The Synodicon in the West Syrian Tradition« (Louvain 1976) nach der Hs. Damaskus Orth. 8/11 heraus und übersetzte ihn ins Englische. In seinem schmalen Heft »An Unknown Recension of the Syro-Roman Lawbook« (laut Impressum: Stockholm 1977, tatsächlich aber wohl viel später erschienen) veröffentlichte er die weitestgehend übereinstimmenden Texte der Hss. Damaskus Orth. 8/11, Mardin Orth. 316 (richtig: 326) und 323 im Photo und fügte einen kurzen kritischen Apparat an; seine frühere Übersetzung druckte er unverändert ab. Vööbus arbeitete jedoch nicht nur recht flüchtig, sondern es fehlten ihm auch die erforderlichen rechtshistorischen Kenntnisse; es handelt sich weder um wirklich kritische Ausgaben noch ist die Übersetzung brauchbar.

Diese Lücke hat Selb mit dem anzuzeigenden Buch nun ausgefüllt. Nach einer Einleitung (S. 13-32), in der vor allem über das geschichtliche Umfeld und die Handschriften berichtet wird, folgt die Edition, für die Selb alle bekannten Handschriften benutzt hat. Die danebenstehende Übersetzung folgt möglichst genau dem syrischen Wortlaut, was hier unerläßlich war, weil der syrische Text offensichtlich eine sehr getreue, manchmal sklavische Wiedergabe der griechischen Vorlage ist; teilweise scheint sogar noch die lateinische Grundlage durch, die Selb als Rechtshistoriker — mit der gebotenen Vorsicht — heranzieht. Trotzdem war die Übersetzung, auch wegen offenkundiger Textverderbnisse, manchmal keine leichte Aufgabe. Der Rezensent hätte deshalb vielleicht an einigen weiteren Stellen Fragezeichen angebracht. Es schließen sich nützliche Verzeichnisse aller syrischen Wörter (S. 69-83) und der griechischen Fremdwörter (S. 85) an, jeweils mit Übersetzung und Fundstellen. Der Kommentar zu den einzelnen Stellen (S. 87-188), der sich im wesentlichen mit dem juristischen Gehalt befaßt, ist sehr klar und systematisch abgefaßt; zunächst erläutert der Verfasser, um welchen Sachverhalt es in dem meist prägnant formulierten syrischen Text geht und wie die Lösung aussieht, dann berichtet er ausführlich über die Regelungen in den bisher bekannten Quellen des römischen Rechts und weist insbesondere auf Paralleltexte oder -formulierungen hin.

Abschließend faßt Selb seine Exegese der Einzelstellen zusammen und behandelt das Werk als Ganzes (S. 189-212). Zum weit überwiegenden Teil handelt es sich um rein römisches Recht der diokletianischen Zeit. Nur ganz wenige Texte sind jünger, der letzte ist eine Konstitution der Kaiser Leo und Anthemius aus dem Jahre 472 n. Chr. Als Quellen nennt Selb vor allem den Codex Hermogenianus, den Codex Gregorianus, den Codex Theodosianus und die Paulussentenzen. Da Justinian die Verwendung der drei Codices 529 verbat, müßte das Werk, jedenfalls die vorliegende Fassung, zwischen 472 und 529 entstanden sein. Wann die Übersetzung ins Syrische erfolgte, läßt sich bisher nicht sagen. In die syrischen juristischen Sammelhandschriften wurden die Sententiae Syriacae und das Syrisch-römische Rechtsbuch nicht nor dem 8. Jhdt. eingefügt.

Selb sagt sicher nicht zuviel, wenn er die Sententiae Syriacae als »bislang völlig unbekanntes einzigartiges Dokument frühnachklassischen römischen Rechts« bezeichnet (S. 18). Es unterscheidet sich erheblich vom Syrisch-römischen Rechtsbuch, das auf einer späteren Stufe des römischen Rechts beruht. Auch wenn die Vertreter des Christlichen Orients mit Genugtuung feststellen können, daß eine neue christlich-orientalische Quelle wesentlich zu einer besseren Kenntnis des römischen Rechts beiträgt, ist diese Zeitschrift nicht der Ort, auf rechtsgeschichtliche Einzelheiten einzugehen; die nähere Diskussion ihres juristischen Inhalts, des Kommentars von Selb und seiner sonstigen Erwägungen muß den Vertretern des römischen Rechts vorbehalten bleiben, die trotz der bereits seit einiger Zeit vorliegenden Veröffentlichungen die Sententiae Syriacae bisher überhaupt noch nicht zur Kenntnis genommen haben. Das wichtige Buch von Selb ist eine solide Grundlage für die weitere Forschung.

Im folgenden einige Bemerkungen nichtjuristischer Art:

Zu S. 20: Die Ergänzung der lückenhaften alten Hs. Vat. Syr. 560, also Vat. Syr. 560 B, wurde 1936 nicht im Iraq, sondern in Beirut oder noch eher im Kloster Scharfeh angefertigt, weil der Kopist, Buṭrus Sābā, damals dort tätig war (s. Kurzbiographie auf S. 175f. des unten S. 274 angezeigten Buches von M. Ǧamīl) und weil er dafür Handschriften des damals noch in Beirut befindlichen Fonds Rahmani verwendete.

Zu S. 23: Die Ausführungen zum Kolophon der Hs. Damaskus Orth. 8/11 erscheinen zumindest mißverständlich. 1204 n. Chr. wurde zweifellos die Handschrift vollendet, nicht etwa nur die Sammlung der darin enthaltenen Texte veranstaltet. Derartige Sammlungen entstanden ja einfach dadurch, daß ein Kopist verschiedene Texte nacheinander abschrieb; Fertigstellung von Sammlung und Handschrift ist deshalb regelmäßig ein und dasselbe. Es liegt hier auch ein ganz gängiger Kolophon vor: der Inhalt der Handschrift wird umschrieben, das Datum der Fertigstellung genannt, dann folgen die zeitgenössischen Hierarchen (entgegen Selb ist nicht Michael der Große gemeint, sondern sein gleichnamiger Neffe), der Schreiber usw.

Zu S. 29: Barhebraeus dürfte für seine Zitate aus dem Syrisch-römischen Rechtsbuch im Nomokanon die Hs. Damaskus Orth. 8/11 oder eine ganz nahestehende Version verwendet haben. Seine Paragraphenzahlen stimmten mit wenigen Ausnahmen mit der Zählung der Damaszener Handschrift überein, viel besser als mit derjenigen der ostsyrischen Hs. R II, die Selb in der Tabelle herangezogen hat.

Zu S. 43: Die Übersetzung von § 24 muß lauten: »Der Sohn kann Sachen der Mutter, solange sie noch lebt, nicht verpfänden (oder: verschenken)«. Der syrische Text ist vollständig.

Zu S. 54/55 (§ 73): Das Fremdwort *d'pwrṭ'ṭ'wst'* ist rätselhaft, auch wenn es zweifellos etwas mit Deportation zu tun hat. Vielleicht ist es die bloße Transliteration des dem Übersetzer möglicherweise nicht verständlichen δεπορτατευέσθω, das — wie mir Herr Professor Spyros Troianos, Athen, mündlich mitteilte — in byzantinischen Rechtsquellen häufiger vorkommt.

Die Sententiae Syriacae wurden auch ins Armenische übersetzt, Fassungen in weiteren orientalischen Sprachen sind — anders als beim Syrisch-römischen Rechtsbuch — jedoch nicht bekannt. Ich hoffe, in absehbarer Zeit eine Ausgabe des armenischen Textes vorlegen zu können.

Hubert Kaufhold

Yūḥanōn Dōlabānī, Maktḇōnūtō ḏ-pāṭrīyarkē ḏ-Antīōk d-suryōyē trīṣai šuḇḥō (Nebentitel: Die Patriarchen der syrisch-orthodoxen Kirche von Antiochien), Glane/Losser 1990. 303 S.

Ǧōrǧ Anṭūn Kirāz, ʿIqdu ʾl-ǧumān fī aḫbār as-suryān (Nebentitel: George A. Kiraz, Ikd-uljuman), Glane/Losser 1988, 119 S., 20,– DM.

Hanna Aydin, Die syrisch-orthodoxe Kirche von Antiochien. Ein geschichtlicher Überblick (mit syrischen Nebentitel), Glane/Losser 1990. 193 S., 35,– DM.

Im syrisch-orthodoxen »Bar-Hebraeus Verlag« in Glane/Holland (vgl. OrChr 72, 1988, 213f.) sind in der letzten Zeit einige neue Veröffentlichungen aus dem Bereich dieser Kirche erschienen. Über sie gibt der deutsch geschriebene Katalog Nr. 3 (1990/1991) Auskunft; er umfaßt einschließlich einiger Publikationen anderer Verlage 88 Titel, außerdem eine von Diakon Hanna Aydin besprochene Kassette für den Unterricht im Altsyrischen.

Noch nicht im Katalog verzeichnet ist die Geschichte der syrischen Patriarchen, die der gelehrte Metropolit Philoxenos Hanna Dolabani von Mardin (1885-1969) 1929 als Mönch in Jerusalem altsyrisch verfaßte und die bisher nicht gedruckt vorlag. Der mit einem Computer gesetzte Text beruht auf dem Autograph im Besitz des Metropoliten George Ṣalība vom Libanon. Der Verfasser hat bei jedem Patriarchen das zusammengetragen, was er über Leben und Werk finden konnte, beginnend bei Simon Petrus. Er beschränkt sich auf die Linie von Mardin; die syrischen Patriarchen von Kilikien oder des Ṭūr ʿAbdīn sind nicht eigens verzeichnet. Leider gibt Dolabani seine Quellen nicht an. Es versteht sich aber von selbst, daß er für die Zeit bis zum 13. Jhdt. vor allem die bekannten Geschichtswerke (Michael der Syrer, Barhebraeus usw.) verwendet hat. Der wissenschaftliche Gewinn für die ältere Zeit ist deshalb natürlich gering. Für die folgenden Jahrhunderte wird Dolabani sich auf Kolophone, Ordinationslisten, Inschriften und ähnliches gestützt haben, weil hierfür kaum geschichtliche Darstellungen vorhanden sind. Darin scheint mir der hauptsächliche Nutzen des Buches zu liegen, sind wir doch bisher über die neuere Geschichte der westsyrischen Kirche verhältnismäßig schlecht unterrichtet. Wissenschaftlichen Ansprüchen kann das Buch in der vorliegenden Form freilich nur begrenzt genügen. Wünschenswert wäre eine kritische Bearbeitung in einer europäischen Sprache mit Quellenangaben. Eine leichte Aufgabe wäre das freilich nicht, denn kaum jemand wird den erforderlichen Überblick etwa über die verwendeten Handschriften haben, die infolge der Ereignisse der letzten Jahrzehnte teilweise wohl auch gar nicht mehr existieren oder verschollen sind. So wird man das Buch Dolabanis, wie es ist, doch dankbar begrüßen. Es stellt jedenfalls — wie auch die Arbeiten des Patriarchen Ignatios Ephräm Barsaum (1887-1957), die teilweise noch der Veröffentlichung harren — eine wichtige Grundlage für die weitere Erforschung der westsyrischen Kirchengeschichte dar. Die Darstellung ist bis in die Gegenwart weitergeführt, vermutlich vom Metropoliten Julius Çiçek von Mitteleuropa, der ein kurzes Vorwort verfaßte. Die letzten Patriarchen, seit Jakob II. (1847-1871), sind auch abgebildet, auf dem Umschlag und zum Teil im Text.

Die Reihe der Arbeiten über die Syrer in Jerusalem vor allem von Dolabani (in der Jerusalemer Zeitschrift al-Ḥikma in den 30er Jahren), Ġrīġūriyus Būlus Behnām (Bait Marqus fī Ūrušalīm, Jerusalem 1962), O. Meinardus (The Syrian Jacobites in the Holy City, in: Orientalia Suecana 12, Uppsala 1964) und Yacoub Koriah (Karkenny) (The Syrian Orthodox Church in the Holy Land, Jerusalem 1976) setzt nun — neben A. Palmer mit seinem Aufsatz in diesem Band — George Kiraz (in arabischer Sprache) fort. Er berichtet zunächst allgemein über Geschichte und Kultur der Westsyrer (S. 1-22). Im zweiten Kapitel behandelt er die syrischen Klöster und Kirchen in Jerusalem (S. 25-41), gibt eine Liste der dortigen syrischen Bischöfe (S. 42-47) sowie kurze Biographien der bekannteren von ihnen, beginnend mit Ignatios IV. (1139-1184) bis zum jetzigen Amtsinhaber (S. 48-65); anschließend beschreibt er die Rechte der syrisch-orthodoxen Kirche an den heiligen Stätten (S. 66-77). Im dritten Kapitel befaßt er sich mit der syrischen Gemeinde im Heiligen Land, insbesondere der Herkunft der Gläubigen und ihrer Anzahl (S. 81-83), ihrem kulturellen Leben (Vereine, Schulwesen) sowie den Kirchen in Jerusalem und Bethlehem in unserem Jahrhundert (S. 84-92), dem Gemeindeleben, den Gebräuchen und kirchlichen Festen (S. 93-103). Zum Schluß druckt er Anweisungen für Pilgerfahrten nach Jerusalem ab (S. 106-115). Soweit der Verfasser, ein Bethlehemer Diakon, aus eigener Anschauung berichtet, ist sein Buch eine wichtige Quelle. Im übrigen stützt er sich auf die historischen Texte und die einschlägige Literatur, die er erfreulicherweise in Anmerkungen und einem Literaturverzeichnis angibt. Es handelt sich zwar nicht um eine zusammenhängende Darstellung der Geschichte der Syrer im Heiligen Land — sie fehlt noch immer —, das Buch bietet aber doch eine Fülle von Nachrichten, geht über das bisher Bekannte hinaus und kann in mehrfacher Hinsicht mit Gewinn herangezogen werden. Es enthält außerdem einige Photographien von Personen und Gebäuden sowie an mehreren Stellen schmückende fromme Zeichnungen, die aber wohl nicht alle jedermanns Geschmack treffen. Verblüfft hat den Rezensenten der hüpfende Nikolaus oder Weihnachtsmann auf S. 47 hinter der Liste der Jerusalemer Bischöfe.

Diakon Hanna Aydin gibt in seinem Buch einen Überblick über die Geschichte der westsyrischen Kirche von den Anfängen bis zur Gegenwert. Er bezieht teilweise die Ostsyrer mit ein; in diesem Zusammenhang erscheint auch die — vom Verfasser verneinte — Frage, ob sich die heutigen Syrer als »Assyrer« bezeichnen können; der Streit darüber, der auch von politischer Bedeutung ist, hat in den letzten Jahren in den Gemeinden für einige Unruhe gesorgt. Das Buch ist für eine breitere Öffentlichkeit gedacht. Der Verfasser will laut Einleitung offenbar auch die als Gastarbeiter (und — wie man hinzufügen muß — als Asylanten) in Westeuropa lebenden Mitglieder seiner Kirche ansprechen. Dieses Ziel bestimmt natürlich Inhalt und Art der Darstellung. Unüberhörbar ist die Polemik gegen den Islam und vor allem gegen die Türken. Das erklärt sich nicht zuletzt durch die Herkunft des Verfassers aus dem Ṭūr ʿAḇdīn und seine dort gemachten Erfahrungen. Die Abschnitte »Die Syrer unter dem Islam« (S. 46-94) sowie »Die Syrer unter den Türken« (S. 95-136) nehmen den breitesten Raum ein. Aydin zitiert darin lange Passagen aus anderen Werken, die sich mit der Lage der Christen befassen, insbesondere aus einem Werk über islamisches Recht (S. 56-71; in türkischer Sprache) und aus Adam Mez, Die Renaissance des Islam (S. 72-94). Interessant sind vor allem die Berichte mehrerer älterer Mitglieder der syrisch-orthodoxen Kirche über selbst erlebte Ereignisse — meist Verfolgungen — der vergangenen Jahrzehnte in der Türkei und Jerusalem, die Aydin aufgenommen und abgedruckt hat (S. 99-129). Sie bieten nützliches, wenn auch kritisch zu benutzendes Material für die jüngste Geschichte der Christen im Orient. Ein eigener Abschnitt ist der Frage gewidmet, ob der Ṭūr ʿAḇdīn am Sterben sei (S. 134-136). Der Verfasser beantwortet sie nur indirekt damit, daß er auf die Verfolgungen und Benachteiligungen hinweist, denen die dortigen Christen ausgesetzt sind, also wohl negativ und damit nicht unrealistisch. Der letzte Abschnitt »Zur heutigen Situation der syrischen Kirche« (S. 137-179) ist eine Dokumentation. Dort bietet der Verfasser eine Liste der Bistümer und Bischöfe seiner Kirche und druckt verschiedene Texte ab, z.B. die Verlautbarungen der syrisch-orthodoxen Kirche mit der römisch-katholischen und die beim Besuch des syrisch-orthodoxen Patriarchen 1972 in Wien gehaltenen Ansprachen. Am Schluß steht ein Literaturverzeichnis. Das Buch hätte noch dadurch gewinnen können, daß der Verfasser — auch wenn er gut deutsch spricht — sein Manuskript einem Deutschen zur sprachlichen Durchsicht gegeben hätte. Auch die Zahl der Druckfehler stört etwas. Zusammenfassend muß gesagt werden, daß diese Geschichte der syrisch-orthodoxen Kirche nicht nur deshalb lesenswert ist, weil wie von einem Mitglied dieser Kirche geschrieben wurde, sondern auch wegen der darin dankenswerterweise aufgenommenen Augenzeugenberichte.

Hubert Kaufhold

Suhail Qāšā, Ta'rīḫ abrašīyat al-Mauṣil li-s-suryān al-kāṯūlīq (Nebentitel: Suhail P. Qasha, History of Syriac Catholic Diocese of Mosul), Baghdad 1985. 488 S.

Mīḫā'īl al-Ǧamīl, Ta'rīḫ wa-siyar kahnat as-suryān al-kāṯūlīq min 1750-1985, a.O., o.J. (ca. 1986). 437 S.

Suhail Qāšā, 1942 in Qaraqoš geboren und als Lehrer an verschiedenen Orten im Iraq tätig gewesen, behandelt die Entstehung der syrisch-katholischen Kirche im Iraq und ihre Geschichte bis zur Gegenwart. Er stützt sich dabei u.a. auf die Archive der Kirchen in Mosul, wo die Unionsbewegung ihren Ausgang nahm und wo seit 1790 auch ein Bischof der katholischen Syrer residiert. Das erste Kapitel gilt allgemein der Geschichte des syrisch-katholischen Bistums Mosul (S. 27-94), das zweite seinen Bischöfen, von Kyrillos Behnām Aḫṭal (1790-1828) bis zu Kyrillos Emanuel Bennī (seit 1959) (S. 95-124). Kapitel 3 enthält mehr oder weniger ausführliche Biographien der Priester im Bistum (S. 125-260). Im nächsten Kapitel (S. 261-360) folgen Lebensläufe zahlreicher aus der Diözese Mosul stammender unierter Syrer, darunter wissenschaftlich so bedeutender Persönlichkeiten wie Patriarch Ignatios Ephraem Rahmani (S. 271-281) oder Metropolit Klemens Joseph David (S. 300-322). Von vielen der behandelten Personen finden sich Portraits oder Photographien. Kapitel 5 (S. 361-392) ist den verschiedenen Kirchen in Mosul, Qaraqoš (einem weiteren wichtigen Zentrum der syrisch-katholischen Kirche), Barṭellī und anderen Orten gewidmet, ferner dem einzigen syrisch-katholischen Kloster im Iraq (Mār Behnām). In Kapitel 6 berichtet der Verfasser über die religiösen Bruderschaften, kirchlichen Schulen und die besonders hervorzuhebende Tätigkeit der Dominikaner im Iraq (S. 393-421). Es schließen sich noch eine Liste arabischer kirchlicher Begriffe mit Erläuterungen (S. 422-443) sowie der Lebenslauf und das umfangreichen Schriftenverzeichnis des Verfassers (S. 445-457) an. Insgesamt ein nützliches und materialreiches Buch, das man für die im Westen zu wenig bekannte Geschichte der syrisch-katholischen Kirche im Iraq und darüber hinaus immer wieder heranzuziehen haben wird.

Eine gute Ergänzung dazu ist das Buch von Chorbishof Mīḫa'īl al-Ǧamīl. Es bietet in alphabetischer Reihenfolge über 550 Biographien der Geistlichen (ohne Bischöfe) der syrisch-katholischen Kirche von den Anfängen bis in die neueste Zeit (die des Verfassers steht auf S. 97-100). Auch hier sind häufig Bilder der Betreffenden beigegeben; am Schluß folgen einige Gruppenphotos. Soweit es sich um Kleriker der Diözese Mosul handelt, sind es dieselben Personen, die auch in Kapitel 3 des Buches von Qāšā aufgenommen sind. Soweit ich sehe, sind die Angaben aber unabhängig voneinander aus den Quellen erarbeitet. Als wissenschaftlich besonders wichtig ist Chorbischof Isaac Armalet (Isḥāq Armala; 1879-1954) hervorzuheben (S. 22-26). Auch dieses biographische Nachschlagewerk kann nur sehr begrüßt werden.

Hubert Kaufhold

XXIV. Deutscher Orientalistentag vom 26. bis 30. September 1988 in Köln. Ausgewählte Vorträge, herausgegeben von Werner Diem und Abdoldjavad Falaturi, Stuttgart 1990 (= ZDMG. Supplement 8). XII, 611 S. und 23 Tafeln. 178,– DM.

In erfreulich kurzer Zeit haben die Herausgeber eine Auswahl, etwa ein Drittel, der auf dem Orientalistentag 1988 gehaltenen Vorträge im Druck vorgelegt. Der dicke Band ist nach den in Köln vertretenen Fachgruppen gegliedert und reicht so vom Alten Orient bis nach Südostasien und dem Pazifischen Raum. Seit dem XIV. Deutschen Orientalistentag 1958 in Halle besteht eine eigene Sektion für den Christlichen Orient und Byzanz. Sie war in Köln mit 21 Vorträgen vertreten. Sieben davon wurden in die Kongreßakten aufgenommen (S. 71-130), zwei weitere sind in Bd. 73 dieser Zeitschrift erschienen (M. Lattke, Sind Ephraems Madrāšē Hymnen; M. Breydy, Richtigstellungen über Agapius von Manbiğ). Darüber hinaus berühren Vorträge anderer Sektionen das Gebiet des Christlichen Orients und sollen deshalb ebenfalls erwähnt werden.

Hansgerd Hellenkemper befaßt sich mit den Stadtmauern von Anazarbos (S. 71-76 nebst 4 Tafeln). Den Inhalt seines Beitrages beschreibt er mit dem Untertitel »Archäologische Zeugnisse aus den byzantinisch-arabischen Kriegen« (7.-10. Jhdt.) selbst.

Peter Engels (»Wilhelm von Tripolis. De statu Saracenorum. Bemerkungen zu einem neuen Textfund«, S. 77-89) stellt eine von der bisher bekannten Textfassung abweichende, in drei lateinischen Handschriften überlieferte Version vor. Er schreibt sie einem anderen, unbekannten Verfasser zu; Wilhelm von Tripolis hätte sie nur überarbeitet. Eine kommentierte Ausgabe beider Fassungen soll folgen.

Anna-Dorothee von den Brincken kommt am Schluß ihres Beitrages (S. 90-98) zu dem Ergebnis, daß »mittelalterliche Karten als Geschichtswerke... Orte vorzugsweise der Heilsgeschichte wieder(geben). ... Erst die spätmittelalterliche Seekarte ... verbindet historische Stätten des östlichen Christentums mit zeitgenössischen Beobachtungen über dieselben«. Insofern deckt vielleicht der Titel »Christen im Orient auf abendländischen Karten des 11. bis 14. Jahrhunderts« den Inhalt nicht ganz ab.

Anton Schall befaßt sich, ausgehend von der Frage, ob Ephräm der Syrer in Ägypten war, mit dem Thema »Die syroaramäische Vita Sancti Ephraem Syri: Geschichtlicher und sprachlicher Ertrag« (S. 99-104). Er diskutiert einige Stellen daraus und leitet z.B. die bekannte lateinische Formel »Iube Domne (benedicere u.a.)« überraschend, aber einleuchtend aus dem Syrischen (*pqoḏ Mār(ī) ...*) und weiter aus dem Mittelpersischen her.

»Der von einem Bischof um 514 geschriebene Brief gegen das Christentum und die Verfolgung von seiten Ḏū Nuwās« ist ein Beispiel jüdischer Polemik gegen das Christentum, die einem angeblichen, zum Judentum übergetretenen Bischof in den Mund gelegt wird. Michel van Esbroeck versucht, »die Glaubwürdigkeit des Dokuments durch eine Reihe von Parallelen zu festigen« (S. 105-1115).

Christian Hannick (»Zur Rezeption des byzantinischen Kirchenrechts in Armenien«, S. 116-122) weist mit Fug und Recht darauf hin, daß die Beschäftigung mit der armenischen Kanonistik im Argen liege, obwohl inzwischen wichtige Textausgaben erschienen seien. Anhand einiger Beispiele legt er dar, daß der armenische Wortlaut dem griechischen Text der ökumenischen und lokalen Synoden keineswegs in allen Punkten folge; dies öffne Einblicke in Kirchengeschichte, Kirchenverwaltung und Liturgie Armeniens.

W. J. Aerts berichtet auf S. 123-130 über den Fortgang eines Vorhabens der Universität Groningen: »Zu einer neuen Ausgabe der 'Revelationes' des Pseudo-Methodius (syrisch-griechisch-lateinisch)«. Eines der bereits vorliegenden Ergebnisse ist, daß der griechische Text eine Übersetzung aus dem Syrischen darstellt. Die Editionen sollen bald erscheinen.

In der Sektion »Altorientalistik und Semitistik« referierte Christa Müller-Kessler über die »Überlieferungsstufen des christlich-palästinensischen Aramäisch« (S. 55-60). Sie hebt die Unterschiede hervor zwischen der »Periode des noch lebenden Dialekts« (5.-8. Jhdt.) — repräsentiert durch Inschriften — und der Periode, als »der Dialekt lediglich als Kirchensprache noch gebräuchlich war« (10.-13. Jhdt.): beim Schriftduktus, der Orthographie sowie im Hinblick auf Einflüsse des Arabischen und Syrischen.

Der in der Sektion Arabistik gehaltene Vortrag von Hartmut Bobzin über »Agostino Giustiniani (1470-1536) und seine Geschichte für die Bedeutung der Arabistik« (S. 131-139) ist hier ebenfalls zu nennen, weil zum Gegenstand der Arabistik natürlich auch die arabische Literatur der Christen gehört und Giustinianis »wichtigste ... Veröffentlichung« (S. 137) eine Ausgabe des arabischen Psalters (1516) ist. Bobzins Beitrag ist eine notwendige Ergänzung zu Johann Fücks

Buch »Arabische Studien in Europa«, in dem Giustiniani nicht vorkommt. Georg Graf behandelt die Psalterausgabe im 1. Band seiner »Geschichte der christlichen arabischen Literatur« auf S. 120ff. (Bobzin zitiert ihn trotz sonst reichlicher Literaturangaben nicht).

Genannt sei auch der Beitrag von Irene Schneider über die Adab al-qāḍī-Literatur (Sektion Islamwissenschaft), weil er Anlaß bietet, auf die dasselbe Gebiet, also die Vorschriften des islamischen Rechts über Richter und Prozeßführung behandelnde Tübinger phil. Dissertation (1989) der Verfasserin hinzuweisen: »Das Bild des Richters in der 'Adab al-qāḍī'-Literatur« (Frankfurt am Main 1990). Erfreulich ist, daß sie in der Dissertation auch auf christlich-orientalische Quellen eingeht, die solche Vorschriften aus dem islamischen Recht übernommen haben (insbesondere aṣ-Ṣafī ibn al-'Assāl und 'Abdīšō' bar Brīkā). Mit beträchtlichem Befremden habe ich aber dort gelesen, daß sie diese Werke »nur als Exoticum am Rande« erwähnen will (S. 151). Wenn ein Islamkundler im Zusammenhang mit dem Orient die dort bodenständigen Christen und ihre Literatur als »exotisch« bezeichnet, ist das eine erstaunliche Einschränkung des Gesichtskreises und zeigt beispielhaft, wie deutsche Orientalisten heutzutage auf den Islam fixiert sind und die orientalischen Christen eigentlich gar nicht zur Kenntnis nehmen.

Mit Interesse wird der Fachmann für den Christlichen Orients auch weitere sein Arbeitsgebiet berührende Aufsätze lesen, z.B.: Christopher Toll, Die aramäischen Ideogramme im Mittelpersischen (S. 25-45); Gerhard Conrad, Zur Bedeutung des Tārīḫ Madīnat Dimašq als historische Quelle (S. 271-282) oder Klaus Sagaster, Die Verehrung Čingis Khans bei den Mongolen (S. 364-371).

Insgesamt also ein erfreulicher und nützlicher Band, der außerdem mit einer ganzen Reihe von Abbildungen versehen ist. Allerdings liegt ein großer Teil der Beiträge weit außerhalb des Gebietes der jeweils anderen Fachvertreter aus dem Bereich der Gesamtorientalistik. Man kann sich deshalb fragen, ob künftig die Kongreßakten nicht besser in mehreren, einzeln käuflichen Bänden — geteilt nach der fachlichen Nähe der Sektionen — veröffentlicht werden sollten. (Die Vorträge der Sektion Afrikanistik sind bereits in einem eigenen Band erschienen). Ein Privatmann, für den nur wenige Aufsätze von unmittelbarer Bedeutung sind, wird sich eher Kopien davon anfertigen als den Gesamtband mit seinem zwar nicht unangemessenen, aber doch stattlichen Preis erwerben. Es ist jedoch schade, wenn die Akten der Orientalistentage nur noch in öffenlichen Bibliotheken und in den Bücherschränken der Rezensenten zu finden sind.

Hubert Kaufhold

Günter Riße, »Gott ist Christus, der Sohn der Maria«. Eine Studie zum Christusbild im Koran. Bonn, Borengässer, 1989, XI-275 S. (Begegnung. Kontextuell-dialogische Studien zur Theologie der Kulturen und Religionen, 2).

Vom theologischen und philosophischen Ausgangspunkt her (S. 16-34), sucht G.R. geschichtliche Verwandschaften zwischen Christentum und Islam zu vertiefen, ohne dabei die Unterschiede aus den Augen zu verlieren. Als Einleitung wird am Anfang die Siebenschläferlegende von koranischer Seite aus als sicherer Boden gemeinsamen Ursprungs erwähnt (S. 10-15), wo der grundlegende Artikel von E. Honigmann über Stephanus von Ephesus (in Patristic Studies, Studi e Testi, 1953) leider nicht auftaucht. Die Märtyrer von Naǧrân und die frühchristliche Periode in Arabien und Äthiopien werden in Anspruch genommen (S. 35-85) und mit einer Notiz über das Christentum von der Seite muslimischer Traditionen aus ergänzt (S. 85-96). Das eigentliche Thema, die christologischen Ausdrücke auf christlichem und koranischem Gebiet, füllt die S. 97-217. Das monophysitische Christusbild soll dem Christusbild Muhammads viel gegeben haben. Als erster Mittler der Überlieferung tritt Ephräm auf, und nach ihm Julian von Halikarnaß als wahrer Phantasiast. Am Ende gibt G.R. einen Rück- und Ausblick für das Gespräch mit dem Islam

(S. 218-228). Ergebnis ist, daß die christologische Formel von Chalkedon im Dialog wie schon früher immerhin von Bedeutung ist.

Man muß anerkennen, daß G.R., den Mut hatte, sich einem so ausgedehnten Forschungsgebiet zu widmen. Die Richtung der Arbeit ist wohl positiv zu deuten. Doch ist nicht zu vergessen, daß zwischen Ephräms Text und dem Koran weitere verlorene Zwischenschriften entstanden sind. Es gibt sehr viele Materialien, die offenbar hier nicht erwähnt werden konnten, und die unmittelbar an die Vorgeschichte des Korans anknüpfen. Was die Julianisten betrifft, kann man kaum ihre Lehre als »Doketismus« auffassen, wenn man die armenischen und weiteren theologischen Entwicklungen berücksichtigt: nur Severus und seine Anhänger haben das Wort »Phantasiastès« gebraucht. In Wirklichkeit hatte der Begriff »Natur« bei den damaligen orientalischen Theologen die Bedeutung einer immer in einer Hypostase verbleibenden Natur; damit konnten sie nicht dem Chalcedonse zustimmen. Müßte man nicht zuerst die Ausdrücke der Monophysiten positiv interpretieren, um danach die Koranausdrücke ihrem richtigen Sinn gemäß zu lesen? Das Buch von Draguet, wird S. 148, Fußn. 177, gleichfalls von G.R. nicht positiv angenommen. Daß G.R. so viel Material in einem einzigen Buch zusammenstellen konnte, ist bemerkenswert, doch sollte der Leser immer wissen, daß hier viele Fragen nicht erschöpfend betrachtet worden sind.

Michel van Esbroeck

K. Weitzmann - H. L. Kessler: The frescoes of the Dura Synagogue and christian art (= Dumbarton Oaks Studies 28). Washington D.C. 1990. Ln., 202 S., 202 schw./weiß Abb.

Die im Syrischen Nationalmuseum von Damaskus befindlichen Fresken haben im großen und ganzen die Zerstörung Duras durch die Perser im Jahre 256 n. Chr. überdauert. Die Datierung der Wandgemälde wird auf den Zeitraum 244/5-256 n. Chr. festgelegt. Das Ziel der detaillierten Studie läuft auf ein Postulat hinaus, das von der Tatsache des narrativen Charakters sämtlicher Fresken der Synagoge von Dura Europos ausgeht. Diese Prämisse wird in einer ausführlichen Untersuchung bewiesen. Es zeigt sich dann, daß die Verbindung zwischen den synagogalen Fresken und byzantinischen Miniaturen der späteren Zeit so eng ist, daß für beide ein früher Archetyp angenommen werden kann. Dieser postulierte Archetyp muß schon vor der Mitte des 3. Jhs. bekannt gewesen sein und es muß sich dabei um Buchillustrationen gehandelt haben. Bis jetzt wurde allerdings noch keine einzige, auch nicht fragmentarische, illuminierte Bibelhandschrift dieser frühen Epoche entdeckt. Dennoch, die Existenz illustrierter Teile der Septuaginta wie des Pentateuch, der Samuel- und Königsbücher, sowie einzelner Propheten dürfte außer Zweifel stehen. Möglicherweise mag man auch an Midrasch- und Targumschriften denken. Ferner kommt Josephus Flavius mit seinen jüdischen Altertümern als weitere Vorlage in Betracht.

Die Methode der bildlichen Darstellung einer Geschichte in rasch aufeinanderfolgenden Sequenzen geht in die späte hellenistische Zeit zurück. Die sog. megarischen Schüsseln aus der Zeit des 3. bis 1. Jhs. v. Chr. bieten Illustrationen der homerischen Dichtung und der Tragödien des Euripides in kurzer Abfolge. Diese können durchaus als formales Vorbild für die Fresken von Dura gedient haben. Weder Juden noch Christen haben demnach die Darstellung von literarischen Texten mittels der bildenden Kunst erfunden. Weitzmann kommt damit auf eine bedeutende These zurück, die erneut mit der ersten umfassenden Publikation der Synagoge von Dura Europos erhärtet wurde: »There was no break between classical art on the one hand and the Jewish and Christian on the other« (S. 150).

Sämtliche schwarz/weiß Fotos zu den Synagogenfresken stammen aus dem Nachlaß von C. H. Kraeling. Sollte das Werk, das Grundsatzdiskussionen auslösen wird, erneut aufgelegt werden können, wäre der Abdruck neuester Farbaufnahmen vom Ist-Zustand der Fresken im

Syrischen Nationalmuseum sehr erwünscht. Den Autoren gilt ein besonderer Dank für die hellen Scheinwerfer auf ein nahezu vergessenes Kunstwerk, dessen Bedeutung kaum zu überschätzen ist.

Wilhelm Gessel

Christianity among the Slavs. The Heritage of Saints Cyril and Methodius. Acts of the International Congress held on the Eleventh Centenary of the Death of St. Methodius Rome, October 8-11, 1985, under the direction of the Pontifical Oriental Institute, ed. by E. G. Farrugia, R. F. Taft and G. K. Piovesana, Rome 1988, IX-409 S. (= Orientalia Christiana Analecta 231).

Eine Auswahl von dreißig Vorträgen und Mitteilungen des über Kyrill und Methodius Oktober 1985 gehaltenen Kongresses liegt hier sorgfältig gedruckt vor. Man bemerkt unter diesen sehr unterschiedlichen wissenschaftlichen Beiträgen einige wichtige Forschritte. M. Arranz ist es gelungen, nicht nur das alte sinaïtische Euchologion durch mehrere Parallelen zu erklären, sondern auch die letzten auf dem Sinaï gefundenen Bruchstücke genau zu identifizieren, und damit den Codex zu vervollständigen. Darin spiegelt sich die Liturgie der Großkirche von Konstantinopel. Die am Ende des Kodex enthaltenen Bußkanones gleichen mehr den lateinischen Pönitentialien, wie man sie aber auch in der Kormčaja Kniga finden kann (S. 15-74). Auf ein ähnliches Alter ist der Palimpsest Vat. gr. 2502 zu schätzen, der ein bisher unbekanntes altbulgarisches Evangeliar umfaßt. S. 261-8 gibt T. Kraštanov, der künftige Herausgeber, einen ersten Überblick. Über die ersten Entwicklungen der slawischen Kultur stellen zwei berühmte Spezialisten, I. Dujčev († 24.V.1986) und F. V. Mareš, ein knappes Panorama vor, Ergebnis einer langen Forschung (S. 83-94 und 119-130). L. E. Boyle beschäftigt sich mit der neuen Hypothese von Dr. Osborne, welche das Grab des Kyrill in San Clemente in Rom anders lokalisiert (S. 75-82). Drei Mitteilungen analysieren die alten Übersetzungen: E. Banfi untersucht die gemeinschaftlichen Spracherscheinungen des Balkan (S. 145-164), H. Keipert die Doppelübersetzungen im methodianischen Nomokanon (S. 237-260), und F. J. Thomson legt eine Klassifikation der falschen Wiedergaben von griechischen Vorlagen vor (S. 351-380). Mehrere Disziplinen haben ihren Spezialisten gefunden: S. Dufrenne für die Ikonographie des Kyrill (S. 187-200), T. Špidlik für den geistlichen Einfluß vonseiten des Gregor von Nazianz (S. 299-304), A. Nazor für die slawischen Frühdrucke (S. 283-290), T. Mrkonič für die kroatischen Ausgaben slawischer Texte (S. 267-282). Mit Recht notiert O. Pritsak, daß die khazarische Legende im Leben des Konstantin fremder Einschub sein muß (S. 299-304). Dem Kult und den Offizien zu Kyrills Ehren sind verschiedene Vorträge gewidmet: M. Japundžić auf dem glagolitischen Gebiet (S. 95-118), A. E. Tachiaos auf dem griechischen (S. 131-144): dort besteht immer die Frage, wie bald Kyrill als Bischof bezeichnet wurde. A. Džurova und K. Stančev beschreiben die slavischen Handschriften des Pontificio Istituto Orientale: wenn auch fast alle erst aus dem 19. Jahrhundert stammen, gibt es doch 30 Codices, und aus einer Anmerkung erfährt man, daß noch 21 weitere auf den Bibliotheksregalen des Instituts gefunden wurden. Ch. Hannick findet einige liturgische Gebräuche aus der griechischen Chersones wieder durch eine genauere Analyse des Slovo über die Translatio des Kyrill auf der Chersones (S. 227-237). Wichtig sind noch zwei Abhandlungen über die Rolle von Bischof Stroßmaier von A. Šuljak (S. 305-314), und die historische Wiederentdeckung von Kyrill und Method seit 1850 von A. Tamborra (S. 315-342). Sieben weitere Mitteilungen beschäftigen sich mit lokalen Traditionen. Wie man sieht, hat sich der Kongreß von 1985 am meisten dem balkanischen Gebiet gewidmet, was für die heiligen Brüder auch geschichtlich voll begründet ist. Die Herausgeber haben das Buch in vorbildlicher Weise zum Druck gebracht.

Michel van Esbroeck

Turchia: la Chiesa e la sua storia. I. Turchia, crocevia di culture e religioni. Introduzione di Luigi Padovese. A cura dell'Associazione culturale eteria e dei Frati Cappucini. Roma 1990, Kart., 175 S.

Es handelt sich um eine Sammlung von Vorträgen, die 1989 in Iskenderum (Türkei) anläßlich von Begegnungen zwischen Christentum und Islam gehalten worden sind. In erster Linie werden kirchengeschichtliche Themen abgehandelt, die in großen Zügen einen Überblick zur kleinasiatischen Kirchengeschichte bieten wollen. Die einzelnen Autoren sind um knappe Darstellung bemüht. Manche verzichten auf den Anmerkungsapparat und ersetzen diesen durch eine Bibliographie, die einige wenige Titel aus der neueren Literatur aufführt. Eine Auswahl von Beiträgen mag das jeweilige Interesse der Verfasser illustrieren. L. Padovese: Il cristianesimo dei primi secoli a confronto con le strutture socio-religiose e le lingue del mondo antico (S. 17-47). F. Cocchini: La recezione di Paolo nei primi tre secoli cristiani (S. 49-60). M. G. Mara: Contributo degli apocrifi alla storia del cristianesimo: lettura e commento dal Vangelo di Pietro (EvPt) (S. 61-77). E. Ludwig: Il concilio di Efeso (S. 109-117). V. Kapitanovic: I crociati in Asia Minori (S. 143-151). Besondere Aufmerksamkeit verdient der Beitrag von M. Bayraktar: La situation actuelle de l'Islam en Turquie (S. 165-174), der einen optimistischen Ausblick eröffnet.

Wilhelm Gessel

Henryk Paprocki: La promesse du Père. L'expérience du Saint Esprit dans l'église orthodoxe. Traduit du polonais par Françoise Lhoest. Les Éditions du Cerf, Paris 1990, Kart., 151 S.

Der Titel des mit schönen Bildern ausgestatteten Buches ist Lk 24,49 entlehnt, ein Brauch, der sich orthodoxen Gelehrten wie P. Florensky oder S. Boulgakov anschließt. In drei Kapiteln wird die orthodoxe Pneumatologie dargelegt: Biblische Grundlegung — Gabe des Heiligen Geistes — Erfahrung mit dem Heiligen Geist. Die beiden letzten Kapitel reihen hauptsächlich Väterstellen aneinander, die kurz interpretiert und thematisch geordnet werden. Mit diesem Verfahren will der Autor zeigen, daß der Heilige Geist die Gläubigen durchdringt, die Einheit der Kirche bedingt und vor allem in seine mystische Dimension führt. Das Werk vermittelt einen interessanten Einblick in orthodoxe Theologie, deren Denk- und Argumentationsmuster der westlichen Theologie weiniger geläufig ist.

Der Bildteil bringt u.a. zwei zeitgenössische Ikonen zur Taufe Christi im Jordan. Beide Ikonenmaler fühlen sich der traditionellen Ikonographie verpflichtet, nach der Christus aufrecht im Jordanwasser steht und der erhöht stehende Täufer Wasser über den Scheitel Christi gießt (also Infusionstaufe), während vom Himmel der Heilige Geist in Gestalt einer Taube über Christus schwebt.

Wilhelm Gessel

Friedrich Heyer

Die Orientalische Frage im kirchlichen Lebenskreis

Das Einwirken der Kirchen des Auslandes auf die Emanzipation der orthodoxen Nationen Südosteuropas 1804–1912

(Schriften zur Geistesgeschichte des östlichen Europa 19)

1991. XIII, 349 Seiten (ISBN 3-447-03082-8), br., ca. DM 108,–

Die Emanzipation der südosteuropäischen Nationen vom Osmanischen Reich veranlaßte die Kirchen im Zarenreich, in Europa und Amerika, zu spontaner Hilfe: so wurden Institutionen gegründet wie die „Slavische Wohltätigkeitsgesellschaft" in Rußland, die Agenturen der „British and Foreign Bible Society", die Stationen der Lazaristen und Asumptionisten sowie die der protestantischen Missionen des „American Board of Commissioners for foreign missions" und die der Methodist Episcopal Church. Gleichzeitig organisierte sich auch der christlich orientierte Philhellenismus.
Die orthodoxen Christen reagierten zum Teil empfindlich auf diese Aktivitäten. Ein Teil der Griechen und Bulgaren übernahm, was ihnen die Kirchen des Auslandes zubrachten, ein anderer witterte die Gefahr konfessioneller Entfremdung und wandte sich dagegen.
Die Balkanhistoriographie hat sich mit diesen Fragen bislang nicht befaßt.

Igor Smolitsch

Geschichte der russischen Kirche Band 2

Herausgegeben von Gregory L. Freeze

(Forschungen zur osteuropäischen Geschichte 45)

1991. 536 Seiten (ISBN 3-447-03059-3), br., DM 178,–

Der erste Teil dieses grundlegenden Werkes erschien 1964 im Böhlau-Verlag, Köln. Die Schwierigkeiten mit dem nachgelassenen Manuskript haben die Veröffentlichung zu einem früheren Zeitpunkt verhindert. Dem Herausgeber ist es gelungen, durch Kürzungen und Aktualisierung des bibliographischen Apparates die in der Fachwelt lange erwartete Veröffentlichung zu ermöglichen.